Contents

	Page
Introduction	vi
Prologue: The Library Press, by Eric Moon	10

Part I: Libraries and Librarians

What Good Are Public Library Standards? by Joseph L. Wheeler	28
Public Libraries and the Network Idea, by Verner W. Clapp	53
Performance Ratings and Librarians' Rights, by David Peele	63
Letter to a Library School Lecturer, by Peter D. Pocklington	74
When a Library Job Ends . . . Find Another, by Paula M. Strain	81
Professional Unions, by Darryl Mleynek	92

Part II: Technical Services/Technical Processes

Shared Cataloging, by Herman Liebaers	106
Photocopying in a University Library, by Robert H. Blackburn	146
History of Library Computerization, by Frederick G. Kilgour	160
MEDLARS: a Summary, Review and Evaluation of Three Reports, by Norman D. Stevens	175

CATCALL, by Ralph R. Shaw   192

Automation Stops Here, by Roscoe Rouse   203

On the Design of Information Systems for Human
    Beings, by M. B. Line   214

Part III: Communication and Education

Book Publishing's Hidden Bonanza,
    by Curtis G. Benjamin   238

Collecting Modern Imprints, by G. Thomas Tanselle   249

Charles Bukowski and the Small Mag/Little Press
    Movement, by Sanford Dorbin   259

Feature Films in Your Library, by Paul Spehr   274

Out on a Limb with the Critics, by Paul Heins   290

Identifications and Identities, by Lloyd Alexander   301

Implementing Educational Change,
    by Henry M. Brickell   308

Part IV: The Social Prerogative

Libraries and the Climate of Opinion,
    by Ervin J. Gaines   320

How Mexican-Americans View Libraries,
    by Robert P. Haro   329

American Indians: Search for Fort Hall's Library
    Service, by Gerald R. Shields & George Sheppard   340

Plus ça Change, by Jesse H. Shera   349

The Disadvantaged Majority, by Anita R. Schiller   369

Law Library Service to Prisoners,
    by O. James Werner   376

When Readers Become Suspect, by Reese Cleghorn   398

LIBRARY LIT. -
The Best of 1970

edited by
BILL KATZ
and
JOEL J. SCHWARTZ

The Scarecrow Press, Inc.
Metuchen, N.J.   1971

Copyright 1971 by The Scarecrow Press, Inc.

ISBN 0-8108-0418-2

Library of Congress Catalog Card Number 78-154842

Contents

	Page
Introduction	vi
Prologue: The Library Press, by Eric Moon	10

Part I: Libraries and Librarians

What Good Are Public Library Standards? by Joseph L. Wheeler	28
Public Libraries and the Network Idea, by Verner W. Clapp	53
Performance Ratings and Librarians' Rights, by David Peele	63
Letter to a Library School Lecturer, by Peter D. Pocklington	74
When a Library Job Ends . . . Find Another, by Paula M. Strain	81
Professional Unions, by Darryl Mleynek	92

Part II: Technical Services/Technical Processes

Shared Cataloging, by Herman Liebaers	106
Photocopying in a University Library, by Robert H. Blackburn	146
History of Library Computerization, by Frederick G. Kilgour	160
MEDLARS: a Summary, Review and Evaluation of Three Reports, by Norman D. Stevens	175

CATCALL, by Ralph R. Shaw	192
Automation Stops Here, by Roscoe Rouse	203
On the Design of Information Systems for Human Beings, by M. B. Line	214

Part III: Communication and Education

Book Publishing's Hidden Bonanza, by Curtis G. Benjamin	238
Collecting Modern Imprints, by G. Thomas Tanselle	249
Charles Bukowski and the Small Mag/Little Press Movement, by Sanford Dorbin	259
Feature Films in Your Library, by Paul Spehr	274
Out on a Limb with the Critics, by Paul Heins	290
Identifications and Identities, by Lloyd Alexander	301
Implementing Educational Change, by Henry M. Brickell	308

Part IV: The Social Prerogative

Libraries and the Climate of Opinion, by Ervin J. Gaines	320
How Mexican-Americans View Libraries, by Robert P. Haro	329
American Indians: Search for Fort Hall's Library Service, by Gerald R. Shields & George Sheppard	340
Plus ça Change, by Jesse H. Shera	349
The Disadvantaged Majority, by Anita R. Schiller	369
Law Library Service to Prisoners, by O. James Werner	376
When Readers Become Suspect, by Reese Cleghorn	398

Up Against the Stacks, by Carolyn Forsman   405

<u>Epilogue</u>:   Library Germule   418

Contributors   427

Introduction

This is what some of us consider to be the best writing about libraries and related topics in 1970. It filters down to 30 articles in almost as many periodicals. Books are excluded.

Selection is based primarily upon the judges' personal and professional understanding of good writing. The author with a new insight, an imaginative approach, and visible conviction is given the nod. We have attempted to exclude the familiar pursuit of hot air. This is to say that scholarship, while admirable, is no longer sufficient in and of itself; it must be paired with the qualities that distinguish good writing in every other field, and that includes fiction and poetry. It is time that this double standard be discredited.

We have tried very hard to cover the widest possible field of librarianship, from children's literature to automation, and all points in between. Some areas are neglected, because the author's method of presentation is of more significance than his subject, and a number of subjects were simply not treated during the year with the flair which we were seeking. Our concern here, then, is more with the literature than the discipline, if the two can in fact be differentiated.

In search of this commitment to excellence, the editors read the full run of well over 200 magazines for the period from November 1, 1969 to November 1, 1970. The slight overlap into 1969 will allow this book to be published early in 1971. Next year the editors begin with November, 1970.

Nearly all the periodicals indexed in Library Literature have been scrutinized, and we also instituted a fairly extensive search through the popular and extra-disciplinary indexes for relevant material. Apropos of this, it is significant to note that the editors began this project with the thought in mind that we would discover vast untapped sources of library literature in the secular press. We were rudely surprised to find that libraries and librarians were conspicuously absent from the popular literature we perused. At any rate, a working corpus of 77 articles was selected, from which the judges later chose the 30 "best."

While 30 is no magic number, it seems quite enough. As Eric Moon points out in his keynote article, the major problem with the library press is proliferation. Too many anthologies multiply the problem. We hope to purify by elimination, i.e., wringing out what Moon calls the "milk and water" from library writings. The result is a shortcut for librarian, student and layman. It is hopefully the crystallization of all that is exciting and progressive in our profession, and it should prove to all that the "best of library literature" need not be a contradiction of terms.

Traditionally, library literature has been the dull and stodgy mirror-image of an equally dull and stodgy profession. Only in the last few years, as librarianship has at last begun to be positively affected by the pace and climate of the times, has the literature accordingly improved to the point where such a collection as this is feasible. Naturally, the present state of the art is far from ideal. Again, reference can be made to the Moon piece, or to any student who has to wade his way through the heap. Conversely, the 30 articles here begin to refute the gripes. Specialists in the fine art of librarianship can be creative in presenting their ideas. Few may be considered men and women of literature, but all are, at least, literate. It is a tricky business to condemn out of hand all those who contribute to library periodicals. Sometimes the curses are deserved, but this side of a timeless masterpiece, a remarkable number of authors do quite well enough. The proof that not all library writing need be pedestrian or dull is found here. And while we are not suggesting that the test of ultimate worth is inclusion in this, or any other, anthology, the editors do hope, at the outset, to restore some real value to the term "library literature."

No one is going to agree entirely with the choices. The diligent reader will think that this or that should have been excluded in favor of a personal favorite or two. Good: we claim no non-negotiable aesthetics. But here is only a beginning. We hope to do this annually. Readers are asked to send the editors nominations for 1971. This start is necessarily halting, and the hope of continuing depends primarily upon the support and assistance of those who think library literature can and should be more than a grim jest.

Perhaps, if reader response is great enough, we might be able to institute some sort of popular selection of material for inclusion in this anthology. Or, an expanded jury could be formed, comprised of experts in various subject areas. The possibilities are endless; given the continued maturity of the literature, selection will become a joyous chore, an embarrassment of riches.

The editors wish to thank the judges who so gracefully (moans and groans aside) donated of their time and talents. The members of the jury, in addition to the editors (respectively professor and student at the Albany Library School), were:

John N. Berry III, Editor, Library Journal

William R. Eshelman, Editor, Wilson Library Bulletin

Eric Moon, President, Scarecrow Press

Finally, the editors wish to thank the editors of the 21 magazines whose initial good sense brought these articles to print and who were kind enough to allow reprinting; and the authors whose work is honoring this anthology and the literature as a whole.

William A. Katz

Joel J. Schwartz

Albany, New York
December 1970

PROLOGUE:

THE LIBRARY PRESS

The Library Press

by Eric Moon

Reprinted by permission from the November 15, 1969 issue of Library Journal (94:20) p. 4104-4109. Copyright 1969 by R.R. Bowker Co., a Xerox Company.

The deadliest disease afflicting the library press is proliferation. The kindest and most conservative estimate I am able to bring myself to make is that there are at least three times as many library periodicals in this country as we can afford or are necessary. Perhaps the most constructive single thing that could be accomplished would be to persuade at least one in three publishers of a library periodical to cease publication.

One might reasonably expect that librarians, who have done so much public wailing about the publications explosion, would be among the chief advocates and practitioners of birth control in the world of print. Instead we find them cavorting as uninhibitedly in the king-size bed of printed procreation as do the denizens of the Sodom and Gomorrah of science and technology. Just about every library of any consequence (and some of little consequence) and, almost without exception, every group or organization within the loose boundaries of our profession, decides, virtually at the moment of its birth, that it cannot survive without a publication of its own--a newsletter, a journal, some regular calling card to announce its presence to the world at large.

The incentive may be a genuine desire to communicate--in itself a healthy desire in a profession which should be a significant element in the machinery of communications. Or this massive outpouring may be just another symptom of man's most desperate struggle in today's enveloping society: the attempt to establish and maintain an identity. The trouble is that when one examines the content of much of this debris (and debris is the main result of most explosions), one is forced to ask: 1) Is it worth the cost and effort? 2) Is it

Prologue   11

communicating anything that anyone really needs to know?
3) Is the identity it establishes one that we really want to
live with? And the answer to all three questions, if we
were honest, would be a resounding NO.

      Proliferation has a very severe impact on the overall quality of the library press. Among its specific evils are:

      1) It spreads too thinly the limited amount of good material, so that all the periodicals (and I exempt not the big three) tend, in greater or lesser degree, to flesh out their pages with material about which they are less than enthusiastic.

      2) It also spreads too thinly the advertising support which otherwise could help sustain a smaller number of stronger, well-staffed, economically and editorially independent magazines.

      3) It occasionally diverts into an obscure publication a piece of writing that deserves to reach a wider audience. This problem is not irremediable, of course, if the big boys will keep their eyes skinned and perform the necessary rescue operation occasionally--though some of them are afraid to do this because they may leave themselves open to charges of unoriginality.

      4) Worst of all, proliferation makes it possible for almost anything on the topic of librarianship, no matter how appalling, to find its way into print somewhere. Almost everything I rejected in nine years of editing LJ subsequently turned up in another library periodical--sometimes as many as four or five pieces in one issue of one periodical (I once counted that many in one issue of College & Research Libraries!). Now, some of this occurred, no doubt, because of poor judgment on my part, and some of it is attributable to the infinite variety of human taste. But much of it was the result of editorial desperation. There is--and everyone who has ever edited a library periodical for any length of time knows it--simply too little quality material to fill all the pages the library profession insists on producing.

      The dearth, the paucity of quality, is most noticeable if you examine only one element among the features of the library press: the articles. Yet this is the element most of our editors are hung up on; they all want to publish articles.

If I may again guess at some motives, I'd say that the most likely reason articles are so popular among editors is that they fill up a lot of space. And the lazy editor, who can close his eyes and conscience, can fill up space this way without much creative effort (or effort of any kind) on his own part. Another possible motive, and a slightly more laudable one, is that many people who become editors have, somewhere inside them, some small residue of literary ambition. If they can't be Truman Capote or John Updike or Norman Mailer, they secretly tell themselves, perhaps they have a chance of becoming a Harold Ross or a Norman Podhoretz. And about as near to a literary form as you can get in a library periodical is the article.

Whichever of these motives is operative the new editor quickly finds himself facing the same bleak landscape. There are articles a-plenty around in librarianship (are all librarians writers manqué?) but the majority of them say nothing, or say what it is no longer necessary to say because it has been said so often, and most of them say it so incredibly badly that the editor who accepts one of this breed is left with only two choices. If he is truly lazy, he may say: "This thing isn't worth any effort; the only thing to do is print it the way it is--it'll soon be forgotten, in any case." Or the more scrupulous editor will find that, even to make the article vaguely comprehensible, entails more work than if he were to start from scratch and write something himself. To make his disenchantment more complete the editor quickly realizes that there are few oil wells to be discovered on this land he has chosen to explore, and that his chances of reflected glory through the discovery of a library Thurber or Baldwin are about as remote as Lyndon Johnson's chances of being remembered as the Peace President.

It's not easy to understand the reasons for this appalling lack of quality, particularly in a profession in such close physical proximity (if not necessarily intellectual proximity) to the printed word. The formal educational system must be held somewhat responsible for the widespread inability to string a few dozen words together in some sort of coherent sequence, and for the paucity of ideas and the cloudy thinking behind this word butchery. I cannot help noting that the library schools, though they certainly cannot hope to correct the ills generated by the educational system at earlier stages, appear to me to have added another awful dimension to the written output of our profession. They have been prominent

Prologue

instigators of what is best described as scissors-and-paste research. The procedure is well known: before you write anything you must first ferret around in the literature of the distant past, extract the thoughts and ideas of another time, then paste them together, using footnotes and references for glue. This grubby composite is then presented as your own work. Original thought, ideas advanced before they have fossilized, are not required--indeed, they may be frowned upon. The most concentrated example of this kind of library "literature" today is Library Quarterly, which is still thought of by some as a "scholarly" periodical but which looks to me more like a collection of rather antiquated gentlemen examining their navels, perhaps in the hope of finding a live appendix.

Most editors in our field, after their first month or two of exposure to this incredible stream of garbage, either go into shock or lapse into a prolonged period of deep despair. Those who recover and begin to look for remedies are likely to adopt various courses of action. For example, Kathleen Molz, after a few months of editing the Wilson Library Bulletin, apparently decided that there was little hope for the library profession and went outside thereafter for the great bulk of her material. I admire the skill and the style and the persuasive ability she brought to this endeavor and I think for a few years she gave us an interestingly different library periodical--but one of little relevance to the library scene today.

She once said at a meeting at which we were both speaking, that she was trying to make the Bulletin the Harper's or the Atlantic of librarianship and that I was trying to make LJ the librarian's Time magazine. If you discount the icepick lurking behind that remark (she knew that Time is my pet hate among all magazines), there was a measure of truth in it. My solution to the garbage explosion was to try to build up a top-level staff of writer-reporters who would look at the contemporary library scene and describe it and criticize it in relatively clear prose, without too many frills or too much equivocation. In that way, I felt, we could begin to reduce the number of public relations releases that librarians write about their own operations and hobby-horses and then try to peddle as articles. John Berry, I suspect, from the evidence I have seen during the few months of his editorship, wants to push further in this direction and to cut the number of contributed articles even more drastically.

So my second suggestion, and I assume the first (that
library periodicals commit editorial hari-kiri) won't be accepted,
is don't be afraid to publish a thinner periodical, be
a lot tougher in acceptance decisions, and deliberately set
out to publish fewer articles than last year. I believe LJ,
for example, is now publishing not much more than half the
number of articles it published per year a decade ago, and
I think it is better for that. I know that in my first year
as editor-in-chief I cut 1000 pages out of the magazine. Nobody
(except the other editors) noticed or complained. Not
only were our economics improved, so was the overall standard
of what did appear.

So far, I must admit, this sounds like an exercise in
weeding run amok. I've suggested that one-third of the library
publishers might kill off their magazines, and the other
two-thirds might cut out half the present content of the remainder.
Another affliction of the library periodicals that
has always been a particular concern of mine is the news
gap. Few professions are as ill-served as ours in the area
of current news and information. One must not, of course,
blame the editors alone; the disease is spread and stimulated
by the profession itself. The majority of librarians are
completely lacking in news consciousness; they do not know
what news is, why it is useful, or that timing is a major
factor in its potential value.

This news blindness, this obliviousness to the value
of recording and reporting what we do--and currently--has
achieved for our profession a social anonymity almost unequalled
among the professions. It has also, among other
things, given us statistical services which are unbelievable
in their incompleteness and inaccuracy. It leads our organizations
and institutions to produce the reports of research
projects or the proceedings of conferences or symposia as
much as seven years after the event. And it allows us to
duplicate research, experimentation, and other efforts, over
and over again, without knowledge of what the other guy is
doing or has already discovered. For a profession which is
supposed to aid others in research and in keeping themselves
up-to-date within their disciplines, we set a resounding example
of near-total inefficiency.

Even taking into account that they can expect little
help from their colleagues in the field, however, the library
periodical editors must take much of the blame for our inadequate
news and information services. Much real news

has been suppressed or has deliberately not been pursued. And much of what is published is canned news, most of it supplied in release form by foundations (CLR), professional organizations (ALA), a few libraries, and a variety of other sources such as publishers, suppliers, and public relations firms. Rarely is any digging done by the editors of most of our periodicals to find out whether there is more to the story than the release reveals. Many of the releases, indeed, are not even edited before they are set in type by the library press. The supreme example is The Indian Librarian, which prints (verbatim) releases from Bowker as though they were either ads (which isn't so far from the truth) or reviews (which is a long way from the truth). But our own press isn't much better. Just check out a few of these release-generated stories in half a dozen periodicals (and you can include some of the national ones). Essentially, you'll find the same stuff, the same wording, in pretty well all of the periodicals. Total waste.

So, third suggestion: one thing to start filling up with after having emptied out some of the tons of garbage is some useful hard news and current information, which our profession needs desperately. I think, indeed, that the library press might be much improved overall if a substantial number of the present journals at state and regional levels were to become newsletters. Too much membership money is spent on printing and playing with the redesign of journals which don't appear often enough to be useful, and the content of which does not justify either the expense or the typographic frills. A newsletter may be less satisfying to the ego of the editor or the association but, cheaply produced and frequently issued, it could get information to members and subscribers while it is needed and useful. A quarterly may be a handsome ornament but as a carrier of information in today's world it is a medieval device.

And now to another, and perhaps even worse, gaping hole in the library press. If the Negro, at the time of Ralph Ellison's marvelous novel in the 1950's, was still the invisible man, the library press, still at the end of the 1960's, is the personification of the invisible position--and not just on broader social issues (which many librarians still think it improper for a professional periodical to discuss) but even on basic professional matters. There are so few exceptions to this generalization that those which do exist are often regarded as either vaguely heretical or deliberately sensational.

It was this flat conformity and dullness, this lack of individuality and viewpoint that struck me as the most pervasive quality of the library press of North America when I took my first really solid look at it after being approached about the LJ editorship. My reaction was a mental echo of Jimmy Porter's anguished cry in Look Back in Anger: "How I long for a little ordinary human enthusiasm."

It was easy to confirm that LJ wasn't stirring up a whole lot of enthusiasm. My first check was one I had carried out on several other magazines I had been associated with. The Letters to the Editor file was virtually empty. This is a good test; if this file does not consistently contain more letters than can be used, it is a fair bet that the magazine is not getting through to its readers. Clearly, at the very least, it is not evoking much response from them. I think the most apparent current example of the relationship between a healthy Letters to the Editor column and the resurgence of a periodical is the ALA Bulletin (now American Libraries)--by far the most obviously improved library periodical in the United States.

So how does one set about stimulating some of Jimmy Porter's "ordinary human enthusiasm"? I don't know that I can give any standard recipe but I can tell briefly some of the elements of the program I set for myself when I took over LJ.

The first objective was to find some writers--other than the few good, well known, established and over-exposed ones--who had not only words (and perhaps style) but passion, writers who would express their ideas and convictions without equivocation. (Too many of those who appear in our literature are Lone Rangers--they never take the mask off.) Having found such authors, of course, one must give them their heads, not constrict them. My gambit was never to ask them to write on assigned topics but to try to find out what moved them. I'd ask: What do you get excited or angry or impatient about? What do you really care about? What's your thing? That's what I want you to write about. I've always regarded Dorothy Broderick, now well known and much in demand, as the first success of this policy. The first piece of hers I published in LJ was so successful that reader response was enough to fill a couple of subsequent issues. Another measure of success was that Miss Broderick was fired by her university.

Prologue

A second element in my program, and a major one, was to give LJ an identifiable editorial stance in relation to the library world. In broad terms this was an easy decision to make. Since the majority of the other periodicals were published by associations or institutions, they tended collectively to present a kind of party line, to be an establishment chorus, very middle of the road, timorous about criticism (of anything!). The way for me to use LJ's independence, I felt, was to make the magazine an opposition voice. I meant opposition in a constructive sense, in Disraeli's terms ("No government can long survive without a forceful opposition"), though few people believed there was anything constructive in my approach.

It seemed to me essential to establish at least one outlet in our professional press where any established virtue could be questioned, where no cow was so sacred that its tail could not be pulled in public, where criticism was more welcome than self-congratulation. The editorial text, for those who wanted one, was Dana's Law: "Where there is a standard method of doing a thing which has been accepted and approved over a considerable period of time, it is safe to assume that it is wrong. Or at least that it is capable of being improved. It is no longer based on the intellect, but has become merely habit and imitation."

Third, since we already had a plethora of periodicals concerned principally with the furniture and techniques of librarianship, and because most of our worst problems seemed to me to derive from attitudes rather than faltering skills, I determined to reduce what Ralph Shaw christened the "how-I-run-my-library-good" articles, and to concentrate more on ideas, philosophies, and opinions than on facts or gimmicks. Like Mortimer Adler, who said "The telephone book is full of facts but it doesn't contain a single idea," I will trade a bagful of facts any day for one good idea. I wanted to get away from some of the too-pat answers and dig up some hard, relevant questions. Questions have a way of leading you on to something else; answers sometimes only stop you cold.

Another item on the editorial agenda was to crack the pervasive domesticity of the library periodicals--and of the profession they served. It was all right to spend some of our time debating which classification scheme to adopt, or how to improve circulation control or the interlibrary loan system, but we had to get our eyes off our navels once in a while and take a look at the world and its changes and forces and what they were doing to libraries' relevance.

Librarians are people, too, and I was sure they couldn't be as unconcerned about the individuals, the communities, the society in which they and their institutions orbit as the library periodicals appeared to indicate. It was already, for example, in my first year at LJ, six years after the Supreme Court decision on school desegregation. It was nearly three years after Little Rock. And it was the year in which the sit-in movement really got under way in the lunch counters of the South. The air buzzed with public concern about equality of access to education, to lunch counters, to swimming pools, and to the front seats of buses, but there was scarcely a murmur about libraries. It was understandable that the Negro who was fighting for much more basic human rights would not put libraries at the top of his priority list, but it was incredible that librarians--and more particularly, the library periodical editors--should be exhibiting such a total lack of concern or interest in what all this meant for libraries and their services. It was with that issue that the involvement of library periodicals in public and social issues in the sixties really began, with the leadership coming from the Wilson Library Bulletin and LJ.

Why, then, are milk and water still the principal ingredients of the library press, why does all the fire and brimstone settle down into the slush of footnotes? One obvious reason, I think, is that ours is, overall, a notoriously timid profession (though that is changing somewhat, as Atlantic City made apparent) and the editors, mostly drawn from that profession, are not too unlike most of their colleagues.

Another reason is that too many of our periodicals are edited by committee or group decision, by consensus rather than out of individual conviction. Whether a periodical is published by a commercial concern or a professional association makes little difference: the editor must be left alone to do his own thing. At such time as that becomes unbearable to those who hired him, the option always remains of firing him. This at least has the virtue of bringing the policy differences into the open. But while he is on board, a group cannot control the editor's decisions and actions--not if it wants a periodical with any identity or individuality. Only the editor, operating freely and insisting on such freedom, can supply these qualities. John Berry did it with The Bay State Librarian, Bill Eshelman with The California Librarian, and Gerry Shields, surrounded by higher walls of bureaucracy than any of you at state or regional levels has to climb, is even managing, gradually, to do it with American Libraries.

Nevertheless, lack of viewpoint remains an obvious feature of most of the library press, and I believe there may be a deeper-seated reason for this. Reared from the first days in the library school womb to believe that the library should be a neutral place where all points of view should be housed and disseminated impartially and dispassionately, too many among us have come to believe that the same rules apply to the librarian as individual. The librarian operating without commitment seems unlikely to me to be much of a useful servant to his society. And the librarian-editor who believes that he should be faceless and neutral on all issues is the certain father of a stillborn periodical.

Total objectivity is death, so far as the editor is concerned. The editorial that states, with equal force, all sides of every question it raises leaves nothing for the reader to respond to. So, rule number one for the editorial writer is, to take out all the ifs and buts and maybes and equivocations, come out from behind the shelter of objectivity and fairness and recognition of the "other" point of view, and state his case forcefully and even somewhat baldly. It does no harm for him to be a bit exposed. In this way, he may generate some response from his audience, both from those who are glad to see someone saying something they haven't had the nerve to utter publicly, and from those who profoundly disagree.

When the disagreement comes in, the editor can demonstrate his cherished objectivity. Providing that the other points of view are literate, or can be made so, he should publish them. There is, after all, a difference between the editorial page and all other pages of the magazine, and this difference must be abundantly clear to the readers. The editorial page should be the preserve of the editor (or the editorial staff) alone. It alone speaks for the magazine; it is the magazine's voice, its identity.

On one occasion during the year when Wyman Jones (now librarian at Los Angeles) was my invited guest columnist in LJ, he sent in a column which was about 180 degrees removed from an editorial which I had just completed for the same issue. I printed the conflicting pieces on facing pages. My point is that I don't believe many of our readers were confused about LJ's position on the issue being discussed because it was clear by then that LJ's position always appeared on the editorial page or over the byline of a staff writer. Wyman's position was his own and his position as guest columnist didn't mean LJ endorsed his views.

It is both surprising and annoying that a profession which discusses its own professionalism so insistently should be so tolerant of amateurism in its so-called professional periodicals. Now I don't really expect that all of our magazines can be manned by people who come equipped with training and experience in journalism, but it does seem reasonable to expect that those who take on jobs as editors should also undertake a little self-education in the processes of journalism, even if they do no more than read some of the professional practitioners with an editorial rather than a lay reader's eye.

Take the matter of headlining. In many of our periodicals the article titles read like catalog entries (or worse). Perhaps the worst offender in this respect, unless you count American Documentation as a library periodical, is College and Research Libraries. Such titles are meant to be helpful and informative but actually they become roadblocks, turning the reader away from the article. The title should be a sort of advertisement for the article. Like a low-cut dress it should make you interested in exploring what's underneath. The purpose of the title, and of its supporting deck or bank, is to lure the reader into the first paragraph of the article.

What journalists and many freelance writers do in the first paragraph is to present what they call a "hook"-- either a teaser or further clue about what's to come, or a very tight summary of what they're going to expand and fill in for the next few paragraphs. But in the library press, the reader who is dogged enough to get past some of the titles is stopped cold in the first paragraph. Too many of our articles read like research reports in which you first have to wade through soggy pages of the writer's methodology. One paragraph from the end you finally reach the one small finding or startling conclusion which resulted from the mechanical processes so laboriously described. But the reader rarely reaches the meat because he is too stuffed by the indigestible appetizer. The author may not know any better, but the editor certainly should, and the article can be made more interesting by a little re-shuffling, by re-titling, and generally by the application of a little journalistic know-how. Whatever its content, the author's article is going to serve little purpose unless people read it. The medium may not be the message, but it has one hell of a lot to do with whether and how the message gets through.

Some of the flaws of our periodicals are not so much the result of amateurism as of editorial laziness. One obvious symptom of lazy editing is the parade of articles which are not articles but speeches--full of the rhetoric of the platform (such as the one you are reading now) and the cute asides from which a captive audience cannot escape but from which a reader can. It usually only requires the simplest surgery to remove the speech and audience aspects from such a paper, but in most of our periodicals you can bet, particularly if the speaker is fairly eminent, not a comma will be touched.

Finally, one flaw which is more annoying and frustrating than anything else. It results usually from an editor's over-familiarity with his field and his material. An editor of a magazine inevitably gets to meet or correspond with a lot of people, to move to places and meetings more than most people, to see more printed material in his field than most. But he must never forget that his job is to _interpret_ much of what he sees and hears for his audience. If he begins to assume that his audience starts from the same point as he does, he begins to look like one of those comedians who shares an in-joke with some of his colleagues who have turned up for the first night and are sitting in the front row. The rest of the audience is left out in the cold, and resents it. The detail must be spelled out, the people and places identified. A follow-up story on an event covered in its earlier development must repeat enough of the gist of the earlier story so that the reader knows what is being discussed. A page reference to an earlier issue is not enough.

To conclude on a more positive note, there are many areas where collaboration between the local and national periodicals might help.

The state and regional periodicals might produce some livelier and more interesting and useful material than

they presently exhibit if they were to select some of the
material in the national press to follow-up with local versions.
For example, some years ago I did a survey of
public library book selection practices as related to some
of the more controversial novels then being published. One
young man in Pennsylvania, recognizing that the results of
the LJ survey might not be typical, since the concentration
was upon the larger metropolitan libraries across the country,
decided to check out the survey's findings against a
sample of small to medium-sized libraries in one area of
his own state. Both the contrasts and the similarities between
the LJ and Pennsylvania surveys were interesting and
revealing. The young man didn't send it to his state periodical
but to LJ, and since it was good, I published it.

But this is the kind of material I am suggesting the
state and regional periodical editors should be commissioning,
and if more of them would do it we would begin to get
a clearer picture of national practices and attitudes than the
big three can hope to divine from Chicago and New York.
If a dozen or more of the local periodicals were to follow
up on the same theme, one of the national periodicals could
then provide a useful service by synthesizing the results of
all these efforts and presenting a story with a broader base
than our present fragmentary efforts are likely to achieve.

The original lead for such a concentrated action
doesn't have to appear in one of the national periodicals.
One state might well produce something which would be
worth following up in others. For example, I have always
been puzzled and a bit disturbed that no other state ever
decided to take up the Fiske Report and check whether its
findings are accurate or valid outside California. Obviously,
a state periodical editor wouldn't have the resources to do
a study in the same depth as Fiske, but there is no barrier
to taking one or two, or half a dozen, of Fiske's more startling
findings or charges, and checking them out against a
representative group of libraries in one state.

The same kind of follow-up would be helpful when
ALA or some other professional body publishes yet another
of its multitude of standards documents. How real or relevant
are some of these things? How real or relevant was
the Access Study? Or Castagna's rush item on the personnel
crisis?

I see other possible areas of useful collaboration

between our periodicals at state and national levels, for example in news coverage. When a story breaks in one state which is obviously of broader than local interest, the state editors would be doing the profession a real service if they would act as news feeder sources for the national periodicals. Even if they did no more than provide a quick lead that the event had taken place it would constitute a step forward. (From personal experience, I can tell you that the state libraries and extension agencies are virtually useless in this respect.)

On some of these local stories, also, the local periodicals should be providing the kind of in-depth coverage that the national periodicals, with their broader range, can rarely spare space for. Cooperation should be a two-way thing, of course, and the national periodicals in some cases might be able to lend a hand to the local editor, in the form of resources, advice or technique. For example, the national periodical might have pictures that would be relevant, or background information in its files on similar cases in other parts of the country, or knowledge of action being taken or contemplated by one or other of the professional associations which would be pertinent to a story on the case.

By way of illustration, take the Ellis Hodgin case in Martinsville, Virginia, which got cover, editorial and front-page news treatment in the September 1 LJ. This isn't a very good--or rather not a very typical--case to illustrate my point, since news about it spread so fast that the details were available on the national scene almost as soon as the most alert local editor could hope to get them. But this is by no means the normal situation, and is unlikely to be until some national library periodical is rich enough to afford stringers in all parts of the country like the New York Times.

But disregard the fact that on this occasion LJ had a man on the spot almost as soon as the story broke. In the normal course of events the local editor would have heard about the story long before it reached New York or Chicago. He could have quickly assembled the bare bones of the story and contacted one or more of the national periodicals to alert them that something important had happened. The national editor could then have decided to follow up the story in depth, or he could have asked the local editor to feed him more material as the story developed. The local editor, in any case, should have pursued the story in depth for his own periodical, getting interviews with Hodgin and local officials, gathering factual background on those involved, and so on. If his deadline were longer than that of the national periodicals (which is likely) he could have continued to feed on the more important items while still putting together the complete story for his own magazine.

And again, the process could have been two-way. Shortly after the Hodgin story broke there was a meeting of the Social Responsibilities group in New York City. There, the Hodgin case was discussed, and various actions vis-à-vis ALA and other channels were considered. Also, a collection was taken up by the group as a sort of informal beginning of a defense or support fund for Hodgin. LJ had an editor at that meeting in New York, and she could easily have been assigned to relay the relevant information on the meeting to Dick Burns for whatever story he might be preparing for The Virginia Librarian.

At about the same time, or a little earlier, ALA, receiving the Hodgin news, finally decided it had better show some inclination to do something so far as a defense fund for librarians was concerned. Gerry Shields, if our editors were working as a network in the manner I am suggesting, could also have fed this information to Dick Burns for incorporation into his story in the local periodical.

My final suggestion is that the state and regional periodicals could do a good deal more than they are doing to supplement the efforts of the national periodicals in providing current information for the working librarian. For example (and this may sound like a note of self-interest), while some of the national periodicals do a reasonably good job of reviewing most of the books published for the professional librarian or the student of librarianship, many of these reviews appear six weeks to a year, or even more, after publication. The state periodicals could supplement this reviewing by publishing, say, monthly lists of new publications in librarianship. This sort of current awareness service would not be difficult to accomplish. Information on the majority of new publications could be obtained from little more than half a dozen publishers--ALA, Bowker, Wilson, Scarecrow, Shoestring, Gale, McGraw-Hill--and I have no doubt that these publishers would be only too willing to cooperate.

The state and regional periodicals, also, ought to

make an effort to round up current data within their own territories; data such as salary levels, new buildings, central processing developments, use of teletype, and a dozen other things. The national periodicals attempt occasional summaries of information of this kind, but the results will be fragmentary until a more sustained effort is made at the state level.

This has been a long diagnosis and a short prescription. Both elements fall far short of any claim to comprehensiveness. There are other symptoms of illness--and surely other cures--along with plenty of material for more conjecture. I am off the news scene now, out of the periodical editor's chair. Perhaps some of what I've suggested has begun to happen. There are some hopeful signs of life despite the general malaise of the library press. I've named a few, you know of others. Perhaps the best advice is to suggest that you support, through your subscriptions and your response, the library periodicals you prefer. With luck, the others will fade from the scene.

PART I:

LIBRARIES AND LIBRARIANS

What Good Are
Public Library Standards?

by Joseph L. Wheeler

Reprinted by permission from the February 1, 1970 issue of Library Journal (95:3), p. 455-462. Copyright 1970 by R.R. Bowker Co., a Xerox Company.

National standards, set forth to contrast with local performance, and adequately publicized, have doubtless done more--more promptly than any other device--to help good administrators improve conditions in public libraries.

Some librarians consider that statistics are a bore, a wasteland,[1] and a time waste, because they fail to use statistics effectively. Any circulation increase, any growth in reference service volume, rates a news story which the public likes to hear. Subnormal staffing and salaries cry for remedy. All the statistics called for by ALA, USOE, and the state agencies have definite administrative and public relations value. Usually they help build the case for better funds. Frequently, they reveal administrative and service weaknesses which need to be uncovered. For example, maintenance salaries in 18 largest cities (according to the Enoch Pratt Library Annual Table for 1968) show a range between 5.5 and 11.3 percent and for other building maintenance costs, from 1.8 to 7.4 percent of total budgets. These wide differences may indicate either a) administrative inattention, b) overbranching, c) excessive janitorial salary and staffing domination, d) political influence to perpetuate it, or e) inattention by trustees to this essential measurement of what their library dollar is getting in public service. Performance or program budgets cannot be substantially based without measurement statistics.[2]

As a California county administrator says: standards "altered to reflect changing times and circumstances, are a widely used stimulus to excellence in public administration."[3] The profession is in great need of several more significant measurements and standards, and of better and prompter statistics on which to base them.

The 1966-1967 revision[4] of ALA's 1956 Public Library Service standards was based on a decided shift from individual libraries to regional systems, despite its incorporation of considerable text from the 1956 booklet. It overlooked the certainty that not all libraries, large and small, will join regional systems for some years ahead. It overlooked the needs for standards for individual libraries. It failed to set up quantitative standards or patterns for either system or city branches. It omitted any standard for reference-informational services, in the face of rapidly increasing public demands for such service. And as discussed below, it destroyed ALA's previous standard as to professional staffing which had been a powerful barrier against unqualified personnel.

Even when libraries are parts of systems, they need definite quantitative standards to show them how they are progressing. Otherwise how do they justify their results and their budget breakdowns and requests when they present them to appropriating bodies through their system heads?

Per Capita Support

Years ago there was hot debate at an ALA Conference when two prominent large-city librarians argued vehemently against adopting the first per-capita standard for support: $1. As these gentlemen aroused the ire of their colleagues, this vital standard was adopted forthwith. In its day it did more than anything else to stimulate better local support everywhere.

ALA's more recent $3.50[5] and $3.82[6] per capita have prodded hundreds of communities into better support. Unfortunately in a state like Vermont, where the state agency has been ineffective for years (the headship just filled after a year's delay), the state's statistical report for 1966 showed 249 towns totalling 390,000, 1960 population, and only 22 of these met the then ALA standard of $3.82 per capita. Nine towns of over 1000 had no library. But weep not; all these adjoin or are within six or seven miles of some town which does have a library. There were 159 Vermont towns with less than 1000 population. It may be argued that towns so small should fold up their libraries and have neither a local library nor a system branch. In fact, a group of nonlibrary surveyors in another state has tentatively suggested that 7000 population should be the breakpoint. Pretty drastic! New Jersey's state agency has wisely taken a stand to prevent more of these "pee-wees." Tables from several states show what is true nationally: that the smaller the community the harder it is to meet per capita standards, and the weaker the collection, staffing, and service per capita. Much can be learned from such a table; library birth control rulings in every state "seem imperative," insists one librarian who read the preliminary draft of this article. Even with the few small libraries with notably good citizenship, or with endowments whose incomes tend to shrink in purchasing power, the day of the little ineffective libraries, or branches, should end. But the Bowker mailing list statistics show that such libraries are still increasing, even in New England where most libraries are so underfinanced. People still can and do drive to a larger town and use its better library, especially in regional systems.

Returns from many libraries indicate a substantial rise in per capita support in the last five years. New York State's statistical report for 1964 shows that average per capita actual support increased, for noncapital costs, from $2.61 in 1959 to $3.66 in 1964. In fiscal 1968, five metropolitan county libraries in Ohio were receiving $5.36 to $8.36 per capita. And in fiscal 1968, in Nassau County, New York (above average in education and per family income), out of its 52 libraries, 27 were supported at better than $7 per capita, and nine more at over $5 per capita. Owing to the national average increase in all salaries and wages, and the increase in book prices,[7] an increase to a minimum of $4.90 to $5.25 expenditure per capita could be considered a fair compromise between average recent actual returns and ALA's new 1968 minimum system averages of $5.80 per capita for systems of 200,000; $5.36 for systems of 600,000; and $5.31 for systems of 1,000,000.[8]

Getting individual libraries into systems seems to create substantial new overhead costs: "In working on current revision of Costs of Public Library Services, we find . . . costs have increased to $6.43, $6.03 and $5.91 for the three population groups, for systems."[9] The question arises: just how much, or what proportion, of total funding should be allowed for system and regional headquarters operation and materials? The several recent studies we have read give no figures or estimates. But, as many systems, perhaps eventually most of them (except city branch systems), will consist of individual local libraries usually with local and, it is to be hoped, county and state tax support, it seems logical that per capita standards for individual libraries, based on population groupings, are essential and they are offered in the table on p. 37.

Effect of Systems and Regionals

Justifiably ALA's standard for support, but for large systems, has recently been upped,[10] and is due for another rise, as just noted, partly due to rising book[11] and salary costs. No standard is given for individual libraries, even of 100,000 people. If anyone questions the dimensions of the new standards, or the economy of systems, he will quickly be reminded that the antiquated idea of economy is really not at issue, for systems are intended to assure much better service to everyone than heretofore, and so the big jump of nearly 40 percent, from $3.82 in 1963 to $5.31 in 1968, is only right and natural. It may be called drastic. And the forthcoming 1969-70 figures are even more so. They raise a host of questions as to the validity of the whole regional system idea and operation.

This writer is an advocate of systems, though to date the term is ill-defined. The development of systems in California, for example, shows, among other things, not only large increases in per capita circulation (and would surely show even larger in reference service if recorded) and better staffing, but the stimulation of local support to justify state aid. The statistical tables cannot measure the notable important strengthening of advisory services.[12] But all this is costing considerably more than ever.

Someone needs to put up a few warning signs: a) the taxpayers have some rights and will assuredly stage a revolt unless librarians pay more attention to economy in operation and in their philosophy; b) the overhead of systems, including some city systems, is running away with the body; it needs to be shrunk and simplified; c) neither system overheads nor collections should be housed in separate-cost buildings, but they should be in or attached to or otherwise combined with local, several-level central buildings in the heart of the region's major city in order to avoid considerable duplication of overhead and materials; d) the emphasis should be placed on developing and promoting improved and more specialized reference-informational services, not on organizational machinery and more elaborate and delayed central processing;[13] e.g. one regional system is expending 35 percent of its whole budget on "processing"; one state college group is having 40 percent of its book funds transferred to pay central processing costs; one state is striving for legislation and funds to create ten costly regional "informational science banks" or centers when two would be much more effective for the money. By including both public and college libraries, they can stop perpetuating the gulf between the two groups. One group of 18 college libraries is asking for $10 million of state taxpayers' money to create a "system." The taxpayers have a right to combat these costly ideas, which in many cases are motivated by "electronic retrieval" enthusiasts with an ax to grind, and by the politically potent idea that somehow <u>all</u> the libraries should get a piece of pie.

Two further points: Increasingly the emphasis in regional systems is rightly placed on their informational and advisory functions. Efficiency and economy come from concentrating funds and strength at the fewest possible major existing libraries. Systems headquarters can and should accomplish what almost no local or branch can afford--system-wide publicity and promotion, by all economical and resultful methods. "Advertising lowers the cost of distribution" is a valid slogan. The New York State Library Extension Division's <u>Statistics 1964,</u> based on 1959 and 1964 population estimates, showed total expenditures more than doubled in five years, for the series of systems which now blanket the state, while estimated population increased 22 percent, and "total holdings" increased 67 percent. But circulation increased only 22 percent, and registration increased only 5.6 percent. That is, circulation per capita stood still and registration per capita actually decreased. Evidently in most states, preoccupation with organizational concerns, automation and vast book buying are diverting attention from the main issue of increasing and improving reader services to a much larger proportion of individual citizens than have as yet been reached. And finally, desirable trained service and subject specialists who are added to the systems' overhead staffs could well spend at least half their time in visiting, observing and counselling with local branch heads and staffs. Otherwise we are headed for more bureaucracy, though few librarians or high-fee consultants seem concerned.

One does not applaud efforts by various committees to attempt pressuring individual libraries into systems by blindly refusing to recognize their problems. A decade has passed since I proposed the so-badly needed series of 16 Small Libraries Pamphlets; and three years and three successive ALA committees before the project was approved. We believe these carefully prepared 16-page informational pamphlets were a godsend and that they have done valiant continuing service in persuading individual libraries to join or contract with systems.

Because no appropriate organization has tried to create an up-to-date set of standards for these thousands of individual libraries, we offer a Table herewith, without apology for its shortcomings. It may encourage appropriate ALA committees (including Trustees and State Agencies) to revise and improve it, as a helpful management tool for all public libraries.

The Population Basis

The logical statistical basis for library calculations and standards is the population of the political unit which provides the basic tax funds to run the library; the population is what the library should be serving--whether or not the local library is part of a system. It has been suggested[14] that size of book collection, or possibly total expenditures, of the libraries from which data are drawn, should be used as the chief measure by which to rate a library, or with which to determine the size categories for public library standards and appraisal. But financing influences everything in the library's operations, including the size of its book collections. Even the best staff cannot build an excellent collection without money.

Financing and the book collection influence services and all else. But they are greatly subject to temporary conditions, especially to the quality of administrative leadership and the devotion and determination of the library board or city manager to see that the library gets fair treatment. Public relations and publicity have a great effect. The budget of a library may double in three or four years, if it has previously been grossly underfinanced. So may the book collection, as numerous recent examples attest, thanks to state and federal aid. A change in the library headship, or in two or three or even one department head, may change the entire local library picture to bring it more closely to standards. Meantime, the community keeps on as an entity, normally increasing annually in population, but perhaps standing still or declining, or in occasional cases doubling or increasing at a spectacular rate. This is the library's service area, and primarily library measurements should be proportionate to its population.

Census population figures for 1960 are now nine-tenths out-of-date compared with the very different data most cities and towns may show in 1970. So per capitas need challenge, even though local or U.S. Census Bureau interim data or estimates may be available. It is hard to find them available on a synchronized basis for all the communities covered by any comparative library tables. That is why 1970 should be a landmark as to reporting all factors at one time.

Also, since 1960 there are increasing per capita demands on large city libraries from an increasing proportion of residents outside their city limits. This makes it difficult to estimate fairly an actual service-area population on which to base per capitas. Examples are Baltimore and Providence, which contract to give adult reference services to their entire states, and Boston which now serves the heavily populated Eastern Massachusetts Region and also provides special materials throughout the state. Many cities of 15,000 and 20,000 are swamped by reference requests from students and adults living miles away, and from school districts not contiguous with city boundaries. This breaking through city boundary barriers is an increasingly good reason for regionalizing, or at least for regional contracts, wherein county, state and federal aid can equalize services and reimbursement therefor. However, all libraries of any size have this problem of out-of-boundaries population served, and the in-city population may be the most realistic for comparative measurement.

Another complication. Obviously, population figures often need a modifying plus or minus factor per quality of the population. Maybe all God's children have wings, but everyone knows what the Library Survey of 1947-50 showed, that people of less than average income and education are in general less than average readers and library users. A coal-mining town has more than the average of underprivileged, with low average reading interest. Among branches in a single city such situations are daily evident. Valiant special efforts by libraries in many communities encourage reading and library use by the underprivileged, and by individuals of latent or obvious talent in deprived groups.[15] Trustees increasingly recognize the library's obligation to this end; good administrators are recognizing staff members who can do this, and are paying increasing attention to this aspect of their service to their communities. But though the high cost of serving the underprivileged is obviously a factor in raising per capita total operating costs, "the ethics of our profession demand that we serve these new publics,"[16] and somehow get the money to do it.

Per Capita Formulas

The foregoing comments influence what ALA badly needs, and what so far has been available only as an amateur attempt--a table of standards, by population-size categories, as to the major factors in local library operations. In our library administration book,[17] Mr. Goldhor and I ventured two tables of suggested standards, the second dealing with building capacities. The Table below raises some of our 1962 Standards for Major Factors, and gives added data, broken into population-size categories. Two other tables in the 1962 book (p. 134-5) plainly show that size of community population has a profound effect on per capita planning, operation and performance, and on building-space requirements. The size-categories given in the Table published here had been used by ALA and by USOE for some years; they are important and valid. All of them should continue in use by USOE, by ALA, and by the state agencies. USOE should omit none. USOE needs to gather and summarize similar data from all the states, in order to establish a national picture of current conditions and trends, and also to compare present and future conditions and performance with those in the recent past.

Inadequacy of Current Statistics

Thorough statistics are a large, expensive undertaking. But one of the major objectives in creating USOE's Division of Library Programs was to assure adequate and more frequent tables of public library statistics. This responsibility now rests with USOE's National Center for Education Statistics. At present: a) the tables are more than tardy--the latest we have are from 1965[18] and 1962 data;[19] b) they fail to include three highly significant items, i.e., real reference questions per capita, registration percentage of population, adult nonfiction vs. fiction circulation; c) some definitions are either not realistic or are not carefully enough worded, so that, for example, we have a host of libraries obviously too small to have a "professional" librarian, yet reporting that they had one; d) data for cities of under 35,000 are broken into only three size-categories and are commented on only to the extent of one column. The 1965 libraries of over 25,000 are in only four or five size-groups. In the case of the libraries of under 35,000 population, some of them are totalled but none are summarized. In other words, those who worked up these statistics appear to have been handicapped in interpreting their meaning to the profession, and their application to the planning and management of the individual library.

To assure action, would it not be in order to urge the Public Library Association and the Library Administration Division:

a) To pressure the appropriate Congressional committees and USOE to put public library statistical reporting on a more understanding and realistic basis, and reorganize their procedures to get the returns into print and issued within eight or ten months of the return of the data.

b) To issue advance instructions in 1970 to all libraries, to keep more adequate 1971 data, and to make preparations for complete returns from all the public libraries for fiscal 1971, and 1975. This entails preparing every library to cooperate and supply the data. These returns should be prepared shortly after release of, and correlated with, the 1970 decennial census figures of population. But advance notice is needed to assure the keeping of the records in 1971, especially as there is great difficulty in getting small libraries to keep and report their figures.

c) To insist that libraries down to the smallest be included. The state and local governmental officials have some responsibility for demanding local response. Because of their great significance, the returns should be separated into the 11 size-categories already followed for some years in tables used by USOE, ALA,[20] and Wheeler & Goldhor. For example, data for libraries, or branches, of under 1000 population for 1970 may very well show these service units to be so unprofitable that they should receive no county, state or federal aid if they are within 15 miles of a larger community; and that if most of them were to be actively phased out within five or six years and their annual income transferred, their larger nearby libraries would or could be correspondingly strengthened and everyone would benefit. The burgeoning of small town school libraries provides an additional argument.

MAJOR FACTOR STANDARDS, BY SIZE CATEGORIES, 1969
(See note, end of article, page 50.)

Population Size Categories	Expenditures Per Capita	Proportion for Salaries*	Bookstock per Capita	Bookstock Proportion of Budget	Circulation Per Capita	Circulation Proportions Adult Fiction & Nonfiction; Juvenile
1. Under 1000	$5.25	50%	7 vols.	25%	10.6 vols	27, 23, 50
2. 1000-2500	5.20	55	6	23	10.4	26, 26, 48
3. 2500-5000	5.15	60	5	22	10.2	25, 29, 46
4. 5000-10,000	5.10	61	4	21	10	25, 30, 45
5. 10,000-25,000	5.05	62	3	20	9.5	25, 31, 44
6. 25,000-35,000	5.00	63	2.7	19	9	25, 32, 43
7. 35,000-50,000	4.95	64	2.4	18	8.7	25, 33, 42
8. 50,000-100,000	4.90	65	2.2	17	8.3	25, 34, 41
9. 100,000-200,000	4.90	66	2	16	8	25, 35, 40
10. 200,000-500,000	4.90	67	1.8	15	7	25, 36, 39
11. 500,000	4.90	68	1.5	15	6	25, 37, 38

d) To include adequate summaries, with per capita totals for each size category, and with a commentary. For instance, detailed analytic commentary is needed on the significance of closely defined reference data, and adult nonfiction vs. fiction circulation, if librarians are concerned with their educational and informational functions in this era of "information explosion" and increasing reference demands.

e) To seek foundation grants if necessary, to supplement federal and state funds, so as to accomplish the foregoing.

Space precludes mention of even recent history of public library statistics, well recounted by Krikelas.[21] The late George F. Bowerman published valuable comparative city tables from about 1905-1920 in the annual reports of DCPL. Around 1947 Emerson Greenaway initiated the Enoch Pratt annual comparative tables which are so helpful to all large libraries, and which fortunately have been continued by his successors. We refer to two other recent studies,[22] also the Williams book[23] which attempts definitions and covers methodology, but contains little on the significance or use of the statistics.

Population Size and Standards

We have already noted why library statistics should be reported by population size-categories. Other factors than population are more or less temporary, even fortuitous, as noted under "The Population Basis" section above. Probably no library factor has increased so rapidly in the last decade as the size of library book collections. But this has seldom been matched by equal increase in circulation, or turnover per book, or in volume and character of reference-informational service.

The smaller the city the more books per capita it needs and generally has, the larger its per capita circulation, the larger the proportion of the population enrolled as card holders, and the larger its expenditures per capita. The larger the city, the larger its volume of reference service per capita, and the larger the proportion of its budget going into salaries. Many examples prove this. Dallas, for its 1968 estimated population, for instance, handled 1.3 reference question per capita. This is a high figure, especially for a library which only 15 years ago was in the doldrums, and was then ill prepared to handle reference service at all.

The most helpful standard-guide which the smaller libraries have had is Interim Standards for Small Public Libraries, issued by ALA in 1962 to all libraries of up to 50,000 population. It covered hours of opening, size of book collections, phonorecords, periodicals, staffing, salaries, and building capacities. It set these forth by realistic size-categories. But no standards were given as to circulation or reference use. These valuable 1962 Interim Standards and the 1966 Minimum Standards..., which had few quantitative standards, were the basis for the more specific quantitative "Statistical Standards" issued in 1967.[24] As the latest from ALA, they are helpful indeed. We refer again also to USOE's 1962 and 1965 tables, the University of Illinois tables, and Tables 8-1 and 8-2 in Wheeler & Goldhor for additional evidence of the overriding influence of population size. We also used for the above standards a special table of data from superior Illinois libraries, by size groups, which Don Wright prepared for us from Illinois annual tables for 1967.

How Are Standards Created?

We have discussed elsewhere[25] the standards which public librarians have to measure costs, methods and results, and which may justly be labelled "so-called standards." The same may be said of college library standards.[26] They do not spring from any deep "scientific" research, but since the beginning have been only empirical. They are developed by individuals who are concerned with the level of excellence of service to the public and with economy. The Table above is based on such factors as: a) recent statistical reports and averages from a large number of libraries; b) the ideals, objectives, and accomplishments of a considerable number of better libraries; c) the steady increase in per capita public demands and services, and better economic conditions, e.g. the decreased purchasing power per dollar and the drastic rise in book prices and salary scales; d) the example and returns of a fair number of libraries which are considerably ahead of the crowd, but which are accomplishing more primarily because of better leadership. Some of these are in communities which have neither the highest nor exceptional average per family incomes nor high average years of education.

Fair and acceptable standards have to be based on a fair compromise between current actual averages, and the current results of a fair number of most successful but not miraculous performance among the better libraries. Finally, the fairness of the standards in the Table in this article is evidenced by the numerous cases where recent statistics indicate that each standard is actually being considerably exceeded. In fact, the libraries from which standards are drawn inevitably use them to upgrade themselves, if possible. Another point cannot be ignored; if a considerable number of libraries, scattered over the country, have already met or passed the "standards," it is not only proof that the standards are fair and attainable, especially as to per capita budgets, but that setting lower standards would create a handicap and thereby pose a threat to these more progressive libraries.

We note also that raising certain of the standards at a local library--support for example--does not guarantee improvement in all performance; there will always be poorly managed libraries and mediocre staffs, no matter how fortunate a library's opportunities. In general, however, fair support and the normal interrelationship of staff, bookstock, and services are all interdependent.

Every factor in total and itemized budgets is debatable and is justifiably under increasing scrutiny by the public. The case for libraries, especially public libraries, and most of all for city libraries of over 50,000 population, is so good that one regrets the still small voice with which libraries make their claims, and the lack of determination and courage of so many trustees and many librarians. In competition with other public expenditures, in their benefit to society and to their communities, few can compare with the contribution being made by public libraries.

Budget Breakdowns

Column 3 of the Table suggests a sliding scale of proportion of salaries to the total budget, and Column 5 shows proportion of total budget which might go into book buying. To a layman, the large slice of salary money compared with the small slice of book money is always a surprise--especially if he has never seen a public library in action in its busy hours. Numerous large city libraries are spending more than 68 percent on salaries and less than 15 percent on book buying (see, for example, the Enoch Pratt annual comparative tables of large city libraries). Ohio's overall salary budget had increased from 52.2 percent of total budgets in 1961 to 59.5 percent in fiscal 1968, while in 1968 salaries were 60.2 percent of total budget in Cincinnati,

64.5 percent in Akron, and 71.5 percent in Cleveland.[27] But these per capitas were based on 1960 census figures. This problem is not limited to libraries, but is found also in most large cities' varied services to the public. The reasons are of great administrative interest, but we only note that the larger the city, the larger the library staff per capita. One reason is the increasing proportion of the local population which asks for a greater volume of more specialized reference service. Such a service cannot be given satisfactorily by other than trained librarians, i.e. five years beyond high school. A second reason is the greater proportion of student-sojourners, adult visitors, and suburbanites who seek information not available in their local public, college, or school libraries, even though these are assumed to be excellent.[28]

Sufficient space is lacking to discuss management problems in minimizing the miscellaneous budget items which fill the gap between salaries plus books and materials, and 100 percent of the budget. Unless someone in the organization's overhead pays attention, these miscellaneous expenses can seriously cut the main-line services. Among hidden causes, for example, is the increasing tendency to waste current due to excessive wattage consumed in various types of currently designed lighting equipment, compared with the maximum properly diffused lighting they <u>could</u> deliver.

Salaries and Staffing

It is doubtful that any factor in good library service is so important as good staffing. Both quantitative and qualitative standards need to set a high enough goal. The fact that many libraries do not meet standards is no proof that they cannot, nor any reason for lowering any standard, especially at a time when reader demands are heavier, more varied, and more exacting than ever.

We are not proposing to subject any library to the typical inflexibilities and arbitrary decisions of civil service, which have slowed the spread of formal civil service, and led a distinguished foundation-financed commission to recommend that "the independent civil service commission...should be abolished or limited to an advisory function."[29] Any good library has more effective means for selecting talent and rejecting mediocrity. This is especially true as to trained staff.

All clerical and part-time workers should be chosen for merit only, by competitive tests and tryouts, including grade marks for the preceding year if they are school or college students. They should receive as large beginning salaries and have as favorable step-increases as are paid for similar qualifications in local business and professional offices. This should be considerably more than the current local per hour rate for underprivileged dropouts. Fair differentials are needed between high school students, college students, and college graduates. In one city library, we recently found a 125 percent turnover among clerical workers, at deplorable per hour pay encouraged by civil service and other city officials evidently intent on creating more jobs for mediocre personnel. Such turnover is a waste of taxpayers' money under the illusion that such a situation can be called "public economy."

We now have the belated ALA standard (Minimum Standards for Public Library Systems, 1966) of one full-time employee or equivalent in part-time (and not including janitorial staff) per 2000 population which we first presented in 1941 after considerable study.[30] The ALA's 1956 standard of one per 2500 population has been a handicap for many libraries; statistical tables more than a decade ago showed that nearly half of the libraries of over 300,000 population and many all the way down in size were already better staffed than one per 2000 population.[31]

In addition, the maintenance staff would normally run to the 1/6 person per 2000 population we set up as a standard in 1941. This turns out fairly close to the 1/7 person in the 1966-68 tables for large city libraries.[32]

No one unacquainted with the operations of many public libraries in many states in the last 20 years can realize how many head librarians and trustees have cited and upheld the ALA standard of 1956 that "one-third of the staff should be trained librarians." This means a well-rounded general background of four years of college education, undiluted and not diminished by library training courses, plus a year, with an M.A. at an ALA-accredited library school (there are now 48 such schools). In many cases library officials striving for more and better personnel have been stoutly supported by Friends of the Library, PTA's, and other citizen groups which take statistics and standards seriously.

But in 1966-67 the "one-third professional" standard

received a body blow. It was undermined by the wording slipped in at the last moment before the new standards were all too hurriedly adopted at ALA's 1966 New York Conference: "the professional and subprofessional staff... is approximately one third of the total personnel." There is no adequate definition and no one feels sure just what "subprofessional" means, except that it does not mean professional. This unfortunate concession, under heavy pressure, to the librarians of little courage, many of whom shrink from any agressive struggle to protect their library's welfare, is sure to open the gates for a swarm of half-educated and half-prepared local would-be librarians, sometimes labelled "technicians," backed by irrelevant political and other influence.

The "one-third professional" standard, so meekly and mistakenly surrendered, was based on the quarter-million-dollar Public Library Survey of 1947-1950,[33] headed by a leading political scientist-educator. Adequately educated and trained persons were needed then. How much more so in 1970, when the per capita informational demands from the public have so greatly multiplied and grown more specialized and consequential.

We suggest that this 1966-67 standard be interpreted as applying only to system headquarters, but not to the individual libraries in systems. Otherwise, the weakened standard should be cancelled and the "one-third professional" standard restored. The current attempt to substitute so-called "library technicians," including many who have had only two years of college including some library training, should not delude any library into thinking that such personnel can give efficient service to readers. If less pretentiously labelled "assistants," there are many things which they can and should do. Such workers should not be considered by the public nor by taxpayer groups as equivalent to better educated and trained professionals. Evidently we need a new analysis of which library operations do and do not call for adequately backgrounded staff, for recent articles reveal unrealistic ideas. Our remarks are based not only on careful observation of library staffs which are failing and succeeding in giving good reader service in nearly 200 libraries, plus half a hundred branches, but on conversations with many head librarians and especially with perceptive head reference librarians.

Books and Other Materials

No longer may we simply say "Bookstock" when discussing library holdings. Audiovisual materials are so much in vogue outside of libraries that libraries are pressured into buying them from funds too small to provide the books which people ask for and don't get, even after waiting a week or a month or two for an interlibrary loan. The Youngstown library, which this writer once headed, may have been the first to lend films and a projector in 1919, as well as a busy phono-record collection in 1918; but they were paid for from gift funds. Based on averages slightly increased, in the respective columns of the Pratt Library's current comparative tables and several state agency reports, we suggest that libraries of over 50,000 population, which have total budgets of over $3.50 per capita and are spending for books not less than the proportions given in Column 5 of our Table, plus 1.7 percent for periodicals and 1.5 percent for binding, might spend 6/10 or 7/10 of one percent of the total budget on A/V materials (whose use also involves the costs of additional staff).

We do not imply that phonorecords and films are not important; many of the more consequential are essential, in libraries which can afford them. Most states now have film circuits at nominal rentals. But if important books cannot be afforded, should A/V materials be afforded? A library cannot do everything. The public and the majority of librarians will doubtless continue to look upon printed matter as the public library's prime obligation, and will not equate A/V materials and related activities and staffing with print and its servicing. "Programming" and excessive A/V use narrow the subject matter and interpretation and lead to more drastic regimentation than does any textbook, and usually by a single mind less well posted than the author of a book on the same subject matter. A/V gives little opportunity for study and reflection, as though these are not essential to intellectual development. The less reading a student does, and the less fondness and facility for reading a pupil may develop, the less well he is preparing himself for a normal life in which intellectual curiosity, an open mind and the daily habit of reading and reflection are bound to play a substantial part, if the person is to foster and broaden his potential.

We suggest that not less than ten percent of the formula bookstock be added annually, and not less than five percent withdrawn for "out-of-dateness," including the passing of public interest in the subject matter. Increasing availability of interloans also influences these two standards.

As to the proportion of bookstock as between adult fiction and nonfiction, and as between total adult and total juvenile, we suggest that 25 percent of total book funds be used for juvenile books; 25 percent for adult fiction; and 50 percent for adult nonfiction, including reference books and periodicals. This may be aided by limiting fiction to fewer and better titles per year, even in the largest cities, and by duplicating copies and supplementing the funds by maintaining a pay-duplicate collection.[34] It is often overlooked that most library books used and borrowed by "young adults" are part of the adult collection, not juveniles.

Reference Service

Because reference statistics are so spotty, or not recorded at all, and are variously defined and interpreted, we have had nothing but the curious though useful 1943 Post-War standard of "one-half to one reference question per capita,"[35] with its hundred percent range between minimum and maximum. In view of recent statistics from several good libraries which have exceeded one reference question per capita, it is unfortunate that ALA's 1966-67 system standards did not call specifically for three-quarters to one reference question per capita, which was first proposed in 1962.[36] The System Standards ignored this important subject. No one really knows, and few seem to care, but it is likely that this reference standard should be placed on a sliding scale. Small libraries, i.e. under 20,000 population, are not equipped to look up reference questions as well as large libraries are, even in proportion to their populations. They cannot afford the materials, and few have adequately trained reference librarians who can concentrate on full-time reference service.[37]

One eighth of the staff, specifically college educated and library school trained, should be assigned to answer reference questions and to select materials therefor.[38] That is, a library serving 16,000 population should have one full-time trained reference librarian. Some large city libraries are doing better than this, including full-time trained reference librarians at branches where circulations run above 80,000. Trained reference librarians should not be called on for cataloging nor for such clerical work as checking incoming periodicals, etc., and they should be backed up by sufficient sub-professional and clerical help.

Cataloging-in-Source can and should replace the deplorable slowdowns, duplication of staffing and effort, at staggering costs, in the present duplication of skilled professional decision-making involved in cataloging and classification details in several thousand public, college, school, special libraries. This includes regional and system "processing." This would release a few thousand catalogers (but not all) for special short term training to become adequate badly needed reference librarians. [39]

One of the present frustrations in recording reference statistics results from wide variations in defining reference questions. We suggest using the printed instructions and definitions developed under Emerson Greenaway and Mary Barton and their successors at Enoch Pratt Library; these have been refined several times in the last 20 years. They are the most realistic and practical that we have seen. The idea of attempting to classify reference questions as to degree of importance, or as to time consumed, is obviously impractical; it only adds to the time and difficulties involved in keeping any reference statistics at all. On the other hand, no record of "reference-informational" questions is accurate if it includes questions which are only directional. The same is true where a definite book or periodical title is requested, or if the patron asks "Do you have Study Notes or a review of" or "May I see" well known books and authors being studied in literature courses, or "Where are your babycare books?," etc. [40]

A recent elaborate article suggests recording success and failure in satisfying reader requests in a medical library. [41] There it might be feasible, but at a hectic public reference desk it would be difficult to judge unless the reader himself wrote or checked his own satisfaction for the record.

Circulation Standards

One of the major measurements of public library service is circulation per capita. We offered revised standards for this in 1962. [42] In the Table in this article we have again raised the figures somewhat, due to the marked increase in most libraries in the last seven years, even though some of the large city libraries show slight decreases since 1966, possibly due in part to the rapid growth of school libraries and the millions of dollars of federal aid poured into school library book collections. In numerous cases, also, this desirable growth of school libraries includes discontinuing the public library's "classroom collections" and deducting the circulation previously credited to the public library. Other librarians point out also the great increase in citizen bookbuying, the wave of periodical reading, and the increased popularity of paperbacks and book clubs. One chief factor has been the failure of city libraries to maintain sufficient printed, radio and TV publicity about the library's adult books and services, and about the everyday help which thousands of citizens could be getting from their library if they were aware of such services. We are convinced that any good metropolitan library could increase its adult nonfiction circulation by half in two years, by a consistent program of more alert improved service plus promotion.

Partly as a result of "drifting," the "Index of American Public Library Circulation" appearing every few months in the ALA Bulletin, shows a steadily increasing proportion of juvenile circulation which, several librarians point out, seems to challenge the argument that it is the school libraries that are cutting down total circulation in numerous larger cities. We would make it clear that service to children continues as a prime objective for good libraries, but this should not be an excuse for neglecting adult services, as is so evident in numerous city libraries, and nearly all small libraries.

Because of this current distortion of public service we consider that the proportions of book circulation as between adult fiction and nonfiction, and juvenile, as shown in our Table, are fair and realistic. Space forbids further discussion of the drop in adult use in some cities, but we find that: a) libraries which really strive for worthwhile goals are still gaining in volume of total and adult nonfiction circulation per capita; b) most of the libraries having highest per capita total circulations have also the highest proportion of adult circulation; and c) percentage of the population registered as borrowers is a far more important measurement than some librarians seem to think, and should be insisted upon in statistical reporting to the state agencies. For example, though ALA has offered no registration formula since its "1/3 the population" in Post-War Standards for Public Libraries, 1943, we suggest that currently this should run to at least 40 percent even in the large cities. Due to excellent administration, Dallas had 52 percent of the officially estimated 1968 population registered within the ALA's standard three-year period. To a layman it would appear more than strange that a public service institution fails, in so many cities, to measure its effectiveness in reaching all the population.

It seems significant in library policies and planning, that nearly 60 percent of the U.S. population is over 21 years old, and we note the Census Bureau's prediction that by 1970 the median age of the whole population will be 26.4 years. Just how much is each local public library doing to reach all these adults, and encourage them to borrow and read good library books?

Costs Per Circulation

Recalling the furor of earlier days when several public librarians analyzed and publicized comparative costs per circulation, we refrain from suggesting standards for this, because a) everyone knows that circulation, though the favorite, the easiest, and still the most significant single measure of library usefulness to its community, needs to be reported in three segments, as discussed elsewhere; neither USOE nor many state agencies are so reporting; b) reference figures, carefully defined, are more frequently reported now and will eventually be recorded and reported by all good public libraries--large and small--and good reference service calls for able well-paid trained personnel; c) cost figures may cover up a totally inadequate proportion of professionally trained personnel, "job-holding," and civil service stalemates, and low salaries.

In other words, the difficulties and time involved to ferret out the pertinent data as a basis for calculating cost per circulation (by dividing total circulation into total annual expenditure) and the temptation of some librarians to distort figures to make a better showing discourage what should be a nationwide concern over the reporting of this circulation cost. Currently this appears of little concern to most library heads, though some take it seriously. For example, the Evansville, Indiana staff bulletin for September 15, 1964, with data for six Indiana cities in the 100,000-200,000 size category, shows Hammond with two volumes per capita; 11 per capita circulation; 5.57 turnover per volume, and 26¢ per circulation, compared with 34¢, 61¢, 63¢, 90¢ and $1.16 cost per circulation for the other five libraries. The heads of the two latter libraries might well point out that in one case the library location cannot possibly attract normal patronage, and in the $1.16 library a great volume of reference service is involved, the proportion of adult nonfiction circulation is high, salaries are above average, numerous A/V and group programs are carried on at considerable salary cost, the library is trying to reach a large underprivileged population, and it is heavily used by nonresidents.

One may hopefully predict that the ALA Public Library Association's Standards Committee will develop a valid formula for Cost Per Circulation, which will weigh and duly allow for the foregoing factors, but at the same time will give a figure administratively realistic and useable. It would serve an important purpose, especially if one believes in performance budgeting. There are great differences between libraries in management's attention to in-library operations and services, among libraries where community-type book collections and some other factors are closely similar, but where staff is well or poorly selected and qualified; where the element of competent supervision is highly developed or lacking; where the public relations performance is large-scale and superior or is neglected; and where the institution is running along with inspired direction or with little planning, undefined objectives, and slight direction or guidance. "No one is keeping things pulled together at the top." These administrative weaknesses, so frequently found, but unheeded, greatly influence "cost per circulation."

Building Size Standards

For lack of space, we omit standards for public library building size and capacities, hoping to cover them in a later publication. However, ALA's 1962 Interim Standards for Small Libraries includes a good space table for populations up to 50,000, set up in five size-categories. For larger as well as these smaller libraries, we refer also to Table 33-1 in Wheeler & Goldhor (p. 554). We would now slightly revise upward its Column 2 on Bookstock, to correspond with the Table in this article, and we would cancel the final 1962 column on costs, as increasingly misleading. (For example, Architectural Record shows each month the steady increase in costs and the great variation in costs by region.)

We have to omit also badly needed criteria justifying the creation of added branches (too many now in many cities, not enough in others) and bookmobile service (usually more productive per dollar than "pee-wee" branches), hours of opening, etc. This article is already too long, so I will conclude my comments.

Note to Table

Sources of Data for Standards: In addition to the numerous statistical tables and standards already footnoted, the 1967 or 1968 tables issued by the state agencies in Vt., Mass., Conn., N.Y., N.J., Ill., Ind., Iowa, Mich., Calif., Wash. have been used; also the comparative tables issued by Baltimore and Fort Wayne; also 1967 or 1968 annual reports from numerous public libraries of varied size. The May 1969 "Index of American Public Library Statistics" (ALA Bulletin, p. 556) shows an average (from 21 out of 41 libraries) of 49% juvenile, 23% adult fiction and 28% adult nonfiction, and shows clearly how adult nonfiction book use is being increasingly neglected in most public libraries.

References

1. "Statistical Wasteland," Library Journal, January 1, 1967, p. 78.
2. Wheeler, Joseph & Herbert Goldhor. Practical Administration of Public Libraries. Harper, 1962, p. 121-122 & Chapter 8.
3. O'Brien, J.P. "Use of Standards by Local Governments," Library Quarterly, October 1966, p. 321-324.
4. Minimum Standards for Public Library Systems, 1966. ALA, 1967.
5. Cost of Public Library Service in 1959. ALA, 1960, p. 2.
6. Cost of Public Library Service, 1963. ALA, 1964, p. 2.
7. Publishers' Weekly, March 10, 1969, p. 38-39. Increases from 1958-1968 of 30-135 percent by subject categories, and substantial rises in the one year, 1967-1968.
8. Just Between Ourselves, October 1968, p. 2-4.
9. Letter from Eleanor Plain, August 12, 1969.
10. Just Between Ourselves, loc. cit.

11. Bowker Library Annual, 1966, p. 102, 279; 1969, p. 45. The latter shows 162 percent average increase, 1947-1965.
12. Sabsay, David. "Statistical Study of California Library Systems," News Notes of California Libraries, Summer 1969, p. 346-359.
13. Wheeler, Joseph. "Top Priority for Cataloging-In-Source," Library Journal, September 15, 1969, p. 3007-13.
14. Lockwood, Charles & Ruth Lockwood. Quantitative Guides to Public Library Operation. Univ. of Illinois Library School, 1967.
15. Wolfle, Dael, ed. The Discovery of Talent. Harvard Univ. Pr., 1969.
16. Letter from Henry T. Drennan, August 6, 1969.
17. Wheeler & Goldhor, op. cit., Chapter 8, especially p. 133-136, and Table 8-3 and Table 33-1, p. 554.
18. Statistics of Public Libraries, 1965, Part I, Over 25,000 Population. USOE, 1968.
19. 1962 Statistics of Public Libraries . . . Less than 35,000. Univ. of Illinois Library School, 1966.
20. Including ALA's 1962 Interim Standards for Small Public Libraries, which separated those under 2500 population. Note that 70 percent of the 8,190 public libraries in 1960 had less than 10,000 population and they should be broken into three size categories, e.g. specifying those under 1000 population. See Wheeler & Goldhor, op. cit., p. 7, 134-135.
21. Krikelas, James. "Library Statistics and the Measurement of Library Services," ALA Bulletin, March 1966, p. 494-499. Also the article which follows by Frank Schick, "A National Conference on Library Statistics."
22. Krikelas, James. Library Statistics and State Agencies: a Comparative Study of Three States. (Illinois, Indiana, Missouri.) Univ. of Illinois Library Research Center, 1968. Also, U.S.A. Standards Institute. U.S.A. Standard for Library Statistics, 1969.
23. Williams, Joel. Library Statistics: a Handbook of Concepts, Definitions and Terminology. ALA, 1966.
24. "Report of the Statistical Standards Subcommittee," Just Between Ourselves, May 1967.
25. Wheeler & Goldhor, op. cit., p. 130-136
26. College & Research Libraries, July 1969, p. 273-280.
27. 1968 Directory of Ohio Libraries, with Statistics for 1967, p. 45-53.

28. Squire, James R. & others. "The High School Library and the Personal Reading of Students," School Libraries, Summer 1967, p. 11-19. Study of 16,089 Illinois students using 104 excellent school libraries, each having a trained librarian; they read or used an average of eight books per month, of which 6.4 were from their public libraries. See also the Arlington, Va. example discussed in Wheeler & Goldhor, op. cit., p. 389-391.
29. Municipal Manpower Commission. Governmental Manpower for Tomorrow's Cities. 1962.
30. Wheeler, Joseph & Alfred Githens. American Public Library Building. ALA, 1947, p. 37, 39.
31. Enoch Pratt Library. Statistics of Large City Libraries, annual tables since 1960; also recent tables issued by USOE and state agencies.
32. Ibid.
33. Leigh, Robert. The Public Library in the United States. Columbia Univ. Pr., 1950, p. 181, 186.
34. For discussion see Wheeler & Goldhor, op. cit., p. 463-464 as to apportionment and p. 468-469 as to pay duplicates; also p. 297 as to the majority favoring pay duplicate collections.
35. Post-War Standards for Public Libraries. ALA, 1943, p. 27.
36. Wheeler & Goldhor, op. cit., p. 332 for further discussion.
37. Wheeler, J. L. "Improving Reference Services," RQ, Spring 1967.
38. Wheeler & Goldhor, op. cit., p. 323-324.
39. Wheeler, "Top Priority for Cataloging-in-Source," loc. cit.
40. Miller, Mary M. "Two Days at the Reference Desk," RQ, Winter 1969, p. 107-111. Only about half of all these requests from readers can be recorded as "reference-informational." The latter word covers also knowledgeable advice to readers as to choices between books on a subject. The idea that "technicians," only half prepared, can give reference or advisory service, is an illusion leading to reader dissatisfaction.
41. College & Research Libraries, September 1968, p. 373-380.
42. Wheeler & Goldhor, op. cit., p. 135.

Public Libraries and
the Network Idea

by Verner W. Clapp

Reprinted by permission from the January 15, 1970 issue of Library Journal (95:2), p. 121-124. Copyright 1970 by R.R. Bowker Co., a Xerox Company.

There is nothing new about library networks except the name. Libraries have collaborated--either within or across jurisdictional lines--for a long time, creating what is euphemistically called the library "system" of the country. The name does, however, as is so often the case, provide new dimensions to the idea.

As currently used, the term network appears to be borrowed principally from telephone practice, reinforced by allusions to systems such as those used for rounding up data needed for forecasting the weather or for detecting invasions by enemy airplanes, involving the data-processing capabilities of computers. In particular, Educom, an organization formed to promote inter-university collaboration, has seized upon the computer as a principal tool. It has developed the notion of Edunet, a computer-based network for performing various operations of common benefit to universities. (Educom has suggested, for example, that Edunet might make available to university hospitals a daily set of computer-generated patients' menus.) In considerable part as a result of discussions of this kind, the President proposed to Congress last February that the Higher Education Act of 1965 be amended to incorporate a new program entitled "Networks for Knowledge." The bill provides $8 million for, among other things, computer-based sharing of library facilities among university campuses.

Now, as you know, valiant (and expensive) attempts are being made to bring computers into the daily work of libraries in such programs as the National Library of Medicine's MEDLARS (Medical literature analysis and retrieval system), the Library of Congress' MARC (Machine-readable catalog), and the New England Board of Higher Education's Nelinet (New England library network). Each of these is concerned with the computer processing of bibliographic information.

The MEDLARS program is in actual operation. With its use a computer processes the index entries made for journal articles (and some other materials) in current medical literature. A first product of this processing is the printer's copy for the Index Medicus, the most extensive record (in terms of numbers of items recorded) in existence of the literature of a subject. Other products are specialized bibliographies of various medical subjects. The use to which the highest hopes were attached was for automatic literature-searching, and such searches are actually being successfully performed.

In MARC the Library of Congress is carrying into practice the conclusion reached more than 100 years ago by Charles Coffin Jewett, the first librarian of the Smithsonian Institution, that the best way to promote library efficiency and to organize the library resources of the country is to provide libraries with a common language or standard of bibliographic description, to develop a technique for cooperative cataloging, and to devise a mechanism for creating a union catalog of holdings as a by-product of routine cataloging operations. This is what Jewett himself attempted to do in 1850 with stereotype plates. It is what the Library of Congress made possible with its printed catalog card service, beginning in 1901. In Project MARC it is merely substituting a machine-readable record for the printed. But nearly a decade has elapsed since LC commenced its search for automation and the end is not yet in sight.

Nelinet, in turn, assumes the existence of MARC. It proposes to use MARC tapes in order to provide a variety of services to a regional group of New England libraries, commencing with the libraries of the state universities and extending to other libraries as feasible. Among the services to be rendered would be the supply of sets of catalog cards, book pockets, book cards and book labels, and the maintenance and searching of a regional union catalog. This program has also been under way for several years and is only beginning to offer basic services while it is at some distance from adding new dimensions to library service.

Libraries and Librarians 55

Whether these and other computer applications are successful or not, it is of course the fact that library networks did not come into existence with the computer and are not dependent on it. They have existed for a long time by dint of teletype, or telephone, or telegraph, or even the postal service.

What are some of the characteristics of communication networks? A communication network may, in the first place, be defined as a system consisting of switching centers (this definition is obviously based on the telephone exchange model). As thus defined a communication network is not merely a distribution system, either linear, like a transcontinental railroad, or hierarchical, like an irrigation system. The definition implies that linkages can be established regardless of a principal direction of flow. In a newspaper network the smallest subscriber may suddenly become the source of news of world interest. Distribution systems may, it is true, be attached to the network, providing it with a third dimension; thus, each telephone exchange, which is the switching center, distributes information to its subscribers, some of whom, like large libraries, have many branches.

In speaking of communication networks, we should distinguish between content and channel. We are so impressed by the telephone as the archetype of the communications network that we forget that it is merely a channel, and that content means nothing to it. You may send anything over it that it is capable of conveying. You can swear into it or pour blessings into it. It will facilitate the chatter of teenagers equally with the conferences of heads of state. It will convey pictures or music or information in digital form. We tend to forget, too, that the telephone no longer consists merely of the overhead wire, the telephone pole, the switchboard and the desk set, and that it is rather the type of any communication network employing electrical frequencies, whether by overhead wire, submarine cable, microwave, or communication satellite.

At the opposite pole from the communication networks in which channel is everything, are those in which content is everything. Such are the networks that link the newspapers of the country, carrying news and news photographs between them as well as other material such as syndicated columns and cartoons. Here the network is named for the content rather than the channel, and the latter is of little moment, so long as it works, and indeed, in any issue of a newspaper, the use of a number of channels may be represented. There are many other communication networks in which the important element is the communicandum rather than the communicator--crops, weather, prices of stocks, race-track results, bank balance clearances, etc.

Another characteristic distinguishing networks from mere distribution systems is the greater independence of the networks' members. They are not merely passive recipients or sources. They are reactive. They may initiate a communication, or respond to one, or participate with others in one. The system by which information typically filters up, down and horizontally in a large organization, usually referred to as "through channels," can usually only by courtesy be called a communication network. Only too frequently it serves as a device for impeding rather than facilitating the transmission of information.

An important element in the success of a communications network is its conspicuity; everyone should be aware of it and what it does. This is preeminently true of the telephone, and it is very tempting to take excessive advantage from the fact. In the process of performing its primary function the telephone was found to contribute certain other useful services--a list of subscribers' names and addresses, a subject listing (the yellow pages), and even, in most communities, the time and the weather. Where should it stop? In some places it furnishes musical pitch, and it could easily provide a wide variety of other information. Indeed, the American Telephone and Telegraph Company recently convened a meeting of consultants to consider what information services it should consider providing in connection with the new international trade center that is being planned in New York City. I would not be surprised if the decision was to offer none beyond those now offered; it is quite enough of an accomplishment to provide an efficient channel of communication without also taking responsibility for generating the information that goes over it. But the suggestion was a tribute to the conspicuity of the telephone. Meanwhile, others take advantage of it, and thus, by calling appropriate numbers, one may in many communities receive any of a variety of communications such as a schedule of airplane flights, a short sermon, a racist speech, or even a list of migrating birds recently seen in the vicinity.

Because of lack of simplicity and conspicuity many networks are not recognized as such. For example, chambers of commerce. The chambers of commerce of this country are closely linked by similarities of function, status, and interest, as well as by a national organization. They have perhaps unequalled capabilities for producing, comparing and disseminating information and for responding to inquiries. Yet I suspect that it would never occur to the ordinary citizen to turn to a chamber of commerce for information until other more conspicuous sources had failed.

Similarly with churches. They too are organizationally interlinked, with fantastic capabilities of assembling and transmitting information, of serving as components of a network. But this capability is suppressed. They prefer to serve either as components in a hierarchically organized distribution system or in a system deliberately organized on an anti-hierarchical principle of complete local independence. Both principles are antithetic to the reticular principle, the principle of networks.

Now go to libraries. In the first place, each library constitutes a quasi-network in itself. I say "quasi" because the components of a library, although they are interdependent members of a system of switching centers, are not alike in form or function. The catalog serves as one switching center, the collection of periodical indexes and abstracting services another, and still others can be recognized in the bibliographic apparatus collectively and the reference services collectively--in other words, the entire network which makes it possible for us to move about in the collections, now easily, now with difficulty, assembling material of interest, utility, pleasure.

But libraries are also, inescapably, components of larger networks. As soon as you discover in one library a reference that leads you to another library, or even to a book in another library, you have identified the essential filament, the uniting thread in the library network: it is bibliography. It was this that C. C. Jewett proposed to exploit in his 1850 attempt to organize the libraries of the country into a network based on stereotype plates; it was this that served as the connecting link when, 50 years later, Herbert Putnam accomplished with printed catalog cards what Jewett had failed to do with stereotype plates. It is still the thread whether the communication concerns cataloging or interlibrary lending or collaboration in the development of library resources. Just as steel is the unifying material though the bridge be constructed of girders or trusses or cables, so bibliography is the stuff of printed catalog cards, or MARC tapes or union lists of serials, whether the network is based on shared cataloging or interlibrary lending or collaborative development of library resources.

With libraries, it is obvious, it is the content rather than the channel that makes the network. For all kinds of channels are or can be used by libraries--the mails, railway express, telephone, teletype, microwave, coaxial cable.

But by the same token the library network lacks the simple conspicuity of, let us say, a network channel such as the telephone, or a network content such as stock market quotations. Try to explain to a layman the working of the Farmington Plan or the value of the Center for Coordination of Foreign Microcopying Projects. If you can hold his attention long enough to get a story across, it is sure to come back and haunt you in some oversimplified and embarrassing version such as the one propagated by Educom which is fond of stating that we now have a means of communication so effective that the contents of the National Library of Medicine can be made available in seconds to any physician in the United States.

The fact is that we have had for many years--at least since the dawn of history--increasingly effective arrangements by which, if one had the time, the energy and sufficient funds, an inquirer could secure information in the form of library material from a distant part. Bibliography and interlibrary loan weren't invented yesterday; examples of both can be found in the fourth century B.C. and no doubt earlier. What succeeding centuries have done is to improve the system, by reducing the amount of energy, time, and expense required to make it operate and by improving the quantity and quality of the information obtainable with its use.

The fact is, however, that the existence of a library network has only an academic interest for most persons because they lack realization of its potential usefulness to themselves. And this in turn is because of the lack of perspicuity of the library itself. As in the case of chambers of commerce and the churches the network is lost to sight because of a flooding of the channels. Everyone knows that you go to a library for books. So far, so good. Unfortunately, people don't know, or too many people don't know, what you can find in those books and how to find books that can be in the widest sense useful, pleasurable, etc. In this respect, libraries badly need a conspicuity that is still lacking--how to convey a sense of the applicability of their wares to the interest in hand, to the daily work of the world. "Even the modern great library," said Vannevar Bush in his famous essay As We May Think, some years ago, betraying in that word "even" his own faulty appreciation of the situation, "Even the modern great library is not generally consulted; it is nibbled at by a few." The fact is that the larger the library, the greater proportion of its collections go unnibbled, so that in the very largest the custodians are frank to confess that a significant fraction of the collection may forever remain unused. The quantities of interesting books that lie on our shelves unread is only less frustrating than the quantity of interests that go unserved for failure to use those very books. How to bring these together?

I like to tell the story told on herself by Miriam Carnovsky who, as an ex-children's librarian, felt she should have known better. She was inviting a Hindu to lunch, and--to assure correct dietary etiquette--called the hostess advisory service of the Chicago Tribune to inquire about Hindu eating habits. The next day the adviser called back to say that they had been researching the question in the Chicago Public Library, with most interesting results. Mrs. Carnovsky was amused, but also mortified.

I can match her story from a recent experience. Having read an interesting article in Science which mentioned knapping (a new word to me at the time; it is the process of shaping by chipping stone implements such as gunt-flints and arrow-heads), I wrote to the authors for more information about this art. As I should have known, I would have done better to have gone directly to the library.

If librarians themselves do not always turn to libraries for the services which libraries can most effectively perform, can we blame the laity? We try to inform them by catching them young, by giving them reading lists, by exhibits and other ways, but not only do our arguments reach too few, but they forget them too easily.

Back in the mid-20's, shortly after I got into library work, the American Library Association, aided thereto by the Carnegie Corporation, took a very serious interest in adult education. As part of its adult education program it launched the "Reading With a Purpose" series, a succession of twenty-five cent pamphlet guides to serious reading on a wide variety of subjects. At the ALA Washington conference in 1929, Dr. Keppel of the Carnegie Corporation characterized this series as "one of the most notable pieces of work in the whole development of library service." I agreed, because I was at that time working at the reference desk in the Main Reading Room of the Library of Congress and I knew at first hand how useful the series was in bridging the gap between "I don't know what there is in a library" and "I'm curious."

However, in spite of the yeoman's work performed by these little books, the program was allowed to terminate only a few years later. Long afterwards I tried to find out the reason for the termination, but failed. Carl Milam, then in retirement, remembered only that the program had been discontinued; and even the files of the Carnegie Corporation failed to describe the reason. I had hoped that it might be possible to revive the series, but instead we have the "Reading for an Age of Change." This is not quite the same thing. As its title suggests it is addressed rather to a selection of important public issues than to a large variety of private interests, to such topics as space science, expanding population, biological frontiers, etc. Ten numbers have now appeared; they are available from the Public Affairs Committee, New York City, at sixty cents a copy; but I do not sense that they are as effective in providing a clue to the contents of libraries as did the older series.

What has this to do with networks?

We are currently being encouraged to talk and act like networks. State library systems are supposed to participate, in some manner dimly perceived but not quite specified, in a national network. When challenged as to what makes these networks, we are only too likely to fall back on tried and true elements--interlibrary loans, pickup and delivery services, regional union lists of serials, union catalogs, etc. But these are all old hat. These are the objectives of library work of a generation ago, and if they are only now achieving reality, that is because it has taken a generation for technology and legislation and funding to catch up with ideals.

But it takes more than interlibrary loan and a pickup and delivery service to make a network. If a library network means anything, it means a system which is regarded as such for the sake of the information which it provides, and not as a conveyor. By the same token its success will be proportionate to its conspicuity, to the degree to which it is recognized to be a source of useful information.

There is a difference, perhaps worth noting, between the library network and some others. Each local branch of the channel network--e.g., the telephone--brings new resources to the total network in terms of subscribers which are unique to itself. No other local, not even the largest or wealthiest, can claim these particular subscribers. The case is different with libraries. Few can bring to the network resources in terms of library materials which are not already available to it. What it does bring is purchasing power--a contribution toward a consumer population large enough to justify an ample and varied service.

Libraries, like bookstores, are naturally anxious to exploit the stock which they have assembled at considerable expenditure of money and effort. It is irritating, to say the least, to have customers reject the particular life of Shelley or the particular editon of Sherlock Holmes that you have stocked in favor of another which must be sent for at additional capital investment.

But yet, taking a leaf from the book of the mail order houses, might it not greatly stimulate cultural communications if we encouraged readers to acquaint themselves with the totality of what is available rather than to assume that our necessarily limited collections represent the totality to which they may have access?

I used to toy with the idea of a book catalog store, similar in concept to the catalog stores maintained by mail order houses--places where you can place orders, though you cannot see the merchandise. My catalog stores would be at crossroads. They would be designated by blue pennants bearing the initial B, for books. All you would find there would be copies of Books in Print with its subject index together with other catalogs of a similar nature, such as the Ulrich's Guide to Periodicals, the lists of the Superintendent of Documents, the Schwann catalog of phonorecords, the Unesco list of art reproductions, the Library of Congress list of map reproductions, etc.--in other words, the major tools for ascertaining the source of almost any kind of in-print library material.

Whether or not such a system could be operated by a public library, it is just such access to the cultural resources of the world that a library should provide. It should extend the minds, the interests and the ambitions of its customers, not restrict them within the compass of its own local collections, no matter how carefully selected. There would be difficulties of course. Interlibrary loan codes do not provide for lending in-print material, and few systems, no matter how wealthy, could undertake to secure all wanted in-print material for their customers. With respect to out-of-print material the picture is probably no easier. While interlibrary loans of out-of-print material are contemplated, they are not expected to be casual, and welcomes are quickly worn out.

Yet it is obvious that membership in a larger system, part of a network, could constitute a giant step toward access to the totality of resources. A number of devices for providing such access on a statewide basis has been contrived and is being tested, involving use of the resources of the state library, of regional or other resource libraries and contractual or other services. One result seems predictable from such programs: state systems will most certainly increase in self-sufficiency. With this increase other effects may in turn be foreseen. One is a relaxation of interlibrary loan demands upon the larger libraries which now receive too many of them, permitting them to be more hospitable to those that continue. For another, libraries will encourage their customers much more than in the past to feel free to request material not immediately available.

And if we handle the situation correctly, if we can prevent bureaucratic rigidity from nullifying the value of the service by delay and red tape, if we can instruct our customers in the art of identifying wanted materials or of asking the questions which lead to such identification, then I think we shall have gone much further than mere interlibrary loan and pickup-and-delivery, and shall be on the way to a new plateau of library service.

Performance Ratings
and Librarians' Rights

by David Peele

Reprinted by permission from the June 1970 issue of
American Libraries (1:6), p. 595-600. Copyright 1970
by the American Library Association.

Library literature is flooded with articles telling us how to educate and train our professional personnel. The flood becomes a trickle, however, when the topic is broached of the best means of rating the performance of these librarians we have guided. Mr. X in the Catalog Division has been with us for a year and a half; how good is he? Miss Y in public service is a three-year veteran. Should she or should one of her colleagues be promoted to a position of more responsibility?

There is, of course, a reason for the small in-print output, and that reason was repeatedly fired at me when I wrote some librarians and asked how they rated their employees. "I am sure that any answers you have received," said one, "...have helped you decide that the entire subject is far more complicated and far more individually oriented than perhaps you had hoped." "I don't feel," said another, "that examples I might come up with would be either terribly helpful or altogether fair." To these correspondents and to those to whom I spoke by phone I now reply publicly that I never imagined the subject would be easy. On the other hand, I do not believe that it is so individually oriented that one can say nothing. In what follows I propose to look at two aspects of the situation: 1) the rating form and some guidelines for filling it in, and 2) the right of the librarian who is being rated to discuss or appeal a rating he believes to be biased.

If any general statement can be made about rating forms it might be that 1) almost all libraries have them, and 2) almost all libraries are dissatisfied with them. The reason for the dissatisfaction has been indicated in the previous paragraph--the difficulty of fitting an individual's performance into such pet phrases as: "Knowledge of bibliographic resources--Excellent, Good, Fair, Poor (check one)." The various methods of rating are given in Kathleen Stebbins' Personnel Administration in Libraries (New York, Scarecrow, 1966) in chapter 8, to which interested librarians are referred; I do not propose to state them all here. As she indicates on page 126, no matter what system is used there are certain traits that appear on most forms--initiative, executive ability, quality of work, quantity of work,[1] dependability, attitude towards patrons, cooperativeness, accuracy, judgment, loyalty, and organization of work. One may assign relative importance to the various terms or indeed disagree with them altogether--as I do with the expression "quantity of work." This phrase is one of the great dividers between public service people and catalogers. After a hard morning spent at the desk just before exams the exhausted Circulation librarian slumps into the Catalog Department on his way to lunch. On the desk of one cataloger he sees one book, the very same book that was on that desk when he came in to work that morning. While he was out there on the line facing real pressure, back here one of those (ugh) catalogers spent an entire morning on one book. One book, my god! No wonder six months pass before we get rush items, and it's one year before regular stuff gets through. The Circulation man may have a justified complaint, or he may not. The important question is not quantity of work but rather--was it desirable that the cataloger spend the morning on that book? Did he use his work time effectively? That is the phrase that should appear on the rating form, and the answer to it can be given only by the chief cataloger and the head librarian who interpret it in the light of the cataloging standards for that particular institution. The question does not apply only to catalogers either. Does one blame the reference librarian for following up on a question simply because he is intrigued, even though the original asker of the question has long since left the library? On a "strict constructionist" interpretation he is not using his work time effectively, but in my book his curiosity is desirable as long as he doesn't leave other inquirers standing at the reference desk while he pursues the more absorbing question.

    The real problem with all of the Stebbins terms, however, comes when we try to answer the question, "What is the standard?" What, exactly, are you rating when you try to assess an individual? Primarily, his performance on the job he is doing (although the wise employer will also pay attention to ability. A given employee may not work out well in one spot in the library due to personal conflicts with superiors or fellow staff members, but this does not automatically disqualify him for another area). But the unanswered question--perhaps the unanswerable one--is, "performance compared to what?" Assume for the sake of argument that the library has a 5 point rating scale on which a 1 represents consistent performance above and beyond the call of duty, 2 is occasional performance on that level, 3 means he performs as expected, 4 indicates that he doesn't quite measure up to the standard and 5 shows he is consistently below what we expect of someone in the position. What would a 3 rating on a Stebbins term such as "judgment" mean? He judges as expected--but what is "standard" judgment? Is the new employee told what the standards are for judgment of his judgment so he has some idea of what is expected? If any librarian answers "yes" to that last question I am sure that American Libraries, and many of the librarian's own colleagues, would be interested in seeing a written statement of those standards. This is where a real difficulty lies; not that individuals are so different that one can't do a rating article but that standards are so difficult to fix.

In an academic institution such as the one at which I work there is the further problem of the context of the rating system. At the City University of New York (of which Staten Island Community College is a part), the library is considered an instructional department on the same footing as the English Department, the Physics Department, etc., and our librarians have the academic titles and salaries of instructor, assistant professor, associate professor, and professor. This is most splendid as far as pay scales are concerned, but it makes for tough competition when the question of promotion comes up. Academic promotions are reviewed by a Personnel and Budget Committee; at Staten Island that committee consists of the president of the college, two deans, and the chairman of each instructional department. For promotion to associate professor, the assistant professor in the Library Department is competing with the assistant professor in Chemistry, in History, in Physical Education, and so on throughout the academic spectra of the college. While the "publish or perish" syndrome is not as bad at a junior college as it is in a four year institution, the Ph. D. is the normal requirement for the assistant professor in

History who wishes to be considered for associate. We have managed in the library to convince most of our faculty colleagues that a second Masters, plus experience, is equivalent in the Library Department to the doctorate. Various other items then enter into consideration for promotion, such as "willingness to cooperate with others for the good of the institution," "satisfactory qualities of personality and character," "interest in productive scholarship and creative achievement," and general service to the college (on faculty committees; helping with extracurricular activities, etc.). All of this is to the good in aiding the never-ending struggle for identification as a member of the faculty.

All this being said, the questions asked about Mr. X and Miss Y in the first paragraph still cannot be relegated to limbo; librarians are faced with them all the time. Take the gentleman first. At a junior college library such as ours, 90-95 percent of the cataloging is LC. That means that Mr. X is spending a major part of his time simply verifying information. How can you rate him on this? Indeed, why even have him do this? Let a clerk do it as he did (does?) at Daniel Gore's library. No cataloger at the University of Pennsylvania even looks at a book unless original cataloging is required--thus spake Mr. Warren Haas, formerly director of libraries at that University, to me in a personal interview.

I disagree. At Staten Island we do have a professional looking at LC books, because in our view there are enough "mistakes" made to justify the time. Let me give three specific examples. The LC card for Lisa R. Peattie's 1968 book The View from the Barrio gives one tracing: 1. Ciudad Guayana--Social conditions. The card for B.J.W. Hill's Football (Oxford, Blackwell, 1961; cataloged by LC in the 1967 NUC) also has one subject tracing: 1. Football--History. On Richard Blum's book Utopiates; the Use and Users of LSD 25 the subject tracing is 1. Lysergic acid diethylamide.

A cataloger who is alert should realize that the value of the LC subject tracing for the Peattie book is nil. He should either replace it with or add a 2. Venezuela--Social conditions. Such action will, of course, violate the LC principle of always using the specific heading, but in the conflict between LC principles and usefulness to our student body we opt for the latter. Alerted, perhaps, by the British publisher, the superior Mr. X will take a close look at the football book rather than simply having his typist copy the LC entry. He will discover that it deals primarily with rugby and secondarily with soccer; only pages 79-82 say anything about American football history. Technically the LC tracing is correct; the book does deal with the history of all these forms of the sport. But for the American student the LC entry is misleading.[2] Finally, one can safely wager that students--and even worried deans--who come looking for book material on the live campus issue posed by the last title will not look under "lysergic." They will try LSD, and unless they find a cross reference there they will miss Mr. Blum's book and perhaps several others. The cross reference should be made as soon as the book is cataloged. Indeed, the whole area of cross references is one in which the superior cataloger can make his presence felt. He does not simply copy the LC list of subject headings; he thinks. The only "see" reference to European Economic Community is European common market (1955--) in the LC list. The junior college student, or any college student, would more likely look under "common market" when he wants material, so there should be a "see" reference from that.[3] I don't mean to make this an article attacking the Library of Congress; the point is that even when the cataloging is largely LC there is a case for looking at it critically and modifying it to suit your own clientele. The superior cataloger is the one who will catch these items.

The rating of Miss Y at the reference desk presents different problems. At the City University of New York one means by which a professor rates an instructor is to go into the classroom and listen to him teach--not once, but several times. Similarly, the head reference librarian could hang around the reference desk with one ear cocked--but where the instructor controls his class the reference librarian is "controlled" by his clientele. The day the head man chooses to listen in will be the day Miss Y is queried six times as to the location of the Britannica; the one good question that comes in is directed at him while she is on her coffee break. It is a most difficult task to come up with an accurate estimate of Miss Y's abilities, and I have no good-for-all-times answers. However, there are some general guidelines. The lady's contribution to book selection, and the kind of job she does in preparing subject bibliographies (done at many academic libraries) can be rated. The reference staff should work under a cooperation principle; if Miss Y can't find the answer herself she should not refer the student to a larger library or assume nothing is available. She should turn to her chief; by learning what sources she used her chief can get an idea of her resourcefulness in using the collection.

Another guideline is most suitable for an academic library. In a statement entitled Standards for Promotion, issued by the previously mentioned S.I.C.C. Personnel and Budget Committee in 1967, there is a sentence reading, "Yet nothing a community college teacher does professionally is as important as his teaching." The outstanding teacher has passed the most demanding of the tests to determine whether he should or should not be promoted. As an instructional department the library's reference function ought to be a teaching function; that ideal one with Mark Hopkins and his log. Giving the answer is not as important as showing the student how to find the answer so he can handle similar questions in the future. It is possible when passing the reference desk to tune in on Miss Y and see how she is helping her questioner. Tuning should be tempered with mercy, remembering the times you have given the direct answer rather than doing the harder teaching when the question came five minutes before lunch hour. More important, as Eugene Sheehy, head reference librarian in Butler Library at Columbia University, said in a letter to me "...you can't teach the reader who isn't interested in learning. Understanding when instruction is in order and when it will be wasted breath is as much a part of reference technique as grasping the reader's problem on mastering bibliographic tools."

Reference personnel will be dealing with the public more than catalogers will, so "deportment" is more important for the former than the latter. It is a plus but it is only that; a charming smile and nothing else will not bring the reader back. Any reference librarian can tell stories of being interrupted, while sitting in his office having lunch, by an inquirer who was helped by him once and who henceforth adopts him as the source of all information, even though the librarian actually on duty might better be able to answer the question. Good bibliographic knowledge is what develops that kind of loyalty.

Another factor relating to both Mr. X and Miss Y is one which is often overlooked in rating professional personnel. It is a point raised by Mr. Boynton Kaiser, associate director of Personnel at Stanford University, in seminars on "Solving Library Personnel Problems" that he has conducted in several U.S. cities. A part of any person's evaluation should be a consideration of that person's effect on other members of his department. The perfectionist as cataloger, reference librarian, or anyone else can well be damaging to the morale of other staff members. The inhumanity of his zero defects conduct may reduce the quality and the output of his co-workers. The other shoe also fits; the chief librarian who comes at ten o'clock and leaves at three o'clock four days a week is hardly setting a splendid example to those under him.

To go on to consider in depth the acquisitions librarian, the serials librarian, the documents librarian, and so on through the other library substrata would require a document the length of an Occasional Paper from the Illinois University Graduate School--and more experienced hands than mine should write that document. I have been limited even in the areas I chose to discuss. The library where more original cataloging is done would need additional criteria to judge a superior Mr. X. Good reference work is good reference work wherever it is performed, but a Miss Y at Berkeley will be getting a far higher level of question there than she will at Staten Island Community College and will require a far greater knowledge of resources.

Before leaving this topic a word should be said on the question of the frequency of a rating. In the ALA publication Personnel Organization and Procedure: a Manual Suggested for Use in College and University Libraries, 2nd edition, 1968, it is stated on page 14 that a report should be made on a new employee during his probationary period every three months with a semiannual report after he is promoted to a new position. Stebbins (op. cit., p. 124) feels that after a probationary period or a promotion an annual appraisal is sufficient, with a cutoff point suiting the needs of the library. While I have taken no formal general survey on this point, conversations with colleagues indicate that the Stebbins annual formula is the one most often used even for new employees. Large library systems such as the Brooklyn Public Library have the first formal review of a new professional person after a six-month period. Clerical personnel are often rated on a three-month basis, but I know of no library that follows the ALA recommendation for its professionals. Almost all libraries I know of have an ongoing informal rating procedure whereby a problem case can be discussed any time it is felt necessary.

It is time now to move on to a consideration of the

topic from the viewpoints of the people being rated. It's a vital matter; increasing union activity in libraries focuses on this as an area of discontent. Two questions immediately occur: should X and Y be informed of the rating and the reasons for it, and what right of appeal do they have if they feel their supervisors have been biased?

The "fair play" concept would certainly seem to indicate that those being rated should be told in what ways they fail to measure up and how they can do better their performance. The aforementioned Mr. Kaiser stresses the importance of not waiting until a formal evaluation session to discuss mistakes. Think of your relationship as similar to that of a coach to a player. As soon as possible after an error tell your man what he did incorrectly; don't do it in front of the other players (librarians) or in full view of the spectators (patrons) but do tell him.

One library system that appears to measure up closely to the ideal is that of the Brooklyn Public Library, while one that seems to vary from it is the City University of New York. At Brooklyn (and in what follows I am quoting and paraphrasing from a letter and literature sent to me by Veronica Boasi, chief of the Personnel Division), "Supervisors are instructed to keep their staff informed of their progress (or lack of it) on a current basis through frequent and informal contacts regarding their work and regular conferences prior to the official service rating." At that official rating "...the ratee has the opportunity to question his raters to learn the basis of their markings for each item. At this time the supervisor would give specific examples to support his overall evaluation." Raters are instructed to avoid isolated incidents or exceptional sections. A rated staff member may appeal a decision of the Promotions Board to the Personnel Director within ten days of its publication by that Board. In presenting such an appeal he may be assisted by a representative of his own choosing.

At the City University, on the other hand, the immediate supervisor is not allowed to discuss a rating with an employee. Only the chief librarian may do this. This ruling stems from <u>Attachment B, Personnel and Budget Procedures to the New York City Board of Higher Education Meeting of December 18, 1967.</u> Once again it must be remembered that this would be true for all the faculty. A new man in the History Department might be observed and rated by several of his colleagues, who would then discuss their ratings with the head of the Department. Only that head, however, could discuss the ratings with the new man. Further, no reason for voting not to recommend reappointment or promotion is to be given to the candidate. Clearly the Board of Higher Education's reasoning should be given in full. Here it is, from page 2, item 2.

> The recommendation that no reasons should ever be given for the action of a committee in voting not to recommend reappointment or promotion of a candidate is a recommendation which was arrived at after a rather careful consideration of the pros and cons.
>
> On the side of giving reasons, the most potent argument arises from a sense of fair play: if a person has tried his best to make good in a position, it seems in accord with our American traditions that he should be told wherein he failed and be given an opportunity to rebut, explain or otherwise appeal. Furthermore, the need to support a non-reappointment by the citation of definite reasons might be conceived of as a barrier to the forces of malice and prejudice, whether personal or ethnic.
>
> On the other side, the necessity to give reasons for non-reappointment, with the consequent receipt of rebuttals, explanations and submission of contrary expert opinion, places the college and its P & B committees in the position of defendant rather than of judge. College officials would soon find their time, energies and talents dissipated in disputes. Academic excellence could not thrive in that atmosphere and a premium would be placed on peaceful mediocrity. Often the reasons have nothing to do with the candidate himself (he may indeed be satisfactory), but rather with the possibility that better candidates, with wider backgrounds, more versatility, or specialties which are more likely to be of use to the department in the years to come, may be available, and the department does not desire to foreclose the opportunity to attract such candidates. More importantly, any requirement that reasons be given for non-appointment would have the effect of instituting a type of presumptive tenure inimical to the conduct of the colleges as institutions of higher learning. It is sufficient that reasons or cause must be proven to terminate the services of a tenured

person. If it is not too paternalistic in tone, still another argument against the giving of reasons for non-reappointment may be urged: it is really not in the best interests of the candidate himself, for it makes a matter of record a negative evaluation which may come back to plague him later.

The argument has some merit, but my overall impression is best expressed in Ben Franklin's words: "So convenient a thing it is to be a reasonable creature, since it enables one to find or make a reason for every thing one has a mind to do." What the Board of Higher Education had in mind was undoubtedly the avoidance of litigation; if you give no reasons for dismissal you cannot be taken to court. The fair play argument, in my view, overrides any of the reasons given--especially the bird-in-the-bush-may-be-worth-more-than-the-one-in-the-hand idea expressed in the sentence beginning with "Often..." Also the rule that only the department head may discuss a rating (not quoted above but it is part of the statement) makes things very difficult for the supervisor as well as the employee. If I see something being done incorrectly do I tell the employee? Or do I wait and tell the chief librarian to tell him? Chief librarians are busy people, so the employee may not be told until his formal rating conference. By that time he may well have forgotten it, but he certainly will (and should) feel aggrieved that he wasn't told at the time.

As far as the right of appeal is concerned the City University employee has a number of steps he can take. If one of our librarians is refused reappointment or promotion by the Library Department, and he feels injustice has been done, he may appeal to the full (college-wide) Personnel and Budget Committee already referred to. There is a special Appeals Committee of that group just to hear such cases. If he is again turned down he may appeal to the president of the college; beyond that to the Board of Higher Education's College Committee; beyond that there is no formal machinery, but a lawyer for the candidate might consider the State Commissioner of Education.

My feeling is that Brooklyn Public and City University are not as far apart in practice as they are on paper. Means are found to get around the rules. I know of one instance in an academic department in which a teacher was told that he would be observed unofficially before the official visits were made. After the off-the-record visit the rater discussed the performance of the rated teacher with him. In subsequent official visits the letter of the law was followed, and the rater reported his observations to the department chairman only. This made for more work for the rater, but the teacher, even though he had to put up with more observation, was most grateful for the extra time. Not only did he receive suggestions for ways to improve his classroom performance, but he also got some idea of exactly what the rater was looking for. Similarly, in the library supervisors tend to make on-the-spot corrections rather than worry about the legal niceties of whether they should or should not do it.

The main practical difference, then, in the total personnel situation at City University of New York and Brooklyn Public is that at the former the employee cannot question his raters or have access to their individual ratings. He must deal only with his chief, and he may have access to any memoranda prepared as a result of any evaluation conference between him and his department head.

I trust that what has been said is only the opening gun in a situation that for too long has received too little attention. Ratings from the points of view of both raters and rated staff need more discussion from a wide representation of libraries.

Notes

1. In my copy of Stebbins the phrase "quality of work" appears twice; I am assuming it was a misprint and she meant "quantity" for one of the two.
2. This same book was also done and appears in the 1963 NUC Author List with the tracing 1. Rugby football--History. In 1963, however, the cataloging was done by a cooperating library; in 1967 LC did it using the tracing as given above.
3. It is true that, for the subject heading European Economic Community countries, LC makes a "see" reference from Common Market countries. But if the library has no books with this subject heading but does have them with the subject European Economic Community, a Common market cross reference will be needed--and would not be made under a strict following of the LC list.

Letter to a
Library School Lecturer

by Peter D. Pocklington

Reprinted by permission from the June 1970 issue of
Library World (71:840), p. 368-371. Copyright 1970
by Library World.

Dear Tom,

No doubt you will be surprised to hear from me after all these years, but I really feel the need to let off steam to someone in authority in the Library School world. Since you and I experienced many a convivial short-list together in our wild youth, I think you will at least be able to understand my feeling of intense irritation at some of the pathetic scribbles I receive that pass for applications for jobs from library school students.

What annoys me especially is that it is quite clear that some library schools are taking the trouble to give a little simple advice to their students on this matter; others-- and yours, I regret to say, is one--do not seem to bother, and it is the applicants, not the schools, who suffer. And perhaps my library system suffers, too, for it may well be that the best candidate for a job here did not get on the short list simply through ignorance of the sort of details a prospective employer seeks.

Now I know you are very much a specialist lecturer and this sort of thing may not be your responsibility to teach but surely someone in your establishment can do something about it if you bring the matter up. As it must now be eight or nine years since you yourself disappeared into your academic tower and stopped drafting applications for jobs, I hope you will forgive me if I remind you of one or two things that practising librarians like to know about prospective members of their staffs. Some of this seems too obvious for words, I know, but I am writing from recent sorry experience, having just waded through 36 applications for a vacancy.

Perhaps it will help to explain my current irritation if I describe one so-called application from amongst this recent batch. It took up precisely one half of one side of a sheet of Basildon Bond notepaper and having read it I knew that the writer was either male or female, had a university degree in something or other and had just completed a Post-Graduate Course at a named library school. The candidate's address was also given. Needless to say, this candidate's application received as little attention here as he or she had obviously given to its preparation. Admittedly, one may argue that anyone who can be so casual about an important matter like this does not deserve to get a job, but I think we must be fair and also admit that until recently this sort of thing was good enough--library school products were in such great demand.

I'm sure that the library schools are fully aware of the recent rapid change in the job situation but I wonder if they all realize their responsibility in helping their students over this difficult hurdle--getting the first job. After all, Tom, when you and I made our first tentative moves up the professional ladder we were already working in libraries and had senior colleagues on hand to give us practical advice. Dare I say, too, that even at that early stage we had learnt sufficient of the workings of chief librarians' minds to have a fair inkling of the sort of things they would like to know about prospective employees? So many of the youngsters now coming onto the library market are direct entrants with no idea at all of how to sell themselves on paper and seem quite at a loss if not given an application form with little boxes for all the "vital statistics."

What about these "vital statistics"--what are the straightforward factual matters that a chief librarian wants to know? Well, to begin with, there's this question of identification. Fortunately, the number of candidates who simply forward a brief handwritten application signed "E. Merriweather" is rare but it is by no means uncommon to hear from "Elizabeth Merriweather." I accept that nowadays it is rarely relevant whether a female librarian is married or single and it is certainly not a factor that I very often take into account when choosing a short list. But it is a little irritating not to know whether to address the applicant as Miss or Mrs. And let's face it, in the competitive situation in which most of the young library school leavers now find themselves, the one thing they do not wish to do is irritate a prospective employer!

Then there's this question of age. I don't think it indicates coyness or genuine reluctance to disclose this fact that is the reason why so many applicants omit it; I think they probably regard it as irrelevant. Here again, the days when age was a contributing factor in determining initial salary for junior professional posts have disappeared and we know that the majority of applicants for such vacancies will be in the 20-24 age-bracket.

Nevertheless, there <u>are</u> students in their late twenties or early thirties in our <u>library</u> schools--some even older, so we do like to know the age of candidates who apply to us for jobs. Generally we are looking for keen youngsters, but from time-to-time situations arise in libraries (perhaps a sudden exodus of older staff) which makes the appointment of a more mature person desirable.

As to education, whilst one doesn't require one and a half pages of curricula vitae, the name of the secondary school attended can be of some guidance as are the subjects in which G.C.E. passes have been obtained. Of far greater importance, of course, is information about the Part II papers taken at library school.

To state simply, as so many candidates do, that "I have passed the Part I Examination and am awaiting the result of Part II" tells a chief librarian little that he does not already know or can assume. I suspect that many candidates leave out some of this information in the belief that it will be passed on by the Head of the Library School when supplying a reference. This is true, but what they possibly do not realise is that nowadays few employers take up references <u>before</u> selecting candidates for interview; in short, if your application seems rather bare, you will probably not be picked for interview and your referee not approached.

Obviously any job-hunter who has already worked in libraries before going to library school should make some mention of this practical experience in an application. Here again, whilst no prospective employer wishes to read through a long rigmarole listing all the different routine duties formerly carried out by the candidate, a bald statement that "I have had two years' practical experience with Blankshire

County Library" leaves something to be desired.

    Incidentally, you might point out to your direct entrants, Tom, that lack of previous practical experience does not necessarily place them at a disadvantage; there are junior professional posts that are ideally suited for library school leavers starting at the bottom but which would be rather limiting for ambitious youngsters who have already "got some time in." Also, most chief librarians are as equally interested in enthusiasm, personality and potential as they are in practical experience when appointing at this level.

    What else is there? So far I have mentioned a number of things that ought to be in every application, so what can the keen job-hunter do to implant his personality and individuality upon the person wading through three or perhaps four dozen applications? I would suggest there are three things he can do: he can make some mention of his hobbies or interests outside librarianship, he can add to the list of "vital statistics" a covering letter of application and he can present the whole in an attractive manner.

    I have no doubt that some young people might regard it as an intrusion upon their personal liberty to be expected to give some indication of their spare-time interests. This could be true if any employer wished to examine them in any detail about say, their political or religious beliefs. These are irrelevant, indeed, but it is surely not irrelevant for a prospective employer to want to know something about a candidate as a person rather than as a librarian.

    An interest in politics indicates to me a concern about the state of society and is something I applaud in an aspiring librarian. And the fact that I am looking for a branch librarian and not a leader of a Himalayan Expedition does not negate the fact that a disclosed interest in mountaineering tells me a bit more about a candidate and what makes him tick.

    In the final analysis, when faced with a score of applications from young people with similar backgrounds and experience, the selection of the final half-dozen may well hinge upon some small personal traits that pick out certain candidates from their fellows--an interest in photography, musical expertise, amateur artist, keen cricketer. Most candidates have something beyond mere professional competence to offer: the wise ones will give some thought to this aspect of the matter.

I have noticed that even those library schools which devote some time to advising their students on how to lay out an application appear to have paid scant regard to the covering letter. I have lately received several applications in which details of name, age, education qualifications, etc., were all nicely laid out in tabulated form (with dates) but which were accompanied by a letter simply formally applying for the post advertised. There is nothing wrong with this, of course, except that these candidates are missing a great opportunity to explain why they are interested in the job!

I am sure you will remember old Freeling, Tom, who had several dozen copies of his application duplicated and merely had to compile a new covering letter for each job he applied for! You and I never went to quite the same lengths but we certainly had a "standard" application ready for instant use, and we spent many a happy hour discussing the wording of each accompanying letter.

The Head of one of our more progressive library schools with whom I discussed this very matter recently said that most of the library school leavers who apply for jobs simply want to start earning some money and they are too honest to invent reasons for applying for a particular post! Far be it from me to encourage deceit in the young, but this strikes me as being a bit too naive.

Chief librarians all cherish the secret belief that their particular library has some special quality (whatever they may publicly say to the contrary!) and they would be less than human if they did not hope that those wishing to work in their libraries felt something of this attraction. This is not to say that I expect every application for a job in my library to be accompanied by a panegyric about the system. What I am suggesting is that in a competitive situation, the candidate who expresses some reason--other than simply to get a job--for applying to me for a post is more likely to strike a responsive chord in my heart than the candidate who is mute on the subject.

I accept that many library school leavers are undecided upon the type of librarianship they ultimately wish to follow but see no reason why this cannot be made plain in the letter of application, together with a comment to the effect that "the post for which I am now applying seems an interesting way of practising librarianship whilst I find my feet."

The manner in which the information given in an application is laid out and presented is very important indeed, for this is what one first notices about an application. It is no use taking the line that "I want to be judged as a librarian--not simply as someone who can look good on paper." Candidates have got to be able to sell themselves to an employer and in the first instance this means getting picked for an interview.

Other things being equal (and at this stage they frequently are), an employer will always opt for the candidate who has obviously taken a bit of trouble to ensure that all the relevant facts supporting his application are presented succinctly and neatly. Few librarians now insist upon handwritten applications and it's a poor applicant who cannot make friends with some competent typist to put a bit of gloss on his image.

Of course, any candidate who is fortunate enough to possess a neat, legible script need not have recourse to a typewriter since good handwriting is so rare in libraries nowadays that it's mere appearance creates a certain warmth in the bosom of most chief librarians.

I could say quite a bit about interview technique, but I know you library school fellows are so busy that if I go on much longer you won't have time to read it all! One thing, though, I must add because there does seem to be some genuine ignorance about the procedure in the minds of many young people selected for interview. This is whether it is the "done" thing to go and have a look 'round a library before one is interviewed for a job there. I know this sounds silly and that you and I would never dream of getting as far as the interview without having a good look first to see whether we really wanted the job.

To dispel any uncertainty on this point, I always mention in the letter inviting candidates for interview that they are welcome to look round in advance and ask any questions of the staff. I believe this is now fairly common practice but where it is not done I see no reason why a candidate should not state his intention of doing this "unless you have any objection" when writing to say that he will be attending the interview.

Well, Tom, there it is; I've got it all off my chest now and I feel heaps better already. I do hope you are able to do something about the matter and I look forward to receiving some super applications from your library school when I next advertise a junior vacancy.

                                        Yours sincerely,
                                              Peter

When a Library Job Ends
... Find Another

by Paula M. Strain

Reprinted from Special Libraries 61:(no. 7) p. 363-367 (September 1970). Copyright 1970 by Special Libraries Association.

The traumatic Spring of 1970 forced an acquaintance with two little-discussed aspects of special librarianship and the problems associated with them. They should be better known.

> Business is so bad that the administration, to keep us competitive, is cutting our services. One of them is the library. Close down library activities as quickly as you can and then spend the time you have remaining on the payroll looking for another position.

The personnel director's order surprised but did not astonish me. In the past nine months, the library staff had been cut two-thirds, and economies had been enforced everywhere. I was shocked. The company sold its services on the premise that they were based on the latest and best knowledge--and where did this knowledge come from if not the library? To close down the library seemed to me a form of slow suicide for my employer. But there's no use in fighting a battle already lost. This one was.

How do you go about closing a library? The professional literature doesn't help. Self-help was the only answer.

First, the library staff had to be told. Even though the administrator to whom the head librarian reported had shifted the responsibility of "firing" the library onto the personnel director, the head librarian had a responsibility to inform the staff. Half of them would be leaving with me; two (the library secretary and the interlibrary loan clerk who

was the most senior member) were being retained for a time
because it might be possible to transfer them to another activity in the company. All had to know the administration's
decision and why it had been made.

    The next obvious step was to cancel any planned ex-
penditures. Recall the bindery order that had been picked
up a day or two earlier. Go through the book order file and
notify the jobbers of the cancellation of all orders outstanding. Check the suspense file for outstanding orders of any
other material that might involve charges; send letters can-
celling the original requests.

    It was necessary to cut back what other long-term
costs we could. Periodical subscriptions were on a calendar
year basis. If cancellation orders got to the subscription
agency by the end of April, about one-half of the publishers
would give a refund for a part-year cancellation. Order a
computer print-out of subscriptions and send a copy to the
head of administration to determine if some of them should
not be cancelled but--rather--be readdressed to individual
offices within the company. Then issue the necessary instructions to the agency.

    That took care of financial responsibilities. What of
other kinds?

    Some operations in the library no longer had any rea-
son for their existence. Suspend the inventory at the point
we had stopped one evening: at the end of one classification
schedule. Expand the notes made on the completed portion
in case anyone ever came back to the records; hope that the
expanded notes were complete enough for a professional librarian to understand them.

    A few projects were so near completion that they
could be finished up in some fashion. This included catalog-
ing--in a hasty fashion--all the books being held for the arrival of LC cards. Better a poor cataloging job and some
records in the files than no records at all. One can't cancel an LC card order so the data on the cataloging done was
recorded on the carbon in the LC card order file in the hope
that the LC cards would be preserved when they came in and
eventually be united with the record. The money in the LC
deposit account was so small that abandoning the account was
cheaper than trying to close it out.

We went over the administrative and correspondence files and wrote notes of explanation on anything that seemed unclear. The intention was to leave adequate records by which other company personnel could trace the library transactions if they had to.

In a defense industry library, much material comes from technical reports distributed by the Defense Documentation Center (DDC) and the Clearinghouse for Federal Scientific and Technical Information (CFSTI). Neither of these institutions care whether a library orders material or not; anyone in the recipient organization may be the official contact and control point. No need, therefore, to close our deposit account. Just determine who the new contact point in the company is to be; change the registration at DDC and CFSTI; and indoctrinate the new contact about the records which have to be kept and the routines the library had been following in procuring material from the centers. The same conditions held for our Government Printing Office deposit account.

Interlibrary loans were a larger part of our operations than in many special libraries. Because we had been offering to colleagues who lent to us duplicate and weeded material from our collections as a small gesture of appreciation for their loans, we had a reasonably up-to-date list of the libraries from whom we borrowed most frequently. The interlibrary loan clerk went through her records and picked up the names of local libraries which occasionally loaned materials to us; the final list included more than 125 libraries with whom we had had lending or borrowing relationships during the past year. To all of them we sent a short letter explaining that we expected to be closing down our library services very soon, thanking them for their cooperation, reassuring them that we expected to return any material we had borrowed from them--but asking them to check their records at once to notify us of material they had recorded as loaned to us for longer than a fortnight. We wanted to clear up all questions of responsibility for return now while someone who knew the records and who remembered interlibrary lending activity was at hand. At the same time, we began to call in all interlibrary loans in the hands of our readers and returned them to the lending libraries.

Now only our library collection itself, and the material from it in the hands of our readers, remained to consider. We could not act without some guidance from admin-

istration, and administration needed information on which to
make its decision on the final disposition of the library collection. Part of that information had to be the dollar value
of the collection; monetary value was both the most easily
obtained and the most meaningful. It was evident that the
information value of the collection to the company was discounted by the administration. The annual estimates made
on the replacement value of the collection for insurance purposes were consulted to get a figure for the financial worth
of the collections. The value of the equipment was estimated
by consulting the completed orders on file for recent purchases of furniture, and by looking at catalogs of library
equipment. The total value of the library collections and
equipment was high--perhaps a surprise to the administration,
but not to the library staff.

A memo was then prepared listing the value of the library and its contents and outlining the courses of action
possible--storing the collection; disposing of it; letting it stay
on the shelves. Advantages and disadvantages of each were
mentioned briefly. Keeping the library in its present location was the least expensive in manpower but would require
that the room be kept locked unless someone was made responsible for supervising both loan and return of the materials. Users of an unsupervised collection, no matter what
good intentions they may have, would fail to charge material
taken or record its return--and the collection would suffer
by attrition. Storing the library would protect the collection
but would require manpower to pack it up. Selling the collection would bring in cash but certainly nothing like the collection's value. The library could be transferred to another
corporate subsidiary which had its own library; this alternate,
too, would cost manpower for packing and shipping. The
memorandum concluded with the request for a decision as to
what course administration wished us to follow, plus the
statement that, until such an administrative decision was
made, the library staff remaining would continue to circulate
our own library material to company personnel.

Those of us who were to be laid off had done all we
could to close down library services. We were now free to
find other employment if we could. Those who remained
"for the time being" continued to take care of incoming mail,
the loan and return of company owned books, periodicals,
and reports, and give what reference help to readers their
ability permitted. Administration had not replied to my
memo by my last day of employment.

Nonprofessional staff from a special library may go to the U.S. Employment Service or to local employment agencies with a fair chance of finding jobs that utilize their clerical skills at an appropriate salary level. The professional special librarian has no such hope. The local U.S. Employment Office at which I registered for employment told me, "Sorry, you're on your own in finding a library job. We can't help."

This isn't exactly true, as we shall see, but it is generally true for finding professional special library jobs. There is no one place--not even three or four places--to which an unemployed special librarian can apply with hopes of finding listed most of what jobs are available.

There are advertisements, to be sure. Library Journal, Wilson Library Bulletin, and Special Libraries carry advertisements of library vacancies. Those in LJ and WLB are mostly in public, university, and occasionally school libraries, with a special library opening appearing infrequently. Special Libraries carries advertisements of special library jobs and some others. The "News-of-the-Week" section of the Sunday New York Times regularly carries advertisements of library openings, mostly in the metropolitan New York area, and mostly public and college library vacancies, though openings elsewhere in the country and in special libraries appear often enough to make it worth buying the paper each week. Some large metropolitan newspapers do advertise library positions; the Washington Post is one that does. The Post's ads are either in the "Help, Men & Women" or "Help, Women" columns (never in "Help, Men"), and are almost always for special library openings in the local area. Generally speaking, the openings listed in their "Men & Women" column will have a higher salary and a greater demand for experience than those in the "Women" column. (Women's Lib, take note!)

The job-seeking special librarian who depends on advertisements for his leads should be aware of at least two things. The time between the submission of an ad to a library journal and the delivery of the issue carrying the ad to the job seeker may be six weeks or longer. Not infrequently the job for which one decides to apply will be filled before the applicant can read the advertisement. Also the job seeker should be cautious about "blind" ads, those which do not name the company seeking to fill an opening. It isn't that the job isn't bona fide; it's just that many times the applicant will get no reply at all to his application. Apparently the use of a box number absolves the prospective employer from the need to be considerate of applicants.

There are some regional clearinghouses for jobs. In some large metropolitan centers, the U.S. Employment Service maintains a Professional Career Information Center, which collects information on openings for professional people, including librarians. The jobs listed as currently open for librarians tend to be few; most public libraries, universities, and employers of special librarians apparently are not much in the habit of going to the U.S. Employment Service for professional employees. The Washington Professional Career Information Center, in the three months when I was visiting it every week or ten days, had only three non-governmental special library jobs listed, but it did carry the monthly Federal Library Vacancy List with more government library openings. Unfortunately, the Vacancy List was displayed as much as three or four weeks after it had been issued. The Centers also display the job openings posted at the ALA and SLA[1] Conferences. This might be helpful if one is out of a job in mid-July or August but is less valuable when one is looking in the spring. There were no dates on the photocopies of the Conference postings to warn the unwary that they were out-of-date.

The Federal Library Committee, whose secretary's office is in the Library of Congress, publishes a monthly listing of vacancies in the federal libraries in Washington and elsewhere. This is sent to most federal libraries and, apparently, to all the Professional Career Information Centers. An interested job seeker may request his own copies of the listing from the Federal Library Committee, but getting on its mailing list may take three months or more--not much help when one is out of work.

It should also be noted that application for a job in a federal library is a waste of time unless one is already on the Civil Service Commission register for librarians. Federal libraries can hire only from the register. For the librarian not presently in federal library work, the register is, in effect, a hunting license and no more. With, perhaps, the exception of the lowest level--that of the beginning librarian--there is very little hiring done directly from the register. Promotion from within, transfer from other government libraries, and hiring applicants already on the register who present themselves at the personnel office of the hiring library and who are persistent seem to be the preferred methods of filling federal library vacancies.

A National Registry for Librarians is maintained by the Illinois State Employment Service, Professional Office, 208 S. LaSalle Street, Chicago, Illinois 60604. The National Registry was established initially as a result of the Joint Committee on Placement of the Council of National Libraries Associations. The registry receives your résumé and will make it available to an employer who contacts the registry. It also maintains a placement service at ALA Conferences; all résumés on file with the registry are available at ALA Conferences. If you attend an ALA Conference, register with the placement office at the Conference so you can be reached for employer interviews. This registry seems to have useful potential for SLA members and their potential employers that could be expanded.

There are also the employment clearinghouses run by individual SLA chapters. The Association's placement service that SLA had attempted to provide was discontinued over a year ago, but individual Chapters still attempt to match up job openings and applicants in their own areas. How well they do it depends on the energy, time, and acquaintances of the Chapter's employment chairman. If he is energetic and has numerous acquaintances, he will encourage employers of special librarians to let him know about openings and will solicit vacancy information from other librarians; more often, when the chairman has limited time, he waits for information on vacancies to come to him on its own. An energetic job-seeking librarian may well know more about what jobs are available locally than the Chapter employment chairman will.

Another source of vacancy information may be library schools. Some schools maintain a very full list of jobs that come to their attention and make these lists available to their students, sometimes merely by posting them on a bulletin board; in one or two cases, by issuing a monthly "Positions Open" bulletin sent to all alumni. Usually these schools have no hesitation in allowing other librarians access to this information. Other library schools are comparatively uninterested in centralizing job availability information for the use of alumni or outsiders. Only inquiry at the school itself will tell which attitude exists and whether leads are available there.

Surprisingly enough, private employment agencies are

sources for some special library jobs. You will have to visit the agency to find out about the job; only general details will be told over the phone. Not infrequently, you will find you already knew about the job from another source. Often, it will be a job which does not require much experience, offers only an average salary, and has a limited scope--but, still, private employment agencies occasionally have the only listing of a really worthwhile job. There are a few employment agencies, especially in New York City, which supposedly specialize in library vacancies. Here I have no experience; I was not interested in moving to that area.

By far the most satisfactory method of finding out about job openings in the special library field is through friends and acquaintances. Having a wide circle of acquaintances who know that you are looking for a job is to assure yourself of hearing what jobs are available or may be opening. Library colleagues will be helpful. Not infrequently, a librarian whom you do not know personally, but whom you have contacted about a vacancy he had, will tell you about another promising opening. Do not fail to inform your friends outside the library field of your interest in library openings; they often know of possibilities within their own organizations--a librarian about to retire, a service being expanded. Leads from non-librarians may be less accurate than those from colleagues, but they sometimes produce a more exciting job possibility. So follow up all leads you get.

In my search for a job, one thing surprised me--how often an application for employment for an advertised position is never acknowledged by the employer. More than a third of the applications I sent out were never acknowledged. The percentage of no replies was higher for vacancies in the government libraries. If an application must be mailed, about two-thirds of the time one never knows whether or not it has been received until some months later when it will be returned with a form checked off to report that the job has been filled and the application is being returned for re-use. Nongovernment libraries which do not reply do not even return the résumé.

Even when you apply in person and have an interview, you may never be informed you are not being considered for the job or even that the job has been filled. A good rule of thumb is to cross the job possibility off if you don't hear within two weeks. We may be professional in our education and responsibilities, but employers treat us otherwise when

Libraries and Librarians

we are job seekers.

The discrepancies between the advertised job and the job you are told about during an interview, and the employer's rigidity or flexibility in the requirements he seeks in applicants are subjects to be left for another time or author. Much could be said!

Problem Areas

There is a real need for a central national clearinghouse for all types of library positions. Since positions in special libraries are less adequately publicized than any others, why does not SLA join with other CNLA member associations in encouraging the use of the National Registry for Librarians?[2]

SLA might also publish each fall the names and addresses of all Chapter placement officers so that applicants wishing to seek work outside their own area would know to whom to apply, and employers seeking applicants could know where to send notices of openings. The Association's Placement Committee might very well encourage the Chapter placement chairmen to act as liaison with the National Registry for Librarians.

This is a problem for action, not thought.

The more serious problem that came to my attention this spring is one of professional ethics. For it I have yet no answer. It is connected with the closing down of a special library (or its opening or operating under certain circumstances).

I mentioned that, by the day the last professional library staff member left the company, the administration had not told any of the library staff what final disposition was to be made of the library collection, and that the clerical staff still working was operating the library on a day-to-day basis with a minimum of library services being offered. A number of months later, clerical personnel are still doing so. They tell me that, at the instance of company personnel--some of them in administration--they are requesting help <u>and are getting it</u> from other local libraries--public, federal, university, and industrial. This raises a question: Is such helpfulness ethical? For the public library, which attempts to serve the needs of all taxpayers, it is--but for the other libraries, which do not have a similar responsibility based on tax support, I feel that it probably isn't.

The problem raised by a library operated intentionally without professional staff requires consideration by the special library profession, indeed by the entire library profession. It involves many questions.

When is a library not a library? Does it cease to be a library when it no longer has any professional librarian directing its operation? Or does the fact that a collection of books exists with a person nominally in charge (regardless of his background) justify its recognition as a library eligible to receive interlibrary cooperative service from professionally operated libraries?

A well-known government librarian told me last year that industrial librarians were parasites on federal libraries. If this is so, are not government libraries encouraging parasitism by extending library services to inadequately staffed and managed libraries?

Should there be standards that libraries must meet before they qualify for help from other libraries? What standards should they be? Indeed, what is a library? Should our professional library associations set standards and enforce them? Are we being less than professional when we avoid defining a library and when we avoid upholding our definition by our behavior?

These are questions that the library profession, especially the special library segment, should consider and determine if we are to become truly professional. Other professions have faced similar problems and have come to some enforceable agreement among themselves, and they try to enforce the agreement. Why have we dodged the issue? Why do we not discuss such matters at our annual Conferences?

Notes

1. SLA has not authorized the U.S. Employment Service (or any of its Professional Career Information Centers) to display job openings listed at ALA's Annual Conferences. Miss Ann Firelli (Manager of SLA's Membership Department), who handles the Employment Clear-

Libraries and Librarians 91

inghouse at the Conference, is interested in knowing why undated photocopies of job descriptions from the 1969 Conference in Montreal were posted in the USES Professional Career Information Center in Washington, D.C. in Spring 1970. --Editor, Special Libraries.

2. In June 1968 the SLA Board did not accept a recommendation from CNLA that all member associations of CNLA use the National Registry for their placement purposes. --Editor, Special Libraries

Professional Unions

by Darryl Mleynek

Reprinted by permission from the April 1970 issue of
California Librarian (31:2), p. 110-118. Copyright
1970 by the California Library Association.

The Librarians' Guild was chartered in August 1968 by the American Federation of State, County, and Municipal Employees, AFL-CIO, thus becoming one of the first professional unions. Then it represented only the librarians of the Los Angeles Public Library, but now also represents the librarians of the Santa Monica Public Library.

The concept of a professional union has obviously already had a measurable affect on many librarians. Recently the Canadian Library Association passed a resolution recommending to their members that when they join unions they do so on a professionals-only basis. It is this concept of a professional union which I wish to explore.

Most people have a fairly clear idea of what constitutes a union. I think we could agree that basically a union is an independent organization of employees dedicated to improving their working situation. In addition, we in the United States have traditionally come to associate the word with those particular employee groups affiliated with the American Federation of Labor-Congress of Industrial Organizations, plus a few other dissident groups which have broken away from the AFL-CIO.

In contrast, however, what do we feel constitutes a profession? Often we do not know with any appreciable degree of precision what we mean when we say "profession." All we could probably agree on is that a profession is something more than merely an occupation. To then add this vague concept to the word "union" seems to leave some people in a state of semantic bewilderment.

All of us in the library world invest considerable energy in promoting the "profession" of librarianship, while at the same time writing ream upon ream about whether we are in reality a profession and what a profession in reality is. To discuss over many years the existence of something which does in fact exist would, I think, be a very serious condemnation of our perceptiveness. However, as each of us knows, these discussions continue only because the existence of a library profession is indeed questionable.

The confusion enters our minds because of the dichotomy which exists between librarians and library administrators. Professional involvement, exposure to new ideas in the field, the freedom to be creative and to experiment, the opportunity to improve services offered to the public, chances to extend one's knowledge, are all characteristics of a profession and, within the field of librarianship, are normally only available to or experienced by library administrators.

Librarians below the administrative level are for the most part employees within a strict employee-employer relationship. In no meaningful sense of the word can they be considered part of a profession. Their jobs are routine when not actually clerical. Their control over their own work responsibilities is nearly non-existent. Their opportunity to make meaningful improvements in the service they offer the public is poor. Their involvement in the profession as a whole--beyond leafing through a professional journal-- is minimal. Their work is not professional, nor are they professionals. Given this situation, we should not be surprised that we have a recruitment problem in the field of librarianship. Nor should we be surprised that there is a growing retention problem: a recent survey of public librarians indicated that 17% of the librarians surveyed were not only actively thinking of changing their jobs, but were actively considering leaving librarianship for a different career.

Put that 17% into personal terms and think of it in connection with the staff of the library in which you work. Then add to it what must be a considerably higher percentage of staff members who are not yet ready to leave the field but do want to change jobs. You can begin to appreciate how much dissatisfaction there is in the field; and, having done that, you will know what the principal motivation is behind the professional union movement. Once our motivation for joining a union is clear, it is less difficult to understand the type of organization we have chosen and the direction in which we intend to move.

At the foundation of our organizational structure are two basic realizations: (1) Members of the recognized professions have relatively equal status with other members of their profession; and (2) Members of the recognized professions have considerable control over their own profession. Presently, neither of these situations exists in the field of librarianship. First of all, librarians work within an employee-employer relationship which does not allow for equality. Secondly, librarians are severely controlled in their careers by a small percentage of their colleagues--that is, library administrators--plus civil service commissions, personnel departments, and a variety of other non-library and restriction-producing agencies.

In creating an organizational structure which would mitigate these problems, we have developed one which is: (1) democratic--that is, all members are equal; (2) independent--that is, it has sufficient strength to exist separately from the institutions in which we work; and (3) locally present--that is, its effective strength is at the local level where the problems are and control of the profession is both feasible and desirable. We chose to affiliate with the union movement in order to develop an organization with sufficient strength to be independent of libraries. The union movement provides us with effective power at the local level to gain control of our own profession, and also guarantees us a basic democratic structure. As a condition of affiliating with a union, we restricted our jurisdiction to librarians in order that our fundamental professional concerns would not become diluted by a broader membership. This is basically what we mean when we use the term "professional union." We are part of a union organized solely along professional lines.

By affiliating with the union movement, we received much more than merely the satisfaction of our basic criteria; that is, a professional, independent, democratic, and locally organized group. We also received the benefits of an organization which has considerable experience with, and is actively involved in, using different methods of achieving objectives. These methods range from lobbying to negotiating and include labor's ultimate weapon--withholding its services. With our knowledge of the library world, we shall set our policy and our objectives; out of the union's experience, we shall choose the methods for attaining our objectives.

By forming a professional union we are saying to the library world that: (1) we do not think librarianship currently is a profession; (2) we think it should become a profession; and (3) we intend to begin actively working to turn it into a profession. As a result of our affiliation, we expect to improve our specific jobs, to give better service to the public, and thereby to strengthen the profession, thus beginning the cycle over again: better jobs, better service, and a stronger profession.

More important, however, than our own declarations of what we believe ourselves to be, is determining the direction in which we intend to move. Our programs and actions will define us more closely than our rhetoric. As a professional union, we have combined our professional interests with traditional union concerns over wages and working conditions to form a philosophy of action which would include the following basic program of ten points. These points will illustrate the area in which our concerns lie.

I. <u>With the Active Participation of Their Professional Staffs, Libraries Should Define Their Function in Society</u>

In this first point, as with the remaining nine points, the intent is to emphasize that the entire professional staff of a library should be involved in setting forth the major philosophical foundations of the library. We contend that the formulation of policy is the right and obligation of all professionals within a library system. To do otherwise is to relegate the librarian to a non-professional position.

To involve a library's professional staff is to bring forth a variety of viewpoints which will of necessity lend greater depth to the policy decisions eventually reached. In addition to developing better policies based on wider and more varied experience and knowledge, the involvement of the librarians will create an understanding of and agreement with the policies which they implement and interpret to the public. The librarian is the public's contact with the library. If he does not understand or agree with the library's policies, he is either consciously or unconsciously subverting them. The easiest way to inform a librarian of the policies of the library, and the only way to be assured of his agreement with the library's policies, is to involve him in the formulation of them.

Considerable thought has to be given to the method of

involvement of the staff, for we are talking about meaningful involvement, not sham involvement. The only reason for greater staff involvement is to improve the library; and the library administrator, as well as the staff itself, must be careful that this involvement is not a deception. The most crucial factors in meaningful involvement are that all participants have a right to be heard and understood and that decisions be reached by consensus wherever possible, and otherwise by democratic vote. Where committees are used, the staff should choose their representatives, preferably through whatever organization represents them. This type of staff involvement will improve the library as the result of the acquiescence of the staff in the library's policy, and as the result of a staff that is far more satisfied with their jobs and therefore more productive, both qualitatively and quantitatively.

With the matter of staff participation more fully defined, it is possible to explore the remainder of the first point, which is that libraries should define what their function is in society. We have not in librarianship ever developed a very clear understanding of what we can offer to the public, nor what our area of expertise is, beyond knowing that libraries deal with the storage and retrieval of information.

Throughout the history of libraries, this imprecisely defined function has kept libraries afloat. I suspect that this is only because information was not important to earlier societies in the same way that it has become vital today. Nearly all segments of society now need information for a variety of important purposes. This poses a significant challenge to libraries if indeed their function is as an information center.

It is important to define the function of a library in order that we as librarians will know what that function is and can build libraries to fulfill that function. There is good reason to believe that we are not now doing so. For instance, many governmental information agencies have been established in recent years which are not libraries, even though their function is to disseminate information to the public. This has occurred presumably because libraries have not identified their function, nor the needs of the government or the public.

Whatever the function of libraries, it should be defined by the public that creates them. We should not forget that; otherwise, we too shall join the ranks of outmoded institutions in our society which exist only for their own edification.

II. With the Active Participation of Their Professional Staffs, Libraries Should List, in Terms of Their Function and by Order of Priority According to the Needs of Society, the Obligations of the Library to Society

For many years now, librarians have talked about the importance of knowing their community. Yet few libraries have accomplished this; how else can we explain the fact that only within the last few years have libraries begun to try to serve culturally deprived areas? The very existence of the term "culturally deprived" is a condemnation of the relevance of libraries. It is libraries, among others of society's cultural institutions, of which these people have been deprived.

It is not sufficient to know which segment of the public a particular library is created to serve. We must also determine what the needs of the public are in terms of the library's function. Once those needs are established, we must then list their satisfaction on a priority basis. Since most libraries have limited resources, they cannot satisfy all of their obligations to the public they are funded to serve. If the best possible use of those resources is to be achieved, the obligations must be listed in priority order. The only possible basis for such an order is the needs of the public.

When resources are limited, it would seem that we should face up to questions which the field of librarianship has largely ignored in the past. For instance, is the need of a ghetto youth to have a book to help him pass a civil service test greater than the need of an elderly woman to have a mystery or true-crime story? Is it possible that one need should be satisfied even before another is partially fulfilled? Do we in reality responsibly serve the public when we ignore such questions? I think not. To fulfill this responsibility will be an extremely difficult task. It is difficult even to define the dimensions of the problem. But, surely, we do not have the right to shirk a responsibility because objective criteria are not easily arrived at and the task is therefore difficult.

We must, then, if we are to build viable, meaningful institutions, determine which segments of society financially support us and therefore have a claim to be served by us; analyze what the needs of those segments of society are; discover the ways in which our functions can satisfy those needs; constitute the resulting combination of functions and needs as the library's obligation to its public; and establish those obligations in order of priority on the basis of society's needs.

III. <u>With the Active Participation of Their Professional Staffs, Libraries Should List, in Terms of Their Obligations to Society and by Order of Priority, Society's Obligations to the Library</u>

This third point is somewhat presumptuous on the part of the library, for in the end the public will determine for themselves what their obligations are. However, it is definitely to our advantage, and I think to the public's advantage, for us to initiate the process of deciding what obligations the public has to the library.

We can do this on a <u>quid pro quo</u> basis; that is, to the extent that the public's obligation is financial, we can state with some precision that to store recorded information will cost a given amount of tax money which will amount to a per capita tax of a given amount. To make this information available to the public through reference service will cost the public a specified amount more. To add telephone reference service, interlibrary loan privileges, research help, or other services beyond the most basic ones will cost more. In other words, if the public can see the value of a certain service, they will know that by asking for it they incur an obligation to pay for it.

This may be the only logical way to obtain the support that libraries need. As matters now stand, the public seems to want the best library service available and at the same time votes down bond issues to provide that service. In these instances, however, I do not think that we can simply assume that the public is being irresponsible. It is much more likely that they are not given sufficient information to make an intelligent decision.

Libraries have developed elaborate methods to provide optimal service while receiving minimal support. In some cases, they charge for extra services such as providing interlibrary loan procedures, an honest method which acknowledges the public's lack of support. Another method, however, which is engaged in by nearly every library in this country, is grossly unfair and throws the burden on the wrong people. That method is to pay librarians low salaries to, in effect, ask them to subsidize a community's library service. The community cannot responsibly ask librarians to do this, nor should librarians be willing to do it.

If we were talking about the usual salary inequities which exist, this argument would be over-stated and therefore largely without merit. However, in the field of librarianship, we are not talking about the usual inequities. The highest paid beginning salaries for public librarians in this country fall fully $200 per month behind beginning salaries for other comparable professions with similar educational requirements.

This nation and most of the communities within it are sufficient wealthy to support the services they want. This is their obligation. However, it is our obligation to tell them what library service costs, including what the service of a librarian paid at an equitable rate costs. Since the quality of the service we offer depends almost totally on the capabilities of librarians, it is short-sighted for us to do otherwise. The public suffers in the end with less service than they might have otherwise been willing to pay for if they had had the information to make an intelligent decision.

IV. <u>The Resulting Document Should Be Publicized by the Library As a Social Contract Between the Library and Its Public, Against Which the Successes and Failures of the Library Can Be Measured</u>

In reality there already exists a contract between a library and its public. It is, of course, an unwritten contract and its provisions are extremely obscure. But, there is one. We should also recognize that that contract is let by the public, not by the library; and the public in its own slow, cumbersome way can cancel the contract whenever it wishes. There is some evidence that it may want to, even now.

The intent of this point is that the contract should be put into written form and should be made more explicit, although of course still leaving it unsigned. It is not a legal contract which is needed, but rather a contract of social obligations. By publicizing this social contract, libraries will have the opportunity to enlighten their constituencies.

Furthermore, the feedback they receive should be an invaluable source of information for making future policy decisions.

Part of that feedback will occur because the social contract will enable the public (and the library staff, too) to judge more accurately the successes and failures of the library. One of the reasons that the public grows disenchanted with libraries is because they judge them inaccurately. What we must do is to provide them with the framework in which to make accurate judgments. Presently, for instance, any lack of service is considered by most of the public to be a failure. Why? Because they judge us against an ideal version of a library which they have constructed in their minds. Would it not be better if we could say, "Here, these are the services that you as a member of the public have been willing to fund. It is only reasonable for you to judge our ability to provide those services. Any other complaints that you have should be directed against the public, not the library."?

The public has the right to judge our performance and they will judge it. We can be sure of that. Therefore, as a matter of preservation, we should do all we can to provide the public with the proper foundation for criticism. This can be accomplished by informing them of the limitations they place on the library.

At the same time, we as librarians also need a better foundation for assessing our own performance. The American Library Association and the state library associations have established many different types of minimum standards which provide a part of the necessary framework. For instance, they establish how many volumes a particular-sized library should contain, but they do not adequately establish a method for determining whether those volumes are appropriate for the public served. To overcome this deficiency, we need to create machinery which will help insure that the right volumes are purchased. The concept of a social contract is part of that machinery. If correctly constructed, every purchase can be judged against its provisions.

V. <u>Through the Use of Committees of Staff Representatives, Libraries Should on a Regular Basis Reexamine Their Social Contracts,</u> with the Method of Reappraisal to Include Public Hearings Regarding Society's Needs, the Library's Obligations to Society, Society's Obligations to the Library, and

the Library's Successes and Failures

Histories of governmental institutions invariably indicate that most are created in response to a public need, but have a strong tendency later to become irrelevant to the public's needs and to continue to exist only for their own ends. However, modern political science also indicates that we can structure an institution against this tendency. This is what this point is designed to do. If its provisions are followed, entrenched ideas will be periodically challenged by the public. This will be to our benefit. Meanwhile, the public will be given the opportunity to express itself.

With the Active Participation of Their Professional Staffs:

VI. Libraries Should Justify All Current Policies in Terms of the Social Contract, Especially Book Selection Policies and Uses of Non-Book Materials

VII. Libraries Should Justify All Current Services in Terms of the Social Contract, Especially Different Types of Reference Services, Interlibrary Loan Programs, and Outreach Programs

VIII. Libraries Should Justify All New Policies and Services in Terms of the Social Contract

Each of these three points deals with the desirability of measuring all policies and services against the established criteria according to which the library is operating. These criteria, as they are set forth in the library's social contract, will form something analogous to a constitution. Therefore, the three points establish the library's intent to make decisions regarding the constitutionality of all existing and newly adopted policies and modes of service.

Quite naturally, the legislative or enacting body should not also be the judicial body. It would be quite appropriate, therefore, to create a committee chosen by the professional staff to sit as a judicial reviewing board for all existing and newly proposed policies and services. As a judicial reviewing board, their power would be only to compare new policies and services against what had already been established as the criteria by which the library is to operate.

In no way would such a judicial reviewing board abrogate the powers or privileges of a board of library trustees or a library administration. What it would do is aid trustees and administrators to interpret the library's role in the community. The practical effect of instituting a judicial review board would be, first, to emphasize to the board of trustees the necessity of working within a framework of acceptable professional guidelines and, secondly, to provide the professional staff with one small check on the general direction in which the library moves. Although there are many good reasons why most public libraries have had nearly all authority vested in a lay board of trustees, nevertheless we should recognize that trustees are normally professionally unqualified to adequately fulfill such a role. Much as trustees serve as a check and balance on city government, a judicial review board would serve as a check and balance on the trustees.

To institute a judicial review board would probably serve to avoid confrontations between the board of trustees and the professional staff because the trustees would be forced by the judicial review board to be more aware of the library's general policy. As an example, it seems possible that in the Richmond, California, censorship case the board of trustees would not have given in to special interest groups and agreed to remove an underground newspaper from the library if there had been a judicial review board there to compare that act of censorship with the library's book selection policy. Quite possibly, in the face of a reversal from the judicial review board, the trustees would have found the courage to stand by their previous policy decisions.

With these three points, as with all of the other points, we wish to establish concrete methods which will aid us--administrators and librarians alike--to build better libraries. We can take a few meaningful steps toward better libraries by structuring them to accomplish their objectives. They are not so structured now. The organizational structure of most public libraries having a board of trustees was built around the single idea of providing a buffer between the library and the city government.

IX. With the Active Participation of Their Professional Staffs, Libraries Should Re-Define the Role of the Librarian

I suspect that most library administrators know that much of the work that a professional staff is asked to perform is far below their capabilities. This situation must be corrected.

A professional librarian has the right to expect a job which makes full use of his capabilities and education. He has the right to expect considerable responsibility, and the authority to match that responsibility.

X. <u>With the Active Participation of Their Professional Staffs, Libraries Should Establish Professional Career Development Programs</u>

Besides redefining the actual work a librarian performs in order that he can work to his full capabilities, libraries should also provide opportunities for librarians to further develop their capabilities. Seminars, sabbatical leaves, in-service training programs, and greater opportunities for librarians to attend professional meetings would be a few examples of this type of activity.

The dialogue which would result from implementing these ten points, plus the future dialogue which would be generated by fulfilling the points themselves, should be very valuable to the profession. It may be difficult at times to define what public is served by a library, what the needs of that public are, and what priorities should be established, for these decisions involve many subjective judgments. Nevertheless, the profession probably has a sufficiently socially-oriented philosophy to deal successfully with such questions.

With these ten points, I hope I have been able to illustrate that the Librarians' Guild, as a professional union, is seeking to build a profession which is responsible to the public it serves and a profession which serves the public with its total capabilities. As an organization formed around particular library systems, we shall begin working to implement programs of this nature at the local level. We shall simultaneously work to incorporate these basic ideas into criteria for accrediting libraries.

PART II:
TECHNICAL SERVICES/TECHNICAL PROCESSES

Shared Cataloguing[1]

by Herman Liebaers

Reproduced by permission from the March-April 1970 (24:2), p. 62-72, and the May-June 1970 (24:3), p. 126-138, issues of the UNESCO Bulletin for Libraries.

Introduction

It is less than four years since the United States Congress decided to amend the 1965 Higher Education Bill to include Title II, Part C so as to authorize the Library of Congress to establish a National Programme for Acquisitions and Cataloguing (NPAC), and it may seem too early to try to assess the results. If this is true of the United States itself, it is even more true of other countries. There was, however, a certain advantage to be gained, in the context of Unesco's bibliographical activities, from treating the problem as a whole. The European observer cannot help being impressed by the American contribution to the development of modern librarianship: the National Programme for Acquisitions and Cataloguing is an exceptionally bold venture, even for the United States. The less wealthy countries should study it and try to increase and pool their own resources so as to derive from the programme the benefits which the United States is quite willing for them to have.

To understand the NPAC properly, one should not see it as an isolated phenomenon. In fact, a series of previous steps led up to it: centralized cataloguing has been practised for some time in America; interest in foreign bibliographical resources has increased remarkably, particularly since the Second World War; and centralized projects on a nation-wide scale have started to become a feature of education, science and culture.

The present study is based mainly on material from the United States (see bibliography), but in addition to consulting certain articles published elsewhere, the author has drawn upon the discussion of the programme which has been taking place since 1966 within the various sections and commissions of the International Federation of Library Associations. IFLA is continuing its study of two forms of co-operation: the use of Library of Congress printed cards outside the United States and the use of certain acquisition techniques, particularly in the developing countries.

The conclusion which the author draws is that the Library of Congress NPAC is at present operating almost exclusively in one direction. Favourable conditions exist for making this co-operative project work in both directions, but this requires first a material and intellectual effort on the part of non-American librarians, at the national and international level. [2]

Part I. The National Programme for Acquisitions and Cataloguing in the United States of America

Origin of the programme

Depending on how one approaches the NPAC, or Shared Cataloguing Programme, it appears to have various origins.

Librarians have long been concerned at the waste of time, effort and money involved when the same books are catalogued over and over again by different libraries. Centralized cataloguing and the distribution of printed catalogue cards are a partial answer. The Library of Congress, home of the NPAC, has been distributing cards in this way since 1901. Centralized cataloguing was devised on a strictly national basis and did not take into account cataloguing work done in other countries.

Particularly since the Second World War, the United States has made a great effort to acquire a greater quantity of the books produced abroad. A co-operative programme known as the Farmington Plan was launched in 1942. A co-ordinated division of the labour involved in the processing of bibliographical resources has been one of the characteristics of recent developments in American research libraries and is certainly not unconnected with the direct origins of the programme.

Lastly, the realization of the need for bibliographical coverage of the developing countries led to the introduction of the PL-480 programme, which was the outcome of an act authorizing the Library of Congress to use American local-currency credits in certain countries to acquire books, bind them, catalogue them and send them to the American libraries participating in the programme. The application of this act may be regarded as foreshadowing the execution of the programme.

However, even the combined effect of the funds of individual libraries traditionally allocated to acquisitions, the co-operative efforts undertaken under the Farmington Plan and the experiment in centralization in the PL-480 programme did not provide the research community with the bibliographical resources it needed to carry out its task.

This led to a re-examination of the question, and it was thus that the idea of a national programme for acquisitions and cataloguing took shape in the Association of Research Libraries (ARL) in 1964-65. The following were the main points presented before a committee of the U.S. Congress on 10 March 1965:

1. The seventy-four major libraries belonging to the association spent $18 million annually on cataloguing, but this sum was only a small fraction of the total expenditure on cataloguing.

2. The forty-seven million catalogue cards sold by the Library of Congress to 17,000 libraries accounted for less than half of the total cataloguing work actually carried out, with the result that more than half of the original cataloguing had still to be done locally, which led to an enormous amount of duplication and--worse still--considerable delay.

3. There was a national shortage of language-specialized and subject-specialized librarians; centralization alone would make it possible to optimize the use of available manpower.

The Association of Research Libraries proposed an addition to the Higher Education Act of 1965 which would establish a national programme for acquisitions and cataloguing. This was enacted as Part C of Title II.

Congress decided to allocate $300,000 to this programme in 1966, $3 million in 1967, $5 million in 1968 and $5.5 million in 1969 (United States fiscal year: 1 July to 30 June). For 1970, only $4.5 million of the sum of $7,356,000 initially included in President Johnson's budget was included in the revised budget of the incoming administration, and the Library of Congress has asked for additional funds. In any case, the funds appropriated to the programme since its inception have generally been considerably less than those authorized to higher education by the substantive committees responsible. In 1969, a marked retrenchment in the programme's development has had to be considered.

Purpose and scope of application

According to the text of the Higher Education Act, the purposes of NPAC are as follows: "(1) acquiring, so far as possible, all library materials currently published throughout the world which are of value to scholarship; and (2) providing catalogue information for these materials promptly after receipt and distributing bibliographic information by printing catalogue cards and by other means, and enabling the Library of Congress to use for exchange and other purposes such of these materials as are not needed for its own collection."

Three further amendments in 1968 authorized the Librarian of Congress: (a) to purchase more than one copy of materials acquired under NPAC; (b) to produce catalogue data not only by means of printed cards, but also to produce other publications necessary for higher education, such as bibliographies, indexes, guides and union catalogues which are also sources of information indispensable to research; (c) to absorb the administrative cost of a co-operative service set up for higher educational institutions or groups of institutions for the acquisition of works published outside the United States in areas where acquisition of library materials is exceptionally difficult.

These amendments have not been implemented because of lack of funds.

Thus, in the most ambitious national project for acquisitions and cataloguing ever known, the programme is trying to cover all books of value to scholarship published throughout the world. The arrangements adopted in each country are dictated by pragmatic considerations. For its acquisitions, for the time being still limited to monographs, the Library of Congress places blanket orders with foreign booksellers or requests other national libraries, subject to various conditions, to acquire books for it, and in addition has regional offices and other sources of acquisition (Table I).

TABLE I.   Sources of acquisition

Regional shared-cataloguing offices[1]	Bookseller
London	Stevens & Brown
Wiesbaden	Harrassowitz
Also receives German-language books published in Switzerland	Helbing & Lichtenhahn, Basle
Oslo	Tanum[2]
Also receives Finnish-language books	Akateeminen Kirjakauppa[3]
The Hague	Martinus Nijhoff[4]
Paris	Stechert-Hafner
Also receives French-language books from: Belgium	Martinus Nijhoff, The Hague
Switzerland	Helbing & Lichtenhahn, Basle
Belgrade[5]	Various sources
Florence	Casalini Libri
Tokyo	Japan Publications Trading Company
Vienna	National Library

Regional acquisitions offices

Nairobi (covering Ethiopia, French Territory of the Afars and Issas, Kenya, Madagascar, Malawi, Mauritius, Somalia, Tanzania, Uganda and Zambia).
Rio de Janeiro (Brazil).
Djakarta (Indonesia).

1. In addition to the countries shown above, the Library of Congress has established shared-cataloguing arrangements functioning without overseas offices with Australia, Bulgaria, Canada, Czechoslavakia, New Zealand, South Africa and the U.S.S.R.

2. Norwegian, Danish and Swedish books.

3. Selected by Helsinki University Library.

4. Also acquires Belgian books, but sends those in French to Paris.

5. In conjunction with PL-480 programme.

For shared cataloguing proper, the Library of Congress co-operates with the body responsible for the country's national bibliography in the following countries.

National bibliographies and list of current publications

Australia (1966--),* Australian national bibliography.
Austria (1966--), Oesterreichische Bibliographie.
Belgium (1966--), Bibliographie de Belgique.
Bulgaria (1969--), Bulgarski knigopis.
Canada (1966--), Canadiana.
Czechoslovakia (1969--), Ceské knihy.
Denmark (1966--), Det danske bogmarked.
Finland (1968--), Suomen kirjakauppalehti.
France (1966--), Bibliographie de la France.
Federal Republic of Germany (1966--), Deutsche Bibliographie.
Eastern Germany (1966--), Deutsche Nationalbibliographie.
Italy (1967--), Bibliografia nazionale italiana.
Japan (1968--), Nōhon Shūhō.
Netherlands (1966--), Nieuwsblad voor de boekhandel, Brinkman's cumulative catalogus.
New Zealand (1966--), New Zealand national bibliography.
Norway (1966--), Norsk bokhandler tidende.
South Africa (1966--), South African national bibliography.
Sweden (1966--), Svensk bokhandel.
Switzerland (1966--), Das Schweizer Buch, Le livre Suisse, Il libro svizzero.
U.S.S.R. (1968--), Knižnaja letopis', Vsesojuznaja knižnaja palata cards.
United Kingdom (1966--), British national bibliography.
Yugoslavia (1966--), Bibliografija Jugoslavije.

* Dates in parentheses show when co-operation began.

After less than four years in operation, the NPAC employed 400 people, but the funds available for the current year have necessitated a considerable reduction in this number. Although the shortage of language-specialized and subject-specialized librarians was one of the reasons why the programme was launched, Washington fairly rapidly managed to recruit and train librarians to cover the many languages involved.

Developments have not been quite so favourable as concerns subject coverage (15 per cent fewer books were processed by the subject cataloguers than by the descriptive cataloguers). Nevertheless, 200,373 titles were fully catalogued during the 1969 fiscal year. The Library of Congress has set up a highly complicated administrative and technical system in its Processing Department. There is a high degree of closely integrated activities, with all the advantages and disadvantages that this implies. Among the advantages might be mentioned the blanket order system and experience gained from the PL-480 programme, whilst among the disadvantages might be mentioned, for instance, the priorities in cataloguing which are not always favourable to the programme. It should however be noted that the United States has never before had a programme as highly centralized as this.

Techniques of collecting bibliographical data

The Library of Congress has concluded agreements with the countries listed above ('National bibliographies and list of current publications') to obtain advance or at least simultaneous printer's copy of the national bibliography entries.

The procedure is for the regional shared-cataloguing offices or the Library of Congress Processing Department to procure the cards used as a basis for the printing of the bibliography or the proofs of the bibliography itself. Catalogue data are received in several copies. Since speed is rightly considered to be essential to the success of the programme, data are sent in weekly, if not more frequently, and by airmail if need be.

This collecting procedure is used in countries which maintain a national bibliography at an acceptable professional level. All entries coming from the national bibliographies are received by the regional shared-cataloguing offices or directly by the relevant department of the Library of Congress.

Technical Services

In countries where there is no rapid and comprehensive national bibliography, the programme relies either on the regional offices set up under the PL-480 programme or on its own regional acquisitions offices, the former of which are located in Ceylon, Cairo, New Delhi, Tel Aviv, Karachi and Belgrade, and the latter in Nairobi, Rio de Janeiro and Djakarta.[3]

From the cataloguing point of view, the results have been considerable, but they cannot be regarded as examples of shared cataloguing. The representative of the Library of Congress tries to train local staff in the techniques of cataloguing, but inevitably runs into the crucial problem of the shortage of skilled personnel. Nevertheless, the accession lists are often used as national bibliographies and are a valuable contribution to the bibliographical equipment of the country concerned. The accession lists which are published in this manner are as follows.

Accession lists

<u>Ceylon.</u> Quarterly. Distribution: American Libraries Book Procurement Center, c/o American Embassy, New Delhi, India.
<u>India.</u> Monthly. Distribution: American Libraries Book Procurement Center, c/o American Embassy, New Delhi.
<u>Indonesia.</u> Irregular. Distribution: American Libraries Book Procurement Center, c/o American Embassy, APO San Francisco 96356.
<u>Israel.</u> Monthly. Distribution: American Libraries Book Procurement Center, c/o American Embassy, Tel Aviv.
<u>Middle East.</u> Monthly. Distribution: American Libraries Book Procurement Center, c/o American Embassy, Cairo, Egypt.
<u>Nepal.</u> Three times a year. Distribution: American Libraries Book Procurement Center, c/o American Embassy, New Delhi, India.
<u>Pakistan.</u> Monthly. Distribution: American Libraries Book Procurement Center, c/o American Embassy, Karachi.
<u>Eastern Africa.</u> Quarterly. Distribution: The Library of Congress, East Africa, P.O. Box 30598, Nairobi, Kenya.

<u>Acquisition techniques</u>

The booksellers responsible for fulfilling the blanket orders select works in accordance with pre-established criteria and within the limits of a fixed budget. These criteria may vary from one part of the world to another, but are fundamentally as follows: one copy of each appropriate new book, in the broad sense of the word, and from four to seven copies, according to the individual case, of certain dictionaries or biographical collections; for a variety of reasons, periodicals, books on medicine and agriculture, children's books, official publications, publications issued by associations and very expensive works are excluded from this automatic selection though. Certain categories of these publications are obtained by the Library of Congress in any case by other channels.

The books selected are bought as quickly as possible, processed using shared-cataloguing techniques and sent every week by air freight to Washington. Procedure differs, particularly in Western Europe, because of different factors. In addition to blanket-order selections, recommendations for acquisitions are made by Library of Congress specialists and by other co-operating libraries.

Co-operation was first established with the United Kingdom, where all orders are placed in London. This co-operation has served as a pattern for the others. For the Scandinavian countries, orders are centralized in Norway and Finland and the books are processed in Oslo. Books published in the Federal Republic of Germany and Eastern Germany are collected and processed by the Wiesbaden Office, which is also responsible for Swiss books in German. French-language books published in France, Switzerland and Belgium are centrally processed by the Paris office. The Swiss books are selected by a bookseller in Basle. The bookseller in The Hague selects the Dutch and Belgian books, those in Dutch being processed in the Hague, while those in French pass through the Paris office for processing. A Florence bookseller has recently begun to select Italian books and a Tokyo bookseller Japanese books. In Austria, the Library of Congress works, not with a commercial firm, but with the National Library. A similar arrangement has just been concluded with the State Library of Czechoslovakia, and another with the National Library of Bulgaria, although the Library of Congress has no centre there. In Belgrade, acquisition for the Library of Congress is carried out in conjunction with the operation of the PL-480 programme. Several suppliers are used.

The programme is not yet operating in Spain or Por-

tugal or in several of the Eastern European countries. The
Library of Congress has long been interested in Soviet books
and has published since 1948 (hence well before the existence
of the NAPC programme) a Monthly index of Russian accessions.[4] Soviet accessions go directly from the numerous
sources to Washington. Australian, New Zealand, South African and Canadian publications are also received directly by
the relevant department of the Library of Congress.

The Rio de Janeiro office draws on a number of
sources to obtain Brazilian books and in fact has to do so
since more than 45 per cent of Brazilian publications are not
published by commercial houses. One acquisition technique
has been for the Library of Congress to sign contracts with
individuals in various parts of the country, usually librarians,
for the acquisition of the books published in those regions.
This method had to be employed because books printed in
other Brazilian towns frequently could not be found in Rio de
Janeiro.

The first regional centre operates in Nairobi and covers ten territories of East Africa: Ethiopia, the French
Territory of the Afars and Issars, Kenya, Madagascar,
Malawi, Mauritius, Somalia, Tanzania, Uganda and Zambia.
Its function is to track down and obtain all significant current
publications in these countries, where there is neither a national bibliography nor an established book trade.

The acquisitions offices supported by PL-480 programme budgets are another important source. The territories thus covered are: Ceylon, India, Indonesia (which has
now joined the NPAC programme), Israel, Nepal, Pakistan,
United Arab Republic and Yugoslavia. As can be seen, these
are countries at various stages of development, and the acquisition techniques vary from one country to another and
even within a single country.

Bibliographical description

The method of preparing bibliographical descriptions
is the very basis of the programme and the reason why it
is referred to as 'shared cataloguing'. Wherever possible,
the regional cataloguing offices make full use of the descriptions of publications prepared for national bibliographies (see
above: 'National bibliographies and list of current publications').

At the local level, the cataloguing centre co-operating with the Library of Congress, whether it is run by an American librarian or not, adapts the descriptions to the cataloguing practices of the Library of Congress. The same procedure is followed for national bibliographical descriptions which do not pass through a regional shared cataloguing office, mainly those from the countries of Eastern Europe, Australia, Canada, New Zealand and South Africa.

The type of adaptation required varies according to the description's country of origin. In spite of the progress achieved since the Paris Conference of 1961 on the principles of cataloguing, many differences in cataloguing practice persist. The IFLA Committee on Cataloguing Rules discussed shared cataloguing at its last session in Copenhagen in August 1969. The conference of cataloguing experts which met in Copenhagen immediately before the IFLA session set up a working party to draft proposals for the international standardization of the content, form and order of the different parts of the bibliographical description.

In principle, the Library of Congress leaves the title and collation of the card unchanged. The procedure is described in bulletins 75 and 85 of the Library of Congress Cataloguing Service (May 1966 and October 1968). Library of Congress practice is followed in choosing the form of the author-heading. Library of Congress and Dewey Decimal Classification numbers and subject-headings are added, as is the number of the description in the original national bibliography. The price, a note indicating translation if applicable, and notes indicating language of the text if it differs from the language of the title are also given. Titles in non-Roman alphabets are followed by a transliteration. The Library of Congress catalogue and number is added and recently the Standard Book Number has also been added, when available.

Four Belgian catalogue descriptions are given below as an example showing the various modifications which may be made in the adaptation of descriptions (see Fig. I).

Distribution of bibliographical data

The Library of Congress was also the obvious choice for distributing the collected bibliographical data, as it has been distributing printed catalogue cards since 1901. The programme explicitly provides for the printing and distribu-

NUYENS (J[ean])

B.D. 19.566 1
Aspects de la mécanique des roches.
(Brux., Presses universitaires de Bruxelles, 1966), 4°, ill., diagr., tab., 30 p. (50 fr.).
(Université libre de Bruxelles. Faculté des sciences appliquées. Institut des constructions civiles. Laboratoire de mécanique des sols. Bulletin, 28.4.66.)

Nuyens; J

Aspects de la mécanique des roches, par J. Nuyens. (Bruxelles, Presses universitaires de Bruxelles, 1966).

30 p. illus., diagrs., tables. 30 cm. (Association belge pour l'étude, l'essai et l'emploi des matériaux. A. B. E. M. Publication groupement no 18) bfr 50.–

(Be 67-417)

Publication A. B. E. M. no 324.
At head of title: Groupement belge de la Société internationale de mécanique des sols et des travaux de fondations. Section de l'A. B. E. M.
Bibliography: p. [30]
1. Rock mechanics. I. Title. (Series: Association belge pour l'étude, l'essai et l'emploi des matériaux. Publication groupement no 18. Series: Association belge pour l'étude, l'essai et l'emploi des matériaux. Publications, no 324)

TA710.A1A75 no. 18 624'.151 77-366048
Library of Congress 69 [10]

GRANDEUR

B.D. 14.812 5 III
Grandeur de la Grèce. (Exposition, Morlanwelz-Mariemont), Musée de Mariemont, 4 mai-31 octobre 1968. Catalogue établi par Guy Donnay.
Morlanwelz-Mariemont, Musée de Mariemont, 1968, 8°, couv., ill., 83 p. (100 fr.).
(Trésors inconnus du Musée de Mariemont, III.)

Morlanwelz, Belgium. Musée de Mariemont

Grandeur de la Grèce. (Exposition, Morlanwelz-Mariemont), Musée de Mariemont, 4 mai-31 octobre 1968. (Catalogue établi par Guy Donnay.) Morlanwelz-Mariemont, Musée de Mariemont, 1968.

83 p. illus. 25 cm. (Trésors inconnus du Musée de Mariemont, 3) bfr 100.–

(Be 68-3261)

1. Sculpture, Greek—Exhibitions. I. Donnay, Guy. II. Title. (Series: Morlanwelz, Belgium. Musée de Mariemont. Trésors inconnus, 3)

N1850.M6A27 no. 3 78-363570
Library of Congress 69 [2]

VERCHEVAL (J[acques])

B.D. 18.662 7
Tabel van de kunstmatige satellieten: 1957-1966. (Nederlandse vertaling van G. Louwet.)
Ukkel-Brussel : Belgisch Instituut voor ruimte-aëronomie, Ringlaan, 3; 1967, 4°, tab., [II]-54 bl. (54 fr.).

Vercheval; Jacques

Tabel van de kunstmatige satellieten: 1957-1966. Door J. Vercheval. [Nederlandse vertaling van M. G. Louwet] Ukkel, Brussel, Belgisch Instituut voor Ruimte-aëronomie, 1967.

54 l. 27 ½ cm. (Institut d'aéronomie spatiale de Belgique. Aeronomica Acta F, no. 7) 54.00

(Be 67-2113)

"This text is a bringing up to date of the table of artificial satellites published in the Aeronomica Acta F, nr. 3, 1966."
Translation of Tableau des satellites artificiels 1957-1966.
Summary in English, French, and German.
Bibliography: leaves 4-5.
1. Artificial satellites. I. Aeronomica Acta. F, nr. 3, 1966. II. Title. (Series: Aeronomica Acta. F., no. 7)

QC851.A26 no. 7 629.43'4 79-363644
Library of Congress 69 [2]

ONTWIKKELINGSHULP

B.D. 16.123 2-3
De ontwikkelingshulp gezien vanuit het standpunt der hulpverlenende landen. Referaten.
Deel 1-2 + Notulen.
(Gent); Seminarie voor toegepaste economie (bij de) Rijksuniversiteit te Gent (Serug, Universiteitstr., 16); 1967, 3 dln, 8°, portr., ill., diagr., tab., XXII-815 + 459 blz. (850 fr.).

(Vereniging voor economie. Achtste Vlaams Wetenschappelijk Economisch Congres. Gent, 19 en 20 mei 1967 — Rijksuniversiteit te Gent . Reeks Verslagen en verhandelingen van het Seminarie voor toegepaste economie).

Vlaams Wetenschappelijk Economisch Congres, *8th, Ghent, 1967.*

De ontwikkelingshulp, gezien vanuit het standpunt der hulpverlenende landen. Gent, Rijksuniversiteit, Seminarie voor Toegepaste Economie, 1967.

3 v. 24 cm. (Rijksuniversiteit te Gent. Reeks Verslagen en verhandelingen van het Seminarie voor Toegepaste Economie) bfr 850.–

(Be 68-63)

At head of title: Vereniging voor Economie.
Includes bibliographical references.
Contents.—[1-2] Referaten...—[3] Notulen.
1. Economic assistance—Congresses. 2. Underdeveloped areas—Congresses. 3. Underdeveloped areas—Finance—Congresses. I. Vereniging voor Economie. II. Title. (Series: SERUG-publikaties. Reeks: Verslagen en verhandelingen)

HC60.V535 1967 76-363646
Library of Congress 69 [2]

FIG. I. Four Belgian catalogue descriptions.

tion of cards, although other means of distribution may be
used. The increase in the distribution of cards was one of
the strongest arguments quoted in favour of the establishment
of the NPAC. Although the library sold 47 million cards in
1965 to 17,000 libraries, these cards covered only 35 to 50
per cent of the major research libraries' cataloguing requirements, and these libraries were spending over 16 per cent
of their total budgets on cataloguing work. After only three
years of shared cataloguing, the percentage of requirements
covered has already increased to between 70 and 80, and
the number of printed cards distributed annually has now
reached 100 million.

The 89 university research libraries which co-operate
with the Library of Congress in the NPAC receive a complete set of printed cards. They are encouraged to reproduce these cards for their own catalogues, and this practice
is becoming increasingly common. They undertake to file
these cards, which are delivered to them daily, so as to be
able to check if all their accessions have been covered.
For the sake of convenience, it is considered advisable to
carry out this filing by calendar year and to get rid of cards
as soon as the catalogue in book form for the corresponding
year appears.[5]

Checking up on gaps noticed by libraries in 1968, it
was found that three-quarters of the works for which catalogue cards were reported missing were in fact already covered by printed cards, had been received and were being
catalogued, or had already been ordered but had not yet been
received. The Library of Congress place orders for the
remaining 25 per cent of missing books, since one of the
objects of NPAC is to provide cards for all books acquired
by major research libraries.

The production and distribution of printed cards is a
complicated operation which still presents serious problems,
even to the Library of Congress with its long experience.
The library has in fact begun a large-scale automation project, the first phase of which is already operational.

Before giving an outline of this project, we should
mention one aspect of the problem which will not be affected
by automation, namely, the difficulty of co-ordinating a book
obtained from one source with its bibliographical description
obtained from another. As early as 1958, with the help of
a subsidy from the Council on Library Resources, the Li-

brary of Congress tried to tackle this problem head-on with
the idea of 'cataloguing in-source'. This project did not,
however, win the general support of publishers and it was
abandoned, mainly for economic reasons.[6] The effort was
not entirely wasted, however, since a certain number of
works, including some important titles, still have the bibliographical description on the back of the title page. Of course,
the great majority of American trade publications give the
preassigned number of the Library of Congress card, which
remains the starting-point for an order for Library of Congress cards. The standard numbering of new books, a practice in which the United States is beginning to follow the example of the United Kingdom, may also help to solve this
thorny problem.

The accumulation of huge stocks of cards produced
year after year by the Library of Congress finally created
major storage and retrieval problems. The automation project was a response to these growing difficulties. The operational phase of the programme is based on optical reading
of order slips, which makes it possible to produce simultaneously and automatically three lists: the first, a readable
list, gives a permanent inventory of orders received; the
second, on magnetic tape, is used for checking inventories,
statistical analysis and invoicing; the third, using fluorescent
code signs on the back of each order, is used for machine
sorting. The orders are then sorted by the numerical order
of the cards. Those in stock are extracted manually from
the reserves and attached to the orders.

The machine automatically re-sorts the orders and
the cards by subscriber number. Packing and dispatch are
done manually. In a year's time, the Library of Congress
hopes to have automated all the ordering, selection, production, packing and dispatch procedures for its cards (60,000
orders are received daily). The new system would ensure
that orders are filled more rapidly, would make it possible
to reduce stocks of printed cards considerably and would, in
the long run, save money.

Automated processing of bibliographical data

Independently of the NPAC, the Library of Congress
began a project, known as MARC, for the development of
machine-readable cataloguing copy. MARC II (MARC I was
experimental), as it becomes operational, is sure to make
an important contribution to the success of NPAC.

Between the end of 1966 and the end of 1968, project MARC encoded 35,000 bibliographical descriptions of English-language books and transmitted them, on 62 magnetic tapes, to 16 North American libraries participating in the programme. The aim of the project was to see how centrally recorded bibliographical data could be used by computers in different libraries.

The libraries wanted to use the tapes mainly for the production of their own catalogue cards, while the Library of Congress wanted a more general idea of what were the most useful services which automated bibliographical records could provide. It very quickly became apparent that certain modifications to the programme were necessary in order to improve the quality of this bibliographical aid, and the structure of the project was redesigned. The new structure was much more flexible. By increasing the range of possible records, it gradually got away from the particular needs of specific transcriptions. MARC II has thus become an all-purpose system for the transmission of descriptions, based on acceptable standardization but leaving it to different libraries to make their own tapes according to their own requirements. As compared with MARC I, the new structure shifts the emphasis from bibliographical processing to transmission, and from compatibility to convertibility, thus becoming progressively better adapted to the differing situations in the libraries taking part, but at the same time requiring that these libraries make a greater effort to do their own programming.

American evaluation of the programme

Very shortly after its introduction, the NPAC programme aroused enthusiasm in the United States. The event was even compared with the introduction of the catalogue card in professional work.

This is clearly the biggest acquisitions and cataloguing venture ever known in library history. Such centralization is somewhat surprising, as it goes against the American tradition: even the Farmington Plan, after the Second World War, was on a decentralized basis; but there has been a general realization that the documentation requirements of the research library community called for action on a national scale.

In spite of this high degree of centralization, probably due to the scale of the resources involved, it should be remembered that the initiative for the establishment of the programme came from a conference held by the Association of Research Libraries, that 89 research or university libraries are participating in the programme and are in fact submitting it to constant evaluation, that the officials in charge of the shared cataloguing programme of the Library of Congress report on its progress at each major professional conference and lastly, that they regularly distribute progress reports.

With regard to accessions, some spectacular results have been obtained. The number of additional monographs which soon began to arrive each week at the Library of Congress was a thousand or more. Cataloguing had to make a concurrent leap forward. The integration of the programme into the already formidable Library of Congress cataloguing structure presented many problems, but from 110,000 books catalogued in the 1965 fiscal year, production has steadily grown until 179,000 were processed in the 1968 and 200,373 in the 1969 fiscal year. However, because of the library's schedule of cataloguing priorities, in which shared cataloguing, though well placed, does not come first, many works, after being sent to Washington at great expense, have to wait their turn. Nevertheless, catalogue cards are available for about 75 per cent of books within four weeks of their arrival in the various libraries. This means that in a relatively short time the coverage of the cataloguing requirements of the co-operating libraries has climbed 50 per cent. This is a remarkable result, considering the delays due to the inadequacy of the manpower available to deal with the volume of work involved. It is also worth stressing that in spite of the complexity of the undertaking and the scale and variety of the work to be done, the initial emphasis on speed has not been lost sight of.

We shall now attempt very cautiously to estimate what percentage of works published in the countries participating in the NPAC are actually acquired. As the Library of Congress processes an average of one thousand English titles (including American books) per week, it can be reckoned that 85 to 95 per cent of such publications are included; this figure will perhaps be somewhere between 30 and 60 per cent for countries where there are shared-cataloguing centres and where agreements exist with the national bibliographies and libraries; and for the rest of the world the aim is not so much to apply selective criteria as to try to obtain all significant current publications.

These figures are imprecise because the national sources are hard to compare: the periods covered differ from one country to another, and local data are of very variable quality. The importance of the statistical data should not however be underestimated as they are essential for judging the programme from an American and from an international point of view. Only quantitative criteria can be applied at the present time, but attention should still be paid to qualitative considerations, which are in danger of being overlooked in the scale and complexity of the programme.

It is too early to assess the probable benefits of the amendments to Title II-C of the Higher Education Act but these are threatened by the projected reduction in funds even before they can be put into practice.

The geographical expansion of NPAC is anticipated and we may therefore conclude that the present limits are regarded as too narrow. The absence of books in Spanish-- 25,000 of which are published annually--is to be particularly deplored. [7]

In conclusion, it should be noted that arrangements have been made to enable two other national libraries in Washington, the National Library of Medicine and the National Agricultural Library, to avail themselves gradually of the facilities provided by the programme.

Part II. The National Programme for Acquisitions and Cataloguing (NPAC) outside the United States of America

The United Kingdom

It was necessary to begin the study of shared cataloguing with the United Kingdom, since the first international meeting on the Programme was held in London in January 1966. In addition to United States and United Kingdom delegates there were representatives present from France, the Federal Republic of Germany, and Norway. The current national bibliography of the United Kingdom, the British national bibliography, can be considered as providing a model of shared cataloguing on NPAC lines. The United Kingdom is also the only country which has so far taken part in the automated cataloguing programme (MARC).

Following the example of the Deutsche Bibliographie (Frankfurt am Main) and independently of shared cataloguing procedures, the British national bibliography had decided to introduce automation, on the basis of the calculation that over and above its normal bibliographical output it could produce magnetic tapes of the MARC type. This proved to be impossible, since the British national bibliography is a bibliography, not a catalogue, and any cataloguing service restricted to books published in the United Kingdom would be considered inadequate by libraries; further, it was essential to have the standard book numbers printed on the books.

The decision was taken to organize a MARC service making use of existing catalogues of foreign material, preferably catalogues which could be read by computer. It was here that the NPAC acquired its full significance. Co-operation between the United Kingdom and the United States relies to a great extent on the new standard book numbering system and the latest edition of the Anglo-American cataloging rules, in the sense that mechanization requires the greatest possible standardization, a development which is essential for the efficient use of computers. It is also necessary to have a standard format for automated catalogue descriptions. The separately devised American (modifications from MARC I to MARC II) and British forms were compared and evaluated, and a common format adopted at the end of 1967 (see bibliography).

The first magnetic tapes were made available in 1969 to some twenty libraries in the United Kingdom. Distribution will continue to be on a small scale for an initial period of one or two years, since the British national bibliography wishes to develop an adequate number of programmes to use them. The United Kingdom MARC service is not an automated system, but is intended for use by an automated system, and is devised to be adaptable to the local requirements of user libraries. Local evaluations of the Programme in the United Kingdom are now being prepared.

Regional shared cataloguing centres

The United Kingdom method of supplying material and bibliographical coverage to the Library of Congress is not essentially different from that of the other countries which have shared cataloguing centres, and they can therefore be

grouped together. It should also be noted that the use of a
common language by the United Kingdom and the United
States constitutes an immense advantage, since differences
of language are one of the primary reasons for the slowness
of work at the international level. This is particularly true
with librarianship, since it uses a vocabulary which is constantly developing. It may be a premature question, but one
may well ask whether shared cataloguing will not tend towards a division of the labour involved in cataloguing by
language rather than by country. It should be noted immediately that this probable trend would produce another problem, that of financing the preparatory work at regional level.
At present, even though the sources of finance are mainly
national, there are already activities which go beyond the
national framework. German-speaking librarians (the Federal Republic of Germany, Eastern Germany, Switzerland,
Austria, Luxembourg) have been meeting regularly since
1964 to study cataloguing problems. The 1961 Paris Conference was preceded by preparatory meetings taking language
as a criterion, and recommended that countries belonging to
the same linguistic region should hold consultations with a
view to standardizing their individual practices as regards
the production of author entries. This recommendation is of
paramount importance.

Table I contained a list of regional shared cataloguing
centres and booksellers responsible for the purchase of
books under the NPAC. Part I of this article set out the
principles governing acquisition procedures, together with the
various ways in which these principles are applied. The
American approach to the problem is essentially of a practical nature, making the best possible use of resources available locally.

American libraries have for many years placed blanket
orders with booksellers. The result depends entirely on the
skill and professional integrity of these booksellers; American libraries consider that the profit motive is a sufficient
guarantee of good service. The fact that this practice is
not widespread outside the United States of America is probably due to fears as to its reliability, and also to the fact
that there are few libraries able to purchase on a scale comparable to that of the United States of America.

Where procurement is effected by booksellers, co-operation by libraries is on a relatively small scale. Libraries generally play an essential part in drawing up the programme for a particular country and providing information on the local book trade; thereafter their action is limited to technical points such as the forwarding of catalogue descriptions or indicating the origin of material which is difficult to identify.

The best system seems to be that of the European libraries which are more directly involved in procurement: Vienna, Helsinki, Prague and Sofia. It appears at first sight that the Finnish system, whereby the choice is left to the library and the purchase to a bookseller, provides the greatest number of guarantees.

It is too early to compare results as between the two methods. The first part of this article attempted, with due caution, to establish a quantitative evaluation, and there is no reason to think that quantitatively the two methods produce different results. A qualitative evaluation of results is however vital to the basic success of the Programme. One major drawback to an evaluation of the alternative sources of selection--library or bookseller--is that too many books are received in Washington. Even when all the preliminary work is done in the regional shared cataloguing centres, the cataloguing finally adopted is governed by criteria which take virtually no account of the intrinsic worth of the book being processed. It seems that until now quantity has prevailed over quality. [8] In passing it should be noted that two years after the inauguration of the Programme, the Association of Research Libraries considered that books of doubtful value still posed no problem. By agreement with the association, the Library of Congress decided nevertheless to eliminate reports from co-operating libraries for material such as norms and standards, calendars, posters, telephone directories, loose-leaf statutes, patents and specifications, comic books, minor juvenilia, tourist brochures, primary, elementary and secondary school-books, university syllabuses, reprints of articles, commemorative postage stamps and related leaflets, certain theses, correspondence courses, 'how-to-do-it' books, expensive reprints previously catalogued by the Library and held in the original, certain translations, and foreign language versions issued by international organizations where English language editions exist.

Co-operation is nevertheless more extensive as regards cataloguing. The meeting in London in January 1966 laid down the basis of such co-operation by recognizing that the similarities in national cataloguing practices were considerable, and that in the past, librarians had been too often blinded by the differences. Apart from the heading, the description proper and the collation could be used much as they were, and merely required mechanical adaptation. Naturally the heading needed to be brought into line with Library of Congress procedures, which include a great wealth of additional information. It is however corporate authors that regularly pose the largest number of problems; and there is often doubt as to whether a publication should be described as official.

It is probable that these procedures will influence local bibliographical practices and gradually bring about an improvement.

The high standard of cataloguing which has obtained for many years among American librarians and their various shared cataloguing centres has a salutary influence, which varies according to the degree of local development.

The Ufficio Bibliografico of the Library of Congress in Florence not only uses the bibliographical information provided for the Bibliografia nazionale italiana, but also lends for listing in the bibliography a fairly high percentage of Italian books which for one reason or another have not yet been received by legal deposit. In Tokyo, there is very close co-operation, owing to the use of Japanese characters. The production of the card to be sent to the Library of Congress involves a somewhat complicated process calling for standing co-operation between the Diet Library and the Library of Congress Centre. In Helsinki, the National University Library co-operates by forwarding the bibliographical copy as well as the official publications, thereby saving valuable time in producing catalogue entries, as well as continuing the traditional exchange of documents.

In Switzerland, where the national bibliography is virtually up to date, the Programme has, however, led to the National Library insisting that publishers should effect the deposit more rapidly. In Vienna, there is very close co-operation between the National Library, the Oesterreichische Bibliographie--which prepares the original card for every work published in Austria--and the Library of Congress Centre. From the American point of view the Austrian solution is rather an exception, though justified for historical reasons.

In Rio de Janeiro, the existence of the centre has promoted closer co-operation between the National Book Institute and the National Association of Book Publishers, both of which are responsible for processing part of the bibliographical information. The result is that the Bibliografia brasileira mensual has become an efficient national bibliography which can be used for the NPAC. Reduced funds have temporarily affected this excellent result. Mention should also be made of the fact that the Library of Congress Centre is also co-operating in the Latin American Co-operative Acquisitions Program (LACAP).

It should be noted that an international network for partial co-operation is being gradually built up between, on the one hand, an area chiefly comprising Europe (though not solely Western Europe) and on the other hand, a part of Latin America. The NPAC nevertheless remains primarily a co-operative venture in one direction. Before studying this question in detail, a rapid survey should be made of the Programme in other parts of the world.

Regional acquisitions centres

The regional acquisitions centre par excellence is that in Nairobi; those in Ceylon, India, Israel, Nepal, Pakistan and the United Arab Republic have for long been operating under the PL-480 programme. As noted already, the centre in Yugoslavia is operated jointly by the two programmes, whereas that in Indonesia has just transferred from the PL-480 programme to the NPAC.

The Library of Congress has set up acquisitions centres, as distinct from shared cataloguing centres, in countries where the book trade and bibliographical coverage are not yet developed. Generally the problems encountered locally by the Library of Congress are due to a shortage of professionally trained staff. In each case where there is a problem of identification, acquisition or cataloguing, the need makes itself felt to increase the number of professionally trained personnel; for Africa and other developing areas throughout the world this remains the primary problem. It is obvious that it is not for the NPAC to provide a solution, but each acquisitions centre is involved, since it inevitably constitutes a local training centre.

While the accession lists published by the various acquisitions centres have probably not yet had a great influence locally, there is no doubt that in these areas of the world they often provide the only substitute for national bibliographies, which can be used both in the United States and elsewhere.

The contents of these lists, which naturally vary since the degree of development varies widely from one country to another, are worth a study by industrialized countries. Many vernacular languages are only now beginning to take shape through the medium of these early publications; methods for teaching Western languages are adapted in each case to the spirit of the locality, and sociological studies are already well advanced.

Two further comments arise in connexion with the presence of the NPAC in the developing countries. Firstly, the NPAC is the embodiment of specific professional procedures. In this sense it is one of the various types of technical assistance available to these countries. Regional study courses, vocational training courses or the provision of libraries or library systems do not generally afford the same opportunity as does the NPAC of applying newly acquired, and therefore to a great extent still theoretical, knowledge. But since all forms of aid are intrinsically important, this should be added to the sum total of all the other forms.

The second comment relates to a country's degree of development. It is undeniable that in some countries the NPAC may be looked on as an entirely foreign element, and in others as a catalyst which influences local practices by its very presence. In some countries the NPAC has very rapidly improved the quality of the bibliographical processing of books being currently produced, and has a salutary influence on the network of professional procedures, which is often still at an early stage of development.

Other areas

The NPAC has had less effect on other areas of the world, and the sole object of referring to it in this connexion is to complete the list of its resources. The Library of Congress does acquire, as quickly as possible, official national bibliography data from Australia, Canada, New Zealand, South Africa, and the U.S.S.R., and uses the data in preparing its catalogues.

Chinese language material is forwarded to Washington

Technical Services   129

from various sources, but is still processed outside the NPAC.

It should again be noted that it is unfortunate that an important language like Spanish is not covered by the NPAC either in Spain or in Latin America; the same is true for Portuguese, except for books of Brazilian origin. Acquisitions and catalogue coverage for this area is provided in the traditional way.

In contrast, the English-speaking countries listed above do make use, to varying extent, of Library of Congress printed cards and printed bibliographies.

International and multinational organizations

At the supranational level, the NPAC has been studied at the last four sessions of the International Federation of Library Associations held in Scheveningen, 1966; in Toronto, 1967; in Frankfurt am Main, 1968; and in Copenhagen, 1969. It was the subject of statements at the International Conference on African Bibliography held in Nairobi in 1967 and at the meeting of the Association of International Libraries on Geneva in 1968; and a paper on it was presented to the Directorate of Education and Cultural and Scientific Affairs of the Council of Europe in Strasbourg in 1968.

There was a brief programme presentation at Scheveningen. Four papers were presented by American speakers in Toronto under the heading of International implications of the Shared Cataloging Program (see bibliography) emphasizing the determination of the responsible United States authorities to make this powerful instrument for bibliographical control available to scholars throughout the world. The speaker who made the most specific proposals was R. Vosper:

> At an initial level, it would seem useful and reasonable for individual libraries in any country, including the United States, to test the Shared Cataloging Program as a selection mechanism for foreign books. If the bibliographical information, including book prices, produced for and emanating from the Program is sufficiently rapid and complete, conceivably it can provide an effective current book selection tool as well as a cataloguing tool.... Full or selective depository sets of Library of Congress cards

are now going to several countries, and it would
seem desirable to explore the fullest possible use
of this information. Eventual access to automated
information might even enhance these values.

Beyond this, we might ask whether parallel or coordinate procurement arrangements to those established by the Library of Congress, in Kenya and
Rio for example, might be useful in behalf of other
countries or groups of countries? The fiscal, management, and political problems in such an international enterprise are not minor, but the possible
advantages should be considered, especially in those
areas where book procurement is a difficult task for
any library.

And beyond this, one might ask whether the concept
of a deposit and central lending facility envisioned
for the Centre for Research Libraries might have
utility elsewhere. The British for some time have
wondered about the possibility of a national lending
library for humanities and social sciences. Would
such an institution now have validity, particularly
for non-European books, working in parallel with
the Library of Congress procurement pattern?

If valid in the United States or in Great Britain,
would one or more central, multi-national deposit
and lending libraries of this type, especially for
non-European books, be meaningful in Europe itself?
The problems of course mount rapidly, and it would
be presumptuous for an American librarian to do
more than raise the question.

These three suggestions--a procurement tool, a cataloguing tool, and a deposit facility for non-European (and non-American) books--did not immediately stimulate the hoped-for discussion. From the American side it was felt that Europeans looked towards shared cataloguing to solve all their cataloguing problems. Obviously, this was not one of the purposes of the NPAC. The Europeans on the other hand were not blind to the fact that the Programme was devised and executed on solely American lines, and that it took no account of the particular situation of European libraries.

The IFLA National and University Libraries Section and the Committee on Mechanization, in which discussion had taken place, decided to put this question on the agenda for the next session, and to invite non-American speakers. The following year, in Frankfurt am Main, a German speaker reverted to it from the point of view of procurement and cataloguing, while a Belgian librarian dealt with methods for setting up a European deposit library for books published in the Third World (see bibliography).

F.G. Kaltwasser of Munich pointed out that the NPAC was in fact a one-way American undertaking, but that its guiding principle actually introduced a type of internationalization which was new to the profession. The efficient use for either procurement or cataloguing purposes of the Library of Congress cards made available to non-American libraries, remained the major objective in mind. The project was attractive in theory, but numerous problems arose in practice: the use of Library of Congress cards as a procurement tool cannot prevent the existence of two systems of selection, which necessarily involves great risks. He studied three categories of procurement: (a) books of national origin; (b) books from developed countries; and (c) books from developing countries.

No library will use Library of Congress cards in selecting books published in its own country; as regards the second category, selection may be either too wide, or in very specialized fields, too restrictive. For the third group, Library of Congress cards and accession lists are undoubtedly a highly important source, and the idea is re-emerging of authorizing regional acquisitions centres to work for non-American libraries.

As regards cataloguing, international use of Library of Congress cards is still difficult, since practices vary from one country, and even one library, to another, notwithstanding some degree of progress achieved since the 1961 Paris Conference. In any case the conference dealt only with alphabetical cataloguing, in which there is already sufficient variety, particularly in the choice of heading, corporate authors, the form of authors' names, transcription and transliteration. As regards subject cataloguing, it should be recognized that Library of Congress cards provide more possibilities, for example Library of Congress Classification, Dewey Decimal Classification, and subject headings. However, the first two classifications are not very helpful, since few European libraries use them; and the fact that the subject headings are prepared in English reduces the use which can be made of them, since a mere translation is generally insufficient. In any case individual libraries need cataloguers, and it appears that automatic entering by subject headings is not feasible.

The possible use of Library of Congress cards poses a major problem of international organization. Is each library to subscribe to them individually, or will a national agency be set up to adapt them? Each possibility raises other questions, the importance of which can only be assessed with experience. The German committee of experts on centralized cataloguing has accordingly suggested to the Deutsche Forschungsgemeinschaft (German Fund for Scientific Research) that it conduct two experiments:

1. A selected set of Library of Congress cards to be distributed to German libraries, according to their specialization, with the object of discovering which works have escaped their selection procedures.

2. A survey, in a more limited number of libraries, to determine: (a) the time factor: the intervals between the dates on which Library of Congress cards are received and the dates of the library's own operations; (b) the extent to which Library of Congress cards are revised; and (c) the percentage of titles based on Library of Congress cards in relation to total production in any given country.

Pending the results of these important investigations, promised for 1970, some preliminary provisional comments can be made.

It would be useful for each national library or bibliographical centre producing catalogue descriptions intended for the Library of Congress to draw up a collection of Library of Congress cards for books published in the country. This collection would provide an answer to some of the questions asked by Kaltwasser:

1. The percentage of 'returns': the figures of 30-60 per cent which have already been quoted are highly conjectural, and refer only to books selected by regional centres; they undergo varying reductions when they pass through the cataloguing bottleneck in Washington. Various factors are the cause of this, such as the lack of cataloguers for certain languages and

for subject processing, the priorities in the Library of Congress general cataloguing programme. Figures are not yet available for books originating in Western Europe (except for the United Kingdom), but it is probable that they will be somewhat disappointing.

2. After the initial selection in the country of origin, these quantitative criteria leave little opportunity for considering the quality of the books for which cards are finally prepared. Specific requests presented by participating American libraries, and the direct intervention of an increasing number of non-American publishers who ask in advance for a Library of Congress card number, influence the number of 'returns'.

3. By building up a collection of these 'returns' it is possible to see how the time factor develops during the execution of the programme. This is of major importance on both sides of the Atlantic.

4. Such a collection would also make it possible to establish a list of the modifications to the original descriptions, and to draw conclusions as to their scope and nature; it would doubtless have an effect on local practices.

It is certain that the building up of such a collection would provide a fairly comprehensive procedure for checking the effectiveness of the application of the programme. The sum total of such national checks should enable the Library of Congress to carry out a continuing evaluation. Since it is in the Library's interest to promote the constitution of such a collection, it sends cards on request to the centre which has produced the original descriptions. These centres should follow the example of participating American libraries by submitting periodical reports with their comments. It is arguable that such a type of participation might be even more useful than that of American libraries.

Kaltwasser shows little enthusiasm for the possible effect of machines on co-operative procedures. It is however relevant to recall the example of Anglo-American co-operation in this field, even bearing in mind the advantage of a common language. The Library of Congress MARC II Project is an experiment aimed at proving that it is possible to produce a standardized machine-readable catalogue which can be handled, revised and adapted in the light of local practices. The United Kingdom experiment also shows that it is already desirable that the American system should cease to co-operate in one direction only, and that participants should be able to communicate directly with each other by machine. It becomes essential to make international arrangements to avoid conflicting local solutions, as is the case with the manual processing of catalogue descriptions. Co-operation between the United States and the United Kingdom has resulted in the creation of a format for an automated card which is sufficiently standardized and flexible to be used as a basis for international discussion.

Though only a few countries have made sufficient progress to take part in such discussion, yet it seems that the time has come to arrange for it, in order to determine the possibilities as regards compatibility and convertibility between the various systems now being worked out. An exchange of views of this type was recently held in 1970 in the Federal Republic of Germany, under the joint auspices of Unesco and IFLA.

A European collection of material from the Third World

R. Vosper and F.G. Kaltwasser have indicated the methods which could be used by the Shared Cataloguing Programme to build up a collection of books from the Third World.

Those responsible for the American programme have proposed on several occasions to share its advantages with non-American libraries, one suggestion being to build up a European collection of books published in the Third World. Given the present state of progress on area studies in Europe relating to civilization, language, and the political, economic and social sciences, it would be sufficient to provide one copy of all books coming from the Third World and intended to form a general collection as complete as possible, to meet research needs. The constitution of such a collection would not have a direct effect on the growth of existing specialized collections in Europe. European libraries have neither the physical resources nor the necessary trained manpower to channel towards themselves the flow of books written in languages that are difficult of access, and published in countries which lack an organized book trade and national bibliographies.

Technical Services 135

In order to carry out this project the following procedure might be adopted:

1. Obtain the official agreement of the American authorities as soon as Europe indicates its desire to act.

2. Find a library in Europe which is capable of housing the collection and of integrating it into an international inter-library lending system.

3. Designate, in each country, the library or libraries responsible for preparing the collection catalogue from the cards provided by the Library of Congress.

4. Calculate and procure the appropriations necessary to cover payment of the European contribution to the American authorities.

5. Calculate and procure the appropriations necessary to pay for the staff responsible for managing the collection.

6. Appoint an ad hoc committee to arrange for co-operation with the Library of Congress and be responsible for managing the collection.

In this way Europe as a whole would be equipped at low cost with a working instrument for speeding up and extending in depth the exchange between the Third World and Europe. This project would also represent a concrete form of co-operation among the major European national libraries and an example of practical collaboration with the United States.

The meeting of the International Federation of Library Associations held in Frankfurt produced the following four resolutions, which bear more or less directly on shared cataloguing.

1. The National and University Libraries Section and the Committee on Mechanization proposed jointly on 18 April 1968 that a contract be drawn up between Unesco and IFLA to examine the possibility of extending the Shared Cataloguing Programme to other countries, particularly developing ones. But the Programme is a complicated system making highly technical demands on its users, which cannot easily

be fulfilled in developing countries. Apart from the enormous technical and organizational problems inherent in the implementation of this project in developed countries, the restriction of the investigation to developing countries raises the additional question as to how these countries can be helped to use the technical mechanism of the Shared Cataloguing Programme. Both questions--the general investigation of the use of the Shared Cataloguing Programme by other countries and the special investigation of the conditions for carrying out this project in the developing countries--seem to call for separate studies. For this reason the National and the University Libraries Section and the Committee on Mechanization recommended that the IFLA Executive Board request Unesco to draw up a contract providing for: (a) a first study, to investigate the general conditions for the application of the Shared Cataloguing Programme to countries other than the United States of America; to be followed by (b) a second study to examine the use of the Shared Cataloguing Programme in developing countries; and (c) on completion of the first study a conference of experts from all interested countries to examine the different conditions in the various countries (Unesco or another international organization should be asked to support this conference financially).

2. The National and University Libraries Section recommended that an approach should be made to the Council of Europe for financial assistance in establishing a European central collection of books published in developing countries and in conducting a preliminary study of the project.

3. The Committee on Uniform Cataloguing Rules proposed to organize a meeting of cataloguing specialists immediately before or after the subsequent meeting of the General Council of IFLA to review progress in cataloguing since the Paris Conference of 1961 and to consider the problems raised at the meeting in Frankfurt in relation to the Shared Cataloguing Programme of the Library of Congress.

4. The Sub-Committee on the Exchange of Official Publications proposed to organize a working session with the chiefs of the European Africa Institutes to dis-

cuss the establishment of a catalogue of the holdings of African official and government publications from the new African states in European libraries.

Insufficient time has elapsed since the adoption of these resolutions for it to be possible to comment on them. However this article can perhaps be looked on as a favourable reaction by Unesco to the first resolution.

It has frequently been noted that the production of uniform cataloguing rules is obviously a powerful control mechanism covering the whole field of shared cataloguing.

Conclusion

Before concluding it may be useful to recall the basic considerations which led the United States to adopt the NPAC: (a) the time-lag which had arisen in cataloguing, due chiefly to the shortage of language-specialized and subject-specialized cataloguers, and (b) the need for a considerable increase in acquisitions of foreign books for the use of the research community. In tackling these two conflicting problems the United States was able to draw on both the long experience of the Library of Congress in centralized cataloguing, and its system of distributing printed catalogue cards. The co-ordinated but decentralized type of acquisition under the Farmington Plan was not however adopted; and for the first time, the United States decided on a massive centralization of collections in the Library of Congress, though the Library had recourse to the help of participating libraries in evaluating its work and thus establishing mutual aid. Congress provided the Library with considerable appropriations to carry out this dual acquisitions and cataloguing programme.

In less than four years the Library of Congress has succeeded in processing annually 200,000 books, meeting 70-80 per cent of the needs of participating American libraries, and enlisting the co-operation of twenty-two foreign national libraries or national bibliography producers, and establishing nine regional shared cataloguing centres and three regional acquisitions centres. This excludes the five previously established PL-480 programme centres.

This system, impressive in itself, must also fulfil other Library of Congress obligations ranging from priority for Congress requirements to partial automation of the distribution of catalogue cards. The result is an extremely

complex organization, encumbered by heavy commitments
due to office administration, and one which it is not always
easy to understand outside the United States.

Even before the National Programme for Acquisitions
and Cataloguing, the United States outstripped European libraries in many fields as regards the scope of their annual
acquisitions and the high level of services to users. The
resources now used by the NPAC will accentuate this gap
even further and the 'American challenge' now extends to librarianship. European libraries, which, notwithstanding
their moderate resources, often work at a level comparable
to that of the United States, live permanently from hand to
mouth. They are not even able to acquire the materials they
catalogue, and in almost every case the Library of Congress
is obliged to finance the limited additional effort it requests
from national catalogue processing sources. These same libraries are also reluctant to accept the 200,000 cards printed
annually and to use them rationally for their own purposes.
They generally lack the staff necessary to classify them in a
usable order and to adapt them to local practices, in order
to benefit from them in the same way as does the Library
of Congress from their catalogue descriptions.

Shared cataloguing in Europe has not yet become an
operating reality. European libraries reap certain side benefits from it where their own bibliographical services are
inadequate. The establishment of a collection of books from
the Third World might prove to be the starting point of a
genuine operation of the system.

The variety of languages and political conditions in
Europe is admittedly a drawback to integration into the powerful monolithic American block, and respect for centuries-
old institutions is a considerable obstacle. On the other
hand, the reasons which have led the United States to carry
out this ambitious programme are <u>a fortiori</u> valid for Europe.
There is thus an overriding need to make a primarily financial effort, both nationally and in European organizations, to
create the structures necessary for making effective use of
the American contribution to bibliography throughout the
world. Here it is significant that the United Kingdom, which
sets the example of the closest co-operation with the Library
of Congress, is also the country which most strongly advocates international co-operation.

A brief reference should also be made to the possible

replacement of bulky cards by MARC magnetic tapes. There is no doubt that such tapes, which only a very few European libraries can use, have their advantages over cards. An important point to begin with is that they are the outcome of a joint Anglo-American effort. In their present form they are of no use without a regional (national) production office. Even with these tapes, technological difficulties are already arising due to the different trends followed by the most modern European libraries; for example, German libraries have opted not for tapes of the MARC type, but for automated catalogues. It is high time to hold an American-European exchange of views in order to avoid incompatible local practices being adopted, with all the attendant disadvantages. Here again the transition from MARC I to MARC II is favourable to an international approach to the problem

There remains the use of shared cataloguing for developing countries. Its advanced technicality rules out for the time being any direct operation by these countries. Indirectly, however, they can draw definite advantages from it, such as world-wide distribution of their publications (and incidentally, the inflow of foreign currency this represents), the beneficial influence of highly qualified services on local development, and in certain cases, practical vocational training. Still more indirectly, the programme can be seen as a form of technical assistance. At a much more general level it provides an example of the interest shown by a highly developed society in its bibliographical resources. There is moreover a simple direct link between this interest and the degree of development.

Two kinds of conclusions can be drawn from the foregoing:

1. The need to hold international meetings at which those responsible for the programme in the United States would come into contact with their counterparts abroad. The agenda might include the following items: (a) the quality of the books for which cards are distributed; (b) the possibility of producing separate complete sets of printed cards, for example on a language basis; (c) the usefulness of authorizing regional centres to acquire additional copies for libraries outside the United States of America; and (d) the internationalization of projects such as MARC. All of these would in fact produce closer integration for libraries participating in the NPAC to which they

already provide reliable support but without the benefit for which they hoped.

2. The need, particularly in Europe, to approach problems from a less nationalist point of view, and to set up multinational centres whose responsibilities may vary but which should be of sufficient stature to enter into a valid dialogue with the United States.

The Library of Congress Shared Cataloguing Programme proves there already exists adequate compatibility to ensure effective, world-wide co-operation. At present, however, the United States are alone in demonstrating this, at the cost of a considerable financial effort. Yet it is not possible to continue to rely on the willingness and resources of a single country to provide a supranational bibliographical service. European countries should now take the Library of Congress Shared Cataloguing Programme as an example in improving their national bibliographical services, and in reconsidering and modifying their current techniques in order to be in a position to make a valid contribution to a common pool.

In conclusion, it should be repeated that the NPAC has not been operating for a sufficient time for us to be able to assess its impact outside the United States accurately, but that reactions to it throughout the world at all professional working levels are an adequate demonstration of the importance of what is at stake.

Notes

1. Written under contract with Unesco.
2. While grateful for the help which he has had from all over the world the author would nevertheless like to express his warmest thanks to all the authorities of the Library of Congress, beginning with Mr. L. Quincy Mumford, Librarian of Congress. The author was invited to examine for himself the organization of the programme, and Mr. E. Applebaum, in charge of the execution of the programme, gave him free access to all material. Had it not been for his help and the devoted work of his staff, the task could not have been achieved, and the author wishes to express his warmest gratitude to him.
3. Djakarta was previously a PL-480 centre but has recently for budgetary reasons become a NPAC centre;

the Belgrade centre is run jointly on behalf of both programmes.
4. Publication of the Monthly index of Russian accessions was discontinued in May 1969.
5. It should be remembered that there will be a time-lag before the December issue appears, as the manuscript is sent to the printer the following month. Many libraries retain all the cards in one pile in order to reduce the number of places they must search.
6. A new effort at cataloguing-in-source is now anticipated by the library.
7. The library does acquire Spanish materials selectively but has refrained from a shared cataloguing programme with the Spanish National Library until increased NPAC funds become available.
8. However, a check of Belgica selecta showed that of 121 titles listed in the first issue, Library of Congress cards had been printed for 88, 24 additional titles had been received and were in process, and the remaining 9 titles were already on order (15 January 1970).

Bibliography

Official documents

U.S. CONGRESS. HOUSE COMMITTEE ON APPROPRIATIONS. Hearings before a Subcommittee on the Departments of Labor and Health, Education and Welfare, fiscal year 1968, 90th Congress, 1st session. Part 3, p. 464, 468; Part 6, p. 74-8.
―――――. HOUSE COMMITTEE ON EDUCATION AND LABOR. Higher Education Act of 1965. Hearings before the Special Subcommittee on Education, 89th Congress, 1st session, on H.R. 3220, p. 368-84, 748-53.
―――――. ―――――. To amend the Higher Education Act of 1965, the National Defense Education Act of 1958, the National Vocational Student Loan Insurance Act of 1965, and the Higher Education Facilities Act of 1963. Hearings before the Special Subcommittee on Education, 90th Congress, 1st session, on H.R. 6232 and H.R. 6265, p. 107-16, 155-81.
―――――. SENATE COMMITTEE ON LABOR AND PUBLIC WELFARE. Higher Education Act of 1965. Hearings before the Subcommittee on Education, 89th Congress, 1st session, on S. 600. Part 2, p. 553-631.

_____. _____. To amend the Higher Education Act of 1965, the National Defense Education Act of 1958, the National Vocational Student Loan Insurance Act of 1965, and the Higher Educational Facilities Act of 1963, and Related Acts. Hearings before the Special Subcommittee on Education, 90th Congress, 2nd session, on S. 3098 and S. 3099. Part 3, p. 1157-83.

_____. LIBRARY OF CONGRESS. Annual report of the Librarian of Congress for the fiscal year ending June 30, 1967. Washington, Library of Congress, 1968. (Latest report.)

_____. _____. Information bulletin. (Various issues from 1965 to 1968.)

_____. _____. The Marc Pilot Project. Final report on a project sponsored by the Council on Library Resources, Inc. Prepared by Henriette D. Avram.

_____. _____. PROCESSING DEPARTMENT. Library of Congress policy on shared cataloging. Cataloging Service bulletin, no. 75.

_____. _____. _____. NATIONAL PROGRAM FOR ACQUISITIONS AND CATALOGING (NPAC). Annual report. (Latest report: 1968.)

_____. _____. _____. _____. Progress reports. (Latest report: August 1969.)

Publications

APPLEBAUM, Edmond L. The National Program for Acquisitions and Cataloging. DC libraries, Fall 1968, p. 75-8.

_____. Developments at the Library of Congress. Library resources and technical services, vol. 12, Winter 1968, p. 18-22.

ASSOCIATION OF RESEARCH LIBRARIES. Minutes of the meetings.

BALNAVES, J. Shared cataloguing. Australian library journal, vol. 15, October 1966, p. 196-9.

BLEAN, Keith C., Jr. Developments at Stanford. Library resources and technical services, vol. 12, Winter 1968, p. 23-5.

BROCK, Clifton. Developments at North Carolina. Library resources and technical services, vol. 12, Winter 1968, p. 25-7.

COWARD, R. E. BNB and computers. Library Association record, vol. 70, August 1968, p. 198-202.

CRONIN, J. et al. Centralized cataloging at the national and international level. Library resources and technical

services, vol. II, Winter 1967, p. 27-49.
CRONIN, John W. The Library of Congress National Program for Acquisitions and Cataloging. Libri, vol. 16, no. 2, 1966, p. 113-17.

──────. Remarks on LC plans for implementation of New Centralized Acquisitions and Cataloging Program under Title II-C, Higher Education Act. Library resources and technical services, vol. II, Winter 1967, p. 35-46.

──────. The National Program for Acquisitions and Cataloging. Louisiana State University Library lectures, second series, nos. 5-8, Baton Rouge, 1968, p. 10-24.

DAWSON, John M. The acquisitions and cataloging of research libraries: a study of the possibilities for centralized cataloging. Library quarterly, vol. 27, part I, January 1957, p. 1-22.

──────. The Library of Congress: its role in co-operative and centralized cataloging. Library trends, vol. 16, July 1967, p. 85-96.

──────. A history of centralized cataloging. Library resources and technical services, vol. II, Winter 1967, p. 28-32.

DIX, William S. Centralized cataloging and university libraries--Title II, Part C, of the Higher Education Act of 1965. Library trends, vol. 16, July 1967, p. 97-111.

──────. Recent developments in centralized cataloging, Library resources and technical services, vol. II, Winter 1967, p. 32-5.

──────. John Cronin and shared cataloging. Library resources and technical services, vol. 12, Fall 1968, p. 395-6.

ELLSWORTH, R. E. Another chance for centralized cataloging. Library journal, vol. 89, September 1, 1964, p. 3104-7.

FIRSOV, G. G. Centralized cataloguing and its importance. Unesco bulletin for libraries, vol. XXI, no. 4, July-August 1967, p. 200-6.

GILJAREVSKIJ, R. S. International distribution of catalogue cards. Paris, 1968. (Unesco manuals for libraries, 15.)

GRØNLAND, E. The role of the national bibliography within the Library of Congress Shared Cataloging Scheme. Bibliotek og forskning, 1967, p. 34-48.

HERATH, K. A. Books from Brazil. Américas, September 1968, p. 36-7.

KOZLOV, V. (trans.). Raspredelenniia katalogizatsiia: novyi vzgliad na staruiu problemu. Teoriia praktika nauchnoi informatsii, March 1969, p. 1-7. (Translation of A. J. Wells, 'Shared cataloguing: a new look at an old

problem', Aslib proceedings, vol. 20, no. 12, p. 534-41.)
LORENZ, John G. International implications of the Shared Cataloging Program; planning for bibliographic control. Libri, vol. 17, no. 4, 1967, p. 276-84.
MUMFORD, L. Q. International breakthrough: an account of the operational beginnings of the shared cataloging program. Library journal, vol. 92, January 1967, p. 78-82.
―――――. International co-operation in shared cataloging. Unesco bulletin for libraries, vol. XXII, no. I, January-February 1968, p. 9-12.
ORNE, J. Title IIC, a little revolution. Southeastern librarian, vol. 16, Fall 1966, p. 164-7.
PIERCY, E. J.; TALMADGE, R. L. (eds.). Cooperative and centralized cataloging. Library trends, vol. 16, no. I, July 1967.
POVES, M. L. Un nuevo programa de catalogación centralizada a nivel internacional. Bibliotheca Hispana, vol. 24, nos. 2-3, 1966.
RAYMOND, Boris; FRANCIS, Derek. Is this trip really necessary? Canadian libraries, vol. 95, no. I, July 1968, p. 35-7.
READY, W. Cards across the water. Library review, vol. 21, no. 3, Autumn 1967, p. 129-31.
ROSS, Ryburn M. Developments at Cornell. Library resources and technical services, vol. 12, Winter 1968, p. 22-3.
SEBESTYEN, G. Namzetközi kataloguscédulak? Könyvtáros, vol. 16, November 1966, p. 629-33.
SKIPPER, James E. Future implications of Title II-C. Higher Education Act of 1965. Library resources and technical services, vol. 11, Winter 1967, p. 46-9.
SKIPPER, J. E.; LORENZ, J. C.; VOSPER, R. International implications of the Shared Cataloging Program. Libri, vol. 17, no. 4, 1967, p. 270-93.
STEVENS, N. D. et al. The National Program for Acquisitions and Cataloging: a progress report on developments under the Title IIC of the Higher Education Act of 1965. Library resources and technical services, vol. 12, Winter 1968, p. 17-29.
SUKIASJAN, E. R. Centralized classification: achievements and problems in regard to future development. Unesco bulletin for libraries, vol. XXII, no. 4, July-August 1968, p. 189-95.
VOSPER, Robert. International implications of the Shared Cataloging Program: planning for resource development, Libri, vol. 17, no. 4, 1967, p. 285-93.

_____. The public interest. <u>Newsletter of the American Documentation Institute</u>, vol. 6, January-February 1968, p. 1, 14-15.

WELLS, A.J. Shared cataloguing: a new look at an old problem. <u>Aslib proceedings</u>, vol. 20, no. 12, p. 534-41.

WESTBY, Barbara M. Library of Congress Shared Catalogue Program and the MARC Project: aspects of international cooperation, <u>NFF-skrift</u>, no. I, Oslo 1969, 9 p.

_____. Shared cataloguing. Dublin, University College Dublin, 1969, 16 p. (School of Librarianship publications.)

WILLIAMS, Lorraine. The Shared Cataloging Program: the importance of being ordered. <u>College and research libraries</u>, vol. 30, July 1969, p. 342-3.

Photocopying in a University Library

by Robert H. Blackburn

Reprinted by permission from the October 1970 issue of Scholarly Publishing (2:1), p. 49-58. Copyright 1970 by University of Toronto Press.

The advent of photocopying machines has coincided with a vast expansion of research activity and publishing in universities and governments and industries, and in many new subjects and new countries. For libraries this expansion has greatly increased the amount and variety of world publication from which to select, and it has multiplied the demands for wider and quicker service; presumably the expansion has posed parallel problems for the publishing industry. In the past ten years the University of Toronto Library has raised its acquisition budget by a factor of 10, but the number of requests which we cannot meet except by loan or copy from other libraries has quintupled. Most research of course implies the quick consultation of many volumes: a glance at the preface or table of contents, a look in the index for certain words, and perhaps some reading and copying from the text. Our users have pressed for shorter loan periods, and for some material (especially journals) to be kept available in the library at all times. The number of graduate students and professors has grown rapidly at our university, and each one has a special subject with special demands on the library. At the same time the load on the library and its research facilities has been increased further by the growing emphasis on independent study by undergraduates, and they too ask for a wider range of service.

In order to minimize the borrowing of journals and other research materials so that they may be kept available, and to assure that paper and bindings are treated as gently as possible, we prefer to have photocopying done by library staff rather than by library users. A booth containing two machines in the main hall is staffed 94.5 hours a week. Copies are made while the user waits or, if he does not

wait, are ready for him by next morning. There are two
other staffed machines behind the scenes, used mostly for
making copies for other libraries in lieu of interloans.
There is also a staff-operated machine in the department of
rare books and special collections. Charges are per page
(not per exposure) in order to facilitate estimating, and especially to avoid insistence by the user that bound volumes
be pressed flat enough to copy two facing pages on one exposure. Charges to users from outside the university are
high enough to approximate the actual cost of making the
copy (though not the overhead or incidental work). Charges
to members of the university are set as low as possible to
encourage use of the service, but high enough to discourage
frivolous use of it; we are in fact interested in a system
which would give each person a limited number of free copies per year. It is important that our charges be kept so
low that it will not be worth a user's while to borrow the
book and have it copied elsewhere. There are at least 152
book-copying machines in various parts of the University of
Toronto; most professors and some students can use departmental machines without charge. Many students also have
access to machines in offices in the city; it is estimated
that there are about 20,000 book-copying machines in Metropolitan Toronto. The library provides one dime-operated
copying machine in the main building and two others in other
buildings; these are all in undergraduate reading rooms
where the books are all duplicate copies which do not have
to be preserved forever.

    The library must assume that those who come in to
read, or to borrow, are familiar with the principles of copyright and fair dealing, and that they will deal fairly with any
work they consult or borrow. We cannot be responsible for
their morals, or for their subsequent publications. At the
same time, we know that research and serious study are
pointless unless the student takes systematic notes and prepares himself to make accurate quotations in context. That
is, copying is implicit in the use of our collections and we
have always facilitated it in some way; in the good old days,
before ball-point pens, we used to provide ink at a penny a
penful. We now provide coin-operated photocopy machines
and a staffed photocopy service, microfilm service and reader-printer service in the firm belief that providing a single
copy of a reasonable portion of any work falls within the
definition of fair dealing for the purpose of research or private study, as defined in Section 17(2)(a) of the Canadian
Copyright Act. We are not offering copies for sale, nor are

we distributing copies as suggested by critics such as Sharp.[1] We are simply providing a service through which an individual reader may obtain an excerpt more quickly and accurately than he could copy it by hand.

The official (although obviously unattainable) goal of our library is to provide any member of the university with access to any work he may wish to see, no matter when or where it was published. It makes no attempt to provide textbooks, which students are supposed to buy, but aims rather at the selective coverage of world publication, mostly in one copy, for purposes of research. Its acquisition program depends heavily on imports through specialized agents in many countries, and each year's accessions represent tens of thousands of publishing sources. Although it ranks only ninth among North American university library systems in the total size of its collection, it has for the past three years ranked first in the amount of material added. It is, presumably, one of the major providers of photocopies.

Until now, discussion of the photocopying which is done by Canadian libraries has consisted mainly of complaints and accusations by publishers, and indignant denials by librarians. Since the matter will have to be dealt with somehow in the revision of Canadian copyright law which is now brewing, there is an obvious need for facts instead of oratory, and first of all some facts about what is actually being photocopied. Accordingly, several of my colleagues at the University of Toronto Library agreed to take and analyse a two-week sample of the traffic. We sent an outline of the plan to a number of other Canadian libraries, and some of them took similar samples which were less elaborate but tended to validate our findings.

Sampling Procedure

To find out what was being copied on our five staff-operated photocopying machines, we made a record of each item copied during the two-week period from 23 February to 8 March, 1970. In order that the record could be made as simply and quickly as possible, it consisted of a photocopy of the title page of each item, with notations added to show the category of user, the number of pages copied, and the date of publication if it appeared elsewhere than on the title-page. At the end of two weeks we had accumulated 1,768 such records at a direct cost of approximately $148 for machine operation and staff time.

Analysis of the records was of course a much more expensive business, and revealed some minor problems. It was not always clear, from the record, whether a title had been published by a government department or by some other agency, although we were trying to separate government publications as one of the categories. Date of publication was missing from some records, perhaps because no date was given or perhaps because the operator, being human, simply forgot to look for it. Because we had noted the number of pages but not the specific page numbers, we could not be certain whether two appearances of the same volume implied that the same passage had been copied twice. The sample did not cover 1,758 microfilm exposures made during the test period, or 278 exposures on the reader-printer, or 2,286 exposures on the coin-operated machines. We had decided that the sample need not record copyright notices, since Section 20(3)(a) of the Canadian Act states that copyright in a Canadian work subsists 'unless the contrary is proved,' and works originating in most other countries are covered by similar words in Article 15 of the Berne Convention; we simply have to assume that any work is under copyright unless its particular term (unknown to our operators) has expired. In spite of these minor uncertainties and omissions, however, our sample was large enough to yield clear and significant results.

The Sample

As shown in Table I, 21,483 pages were copied from 1,768 items, an average of 12 pages per item. Of the pages copied, 11% were from Canadian publications, 45% from American, 17.1% from British, and 26.9% from others. The total number of different publishers represented was 1,108 as shown in Table 2, 909 of them represented by one title each. The six most-copied publishers were the University of Chicago Press, American Psychological Association, Springer-Verlag, University of Toronto Press, Academic Press of New York, and Cambridge University Press, in that order.

The age distribution of serials and monographs proved to be about the same for monographs as for serials, except for very new and very old serials (Table 3). About 56% of

TABLE I

Summary of copies made, by country of publication and category of material

		monographs	serials	govt. pubs.	theses	other	total	per cent
Canada	ITEMS	54	119	43	8	1	225	12.7
	PAGES	461	1,124	329	467	1	2,382	11
U.S.A.	ITEMS	180	634	3	--	--	817	46
	PAGES	1,832	7,782	30	--	--	9,644	45
Britain	ITEMS	80	230	2	--	--	312	17.7
	PAGES	688	2,981	14	--	--	3,683	17.1
Other	ITEMS	58	351	5	--	--	414	23.6
	PAGES	823	4,932	19	--	--	5,774	26.9
Total	ITEMS	372	1,334	53	8	1	1,768	100.0
	PAGES	3,804	16,819	392	467	1	21,483	100.0

TABLE 2

Summary by number of items copied per publisher

number of publishers	% of total publishers	number of items per publisher	total items copied	% of all items copied	cumulated % of items copied
909	82.04	1	909	51.32	51.32
86	7.77	2	172	9.72	61.04
34	3.07	3	102	5.77	66.81
29	2.62	4	116	6.57	73.38
12	1.08	5	60	3.40	76.78
7	.63	6	42	2.38	79.16
11	.99	7	77	4.36	83.52
4	.36	8	32	1.82	85.34
1	.09	9	9	0.52	85.86
3	.27	11	33	1.86	87.72
1	.09	12	12	0.68	88.40
1	.09	13	13	0.73	89.13
3	.27	14	42	2.37	91.50
1	.09	15	15	0.85	92.35
1	.09	16	16	0.91	93.26
1	.09	18	18	1.09	94.35
2	.18	20	40	2.26	96.61
1	.09	25	25	1.41	98.02
1	.09	35	35	1.98	100
1,108	100		1,768		

all items were published in the last ten years and 37% in the last five. In the Sophar study, which was dominated by scientific journals, the corresponding figures are 90% and 50%.[2] That is, our sample includes a much higher proportion of older material, especially older books.

    Serial titles accounted for 75.5% of the sample, and outnumbered books in a ratio of 3.6:1. In Sophar's study the corresponding ratio is 10:1, presumably on account of the strong bias towards scientific and technical libraries.[3] He states that 'library copying is mainly from journals, and mainly from non-profit.'[4] The preponderance of journal titles in both samples is interesting because of the special relationship among the authors and publishers and users of journal articles. If authors receive any payment at all from the publishers it is a lump sum, and not a royalty affected by the number of sales. The authors of scholarly and scientific articles seldom receive any payment at all, and in fact most of the principal scientific journals in English now ask their authors to pay a "page-charge" which may be anything from $20 to $75 per page. That is, the author's object is to achieve wide distribution of his ideas, even if he has to pay for it. Ordinarily he obtains a supply of reprints of his article from the publisher at cost at the time of publication, and mails them out to his colleagues or in response to later requests, although I am told that the sending of 'reprint request cards' has diminished greatly since photocopy began providing a quicker source of copies. The publishers of learned journals, most of them subsidized by governments or by professional associations, print enough copies to fill their subscriptions and usually a few more, enough to meet claims and new subscriptions for a few months or perhaps a year or two.[5] Apparently it has never been financially feasible for a journal publisher to serve the diminishing public demand for more than a short time after publication date, and yet the author's wish for dissemination and the user's wish for access continue to exist. The holdings of our library, for instance, include files of about 37,000 serials which amount to about 500,000 volumes containing at least 15 million separate articles, yet several times a day we find that the needs of a particular reader cannot be met unless some other library can send us a copy of the article he wants. At the same time we are kept busy making photocopies of articles in our own collection, many for users in other libraries and many for our own users who want copies to mark up and to keep for a time far beyond any normal period of library loan.

TABLE 3

Monographs and serials by date of publication

		pre-1900	1900-49	1950-59	1960-64	1965-68	1969-	no date	total
Canada	MONOGRAPH	4	11	7	6	16	7	3	54
	SERIAL	3	31	22	19	21	21	2	119
U.S.A.	MONOGRAPH	2	16	28	35	50	11	38	180
	SERIAL	2	97	142	134	132	109	18	634
Britain	MONOGRAPH	12	18	8	10	16	--	16	80
	SERIAL	5	45	59	39	46	31	5	230
Other	MONOGRAPH	7	15	6	5	17	1	7	58
	SERIAL	22	79	70	51	70	54	5	351
Total	MONOGRAPH	25	60	49	56	99	19	64	372
	SERIAL	32	252	293	243	269	215	30	1,334

	monographs	serials	total
total items of known date	308	1,304	1,612
per cent published: 1900 onward	92	97	96.5
1950 onward	72	78	77
1960 onward	57	56	56
1965 onward	38	37	37
1969 onward	6.2	16.5	14.3

TABLE 4

Items and pages copied by category of user

user category	number of items	% of total	number of pages copied	% of total	average pages per item
other libraries	592	33.48	9,012	41.95	15
graduate students	452	25.57	4,978	23.17	10
undergraduate students	390	22.06	3,562	16.58	9
faculty	154	8.71	1,929	8.98	12
general public	79	4.47	738	3.44	9
library-collection	53	2.99	890	4.14	17
library - staff	48	2.72	374	1.74	8
TOTALS	1,768		21,483		12

Table 4 shows that other libraries (Canadian and foreign) form the largest single category of users served during the sample period, accounting for 33% of the items and 42% of the pages. Graduate students were the second largest group, followed by undergraduates and then by faculty members. Members of the general public who use the library accounted for about 5% of the items, almost as many as the combined total for library staff and the library collection.

The 'library collection' category deserves some explanation. When a vandal tears a page or a short section out of a monograph or encyclopaedia, or an article out of the bound file of a journal, obviously the quickest and most practical way of mending the damage is to replace the missing pages with a photocopy from a second set. When the library acquires an unbound file of a journal as a duplicate set, and the annual index sections and title pages are missing, then the only way to complete the set for binding is to insert photocopies from the existing bound file. More frequently, when the library has only one bound file of a journal and discovers that a professor has referred his class to a particular article in one of the volumes, then the only way of serving the class and protecting the volume from theft or mutilation may be to make a few photocopies of the article immediately and place them on the short-term loan shelf. During the past two years we have copied about 1,400 articles per year on this basis, or something less than one hundredth of one per cent of the journal articles in our collection, at an average of 2.5 copies per article. We do not copy chapters of books in this way, though professors occasionally present us with duplicated chapters of books (even forthcoming books!) which they are recommending to their students.

Since some people seem to imagine that libraries have whole classes of students lined up to get photocopies of a new textbook, it is worth noting that only 18 volumes, or about one per cent of the sample, were copied more than once.[6] Sixteen volumes were used twice, one four times, and one seven times. In only three instances does it seem likely that the same pages were copied more than once. Two of these instances involved two copies each. The other involved six pages of the 12 January, 1970 issue of Nation, copied for six undergraduates and one graduate over a period of nine days. This issue, which was six or seven weeks old at the time, must have been sold out in Toronto and a professor must have recommended an article on prison reform, the only six-page piece in that issue. Otherwise, in 1,758 out of 1,761 different items photocopied, there was no overlapping of pages copied.

While photocopying is an important service in a research library, the sample can be put alongside other figures which show it to be a very small part of the whole pattern of use. A door-count taken during the sample period showed that about 66,000 persons entered the building. If we count all photocopies which were made, including those made for other libraries, there were 26 items copied for every 1,000 people who entered the building. Obviously an open-shelf library can never have a complete record of book use, and we reckon that recorded loans represent only one-fifth to one-tenth of the books which are actually consulted. The number of recorded loans in our library, over the past ten years, has consistently shown a greater increase than the rise in student enrolment, and the 34,303 loans recorded during the test period yield some useful comparisons with the photocopy sample. Table 5 shows that use by photocopying, compared to use by borrowing, ranges from 23 per 1,000 (for undergraduates) up to 1,342 per 1,000 (for other libraries). Local users account for only 33 photocopies per 1,000 loans.

One wonders what these users would have done if they could not have obtained photocopies. According to 181 responses from photocopy users who were asked this question in a recent survey at the University of British Columbia:[7]

72% say they would copy by hand
19% say they would forget the whole matter
5.5% say they would attempt to purchase
3.5% say they would steal or tear out the wanted pages

If indeed 5.5% should seek to buy copies, one wonders whether the titles would be in print and available. Checking 54 titles indicated that about 4.4% of the 1,768 items were in print, though not necessarily available in time to meet the need. If 5.5% of them had actually been available and bought, purchases would have amounted to 0.055 x 4.4 or 0.24% of the whole sample, or four items altogether. If the authors or publishers of these four items were to show that their rights had been infringed or that they had been damaged in any way by the copying which took place, then a system of payments would have to be established; but the

TABLE 5

Recorded loans compared to photocopies by category of user

users	recorded loans	items from which pages were copied	items copied per 1,000 items borrowed
undergraduates	16,999	390	23
graduate students	11,707	452	39
staff members	4,538	202	45
general public	618	79	128
SUB-TOTAL local users	33,862	1,123	33
other libraries	441	592	1,342
TOTAL	34,303	1,715	50
TOTAL per 1,000 persons who enter the library	502	26	

system would have to take account of the costs of accounting, as Nimmer points out.[8]

Summary and Observations

1. It seems clear from the sample, and from the Sophar study referred to, that library copying deals mainly in serial publications, an area from which authors derive no royalties, and in which publishers have never attempted to meet the public demand for more than a few weeks or months after the production of each new issue.

2. If our institution is a fair sample, the library's copying operation is only a drop in the bucket compared to that which is done in other parts of the university, and in the city. Sophar estimated that three billion published pages a year would be copied by 1969.[9] Nimmer quotes a guess of 25 billion 'impressions' by 1969 in the United States.[10] Whatever the rate of copying in Canada, it is my untested impression that there is more copying of recent publications in laboratories and in business offices than there is in libraries. Even those machines which are used for copying correspondence and interoffice memos are of course dealing with material which is copyright under Section 6 of the Canadian Act. If any sort of fee or licence were to be imposed on copying machines, for any reason, then it should apply equally to all machines unless, as Nimmer suggests, there were a discount to non-profit educational institutions.[11]

3. It is clear that libraries need to make or obtain single copies of journal articles and of sections of books for purposes of research and private study. They need to make or obtain photocopies to replace missing pages. They need to copy whole volumes of rare or fragile material, either in microfilm or in full size, either to preserve as record copies or to lend in lieu of the rare original volumes. They sometimes need to make multiple copies of journal articles which are out of print, to meet a surge of demand and to preserve the original copy. They need to do all these things and to make the most effective use of all available techniques if they are to meet the public need for information. The current efforts to estab-

lish regional and national specialization of collections, and co-ordination of information systems, would be completely negated if libraries could not continue to do these things without fear of breaking the law.

4. It is clear that the unauthorized production of an edition of any copyrighted work for purposes of sale or classroom use or general distribution without charge must be illegal and subject to effective penalties.

5. I think it is a mistake to think of photocopy and computer-storage as similar in relation to publishing. It will be a very long time before it will be feasible for the text of all books and journals (as we know them) to be stored in digital form and called forth by a user at the touch of a dial on his television set. If that day comes, authors will no doubt receive their royalties out of toll charges built into the dialling system, while both publishing houses and libraries as we know them may have gone the way of the dinosaurs.

Notes

1. Roy C. Sharp, "Licensing the photocopier," Scholarly Publishing, v. 1, no. 3, p. 248.
2. G. B. Sophar and L. B. Heilprin, The determination of legal facts and economic guideposts with respect to the dissemination of scientific and educational information as it is affected by copyright: a status report (Washington, D.C.: Bureau of Research, Office of Education; U.S. Dept of Health Education & Welfare, 1967), p. 65.
3. Ibid., p. 60.
4. Ibid., p. 68.
5. See M. B. Nimmer, "New technology and the law of copyright: reprography and computers," UCLA Law Review, v. 15, no. 3, p. 945.
6. Sharp, p. 248.
7. Private communication from Basil Stuart-Stubbs, 2 April 1970.
8. Nimmer, p. 966.
9. Sophar, p. 84.
10. Nimmer, p. 943.
11. Ibid., p. 974.

History of Library Computerization

by Frederick G. Kilgour

Reprinted by permission from the September 1970 issue of Journal of Library Automation (3:3), p. 218-229. Copyright 1970 by American Library Association.

This historical scrutiny seeks the origins of library computerization and traces its development through innovative applications. The principal evolutionary steps following upon a major application are also depicted. The investigation is not confined to library-oriented computerization, for it examines mechanization of the use of library tools as well; indeed, the first half-dozen years of library computerization were devoted only to user applications.

The study reveals two major trends in library computerization. First, there are those applications designed primarily to benefit the user, although few, if any, applications have but one goal. The earliest such applications were machine searches of subject indexes employing post-coordination of Uniterms. Nearly a decade later, the first of the bookform catalogs appeared that made catalog information far more widely available to users than do card catalogs. Finally, networks are under development that have as their objective availability of regional resources to individual users.

The second trend is employment of computers to perform repetitive, routine library tasks, such as catalog production, order and accounting procedures, serials control, and circulation control. This type of mechanization is extremely important as a first step toward an increasingly productive library technology, which must be an ultimate goal if libraries are to be economically viable in the future (1, 2).

Historical studies of library computerization have not yet appeared, although some reports beginning with that of L. R. Bunnow (3) in 1960 contain valuable literature reviews. Both editions of Literature on Information Retrieval and Machine Translation by C. F. Balz and R. H. Stanwood (4, 5) are extremely useful. In addition, J. A. Speer's Libraries and Automation (6) is a valuable, retrospective bibliography of over three thousand entries.

Origins

The origins of library computerization were in engineering libraries newly established in the 1950's and employing the Uniterm coordinate indexing techniques of Mortimer Taube on collections of report literature. The technique of post-coordination of simple index terms proved most suitable for computerization, particularly when the size of a file caused manual manipulation to become cumbersome.

Harley E. Tillitt presented the first report, albeit unpublished at the time, on library computerization at the U. S. Naval Ordnance Test Station (NOTS), now the Naval Weapons Center at China Lake, California. The report, entitled "An Experiment in Information Searching with the 701 Calculator" (7), was given at an IBM Computation Seminar at Endicott, New York, in May 1954. The system was extended and improved in 1956, and a published report appeared in 1957 (8). Tillitt subsequently published an evaluation (9).

The NOTS system mimicked manual use of a Uniterm card file. This noteworthy system could add new information, delete information related to discarded documents, match search requests against the master file, and produce a printout of document numbers selected. Search requests were run in batches, thereby producing inevitable delays that caused user dissatisfaction. When the user did receive results of his search, he had a host of document numbers that he had to take to a shelf list file to obtain titles. Subsequent system designers also found that a computerized system could cause user dissatisfaction if it did not speed up and make more thorough practically all tasks. Because use of the system dwindled, it was not programmed for an IBM 704 that replaced the 701 in 1957. However, a couple of years later, when an IBM 709 became available, the system was programmed and improved so that the user received a list of document titles (10).

Tillitt, Bracken, and their colleagues deserve much credit for their pioneer computerization of a subject information retrieval system. The application required considerable ingenuity, for the IBM 701 did not have built-in character representation. Therefore it was necessary to develop subroutines that simulated character representation (11). Moreover, the 701 had an unreliable electrostatic core memory. On some machines the mean time between failures was less than twenty minutes (12).

In September 1958, General Electric's Aircraft Gas Turbine Division at Evendale, Ohio, initiated a system in an IBM 704 computer (13) that was similar to the NOTS application. Mortimer Taube and C.D. Gull had installed a Uniterm index system at Evendale in 1953 (14, 15). The GE system was an improvement over the then-existing NOTS system because it printed out author and title information for a report selected, as well as an abstract of the report. Like the NOTS system, however, the GE application provided only for Boolean "and" search logic.

The celebrated Medlars system (16) encompassed the first major departure in machine citation searching. The original Medlars had two principal products: 1) composition of Index Medicus; and 2) machine searching of a huge file of journal article citations for production of recurrent or on-demand bibliographies. The system became operational in 1964.

The NOTS and GE systems coordinated document numbers as listed under descriptors. Medlars departed from this technique by searching a compressed citation file in which each citation had its descriptors or subject headings associated with it. The Medlars system also provides for Boolean "and," "or," and "not" search logic.

The next major development was DIALOG (17), an online system for machine subject searching of the NASA report file. Queries were entered from remote terminals. The SUNY Biomedical Communication Network constitutes an important development in operation of machine subject searching and production of subject bibliographies of traditional library materials. The SUNY network went into operation in the autumn of 1968 with nine participating libraries (18). Its principal innovation is on-line searches from remote terminals of the Medlars journal article file to which book references have been added. The SUNY network eliminates the two major dissatisfactions with the NOTS system and all subsequent batch systems, in that it provides the user with an immediate reply to his search query.

Catalog Production

In 1960, L. R. Bunnow prepared a report for the Douglas Aircraft Company (3) in which he recommended a computerized retrieval system like the NOTS and GE systems that would also include catalog card production. Bunnow's proposal was perhaps the first to contain the concept of production of a single machine readable record from which multiple products could be obtained, such as printed catalog cards and subject bibliographies produced by machine searching. Catalog card production began in May 1961 (19), the cards having a somewhat unconventional format and being printed all in upper-case characters as shown in Figure 1. Cards were mechanically arranged in packs for individual catalogs, and alphabetized within packs--an early sophistication. Accompanying the production of catalog cards was production of accession lists from the same machine readable data.

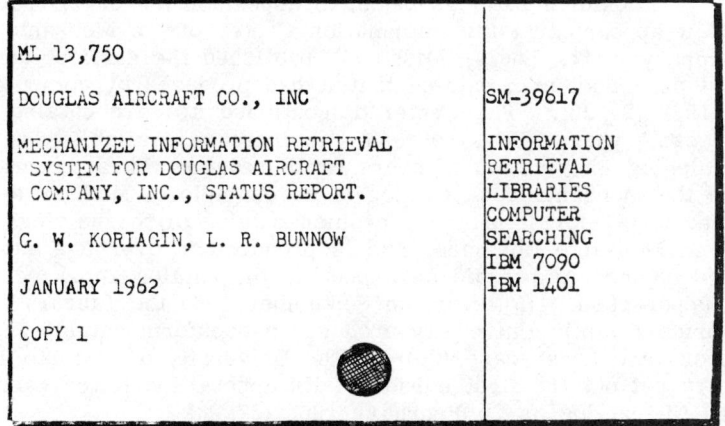

Fig. 1. Sample Catalog Card

The next development in catalog card production occurred at the Air Force Cambridge Research Laboratory Library, which began to produce cards mechanically in upper- and lower-case in 1963 (20). A special computer-like device called a Crossfiler manipulated a single machine readable cataloging record on paper tape to produce a complete set of card images punched on paper tape. This paper-tape product drove a Friden Flexowriter that mechanically typed the cards in upper- and lower-case. Two years later, Yale began to produce catalog cards in upper- and lower-case directly on a high-speed computer printer (21). The Yale cards were also arranged in packs, as had been those at Douglas, but were not alphabetized within packs.

The New England Library Information Network, NELINET, demonstrated in a pilot operation in 1968 a batch processing technique servicing requests from New England state university libraries, via teletype terminals, for production of catalog card sets, book labels, and book pockets from a MARC I catalog data file (22). The NELINET system became operational in the spring of 1970 employing the MARC II data base. Also in 1968 the University of Chicago Library brought into operation catalog card production with data being input remotely on terminals in the Library, and cards being printed in batches on a high-speed computer printer centrally (23).

Bookform catalogs began to appear in the early 1960's, and it appears that the Information Center of the Monsanto Company in St. Louis, Missouri, published the earliest report on a bookform catalog that it had produced by computer in 1962 (24, 25). The Center discontinued its card catalog in the same year. Book catalogs can increase availability of cataloging information to users while reducing library work, and the Monsanto book catalog is an example of such an achievement, for it provides a union catalog of the holdings of seven Monsanto libraries, and is produced in over one hundred copies. As would be expected, the catalog appeared all in upper-case. However, in September 1964 the Library at Florida Atlantic University produced a bookform catalog in upper- and lower-case (26) and the University of Toronto Library put out the first edition of its upper- and lower-case ONULP catalog on 15 February 1965 (27, 28).

The Monsanto catalog format called for author and call number on one line, with title and imprint on a second, or second and third, line. Both Florida Atlantic and Toronto catalogs were essentially catalogs of catalog cards. Under the leadership of Mortimer Taube, Documentation, Inc. was first to produce a bookform catalog in upper- and lower-case, with a format like that of bookform catalogs in the nineteenth century (29); Documentation, Inc., prepared the catalog for the Baltimore County Public Library. Entries were made once, with titles listed under an entry if there were more than one. The Stanford bookform catalog appeared late in 1966, introducing a new type of unit record, whose first element is the title paragraph.

H. P. Luhn proposed selective dissemination of information (SDI) in 1958 (30), and perhaps the first library application of SDI was in the spring of 1962 at the IBM library at Owego (31), where special processing was given to new acquisitions for input into the SDI system. At about the same time, the library of the Douglas Missile & Space Systems Division instituted an SDI system that employed as input a single machine readable record from which catalog cards and accessions lists were also produced (32).

The introduction of SDI into library operation is a major, historic innovation, for SDI is a routine but personalized service in contradistinction to the depersonalized library service characteristic of all but the smallest libraries. Selective dissemination of information is one of the few examples of library computerization that takes full advantage of the computer's ability to treat an individual as a person and not as one of a horde of users.

Circulation

The Picatinny Arsenal reported the first computerized circulation system (33). The Picatinny application produced a computer printed loan record, lists of reserves, overdues, lists of books on loan to borrowers, and statistical analysis, in a system that began operation in April 1962. The charge card at Picatinny was an IBM punch card into which was punched the bibliographic data and data concerning the borrower each time the book was charged. In the fall of 1962, the Thomas J. Watson Research Center (34) activated a circulation system much like the Picatinny system except that bibliographic data was punched into a book card by machine, but information about the borrower was manually punched.

The next step forward occurred at Southern Illinois University (35), where a circulation system like the two just described began limited operation in the spring of 1964 employing an IBM 357 data collection system. By using the 357, it was possible to have a machine punched book card and a machine readable borrower's identification card that could be read by the 357, thereby eliminating manual punching. The

Southern Illinois system became fully operational at the beginning of the fall term of 1964, as did a similar 357 system at Florida Atlantic University (26).

Batch processed circulation systems periodically producing a listing of books on loan have a built-in source of dissatisfaction, particularly in academic libraries, for current records are unavailable on the average for half the period of the frequency of the printout. Such delay can be eliminated in an on-line system, wherein information about the loan is available immediately after recording the loan. However, not all circulation systems with remote terminals operate interactively.

In an on-line system introduced at the Illinois State Library in December 1966 (36) the transactions were recorded on an IBM 1031 terminal located at the circulation desk, data transmitted from the terminal being accumulated daily and processed into the file nightly. As first activated, the system did not permit querying the file to determine books charged out, but this capability was added in 1969. Also in December 1966, the Redstone Scientific Information Center brought into operation a pilot on-line book circulation system based on a converted machine readable catalog consisting of brief catalog entries. This pilot system remained in operation until October 1967, and was capable of recording loans, discharging loans, putting out overdues, maintaining reserves, and locating the record in the file (37).

The BELLREL real time loan system went into operation at Bell Laboratories Library in March 1968 (38). BELLREL has a data base consisting of converted catalog records, so that in effect it also is a remote catalog access system. BELLREL serves three libraries remotely from two IBM 1050 terminals in each library. BELLREL is a sophisticated on-line, real time circulation system that not only records and discharges books, but also replies to inquiries as to the status of a title, and the status of a copy, and will display the full record for a title, as would be required for remote catalog access.

Serials

The Library of the University of California, San Diego, activated the first computerized serials control system (39). This system has as its objective production of a complete holdings list, lists of current receipts, binding lists, claims, nonreceipt lists, and expiration of subscription lists. Checking in was accomplished by manual removal from a file of a prepunched card for a specific title and issue. The check-in clerk sent this card to the computer center for processing and the journal issue to the shelves. This technique of prepunching receipt cards has generated new problems in some libraries, for professional advice is often needed as to action to be taken when the issue received does not match the prepunched card. Nevertheless, the San Diego system still operates, albeit with modifications.

The Washington University School of Medicine Library activated a serials control system in 1963 (40) that was essentially like that at San Diego. A series of symposia held at Washington University, with the first in the autumn of 1963, widely publicized the system and led to its adoption elsewhere. The University of Minnesota Biomedical Library introduced a technique of writing in receipts of individual journal issues on preprinted check-in lists (41). Check-in data was then keypunched from the lists. This system obviated the problem generated by prepunched cards that did not match received issues, but, of course, reintroduced manual procedures.

Difficulties with check-in procedures, and delays in receipt of printed lists of holdings made it clear that an on-line real time circulation control system would be superior to the batch systems described in the previous paragraph. Laval University in Quebec introduced the first on-line, real time system in 1969 (42). In September 1969 the Laval on-line file held 16,335 titles. Access to the file from cathode ray tube terminals is by accession number, and the file, or sections thereof, can be listed. The system also produces operating statistics and contains the potential for automatic claiming.

The Kansas Union List of Serials (43), which appeared in 1965, was the first computerized union list to contain holdings of several institutions. The Kansas Union List recorded holdings for nearly 22,000 titles in eight colleges and universities. Reproduced photographically from computer printout and printed three columns on a page, this legible and easy-to-use List set the style for many subsequent union lists.

Acquisitions

The National Reactor Testing Station Library was first to use a computer in ordering processes (44). A multiple-part form was produced for library records and for dealers. The Library of the Thomas J. Watson Research Center activated a more sophisticated system in 1964 that produced a processing information list containing titles of all items in process, a shelf list card, a book card, and a book pocket label (45).

The Pennsylvania State University Library put a computerized acquisition system into operation in 1964 (46). This system produced a compact, line-a-title listing of each item in process, together with an indication of the status of the item in processing. A small decklet of punch cards was produced for each item on a keypunch, and one of these cards was sent to the computer center for processing each time its associated item changed status. The Pennsylvania system also produced purchase orders.

In June 1964, the University of Michigan Library (47) introduced a computerized acquisitions procedure more sophisticated than its predecessors. The Michigan system produced a ten-part purchase order fanfold, an in-process listing, and computer produced transaction cards to update status of items in process; and carried out accounting for encumbrance and expenditure of book funds. In addition, the system produced periodic listings of "do-not-claim" orders, listings of requests for quotation, and of "third claims" for decision as to future action on such orders.

In 1966, the Yale Machine Aided Technical Processing System began operation (48). It produced daily and weekly in-process lists arranged by author, a weekly order number listing, weekly fund commitment registers, and notices to requesters of status of request. Subsequently, claims to dealers were added, as well as management information reports on activities within the system. Like the Pennsylvania and Michigan systems, its in-process list recorded the status of the item in processing.

The Washington State University Library brought the first on-line acquisition system into operation in April 1968 (49). Access to the system was by purchase order number, with records arranged in a random access file under addresses computed by a random number generator (50). The Stanford University Libraries on-line acquisition system began operation in 1969 (51), and employed a sequential file of entries having an index of words in author and title elements of the entry. The Stanford system calculated addresses of index works by employing a division hashing technique on the first three letters of the word.

Standardization

By 1965, a dozen or more libraries had a dozen or more formats for machine readable bibliographic records, and an impenetrable thicket of such records was evolving. Fortunately, the Library of Congress, with the help of the Council on Library Resources, took the initiative in standardization of format of bibliographic records and produced the now familiar MARC format (52). Just as standardization of catalog card sizes enabled interchange of catalog records, so has MARC made possible interchange of machine readable catalog records.

This standardization has encouraged developments of networks, such as the SUNY Biomedical Network, NELINET, the Washington State Libraries network, and that of the Ohio College Library Center. With each of these regional networks employing the MARC bibliographic record, it will be possible to integrate these regional nodes into a future national network.

Substance and Sum

The first half of the first decade and a half of library computerization was confined almost entirely to two major mechanizations of Mortimer Taube's Uniterm coordinate indexing. The computerization of single descriptors with attendant document numbers was a relatively easy task.

The first breakaway from computerized subject searching came at the Douglas Aircraft Corporation, where the technique of producing one machine readable record from which multiple products could be obtained was introduced in 1961. The last half of library automation's decade and a half has been largely consumed with efforts to automate existing library procedures.

Although notable departures have occurred that take advantage of the computer's powerful qualities, on-line, real time techniques introduced at the very end of the historical period under review began again to use individual words as words, not unlike the logic in which the first applications employed Uniterms; and it seems likely that the immediate future will witness increasing degrees of computerization based on individual words in bibliographic descriptions rather than on the record as a whole.

Acknowledgments

The author is grateful to Sheila Bertram for identifying, searching out, and gathering most of the references used in this paper. Cloyd Dake Gull furnished in correspondence invaluable information about events of the fifties and early sixties, and various librarians supplied photocopies of early documents.

References

1. Kilgour, Frederick G.: "The Economic Goal of Library Automation," College & Research Libraries, 30 (July 1969), 307-311.
2. Baumol, William J.: "The Costs of Library and Informational Services." In Libraries at Large (New York: R. R. Bowker Co., 1969), p. 168-227.
3. Bunnow, L. R.: Study of and Proposal for a Mechanized Information Retrieval System for the Missiles and Space Systems Engineering Library (Santa Monica, California: Douglas Aircraft Co., 1960).
4. Balz, Charles F.; Stanwood, Richard H.: Literature on Information Retrieval and Machine Translation (International Business Machines Corp., November 1962).
5. Balz, Charles F.; Stanwood, Richard H.: Literature on Information Retrieval and Machine Translation. 2d. ed. (International Business Machines Corp., January 1966).
6. Speer, Jack A.: Libraries and Automation; a Bibliography with Index (Emporia, Kansas: Teachers College Press, 1967).
7. Tillitt, Harley E.: "An Experiment in Information Searching with the 701 Calculator," Journal of Library Automation, 3 (Sept. 1970), 202-206.

8. Bracken, R.H.; Tillitt: H.E.: "Information Searching with the 701 Calculator," Journal of the Association for Computing Machinery, 4 (April 1957), 131-136.
9. Tillitt, Harley E.: "An Application of an Electronic Computer to Information Retrieval." In Boaz, Martha: Modern Trends in Documentation (New York: Pergamon Press, 1959), p. 67-69.
10. Zaharias, Jerome L.: LIZARDS; Library Information Search and Retrieval Data System (China Lake, California: U.S. Naval Ordnance Test Station, 1963).
11. Bracken, Robert H.; Oldfield, Bruce G.: "A General System for Handling Alphameric Information on the IBM 701 Computer," Journal of the Association for Computing Machinery, 3 (July 1956), 175-180.
12. Rosen, Saul: "Electronic Computers: A Historical Survey," Computing Surveys, 1 (March 1969), 7-36.
13. Barton, A.R.; Schatz, V.L.; Caplan, L.N.: Information Retrieval on a High Speed Computer (Evendale, Ohio: General Electric Co., 1959), p. 8.
14. Gull, C.D.: Personal communication, (22 August 1969).
15. Dennis, B.K.; Brady, J.J.; Dovel, J.A.: "Five Operational Years of Inverted Index Manipulation and Abstract Retrieval by an Electronic Computer," Journal of Chemical Documentation, 2 (October 1962), 234-242.
16. Austin, Charles J.: MEDLARS; 1963-1967 (Bethesda, Maryland: National Library of Medicine, 1968).
17. Summit, Roger K.: "DIALOG: an Operational On-Line Reference Retrieval System." In Association for Computing Machinery: Proceedings of 22nd National Conference. (Washington, D.C.: Thomson, 1967), p. 51-56.
18. Pizer, Irwin: "Regional Medical Library Network," Bulletin of the Medical Library Association, 57 (April 1969), 101-115.
19. Koriagin, Gretchen W.: "Library Information Retrieval Program," Journal of Chemical Documentation, 2 (October 1962) 242-248.
20. Fasana, Paul J.: "Automating Cataloging Functions in Conventional Libraries," Library Resources & Technical Services, 7 (Fall 1963), 350-365.
21. Kilgour, Frederick G.: "Library Catalogue Production on Small Computers," American Documentation, 17 (July 1966), 124-131.
22. Nugent, William R.: "NELINET--The New England Information Network." In Congress of the International Federation for Information Processing, 4th,

Edinburgh, 5-10 August, 1968: Proceedings (Amsterdam: North-Holland Publishing Co., 1968), p. G28-G32.
23. Payne, Charles T.: "The University of Chicago's Book Processing System." In Proceedings of a Conference Held at Stanford University Libraries, October 4-5, 1968 (Stanford, California: Stanford University Libraries, 1969).
24. Wilkinson, W. A.: Personal communication (November 1969).
25. Wilkinson, W. A.: "The Computer-Produced Book Catalog: An Application of Data Processing at Monsanto's Information Center." In University of Illinois Graduate School of Library Science: Proceedings of the 1965 Clinic on Library Applications of Data Processing (Champaign, Illinois: Illini Union Bookstore, 1966), p. 92-111.
26. Heiliger, Edward: "Florida Atlantic University Library." In University of Illinois Graduate School of Library Science: Proceedings of the 1965 Clinic on Library Applications of Data Processing (Champaign, Illinois: Illini Union Bookstore, 1966), p. 92-111.
27. Bregzis, Ritvars: Personal communication (November 1969).
28. Bregzis, Ritvars: "The Ontario Universities Library Project--An Automated Bibliographic Data Control System," College & Research Libraries, 26 (November 1965), 495-508.
29. Robinson, Charles W.: "The Book Catalog: Diving In," Wilson Library Bulletin, 40 (November, 1965), 262-268.
30. Luhn, H. P.: "A Business Intelligence System," IBM Journal of Research and Development, 2 (October 1958), 315-319.
31. Stanwood, Richard H.: "The Merge System of Information Dissemination. Retrieval and Indexing Using the IBM 7090 DPS." In Association for Computing Machinery: Digest of Technical Papers (1962), p. 38-39.
32. Young, E. J.; Williams, A. S.: Historical Development and Present Status--Douglas Aircraft Company Computerized Library Program (Santa Monica, California: Douglas Aircraft Co., 1965).
33. Haznedari, I.; Voos, H.: "Automated Circulation at a Government R & D Installation," Special Libraries, 55 (February 1964), 77-81.
34. Gibson, R. W., Jr.; Randall, G. E.: "Circulation Con-

trol by Computer," Special Libraries, 54 (July-August 1963), 333-338.
35. McCoy, Ralph E.: "Computerized Circulation Work: A Case Study of the 357 Data Collection System," Library Resources & Technical Services, 9 (Winter 1965), 59-65.
36. Hamilton, Robert E.: "The Illinois State Library 'On-Line' Circulation Control System." In University of Illinois Graduate School of Library Science: Proceedings of the 1968 Clinic on Library Applications of Data Processing (Urbana, Illinois: Graduate School of Library Science, 1969), p. 11-28.
37. "Redstone Center Shows On-line Library Subsystems," Datamation, 14 (February 1968), 79, 81.
38. Kennedy, R.A.: "Bell Laboratories' Library Real-Time Loan System (BELLREL)," Journal of Library Automation, 1 (June 1968), 128-146
39. University of California, San Diego, University Library: Report on Serials Computer Project; University Library and UCSD Computer Center (La Jolla, California: University Library, July 1962).
40. Pizer, Irwin H.; Franz, Donald R.; Brodman, Estelle: "Mechanization of Library Procedures in the Medium-Sized Medical Library: I. The Serial Record," Bulletin of the Medical Library Association, 51 (July 1963), 313-338.
41. Strom, Karen C.: "Software Design for Bio-medical Library Serials Control System." In American Society for Information Science, Annual Meeting, Columbus, O., 20-24 Oct. 1968: Proceedings, 5 (1968), 267-275.
42. Varennes, Rosario de: "On-line Serials System at Laval University Library," Journal of Library Automation, 3 (June 1970).
43. Kansas Union List of Serials (Lawrence, Kansas: University of Kansas Libraries, 1965), 357 pp.
44. Griffin, Hillis L.: "Electronic Data Processing Applications to Technical Processing and Circulation Activities in a Technical Library." In University of Illinois Graduate School of Library Science: Proceedings of the 1963 Clinic on Library Applications of Data Processing (Champaign, Illinois: Illini Union Bookstore, 1964), p. 96-108.
45. Randall, G.E.; Bristol, Roger P.: "PIL (Processing Information List) or a Computer-Controlled Processing Record," Special Libraries, 55 (Feb. 1964), 82-86.
46. Minder, Thomas L.: "Automation--the Acquisitions Pro-

gram at the Pennsylvania State University Library."
In International Business Machines Corporation: IBM
Library Mechanization Symposium, Endicott, New
York, May 25, 1964, p. 145-156.
47. Dunlap, Connie: "Automated Acquisitions Procedures
at the University of Michigan Library." Library Resources & Technical Services, 11 (Spring 1967), 192-206.
48. Alanen, Sally; Sparks, David E.; Kilgour, Frederick G.:
"A Computer-Monitored Library Technical Processing
System." In American Documentation Institute, 1966
Annual Meeting, October 3-7, 1966, Santa Monica,
California: Proceedings, p. 419-426.
49. Burgess, T.; Ames, L.: LOLA; Library On-Line Acquisitions Sub-System (Pullman, Wash.: Washington
State University Library, July 1968).
50. Mitchell, Patrick C.; Burgess, Thomas K.: "Methods
of Randomization of Large Files with High Volatility,"
Journal of Library Automation, 3 (March 1970).
51. Parker, Edwin B.: "Developing a Campus Information
Retrieval System." In Proceedings of a Conference
Held at Stanford University Libraries, October 4-5,
1968 (Stanford, California: Stanford University Libraries, 1969), p. 213-230.
52. "Preliminary Guidelines for the Library of Congress,
National Library of Medicine, and National Agricultural Library Implementation of the Proposed American
Standard for a Format for Bibliographic Information
Interchange on Magnetic Tape as Applied to Records
Representing Monographic Materials in Textual Printed
Form (Books)," Journal of Library Automation, 2
(June 1969), 68-83.

MEDLARS: A Summary, Review
and Evaluation of Three Reports[1]

by Norman D. Stevens

Reprinted by permission from the Winter 1970 issue of
Library Resources & Technical Services (14:1) p. 109-
121.

The MEDLARS (Medical Literature Analysis and Retrieval System) system at the National Library of Medicine (NLM) has over the past few years been one of the most significant and one of the most publicized automated bibliographic information retrieval systems. Over two hundred articles on it have appeared in American newspapers and popular magazines, in specialized medical journals throughout the world, and in a variety of library journals. The publicity that has attended this project has, in a way, been unfortunate, for it has presented an exaggerated picture of the system and its accomplishments which has only made the skeptics more skeptical; and it has obscured in part the examination of MEDLARS real accomplishments. There has to date been very little careful outside analysis and evaluation of MEDLARS. Over 50 percent of all of the articles listed in the bibliography in Austin's report, and virtually all of the substantive ones, represent the work of persons closely connected with NLM or the development of the MEDLARS system. Their judgment on the effectiveness of the system and its overall value cannot help but be colored by this connection.

With the recent publication of Austin's report and Lancaster's study to accompany the initial preliminary document and to mark the coming to an end of MEDLARS, it would seem timely to have a review and evaluation of that system, as presented in those three major documents, by someone not directly connected with that system. That is what this paper will attempt to accomplish. It represents one individual's views and is designed to raise some of the questions that arise from a careful reading of those reports.

175

While it is critical, its criticisms are designed to bring up for consideration and discussion some of the points that have arisen out of the development of MEDLARS which are extremely important to the field of automated bibliographic information services, and indeed for cataloging and bibliographic services in general. MEDLARS has been one of the most significant library developments of the past decade and there is much to be learned from it.

Taken together these three documents present the best picture yet available of the scope and accomplishments of MEDLARS. The first preliminary document, The MEDLARS Story, was published before the system was operational. While it is the least substantive of the three, it does outline the goals and objectives of MEDLARS as they were then seen and, thus, is an invaluable and honest starting point. Austin's report is a good companion piece for it is a review and final description of the actual operation of MEDLARS done at a time when it is in its final stages and when NLM is in the process of designing a new system to replace it. Although it contains a wealth of detail about the operation of the system, its main thrust is a broad scale evaluation of MEDLARS as it now operates and of the extent to which its objectives have been met. Lancaster's study is a careful evaluation of one aspect of MEDLARS--the demand search bibliographical service. For those interested in the automation of the technical operations of libraries these three volumes are indispensable for they describe the largest computer-based store of bibliographic data yet produced and some of the problems encountered in the development, operation, and manipulation of it.

The first section of this paper will review the nine objectives of MEDLARS as outlined in The MEDLARS Story, as evaluated and commented upon by Austin, and with additional comments by me on those objectives and specifically on Austin's evaluation of how they have been met. In the point-by-point consideration of the nine objectives, the format is: (a) the original objective; (b) Austin's evaluation and comments; (c) my comments on (a) and (b). The second section of this paper then will consider in greater detail Lancaster's study and some of the questions it raises about the demand bibliographic search services and, by extension, about MEDLARS as a whole.

1. (a) "Improve the quality of and enlarge (broaden the

scope of) Index Medicus and at the same time reduce the
time required to prepare the monthly editions for printing
from 22 to 5 workdays."

(b) "For the most part, this objective has been met.
The quality of Index Medicus has been improved through improvements to MeSH (Medical Subject Headings), improvements in the journal selection process, and constant attention to indexing accuracy. The scope has been broadened
considerably from 129,908 articles from 2,275 journal titles
in 1963 to 163,077 articles from 2,300 journal titles in 1967.
Processing time has been cut to about five days."

(c) Whether or not the quality of Index Medicus has been
improved is a question of subjective judgment and no concrete
evidence has been, or probably can be, presented to support
this claim. The broadening of the scope, however, is measurable and Austin's claim of success is open to question.
The initial projections called for the indexing annually of
237,000 articles from 6,000 journals by 1969. Considering
the levels reached in 1967 it is unlikely that those figures
will be met. In any case, those levels represent only a 25
percent increase in the number of journal titles covered.
In an era when the explosion of knowledge is such a widely
discussed phenomenon, increases of this size hardly represent an enlargement; especially when compared to the coverage, however crude and slow it may have been, of more
than 10,000 serials in the old Index-catalogue..., and to
NLM's current intake of between 18,000 and 19,000 different
serial publications of all types.

This all assumes, of course, that a broadening of the
scope of Index Medicus was a desirable goal, and that ought
to be considered. In any index comprehensiveness is, in
one sense, to be desired for then the user can be assured
that he has covered all sources of information. On the other hand, investigations into the use of scientific journals,
particularly of medical journals, indicate that a relatively
few journals account for a very high percentage of the actual
use. Lancaster's study, for example, found that about 75
percent of the items retrieved in the searches he analyzed
came from one-third of the journals indexed. At the same
time, although the indexing of foreign language articles consumed about 45 percent of the input effort, they accounted
for not more than 16 percent of the total usage in those
searches. Perhaps NLM should experiment with producing a
printed Index Medicus that is narrower, rather than broader,

in scope for everyday use, relying on computer based searches and recurring bibliographies (see below) for more comprehensive searches.

2. (a) "Make possible the production of other compilations similar to Index Medicus in form and content."

(b) "This objective has been accomplished through the production of recurring bibliographies. However, the original estimate of fifty recurring bibliographies was too high and only nine were in production on January 1, 1968, with some others in the planning stage. Because of the difficulties in the intellectual effort required, the development of recurring bibliographies turned out to be a much larger job than was originally estimated."

(c) The concept of recurring bibliographies ("a periodic selection of citations from current input, structured by a predetermined pattern according to the interest profile of a group"--Austin, p. 37) is an interesting one that is now being widely developed. In addition, for example, to the NLM products, Abstracts of Mycology is now published as an extract from Biological Abstracts. There has been, however, no examination of the rationale behind such bibliographies. Perhaps if the general bibliographies were more limited in scope, as I have suggested, these recurring bibliographies would be more useful. But there are problems. What is a "group"? Do these bibliographies really serve the best interests of "a group"? Are the costs of production justified, or would it be more efficient and less expensive for each user to do his own searching, utilizing the larger and more comprehensive bibliography? Should these be envisaged as nonpermanent, noncumulated tools designed primarily for the personal use of research workers? If this is the case, the use of less intellectual effort and the production of bibliographies for smaller and more highly specialized groups should be considered. Once the basic information has been put into machine-readable form the possible permutations are many and varied and too little attention has been paid to what pattern of printed index services we expect or need to have emerge from this new production approach. Incidentally these recurring bibliographies present a new acquisition problem for libraries. If a library subscribes to the larger, more comprehensive bibliography (Index Medicus), does it need to subscribe to the smaller, more selective bibliography (Index of Rheumatology) production from the same store

Technical Services

of information? Probably not, but the library that does not is likely to find itself facing demands from users who find the selective bibliography more convenient to use as it is tailored to meet their more specific needs.

3. (a) "Make possible for Index Medicus and other compilations, the inclusion of citations derived from other sources, as well as from journal articles."

(b) "The system capability to include citations to monographs in MEDLARS was provided through reprogramming for the Current Catalog."

(c) Austin begs the question here for by no stretch of the imagination can the original objective be said to have been met. The original intention was clearly to combine the indexing of monographic material, theses, and serial titles with that of journal articles in Index Medicus. The MEDLARS Story, in fact, maintains that, "MeSH is based on the concept that subject cataloging of monographs and subject indexing of periodical articles are essentially like operations" (p. 47). Reprogramming the Current Catalog does not meet that initial objective. Austin does point out that that objective was dropped because system limitations would not permit publishing citations without extensive modification, because books and serial titles are not indexed in sufficient depth to be mixed with the detailed indexing given articles, and because there seemed to be certain advantages in a book-form catalog. This was one of the most interesting concepts of the original MEDLARS program. It ought to have been pursued more vigorously. Given the system limitations was the question of what constitutes acceptable form thoroughly considered? The advantages of having an articulated system might well outweigh the disadvantages of having to modify our concept of what constitutes a proper and necessary catalog entry for a monograph. Could books, if not serial titles, be effectively indexed in the same depth as journal articles? Taking again Lancaster's findings on the relative lack of use of the foreign language journal articles, one wonders if NLM ought not to have considered indexing English language monographs in more detail in lieu of indexing foreign language journal articles. In Project Intrex and other proposed advanced automated library systems, the concept of the "augmented catalog" with more detailed approaches to monographic material plays an important role. Does NLM's failure to achieve this in Index Medicus mean that the "augmented catalog" cannot be effectively achieved? One hopes that it will not, in any case, put an end to further experiments along these lines by NLM or other interested parties. Finally the inclusion of detailed indexing for monographs in Index Medicus would not seem to prohibit the publication, as a recurring bibliography, of a book-form catalog with more general entries for monographic material.

4. (a) "Make possible the prompt (a maximum of two days) and efficient servicing of requests for special bibliographies, on both a demand and a recurring basis, regularly searching up to five years of stored computer files."

(b) "It has not been possible to accomplish a two-day search turnaround time with the present batch processing system. Also, because of computer time limitations, demand searches beginning in early 1968 include only references from January 1966 on, instead of references from the entire file."

(c) This was, of course, one of the major objectives of MEDLARS and certainly one of the most publicized. The major limitation of the previous mechanized system was that it provided only for the publication of Index Medicus. It could not provide for "growing demands for rapid retrieval of complex requests specified according to multiple subject axes. Some way had to be found to accomplish more--to do it better, to take less time, to operate more efficiently, and generally to provide a greater all-round versatility" (The MEDLARS Story, p. 2). In a number of respects this objective has not been accomplished. Service is not prompt; instead of a two-day turnaround time the average is now about two weeks. This is a major weakness especially when users now increasingly expect real-time access to computer-based information stores. Only a two-year base is now searched. This is also a major weakness when a manual search in the biomedical field would normally cover at least five years. Here again, while comprehensiveness is desirable, it is perhaps less important than a broader-based search in terms of time. NLM might have investigated, when it became apparent that system limitations prevented searching the entire file, restructuring the file so that a longer file of, say, the English language citations could be searched. Finally, the original projections called for 22,500 demand searches to be provided in 1969 but, in 1968, only approximately 9,200 demand searches were provided. This, too, is a major weakness, for much of the justification for such a system ought to be its ability to handle an increasing number of demand searches. Despite this general failure to meet the original objectives, the MEDLARS demand search service has been the most significant real-life experiment in computer-based bibliographic searching yet conducted.

5. (a) "Increase the average depth of indexing per article by a factor of five, i.e., ten headings versus two."

(b) "This objective has been achieved for depth journals to which an average of about ten subject headings per article are assigned. However, nondepth journals are indexed to an average depth of only about four terms."

(c) In recent years most designers of information systems have placed a high priority on a general increase in the number of subject headings assigned for each item. Depth indexing would seem to be of value in providing for greater specificity in the use of index terms and for better coverage of secondary topics dealt with in an article. One basic concept in MEDLARS was that a distinction could be made between depth journals (those that generally carry reports of greater significance) and non-depth journals (those that generally carry reports of lesser significance) and that the number of index terms could be assigned accordingly. This is an unreal distinction and, indeed, one of Lancaster's recommendations is that it be abolished. His study found that non-depth articles constitute 45 percent of the MEDLARS file but account for only 25 percent of the items retrieved because the limited number of terms assigned provides for too generalized indexing. He recommends that this distinction be abolished and each article be treated on its own merit and assigned as many index terms as are necessary to provide for adequate access to its contents. As many as 30-40 percent of all relevant non-depth articles presently missed in MEDLARS searches might be retrieved if they were indexed at the same level as depth articles. On the other hand, an increase to 25-30 terms per article would be needed to provide for a significant increase in the retrieval of depth articles presently missed because of lack of sufficient indexing depth. Lancaster concludes that although 20 percent of the recall failures in MEDLARS demand searches are attributable to insufficient depth of indexing and only 11.5 percent of the precision failures are attributable to too great a depth of indexing, an overall increase in the number of terms assigned per article does not seem justified. Much more needs to be done in the way of objective research on the basic question of how many terms it is desirable to use in the indexing of articles. The two to three terms traditionally assigned and the ten terms used in MEDLARS are both based primarily on subjective judgments, as well as limitations of resources, rather than on an objective consideration of users needs. Lancaster's analysis of the number of headings needed to provide for effective recall of articles is noteworthy as being perhaps the only objective investigation available.

6. (a) "Nearly double the number of articles that may be handled annually from 140,000 now to 250,000 in 1969."

(b) "Production has increased with MEDLARS to 165,000 articles input in 1967. Library management hopes to meet the goals of 250,000 articles by 1969, but the attainment of this goal remains uncertain."

(c) See (1.) (c) above.

7. (a) "Reduce the need for duplicative total literature screening operations."

(b) "This objective is difficult to evaluate. However, all indications point to its being met. Index Medicus and other MEDLARS bibliographies are used extensively in libraries and information centers as literature screening tools. No other medical indexing operation comparable in size to MEDLARS has come into existence. Hence, it can reasonably be assumed that a good deal of expensive, duplicative indexing has been avoided."

(c) This is the most artificial objective imaginable. Was there ever any real prospect of a rival system to Index Medicus being instituted even prior to the conception and development of MEDLARS? Once a major bibliographic tool has been established in a field--no matter how inadequate and expensive it may be--the likelihood of another system being established in the same subject field is extremely small. Presumably then it is in the area of recurring bibliographies in specialized subject fields that MEDLARS has most effectively reduced the need for other literature screening operations; but only nine of a projected fifty such bibliographies are being produced and there is still no competition. Perhaps this only indicates, however, that the recurring bibliographies are not as essential as the original MEDLARS concept envisaged. It hardly seems reasonable to assume that "a good deal of expensive, duplicative indexing has been avoided" by the development of MEDLARS.

8. (a) "Keep statistics and perform analyses of its own operations, to provide the information needed to monitor and improve system effectiveness."

(b) "This objective has been partially accomplished through the Statistical Module Reports.... Other reports have been identified that could be very useful (e.g., statistical data on demand searches). However, for the most part, NLM programmers have been too busy to work on these reports."

(c) How typical! In the initial justification of all automated systems the unlimited possibilities of statistical analysis are cited as an important objective, but once a system is operational these analyses somehow become less important and this objective is the first to be sacrificed. MEDLARS is no exception. It is just as well for one has the feeling that this is as usual a poorly thought-through objective which would only result in the production of a wide variety of meaningless statistics if it were carried through.

9. (a) "Permit future expansion to incorporate new and as yet not completely defined and hence secondary objectives."

(b) "This has been accomplished. Installation of MEDLARS has provided a base of data processing equipment and experienced system personnel at the Library for work on new systems and extensions of MEDLARS."

(c) The development of new systems and extensions of MEDLARS hardly qualifies as meeting an objective that specified an expansion of the system. How effectively has this objective been met when, even though most of the original target figures have not been approached, "work loads approaching machine capacity" (Austin, p. 9) already exist, and MEDLARS is being abandoned in favor of "a new, more powerful approach to the problems of literature control and information retrieval in the biomedical sciences" (Austin, p. 69)?

The secondary objectives were not altogether incompletely defined. Some of them were: "(1) the requirements of a national, decentralized, medical bibliographical system; (2) the possibility of storing and retrieving graphic images of textual material; and (3) the mechanization of other library functions" (The MEDLARS Story, p. 61). Probably the worst error of judgment in the planning of MEDLARS was the selection of Honeywell, rather than IBM, equipment in view of the requirements of a national decentralized, medical bibliographical system. This error was not as critical as it might have been only because of the failure of the demand search service to develop as rapidly and as extensively as was anticipated. Honeywell equipment is not readily available and, in fact, only the MEDLARS Station at the University of Colorado has had access to it. Although extensive work on reprogramming the MEDLARS files for the more commonly available IBM equipment has been done, "the time and effort involved was badly underestimated by NLM staff" (Austin, p. 57). As of January 1968 only the Colorado MEDLARS Station was processing demand searches. The other five MEDLARS Stations, all of which had been in operation for from two to three years, were sending formulated searches to NLM for processing. A variety of other problems, many of them related to the basic difference in available equipment, exist, and all have greatly increased the developmental time and costs for the decentralized system.

While the development of the demand search service and the need for a decentralized system to support that demand was overestimated, the development of a widespread demand for electrostatic reproduction of articles based on the use of Index Medicus was probably underestimated. Fortunately the development of a decentralized system has helped to provide adequate coverage. In view of that demand, however, one must also judge the failure of MEDLARS to meet the secondary objective "of storing and retrieving graphic images of textual material" as a major weakness. Since NLM has had difficulty in meeting the basic projected goals of MEDLARS, the development of such a capacity within MEDLARS would seem to be nonexistent. This is presumably one of the major reasons for the abandonment of MEDLARS and the development of a new system. Hopefully it will attempt to meet the objective.

MEDLARS has achieved a great deal, but has not met many of its original goals and objectives. This is not altogether unexpected in a project of this size and magnitude. In a more particular way MEDLARS has been successful for it has provided for the prompt publication of Index Medicus, which was an essential requirement, while permitting NLM to gain a great deal of experience with the use and problems of a large-scale automated bibliographic retrieval system. This is probably the most that really should have been expected from the first venture into a program of this scope and magnitude.

Lancaster's evaluation of the demand search service is one of the most important documents published to date in the area of analysis and evaluation of bibliographic information retrieval systems. It is so important not only because it deals with a real-life experiment as opposed to the artificial experiments of many other projects, even the Cranfield studies, but because it raises a number of interesting questions about the use and development of such systems. Unfortunately it is not well organized and is, therefore, somewhat difficult to follow. His synopsis "MEDLARS: Report on the Evaluation of Its Operating Efficiency," in American Documentation (20: 119-42, April 1969) is much better organized, and is considerably easier to follow and comprehend; it does not, of course, provide quite the same detail as the full report, but I recommend it to those who do not have the time or patience to read the full report.

Basically Lancaster is reporting on the precision and recall performance of MEDLARS operating in a demand search service mode in 302 actual requests made by users representing the full range of potential users during 1966 and 1967. His test program, whose design and execution was reviewed by a MEDLARS Evaluation Advisory Committee that included Austin(!) but also Cleverdon (who also acted as a special consultant on this project) and Mooers, consisted primarily of an evaluation by the ultimate user of the relevance of the citations supplied to his needs (precision) as well as an evaluation of how successful MEDLARS was in supplying citations that had been identified in a number of other ways as being relevant (recall). Each of these requests was then analyzed in great detail; the reasons why 3,038 items not relevant were supplied in 278 of the searches, and why 797 items known to be relevant were not supplied in 238 of the searches were identified and examined. Much of his report is devoted to an analysis of the reasons behind each of these 3,835 errors grouped under the general headings of failures attributed to searching, failures attributed to indexing, failures attributed to index language, and failures attributed to inadequate user-system interaction. The analysis of these is careful and detailed and sheds much useful, and sometimes amusing, light on some of the problems encountered. For example, among the most heartening reasons for failure are a number of cases of human-like failures on the part of the computer, including one in which five articles that precisely matched the search formulation were overlooked and not recalled in the initial search although they were recalled in a later rerun using the same formulation. These accounted for only an insignificant proportion of the failures (1.4 percent of recall and 0.1 percent of precision failures), but they are somehow encouraging kinds of errors. On the other hand, in a number of cases, real human errors, including the failure of terms assigned by the indexer to be included in the final input and the failure of single issues, or even whole volumes, of a journal to be indexed, also occurred and they can only be classed as discouraging kinds of errors.

The general findings are that, on the average, MEDLARS is operating at 57.7 percent recall and 50.4 percent precision ratios, but that the results are widely scattered, with some searches achieving high recall and precision ratios and others totally unsatisfactory recall ratios. About 25 percent of the articles retrieved were judged to be of major value by the users (precision) and about 65 percent of the known articles of major value were retrieved (recall).

The general validity of these specific recall and precision ratios is open to serious question, and raises a question about NLM's continuing lack of perceptiveness in the use of statistical techniques. In 1962 NLM published a report on the use of its loan system[2] in which a complete year's file of loan requests was examined. There was no statistical analysis in that report, but the sample size was probably large enough, indeed it seemed unnecessarily large, to make that survey statistically valid. There is no statistical analysis in Lancaster's report either, but it would be useful to know what degree of statistical validity there is with a sample size of only 302 when as many as 18,500 searches may have been handled in 1966 and 1967.[3] The statement that "it was felt that the approximately 300 searches that would thus be fully completed would be adequate to allow a meaningful performance breakdown by processing center, subject field, originating organization, and mode of interaction" (Lancaster p. 15) is not justified in a scientific report. This is especially true when many of the final results are described in percentage terms and are, therefore, presented as being representative of all searches.

Lancaster indicates that these recall and precision figures could be altered by a broadening of the search strategies which would provide for a higher recall ratio but only at a much lower precision level. MEDLARS, as it presently exists, can be operated at any point on or near a recall/precision plot that allows for considerable variation in performance ranging from 90 percent recall with less than 20 percent precision to only 19 percent recall with over 80 percent precision. For the most part the searchers have been operating the system at about the midpoint in order to obtain a satisfactory recall level at an acceptable precision point. Too little attention has been paid to the user's requirements in a particular search. One of Lancaster's main recommendations, and one of his most sensible, is that the MEDLARS search request form be specifically redesigned to allow for the user to indicate his recall requirements and precision tolerances within the framework of the possible relationships. The search strategies could then be adjusted to meet these requirements. If there is a choice to be made, certainly it should be made by the user rather than by the search analyst or system designer.

The present pattern shows a variation in performance between individual searchers as well as between the five MEDLARS centers that formulate searches. The ranking by centers, in fact, shows a completely inverse relationship between recall and precision (i.e., the center with the highest recall level had the lowest precision level) which tends to confirm, as Lancaster puts it, "the inevitability of the inverse relationship between recall and precision... known to research workers for some years" (p. 128). This assumption, which is widely held, that there is a direct fixed relationship between the two elements in a system and that once that relationship is established an improvement in one can only be accomplished at the expense of a deterioration in the other also needs to be carefully examined. Too often it is accepted as an inalterable condition and the question of whether or not there are ways of improving the two ratios simultaneously within a system is ignored. Fortunately, even though Lancaster calls this inverse relationship "inevitable," a number of his recommendations are designed to improve the general performance level of MEDLARS (i.e., provide higher recall with better precision).

Since 25 percent of the recall failures and 16.6 percent of the precision failures were directly attributable to the defective interaction between the user and the system, Lancaster recommends a complete redesign of the search request form to capture the user's initial request before he has discussed it with a search analyst. His earlier analysis of this problem is one of the most interesting and arresting parts of the report. "Unless the requester is first required to write down a narrative statement of need, this requirement may well become distorted in an oral interview between requester and librarian, and the request, as recorded by the librarian, thus becomes an imperfect representation of what the requester is seeking. It is for this reason that MEDLARS performs, on the average, less well for searches in which the local librarian has participated actively in request formulation than for searches in which the librarian acts as carrier only" (p. 113). This conclusion is based on a careful examination of the test searches and seems to be warranted. Lancaster's reasons as to why this should be so are worth quoting.

> When he (the requester) makes a personal visit to a MEDLARS center, we do not normally have the benefit of this written, natural language statement. Rather, the requester is invited to discuss his needs with a search analyst. Unfortunately at this point, his information need tends to get distorted. The problem appears to be at least partly due to the fact that the requester's need is discussed in terms of, and unduly influenced by, Medical Subject Headings. When the requester is writing down his request, he is forced to think of what exactly he is looking for. In this, he is not particularly influenced by the logical and linguistic constraints of the system. When, however, he approaches a MEDLARS center, if he has not already gone through the discipline of writing down his request, he has a less well-formed idea of what he is seeking (i.e., of the scope and constraints of the search). When this somewhat imprecise need is discussed with a search analyst, in terms of Medical Subject Headings, it tends to become forced into the language and logic of the system. The final "request," rather than representing what the requester wants, represents what he thinks the system can give him, phrased in a way that the system will search for it. In many cases the "request," as recorded by a search ana-

lyst, is not a true request at all (at least it resembles nothing that a requester would submit in his own natural language terms). Rather, it is a "pseudo-Boolean statement": a string of MeSH or MeSH-like terms put together in some relationship (p. 111).

This is startling! It certainly seems to contradict our normal and traditional view that the user has an imperfect representation of what he is seeking that can only be improved and clarified in an oral interview with a trained reference librarian. If Lancaster's reasoning is correct, and he certainly makes a strong case, the whole question of how the ultimate user will approach computer-based stores of bibliographic information will need to be carefully reexamined.

While the traditional library approach generally calls for the analysis of all approaches to a system to take place as a function of the input system, possible approaches to a system through manipulation and analysis of the output system need to be considered. Lancaster recommends, for example, changes in the MEDLARS searching strategies which would formalize into pre-established search strategies the "hedges" (informal collections of headings which cut across several MeSH categories in a horizontal pattern) that have been developed by the searchers.

The most obvious solution, though, is that the input ought to be in natural language terms so that the user, especially in an on-line system, can approach the system directly and in his own terms without the constraints imposed by an intermediary and an artificial language. Lancaster recognizes this. One of his recommendations concerns changes in the index language of MEDLARS designed primarily to provide for the up-dating of MeSH by an analysis of the demands placed on the system as reflected by the actual terminology encountered by both indexers and searchers rather than by the use of an external advisory committee on terminology. Finally in his general concluding recommendation that the material gathered in this study be used for further investigations, Lancaster specifically suggests that "natural language, free-text searching of abstracts would be ...well worth investigating" (p. 202).

These are only a few of the more salient topics dealt with in Lancaster's study. He deals with a number of other topics including factors critically affecting the performance of a MEDLARS search,[4] the indexing coverage of MEDLARS, the general question of journal usage factors, the effect of delays in response time on the value of a search, the serendipity value of MEDLARS searches, output screening, indexer consistency, and requests rejected by MEDLARS. Each of these is treated briefly but concisely and yet a wide range of interesting points is raised. One page, for example, is devoted to a consideration of the extent to which the requester found the items supplied which were irrelevant to his specific need of interest because of some other need or project (serendipity value). There was wide variation but the combined sample indicated that 18 percent of the irrelevant articles supplied were of value in relation to other needs. Lancaster feels that this figure is high because in this test the requester was supplied with photocopies of the articles which he might not have looked up had he been supplied only with the citations. I disagree. I suspect, based primarily on personal experience, that in many literature searches, both manual and machine, an important by-product is the supply of useful information not directly related to the immediate need which prompted the search. In fact one of the weaknesses of machine searching may be its inability to provide for the totally unrelated kind of serendipity value that can come in a manual search when one happens to notice, almost as it were by accident, other items simply because, for example, they are on the same page.

This review and evaluation has attempted to summarize and comment upon some aspects of MEDLARS and the questions it raises. It has touched upon only a few of these aspects especially with Lancaster's study. Much remains to be done and a number of other aspects of MEDLARS, including several not adequately dealt with in any of these reports, need further investigation. Except for some limited comments, for example, in The MEDLARS Story and Austin's report about the number of man-years required to operate the former mechanized system for producing Index Medicus (40 man-years per year) and MEDLARS (projected at 60 man-years per year; actually about 90 man-years per year as of January 1, 1968), there is virtually no indication of the time or costs involved in the operation of MEDLARS in any of these reports. One can only assume that the social benefits of a medical information system outweigh any cost considerations. This is unfortunate, for an essential element in the evaluation of any operational program of this size ought to be a careful consideration of the cost and time element. Lancaster recommends that NLM consider establishing a program of "continuous quality control" for MEDLARS (which would provide for the monitoring of all search requests in order to discover further inadequacies of the system) and that, as I have indicated, the data collected in his study be used as the basis for further investigations. This is a start. At some point NLM might hopefully be in a position to make its complete file and records on MEDLARS, especially those relating to costs, freely available to independent researchers. There must be at least a dozen excellent doctoral dissertations there.

Notes

1. The MEDLARS Story at the National Library of Medicine. Washington, D.C., U.S. Public Health Service, 1963. vii, 74 p.; Austin, Charles J., MEDLARS 1963-1967. Bethesda, Md., National Library of Medicine, 1968. vii, 76 p.; Lancaster, F.W., Evaluation of the MEDLARS Demand Search Service. Washington, D.C., U.S. Public Health Service, 1968. viii, 276 p.
2. William H. Kurth. Survey of the Interlibrary Loan Operation of the National Library of Medicine. Washington, D.C., Government Printing Office, 1962.
3. The actual figure is difficult to ascertain because neither Austin nor Lancaster indicates much about actual performance levels attained for the demand search service. Austin provides one table (Figure 29) that shows that 2,300 searches, including 600 handled abroad, were completed in the first quarter of fiscal year 1968. My figure of as many as 18,500 searches for the two-year period is based on a projection of those figures. Lancaster provides no such information whatsoever.
4. These are: (1) the quality of interaction between the requester and the system; (2) the complexity of the request; (3) the ability of the index language to precisely express the notions involved; (4) the subject field of the request; (5) indexing policies and practices; and (6) the adequacy of the search formulation.

CATCALL

by Ralph R. Shaw

Reprinted by permission from the March 1970 issue of
College & Research Libraries (31:2), p. 89-95.

Yes, the title of this talk is CATCALL. That signifies Completely Automated Technique [for] Cataloging [and] Acquisition [of] Literature [for] Libraries. If there is one absolutely indispensable step in any program of automation, it is the initial step of coining a peachy, and preferably mnemonic, acronym. In many cases that can be the final step, so far as getting anything useful done is concerned, because knowing acronyms that someone else does not know immediately establishes you in the inner circle of the mystique.

But after this promising beginning, I am afraid that the cognoscenti in the art will be disappointed in me again, because this paper is going to deal with a prosaic subject like getting some useful work done. If it were a really imaginative program for testing the limits of the computer to prove that we need newer and bigger computers (rather than something prosaic like making use of them to do routine chores, as in this paper), I should have given it a fancier name, such as IRON CRAB POT which obviously stands for Instant Reproduction Of New Catalog Regularly As Book Purchase Order [is] Transmitted. The IRON CRAB POT system would be a real imaginative contribution, and typically it would have to wait for creation of new hardware (probably two or three more generations of quick access memory capable of storing hundreds of trillions of bits at a fraction of a penny a bit so the cost for the memories would come down to a couple of hundred million dollars, and thus would become available to every elementary school library). Economical? Of course not. Nobody who is anybody in this field worries about sordid little details like that. The important thing is that the IRON CRAB POT would print out for you a completely new catalog instantly every time you ordered a book, and think of how that would improve the qual-

Technical Services 193

ity of service, which is the important thing! It would have another great advantage. It would also solve the shortage of librarians because when this wonderful new computer is available at the Library of Congress (for example), and it prints out a completely new catalog (card, book, sheaf form, or what you will) instantly, every time a new book is ordered, the old catalogs are going to have to be hauled off. This would require so many janitors to haul the catalogs off that we would not have any money to waste on frivolities like librarians, and who would need these carping fuddyduddies anyhow, because the catalog would always be in the dynamic state of producing a new edition and no one could reach into it fast enough to look up anything anyhow.

Now, having established my bona fides in this racket, I shall revert to the original topic of this paper and midst the catcalls from the buffs, shall talk about the mundane matter of CATCALL.

The useful potential of CATCALL starts with the SBN. (Now let us not let our imaginations run riot; SBN is not even an acronym; it is just an abbreviation for the words Standard Book Number.) The program of industry-wide uniform numbering of books originated in England, and after a good deal of study has begun to be applied in the United States. Book numbering has been used by individual publishers for a long time, but each had his own numbering system. Under the SBN program the SBN is always nine digits in length. These nine digits are always divided into three parts which are separated by a space or a hyphen. The first unit of the SBN identifies the publisher, the second part identifies a particular edition of a particular book and the third part, which is always a single digit, is the check digit-- a device used almost universally in computer technology to guard against manual mistranscription of numbers.

None of this is new except for standardization. Publishers have used book numbers (and check digits if they have computers), as have jobbers and warehouses, for a good many years. The thing that the SBN achieves is a standardized and unique number for every volume that is sold as a separate unit. It a work in multiple volumes is sold only as a single unit, it gets a single SBN for the entire set. If the individual volumes are sold separately, then each volume gets its own distinguishing number. And if a new edition is published, it too gets a distinguishing SBN. As the program develops, these numbers will be published in all trade sources and will eventually cover a large and increasing proportion of all trade and nontrade books in the English language, or published in England and the United States.

As this happens, it will become increasingly possible for libraries and bookstores to handle orders for particular titles in particular editions by writing the SBN for the pieces or piece wanted. It might be desirable to add the first letter of the author's surname, or his surname, as a further check, but the probability is that 99 percent of all errors resulting from transposition of numbers in using the SBN will be caught by the computer parity check (which is probably better, on the average, than we achieve in manual production of the author, title, edition, place, publisher, date, and price).

Now if we would go just one step further and agree to a standardized customer number, the process of ordering a book would become very simple. We now have customer numbers. If you will examine the bills you receive from any of the major jobbers, you will find a customer number on it; just as those of us who have been using the computer to do our bookkeeping assign dealer numbers to our various sources of supply. Under the SBN program we will have a standardized publisher and book number; what we need next is a standardized jobber or bookstore number and a standardized customer number. So far as American libraries are concerned, the customer number could be as simple as using our zip code, subdivided by a further three- or four-digit number to identify up to 1,000 or 10,000, if needed, different libraries, bookstores or jobbers in any given postal zip code area, and we should, of course, add a parity number.

Given the customer number and the SBN, even the smallest library could obtain cards that are prepunched with its customer number, and all that would be required to order a book would be to punch in its nine-digit SBN. This does not even require rental of a keypunch; we could use a pad and stylus, like those we use in voting in an increasing number of jurisdictions, and at a capital investment of $1.00 or so, the process of book ordering would be automated.

Carrying this one step further, if we wanted to order through a particular bookstore or jobber, we could establish a third zone into which we would punch the supplier's number, and I daresay that most jobbers would be delighted to supply us with stacks of prepunched cards bearing both our

Technical Services 195

customer number and the jobber's supplier number. All we
would have to do to complete the order would be to punch the
SBN with a stylus. An alternative, in order to avoid the investment
of $1.00 or so in the stylus and pad, would be to
use the conventional mark sensing pencil to mark the digits
of the SBN on the card, but this might cost more in the end
because we might conceivably use up $2.00 or $3.00 worth
of mark sensing pencils over a year or two.

    O.K. Now we have the order typed by punching or
marking the magic digits of the SBN on the card prepunched
with our customer number and our supplier number, if any.
How do we get it to the supplier? Well, it may be cheap
enough when Western Union and Mama Bell have central
transmission units in every town, to have it sent via satellite;
but having saved a week or so in avoiding typing our orders,
we could now put the daily (or weekly, or other) batch
of orders into an envelope (and again I suspect the supplier
might even supply preaddressed envelopes if we were to insist)--add
airmail postage--and the book orders should travel
to the office of the supplier within two to three days as a
maximum, from any point in the United States. Given half a
dozen or so order cards per ounce, with domestic air mail
at ten cents per ounce, we would have to figure it pretty
close to justify sending a messenger, costing $1.50 per hour,
to the central transmitting office, even if we did not have to
pay the cost of shortwave transmission; so it would have to
be fairly urgent, as compared with our usual delays in getting
orders out, in order to justify the overall cost of transmission
at higher speed than air mail.

    On the other hand, very large libraries might well
find that their volume of work might justify on-line transmission
to a central computer. They might, but I should certainly
want to see the arithmetic in full, and to study it carefully,
before I should be inclined to believe it. The basic
point here is that we do not have to get very fancy or very
much involved in sophisticated hardware to start getting some
benefit from computer technology; and that it is becoming feasible
even for the one-man school library at the elementary
level to benefit by simply applying that most uncommon commodity
which, for some reason, has become known as common
sense.

    Well now, it ought to be fairly obvious that if we could
mark or punch a nine-digit SBN on a card prepunched with
our customer number and a dealer number, and send it off

and get our book, that should save a good deal of work as compared with typing orders complete with author, title, etc., in full. If it did no more than that for us, it would save some time.

If the books any library bought were recorded in an electronic memory, this would represent a shelflist of the library in SBN form and any future order could be searched automatically to see whether it was in the library or on order. Thus, as soon as this had been in operation for a few years, it would be possible for the computer to do searching for the library automatically, and, if the book was found to be in the collection or on order, the order would be returned with the proper indication of its status unless the order was clearly marked as requiring an added copy or copies. This in time could eliminate substantially all searching of the catalog, the outstanding order files, the in-process files, trade sources, etc., when that book has an SBN and has been published during the time span covered by the computer ordering procedure. Since LC is producing machine-readable cards, the computer could also convert from SBNs to LC numbers and locate cards in the MARC data bank for reproduction and shipment to the library.

And, as would appear to make sense, if LC could change from the use of its own special machine number to the use of SBNs when they are more generally available, then conversion from the SBN to an LC number would be eliminated. In either case all that would be required of the ordering library to obtain LC cards with the books would be to indicate by a proper mark or punch, in the assigned column, whether cards are wanted or not.

With thousands of libraries and booksellers ordering their books in this way through the same central mechanism, a fairly sophisticated computer could be kept busy and it could, if desired, serve as the bookkeeping department for all the libraries, bookstores, and publishers making use of it.

It could also, if desired, serve a central banking function; transferring funds from the account of the bookseller or library to the account of the publisher, either instantly or after any agreed upon period of grace. This is not new. Voucher orders which combine a check with the order are common in the book trade. This alone would save hundreds of thousands of dollars a year for even a medium-sized publisher. Carrying even a million dollars of accounts receivable for sixty days, a normal time lag in payment by libraries, costs the publisher around $12,500 at current interest rates. If this time lag could be cut in half and applied to even half the receivables from sales to libraries, it would produce a tremendous saving for publishers. This banking function is not new. A large percentage of checks are cleared in just this way, and our personal checking accounts in the larger banks are all computerized. The end product to the library would be the equivalent of a bank statement, indicating what books have been bought, the amount paid for each, and the balance remaining in the account. This could keep track of our monthly and quarterly expenditures and it could be designed to keep us from over obligating during the designated periods for which funds are available. A great deal of backroom work would be saved in publishing houses, in bookstores, and in thousands of libraries.

The same routine could also be used to check each publisher's inventory of each book as each copy was sold, against the anticipated rate, and let him know when a reprint is required, as well as doing a good many other similar operations for booksellers and for libraries.

Where do we stand on all this right now? Hardly at the beginning. Publishers have just begun to assign SBNs, and that does not appear to be proceeding very rapidly. Some, hopefully many, may include SBNs for all their backlist in the next volume of the Publishers' Trade List Annual.

To be sure, a few jobbers have set up automated systems for a few of their customers, but these systems appear to be primarily a method for capturing large customers rather than a method for making savings in time or effort. Since this approach requires a substantial amount of makeready for each case and does not affect adoption of standard numbering, it is not of particular interest to the average library.

The only thing really holding back the SBN program is apathy. The publishing industry must be encouraged to speed up the adoption of SBNs and the assignment of these SBNs to all books in print as well as to all books published from now on. Given any real effort by the publishing industry in that regard, we should be able to handle any book in print in the United States or in England by SBNs in less than a year. During that time, if we want it, we could insist on

standardized customer numbering for all libraries, and in the
next six months to a year we could be ordering all English
and American books in print without typing, and possibly with
reduced searching, bookkeeping, and related record keeping.

Each library could make as much use as it wanted of
the full range of the service, with the small library using
the mechanisms that are suitable and practical for it, and
the large library using what serves it economically. There
would be no requirement that anyone accept LC copy in order
to use the service, nor would automatic bill paying, etc., be
required. Its use could vary from library to library.

While this would save fewer man-hours for the small
library than for the large one, it could free manpower for
other work, even if it is limited to SBN ordering, with the
orders sent in by first class mail. In a library with only
one staff member, who has to do everything, it would free
added minutes or hours to provide the services for which the
library exists.

In the long run, it may be that this might change the
structure of the book business, since a few strategically located warehouses could supply all the books that tens of thousands of libraries around the country need, and could do it
faster and better and cheaper than going through intermedi-
aries, but it is doubtful that this would affect trade book
sales, which require display of books to the public. So,
while it might change library buying patterns and it might reduce costs for jobbers supplying bookstores and costs for
bookstores, it is doubtful that this will bring about any radical change in general book distribution channels in the foreseeable future.

The possible advantages to libraries would appear to
be quite great. Speedier and cheaper book ordering and
checking, with immediate reports on o.p. items and on items
temporarily out of stock are the minima that we could expect, and this would require a negligible investment, or no
investment, in either purchase or rental of equipment by libraries or in staff training.

It should achieve better use of the equipment already
in use by the publisher or jobber who already has electronic
data processing equipment, because he would not need to go
through the step of converting our orders to machine readable form before he can handle them in his equipment.

This does not, of course, lay out a complete program for use by anyone, in all the ways in which it could be used. We have said nothing, for example, about ordering multiple copies at one time (one to two punches in the assigned column or columns would take care of that); nor about allocation of funds by departments or to branches--again a simple routine requiring not more than two punches in two assigned columns to take care of as many as one hundred accounts or branches, and with computer programs in existence taking it from there, even with a relatively inexpensive computer such as the IBM 1401.

There is no point, however, in going any further with the potential advantages and usefulness of this system, or any of the other ways in which it could be used, because the fact of the matter is that it is not usable for anything at the moment. The reason that it is not now usable is not lack of computers, or lack of big enough computers, or lack of suitable software, or the cost of equipment in the individual library, or lack of training of staff in new techniques. It is simply that there has not been any sense of urgency about getting all publishers in the United States to assign SBNs to their books in print or to set up a standardized customer number for all libraries, and book jobbers, and book sellers. If standard book numbers were assigned for libraries only, jobbers and booksellers would have to follow suit if they wanted any library business.

If these two steps were taken promptly, any library, with or without electronic data processing capabilities, and regardless of its size, could make the job of book ordering easier and faster for itself and for its suppliers, and should get faster service and faster reporting. We would not even have to wait for other services to be built into the system before we started to use it, since programs for accounting, billing, reporting, backordering, and the like are in existence now and could be added to the system as they are required.

This would not, of course, cover all book buying for any library for many years to come. It does not include books in foreign countries, other than England and possibly Canada, and there does not appear to be any special drive for broadening it to cover all foreign countries. Furthermore, there will probably always be difficulty in achieving complete coverage, by any mechanism, of all privately published books and pamphlets, such as works published by the author or by societies for distribution to members only.

Nevertheless, it would appear that a very high percentage of the books bought by all except the largest public and scholarly library could be ordered this way; the average elementary school library does not order very many foreign or specialized or o.p. items, nor does the small or medium-sized public or high school library, and even college and research libraries order substantial numbers of titles from the ranks of English and American trade or scholarly books which are in print. There is nothing about this approach that requires an either/or answer, and there is no reason why the large amount of buying that can be simplified should not be, simply because some book buying will still require manual processing.

The process will not of course have any appreciable, foreseeable impact on the intellectual processes involved in book selection, except that it might free some time for doing it. It will not replace the card catalog, or the reference librarian, or the readers' adviser, and they will not even have to learn to use a new lingo to make use of it.

It does represent one way in which we can use one or more central computers to do work that is arduous clerical work, which the machine can do, and in which a single input can eliminate a large number of succeeding inputs into the routines we have to carry out in order to get a book into the library and ready for use.

This may not be very glamorous, and it runs the risk that it might work, thus diverting attention from more "sophisticated" problems such as machine searching of the literature and the like, but there is nothing in this proposal that requires limiting the computer to this sort of intellectually sterile operation, and it is hard to see why this sort of intellectually sterile operation should be reserved for humans.

It certainly should not slow down the more sophisticated operations that fill the literature, since, assuming we could really get it going, this would provide a key to the collection in machine readable form from the moment of placing the order for any material. Thus if anyone ever figures out any really viable ways in which we can do such things as automatic indexing, searching, and the like, he would be saved at least part of the job of turning the library's records into machine readable form. The part of the collection ordered by SBN could be converted into LC cards pulled from MARC.

However, we are stepping out of character here, and out of our subject, so let us return to it for a moment. If we could get SBNs supplied for all books in print by all, or almost all, American publishers, and SBNs assigned for substantially all American books published in the future; and if we could get standard customer numbers assigned, we could immediately start using central computer services advantageously, in any of our libraries, regardless of their size, for book ordering and receiving and reporting services, and we could do that without any (or any appreciable) investment in either hardware or in retraining of staff. We could then let it grow from there, variably for different types and sizes of libraries, as that appeared worthwhile.

Some twenty years ago we ran an experiment in the use of photography for clerical routines in half a dozen libraries. One of these was Yale, where the camera, called the Photoclerk, was housed in the catalog department. One of my more memorable experiences occurred when I went back to check on progress of the experiment and as I was leaving, one of the sweet old ladies said to me, definitely more in sorrow than in anger, and with the greatest gentility, "Dr. Shaw, why do you want to do away with catalogers?"

Then two weeks or so ago, when I went over part of the program I have outlined above with my class in documentation, citing it as one of the types of things the computer should be able to do effectively, one of the students, positively stuttering in outrage (note the sign of the changing times), "But Professor Shaw, why do you want to relegate the computer to nothing but routine operations!?"

The answer to both is the same and it is simple. We are employed to operate libraries. We should use any tool or method that helps us to do that more effectively in whatever way it is most useful under the current state of the art. Using a camera to photograph a card cannot denigrate the intellectual work of cataloging and using a computer to compute cannot paint the computer black either.

The approach outlined above appears to promise one of the easy and available ways in which all types of libraries (as well as all types of publishers and all types of booksellers) can profit from the use of available computers with a minimum of change in methods or routines and with a minimum of investment in time or equipment, and it appears to present an evolutionary potential, starting with simple book ordering and adding steps as these appear feasible. I think we ought to get on with it.

Automation Stops Here:
A Case for Man-Made
Book Collections

by Roscoe Rouse

Reprinted by permission from the May 1970 issue of
College & Research Libraries (31:3), p. 147-154.

This is intended to be a case study but it may be more than that. A brief affair with an automatic book-buying plan proved a disappointing experience for the Oklahoma State University Library, and it is the purpose of this paper to relate that experience and to consider the reasons why it was unfortunate.

The observations made here have no implications or applications for other libraries. I speak for one library only. The OSU Library experience was a unique one but not an exclusive one; other libraries have discontinued approval and blanket plans.

A brief description of the book selection policy as practiced before the adoption of the plan is necessary for an understanding of the situation. The procedure was a very smooth one, it moved without friction, it was expeditious, and there was little need for conference or discussion between individuals. Each member of the staff involved had his own specific assignment, and he knew what it was; the faculty knew the individuals responsible for selecting in their respective fields and had confidence in them.

The OSU Library is organized on the divisional plan, and it was the divisional librarians and their staff members (public services personnel) who were responsible for virtually all book selection before the plan was adopted. These were the people who worked with the students and faculty and knew their needs. These were the people who helped undergraduates with their reference questions, who aided the faculty in becoming familiar with holdings in the respective divisions, who serviced the thesis and dissertation collection, who aided graduate students in gathering materials for their theses, who procured materials for them from distant libraries, who knew the holdings of other libraries well enough to direct interlibrary loan requests for a good bull's-eye percentage. Most of these librarians held a graduate or undergraduate degree in the field in which they were working in the library, and all of those involved in the book selection process had long tenure, the average being 14.7 years in the OSU Library at the time the approval plan was instituted. A key number of the staff, although promoted in rank and salary at regular intervals along with increased responsibility, has held the same position and title for twenty-three years.

The book selection routine at OSU was indeed unique. It was tried and found true. There were no complaints of consequence about the acquisition of books and journals, and our files include some letters complimenting the staff on this aspect of their work. The librarians handled about 80 percent of all book selection and the faculty the remaining 20 percent. We sometimes heard faculty comments to the effect that new publications were often ordered before they were aware of the need for them. There was a satisfactory relationship between the librarians and the faculty in the building of the book collection.

The basic book selection tool for current titles was LC proof slips. Upon receipt of the new proof slips, the acquisitions librarian sorted them into categories for distribution to the divisional librarians. Other selection media were used, of course, such as Publishers' Weekly, Choice, mailed advertisements, dealers' catalogs, reprint catalogs, foreign listings, and specific standard lists such as Books for College Libraries. Staff members felt a direct and personal responsibility for the quality of their respective areas and worked very conscientiously to build them and round them out well.

The approval plan agreement was made with a reputable dealer, and the contract specified that the library would be supplied one copy of every monographic U.S. imprint book within categories stipulated as well as all of the library's standing orders. It was the usual kind of arrangement: excluded were general works, juveniles, introductory textbooks, reprints, fiction, medicine, and religion. The staff held the responsibility for selecting newly published works desired in the fields that were excluded and this they did through proof slips and other sources.

    Despite the satisfactory situation they were enjoying, the library staff was willing to relinquish the selection responsibility to an outside party so long as they were assured that the job would be done as well, if not better. At the outset I shall admit to the possibility of unfairness in an experience of only four months but also point out the fact that this was one month longer than the agent said was needed to have the plan fully operational and going satisfactorily. The relationship was indeed of short duration but it was not entered into as an experiment; the contractual agreement was a sincere one made on the basis of expected longevity. Full cooperation was given to the effort by the librarians who had every reason to believe that this was their acquisitions procedure for the future and evermore.

    In fairness to the dealer, it must be noted that his service to the region was new but nevertheless we did not contract with him on the basis of expecting poor service for this reason. The lack of organization and the obvious use of untrained personnel indicated that the company was not ready to take on customers. The failure can thus be tied in to two basic causes: the good climate that had previously prevailed in book selection at OSU and the lack of good organization on the part of the approval plan jobber. The possibility of future improvement of operations by the dealer was an unknown factor; the satisfactory operation of the system formerly employed by the library staff was a known factor.

    One major complaint against the approval plan was that the library found it was at times returning 50 percent of the titles sent. Many of these were already in the library, doubtless the result of an overlap in the staff selection procedure and the new plan but it did give the impression that the books received from the dealer were not new imprints. A large number of books were sent which did not classify in the categories specified in the agreement. Some titles duplicated others previously shipped by the plan jobber. Still others should not have been sent because they were not monographs but serials. There was also the inclusion of many older titles, a source of real concern to the librarians. These seemed to classify as remainder stock, titles that were in some instances six to eight months old, many shelf-worn and faded. The dealer admitted that he purposely did not order enough books for all his customers, knowing that all

libraries did not want all books. He would wait until some
had been returned before shipping them to other libraries
wanting them, which may account in part for the age and
worn appearance of some volumes.

The staff testified to the shipment of every kind of
book in or out of designated categories. Received were
textbooks, juveniles, reprints, and even some foreign titles.
And, of course, there were many books received within categories properly chosen in the agreement which did not qualify as titles needed in the OSU Library. Such titles would
not have been selected by the staff under the former procedure and these were returned. The overall quality of books
received seemed very poor, especially to librarians who had
previously been quite discriminating in the selection of titles.
The instructions given for our library simply were not followed.

The librarians were more dissatisfied with the books
not sent than with those received. A number of good pertinent titles slipped by the dealer for one reason or another
and were not supplied to the library; the staff learned that
they could not place complete dependence upon the plan service, and this loss of confidence was the beginning of the end.
It was known that the jobber did not have good relations with
some publishers. Through all this, the staff was never able
to tell a faculty member the status of a book at a given
time. Whether or not the dealer would ship a particular
title was not known for certain, whereas under the former
procedure one could tell immediately that the book had been
ordered and its exact status in the order routine.

As the librarians became aware of the newly published
books that were not sent by the dealer, they felt the need to
make selections from the proof slips in the same manner as
before. This was the only alternative to haphazard, incomplete collection building. So it was that the staff found itself
back at the old task of selecting books as they had previously
done. The all-books plan then became redundant. A ream
of correspondence between the library and the dealer gives
evidence to efforts by both to resolve the highly unsatisfactory situation. Visits to the library were made by company
representatives.

One basic difficulty in receiving books "unsolicited"
through a dealer was in regard to bibliographic entry. The
Head Cataloger at OSU names this problem as the prime one

in the failure of the plan. Prior to using the approval plan, 80 percent of our orders had been made from proof slips and for these no verification was necessary. The books arrived already identified with main entry established, whereas books arriving from the approval jobber required verification of authors and titles. Books were received with multiple order forms prepared but the entries were so unreliable that the staff had to ignore them.

The OSU Library is one of the ninety-seven cooperating PL 480 libraries in the country and therefore receives a depository LC card for every book cataloged by the Library of Congress Cataloging Division or one of the cooperating libraries. Once a book is received in the library it is a relatively easy task, if a proof slip is stapled to the order card in the orders-outstanding file, to find and pull the depository card, type the call number, and make a full set for the catalog. There is no bibliographical or entry problem encountered.

Books arriving unordered, on the other hand, must be matched with the cards in the depository file. This becomes almost a professional task unless one has a clerical person who has had good experience with corporate entries and other bibliographical intricacies. Books and depository cards did not, of course, arrive at the same time, the cards almost always arriving much later. The books would therefore wait in the cataloging department until the Library of Congress had prepared and distributed cataloging copy for them. These books had to be temporarily controlled unless they were treated simply as not having been received. Cards had to be checked against many shelves of books, or books had to be checked against many drawers of cards over and over again until the docking in space was complete. In other words, each time a shipment of books was received, the books had to be checked with the depository catalog; each time a shipment of LC depository cards was received, these had to be checked with the books awaiting LC copy. A given book might be checked against the depository file a dozen times or more before it was matched with the proper card. In some instances cards never appeared and the searching continued for an extended period, in which case the cataloger would eventually prepare original copy for the book. In short, the processing staff found itself in trouble from the beginning with no let-up seen after four months. The books were not getting on the shelves any faster and additional burdensome tasks were found necessary under the new system. The library was not buying any more titles than before but the processing work was much heavier.

The division librarians, who hold the greatest responsibility for the selection of titles, maintained that the greatest shortcoming of the plan was the narrow bibliographic base upon which the agent operated. The public services librarians found it necessary to search the proof slips anyway, because so many good works were overlooked by the dealer. The agent's staff (or computer) did not send everything in the fields shown in our profile. An example given was concerned with the laser beam. We were in need of everything, literally, published on the subject as a physics graduate student at our institution designed the instrument that sent the laser beam to the moon and back last July. The library found that it could depend upon receiving through the plan only a small part of the material needed because the jobber did not furnish materials from a number of U.S. publishers or from numerous societies, institutions, and associations which issue scholarly publications.

The same librarian who gave the laser beam example said he found it much faster and more satisfactory to choose books from LC proof slips than by using the books themselves. He felt that there was too much time involved in reading tables of contents, prefaces and such, whereas the LC card with its call number, subject headings, and full title gave all that was needed to make a decision, in most cases, especially in the sciences.

The conclusion was reached that only the OSU faculty and library staff knew best which editions the library should have, which publishers were best for specific titles, which editors it preferred. Oklahoma State librarians were better and more currently informed about their degree programs, departmental projects and studies, thesis topics, and specialties of the faculty. There is no time lag in altering the profile when the job is done by a well-advised librarian right at the source of information.

Disenchanted with the whole idea, the OSU Library staff, almost to a man, was pleading to return to the former method of selecting and ordering books. The approval plan was cancelled and the proof slip routines reinstated. When this was accomplished, the staff found that they were still trying to extricate the library from the red tape of the plan a year and a half later. Today the book selection procedure is as good as it ever was. The librarians and the faculty are content with this routine, and they are of the opinion that the development of the collection in the various fields and disciplines is as good as can be expected for a library with a limited budget.

The writer recently received a long-distance call from a million-volume library in the far West. The caller said he needed advice about his acquisitions program. The library had been on an all-books plan the year before but the supplier did not furnish materials as promised. The librarian was unable to answer the faculty's questions as to whether certain titles were coming, and a large percentage of new titles never reached the library. There was much confusion regarding the serials that the dealer should supply and those that would come through the library's own standing orders; it was obvious that the supplier could not differentiate between serials and monographs. The librarian said too much time was wasted in reviewing the books that were received. It was therefore decided to discontinue the plan, and the staff returned to their former method of selection with faculty consultation. The librarian said they soom found themselves in trouble again and were desperately seeking a solution. Further inquiry brought out evidence that the present dilemma stems from a staff shortage. In this case the all-books plan had been turned to as a panacea, which it was not, and a return to the old manual system was a nightmare of another kind--for reasons that were easily identified.

The Council on Library Resources is supporting a two-year study of an experimental model engineering library at MIT incorporating "new technological developments." The physical remodeling alone for the project, which will be carried out under INTREX, has cost $2 million, and the council made grants of more than a million dollars to MIT to support INTREX. The library will incorporate such software as the text access system and the augmented catalog, which is a computer-based bibliographic mechanism utilizing the cathode ray tube to rapidly and interactively search a remotely stored catalog in which each document is cataloged in great depth. The text access system can be used to retrieve those documents from a remotely stored microform file. Programmed teaching machines will also be a part of the library system. We can expect to see a computer age library and retrieval system emerge from this kind of investment and experimentation.

I was interested to know if this, the nation's most forward-looking library (the adjectives are mine), acquires its books through a blanket or approval plan. In my communications with them I almost felt like apologizing for even suggesting a manual procedure in their operations. In correspondence and by telephone conversation with the librarian I received a response which was in good humor but very positively and emphatically stated: the library now employs and expects to continue to employ the manual, individual, and personal form of book selection, all done by members of the library staff and faculty. No approval or blanket plan is foreseen in their library. About 95 percent of the titles are selected by librarians and the remainder by the faculty. This highly mechanized library is quite satisfied with this arrangement, and there seem to be no plans to change it.

The Stanford University library utilizes about seventeen various blanket and approval plans. Still the library employs a number of librarians who are book selection specialists, a staff which makes up, to use their wording, "a network of acquisitional interests." Their specialists use Publishers' Weekly and proof slips for selection purposes. How else would a great library system have full coverage from societies and associations, private presses, little-known publishers, U.S. and foreign governmental agencies, vanity presses, the U.N., publications from underdeveloped countries and near-print materials? Such a vast selection and acquisitions program could not today be successfully handled in toto by a commercial firm, even seventeen of them.

David O. Lane, in preparing his paper "Approval and Blanket-Order Acquisitions Plans," queried sixty-six medium-size academic libraries and received forty-six replies.[1] Thirty-one of those replying used approval plans (three of these were dissatisfied, two undecided). Thirty-eight of those replying used blanket-order plans (five of these were dissatisfied, four undecided). Some of the reasons given for the dissatisfaction by those who expressed it were as follows: serials present a problem, duplicates were received, too much junk was received, too limited, takes too much time, pertinent books not received, late receipt, guidelines not followed, and problems in billing and invoicing.

In regard to Lane's inquiry concerning the satisfaction of the faculty with the plans, only thirty-nine librarians out of the forty-six who responded gave an answer and twenty-eight of these replied in the affirmative. It is interesting to note that his research showed that the median percentage of current imprints added by the operation of the approval/ blanket order plans in these libraries was 28 percent. The largest number of those on the plans indicated their interest in retaining them and most expected to expand to other plans. Three libraries expressed their intention to do away with blanket orders.

In the Summer 1969 issue of Library Resources & Technical Services, Ian Thom wrote of the added work involved with blanket and approval plans.[2] "This method of procurement," he wrote, "other things being equal, does not result in 'less work' for the acquisitions people. On balance, the acquisitions department will require more man-hours to process a given number of titles received on blanket order than it would if these same titles were ordered conventionally." He modified his use of the word "acquisition" to exclude the selection of books, meaning procurement only. He further says, "While it eliminates some operations, however, blanket ordering creates others."

Margit Kraft in her paper, "An Argument for Selectivity in the Acquisition of Materials for Research Libraries," makes the point that the machine will undoubtedly handle quantity for us better but that it does not differentiate between quantity and quality, noting that this requires human intellect.[3] She points out the fact that one feels like a heretic even to question the arguments put forth by virtually all U.S. academic libraries for the building of giant book collections and goes on to say that the urge to preserve an object assumes it has value. Her paper is a sound and solid treatise which will give most of us pause regarding our use of all-books-current plans as we acquire, process, and preserve at great cost the good, bad, and indifferent.

Gordon Williams published a study in 1966 in which he refers to a source which asserts that the technology library at Northwestern University could be reduced by 75 percent and still satisfy 99 percent of its present users, and the general library could be reduced by 60 percent and satisfy 99 percent of its users.[4]

At the Symposium on Approval Order Plans sponsored by the Pacific Northwest Library Association in 1967, the fact was brought out that United States libraries acquired twice as many books in 1966 as they did in 1960. The rate of increase between 1965 and 1966 was 29 percent. About fifty new institutions are established each year and by 1975 academic libraries will be spending $300 million a year for materials. Perry D. Morrison said at this conference. "We hope that the computer's tail will not wag the intellectual dog."[5] He points out three advantages to using an all-books plan and seven disadvantages, including the fact that the automatic plan builds an uncritical collection, and he remarks that one becomes too dependent upon a single supplier and "subject to the tyranny of his computer." The writer, a faculty member himself, said he did not feel that his interests were being served if it were all to become automatic and superficial.

At the same conference, LeRoy C. Merritt presented a paper entitled "Are We Selecting or Collecting?" in which he said, "My contention is that the quality of the collection produced, not the promised increase in efficiency or ordering procedures, is the true issue."[6]

When the Michigan State University library left the divisional plan of operation, Dr. Richard Chapin lamented the loss of the advantages that plan offered in the development of the book collection.[7] He said he found it necessary to redefine their efforts for resource development, and specific discipline assignments were passed out to members of the staff. A book selection department was created in the library.

A recent issue of College & Research Libraries includes a paper titled "Book Selection in Academic Libraries: A New Approach," by J.G. Schad and Ruth L. Adams.[8] These writers advocate a working combination of faculty and librarians to build the most satisfactory and relevant book collection. There is no reference whatever to any kind of approval or blanket or all-books plan.

A complex operation can be automated if it is consistent and standardized. Book selection is neither. The information flow emanating from large numbers of books as they are issued forth is made up of many unique and varying parts with shades of difference that may be extremely important to a particular library situation. A machine cannot deal properly with this kind of fluctuating subject matter, with linguistic and semantic materials; at least the machines in use today cannot. A book is the result of the thinking process of a man, and a machine will treat words just as though they were static, inflexible, sterile, categorical bits; the human mind extracts much more than this from the printed page. It is almost as though one were attempting to put a man's thinking process into a machine for recall as needed. We may try, but I hardly think we can be successful, really successful, in building a good, really good, library collection by automatic book selection alone. We can, I think, do this very well with a combination of machine and human intelligence.

The OSU Library approval plan experience was an unfortunate one, but it did occur at one point in time under a specific set of circumstances. Today it might well be that those circumstances do not exist and the same set of problems would not arise. The OSU Library may very well one day come back into the fold and employ some kind of gathering plan, but if we do, I think we shall still use the human touch to tailor a book collection to fit our own particular needs.

References

1. David O. Lane, "Approval and Blanket Order Acquisitions Plan" (A paper read before the Institute on Acquisitions Procedures in Academic Libraries, Univ. of California, San Diego, Aug. 25-Sept. 5, 1969).
2. Ian W. Thom, "Some Administrative Aspects of Blanket Ordering," Library Resources & Technical Services 13:338-42 (Summer 1969).
3. Margit Kraft, "An Argument for Selectivity in the Acquisition of Materials for Research Libraries," Library Quarterly 37:284-95 (July 1967).
4. Gordon Williams. "Academic Librarianship: The State of the Art," Library Journal 91:2417 (15 May 1966).
5. Perry D. Morrison, "A Symposium on Approval Order Plans and the Book Selection Responsibilities of Librarians," Library Resources & Technical Services 12:133-39 (Spring 1968).
6. LeRoy C. Merritt, "Are We Selecting or Collecting?" Library Resources & Technical Services 12:140-42 (Spring 1968).
7. Richard E. Chapin and Ralph E. McCoy, "The Emerging Institutions: Michigan State University and Southern Illinois University," Library Trends 15:266-85 (Oct. 1966).
8. Jasper G. Schad and Ruth L. Adams, "Book Selection in Academic Libraries: A New Approach," College & Research Libraries 30:437-42 (Sept. 1969).

On the Design of Information
Systems for Human Beings

by M. B. Line

Reprinted by permission from the July 1970 issue of
Aslib Proceedings (22:7), p. 320-335. Copyright 1970
by Aslib.

Planning of any kind can be motivated by a pressing practical problem which has to be solved--for example, an increasing number of people may have to be housed in the same area; or by a long-term idealistic vision; or by both (the idealist seeing the long-term implications of an immediate problem). In short-term planning, the danger exists that the more technical problems may be solved, without attention to their implications for human beings; to take my housing example, higher and higher flats may be built, without considering the possible effects (e.g. the effect on social groupings). In long-term planning, Utopian or ideological blueprints may be produced.

We have some idea of what can happen in both short- and long-term planning. In the first case, people may avoid high flats wherever possible, and where not, they may express their feelings by wrecking them (whether deliberately or by trying to make them conform to what they were used to before). In the second case, attempts to construct Utopian communities have all failed,[1] as have more ambitious attempts to design an ideal state. In both cases, the result is due to a failure to take account of human needs and preferences.

At the other extreme, development can take place entirely in response to known human needs and preferences: not a few human institutions have been designed or have evolved in this way (brothels, gaming-houses, bingo-halls, etc.). The reaction then may be that such institutions are among the 'worst' features of society, that they betray human nature by pandering to its lowest elements, and so on.

These criticisms imply a view of what human nature "ought" to be.

The fact that plans which do not take human beings sufficiently into account are inadequate may mean not that they are basically wrong, but that they have been introduced wrongly. Human beings appear to be extremely flexible, and will adapt themselves to almost anything if it is done gradually. There are obviously biological and physical, as well as economic, constraints which limit adaptability; how strong and permanent these are is not really known. (Desmond Morris[2] may exaggerate their strength and basic nature, but this is probably a useful corrective at the present time.) Whether human beings adapt to a system or not, any system is bound to affect them, perhaps in ways which no one predicted or wanted.

All three main approaches to system building--the short-term solution, the planned Utopian and the unplanned evolutionary--have serious disadvantages. If a system can be planned, but planned in accordance with knowledge of human behaviour and needs (individual and social), as a basis for seeing both what may be usable and what may be the effects of the system, it should be able to have most of the advantages of both the Utopian and the evolutionary without their deficiencies.

This does not solve the dilemma of "is" versus "ought." How far human behaviour can be changed is one question (presumably answerable, though very hard to answer); how far within these limits it should be changed is quite another, which brings in value judgments.

The present information system is mainly of the evolutionary kind; though a lot of detailed and short-term planning has gone into bits of it, there has been almost no attempt at overall planning, and the planning has been aimed mainly at the solution of technical problems (or at mere technical refinements--problems have not always been there to solve). There is certainly a very serious general problem to be solved (if one takes the primary publication system as given-- if one doesn't, there are a lot of bigger practical problems to be solved!) from the volume of literature, its scatter, language problems, and other well-known factors.

Information systems, and to a lesser extent, library services, are undergoing at the present time more rapid changes than ever before. These changes have been caused by technological advances, social pressures, and the sheer growth of recorded knowledge. These three factors are of course interlinked. I will not go into their nature and relationship here, merely note that they exist. My point is that changes in the information system are mostly unplanned in any but a short-term sense, and that they take no account of people as they are. Long-term Utopian planners like Licklider,[3] on the other hand, seem to be planning systems for Utopian planners like Licklider to use.

If we look at some of the problems associated with libraries and information systems, it may become apparent how they could be approached with the help of psychology and sociology.

In the first place, what attracts people, or does not attract them, to libraries? The factors that draw them in initially may be rather different from the factors that induce them to come again. It is known that the public library's clientele is selective, and that even within the selective groups some people never come near the library. Some of the explanation may lie in the physical siting of the library, but even here the distance people are prepared to travel to libraries is at least partly a psychological and sociological matter. To quote from one of the reports commissioned for the U.S. National Advisory Committee on Libraries:[4]

> But even if consensus is reached on defining users descriptively there still remains the problem of finding out why particular classes of users and non-users behave as they do. The why question is far more difficult to deal with than is the how many. In order to find out why library users and non-users behave as they do we must begin to focus attention upon the complex inner structure of individual motivations along with determining their social characteristics.
>
> Let us cite an example. If we know that proportionately fewer Negroes than Whites borrow books from public libraries, we can explain this on one level. Negroes do not have the same educational opportunities as Whites, they therefore are not as 'book-orientated' as Whites; therefore Negroes 'use' libraries less frequently. This is a plausible 'why' interpretation; but it does not explain the fact that

Technical Services 217

many Negroes do use public libraries, while many Whites do not.

Obviously we need more than demographic descriptives here.

In the very least we must look into the following form-types of psychological variables that would go a long way in answering why different sub-groups in the population behave as they do. Critical to the <u>why</u> question are observations relating to people's

1. Assumptions, beliefs, and presuppositions. These often are more determinant of behavior than 'objective' facts.

2. Frames of reference attitudes. These are psychological 'tendencies' or dispositions to react and to behave in certain relatively fixed ways.

3. Sensations, images, and feelings. These relate to the inner experiences and 'pictures in the mind's eye' that various stimuli (i.e. libraries) generate, and they are most important in motivating people to react to the stimuli either positively or negatively.

4. Gratifications. These are the symbolic as well as actual satisfactions that are derived from given experiences.

The hoary argument as to whether academic libraries should be centralized or decentralized has many facets. Most librarians seem to regard it as closed, except that academics <u>will</u> go on wanting books near to them, in smallish compact collections. Rosenberg's[5] and Allen's[6] work should be taken into account here before we decide once and for all that academics are being lazy or obtuse. We have after all tried to convert them to better habits over the years, and the fact that, in some conditions at any rate, we have not succeeded should be a warning that we may be dealing here with some immutable characteristics of people, which we must simply accept. If, for economic or other reasons, centralized libraries are necessary, it may be possible to keep users happy by a rather different organization of the Central Library in accordance with their requirements--once we know what these are.

Within the library, how should seating be arranged in relation to bookstacks? Sommer's[7] work on seating preferences is of relevance here; he shows, not surprisingly, that needs are very varied, and the conclusion I would draw is that libraries should offer a much wider variety of choice than is usual, from six-seater tables to hermit cells. (A later piece of work,[8] which shows that working on a bed produces similar academic results to working at a desk, would suggest that the installation of beds in libraries would be desirable, and would help at the same time to solve the accommodation crisis in higher education.)

I am not suggesting that librarians are not conscious of the importance of psychological and social factors; it would be hard otherwise to explain why we pay so much attention to library display and aesthetic appearance. What we do not know is whether our efforts work, or whether they are made in the right direction at all. We do not know what part pleasant service plays, compared with a large stock, an attractive building, or sheer efficiency. A little effort in the right direction might do more to attract and retain users than any amount of well-intentioned effort in wrong directions.

Another old issue is the broad versus detailed shelf arrangement. There are several facets to this particular problem, which I have touched on elsewhere;[9] I would only say here that I do not see any way of solving it without the help of psychological studies, for example into the memorability of shelf-marks, the ability of users to comprehend their order on the shelves, the number of books within a category that can be readily comprehended by users, and so on.

It would be useful here to distinguish between what I might call subjective and objective usability. Subjective factors decide whether something is used at all, or used more than once, or used with pleasure. Some things--e.g. UDC classification numbers--<u>look</u> offputting, and if users are put off something, they never have the chance to find out whether it is in fact easy to use or not. Objective factors include memorability, comprehension, error rates, speed of use, etc. These are technically easier to determine, though the work involved in determining them can be very large and require complex controlled experimentation.

More fundamental questions in classification relate to the conceptual structures by which people organize knowledge within their minds, and how these relate to the subject arrangement, not merely of libraries, but of indexing and abstracting tools. It may be that the conceptual structures of users exhibit so much variety that few useful conclusions can be drawn; or that, if they show a strong resemblance to Dewey, it is because prolonged exposure to libraries has made them look at knowledge Dewey-eyed. The actual structures (which could be partially studied by an examination of the personal indexes and reference systems of those users that keep references) are different from the structural patterns of knowledge: the way in which the human brain organizes information in order to store and retrieve it. The suggestions made in this connection by Norman[10] are most interesting: he considers the operation of memory (both short- and long-term), and the mechanisms of storage and retrieval, and then discusses the implications of this for the design of future libraries and information systems. His views are not universally agreed among psychologists, by any means, but his approach seems to me potentially a very valuable one. For example, if his view is correct that we "organize into categories with a limit of about five items in one category" and that hierarchies have to be established in the memory, with no more than five items in each group, sub-group, or sub-sub-group, this is surely of extreme importance for the design of classifications.

To move from classification to catalogues. Some of the major problems include whether catalogues should be primarily arranged by author or by title, and whether subject catalogues should be classified or alphabetical. We now know from several studies that people remember title more accurately than author.[11, 12] A few well-designed studies into the classified/alphabetical subject catalogue question could help settle this question too (I say "help settle," because there is also the question whether subject catalogues are intended for users to operate direct, or for library staff to operate on behalf of users). The Aslib/Cranfield studies, among others, have already shed some light on the relative effectiveness of different methods; we now need light on the relative usability, bearing in mind the distinction I made earlier between subjective and objective usability.

The physical structure, layout and appearance of catalogues have received little detailed attention so far. Again, I am not saying that librarians do not consciously try to make their catalogues as beautiful and functional as possible, only that they (and "they" includes me) have little or no idea whether their beauty appeals to the beholder or how they work in practice. What, for example, is the relative speed of access to a printed as opposed to a card catalogue? What errors of use are made in each case? It may be that a card catalogue is best for a specific item search, a book catalogue for a subject search: we do not know. What filing arrangements are comprehensible to users? Would some of the simplified filing rules suggested for computer sorting really make things better or worse for the user?

This leads me on from conventional library tools to secondary information tools such as abstracts, indexes, and so on. The points I made earlier about the subject organization of information within the mind are relevant here. Indexing and abstracting tools, and for that matter bibliographies in book form, exhibit a wide variety of arrangements. It is highly improbable that, for example, chemists organize information in totally different basic patterns from engineers, or that the users of Sociological Abstracts are a different breed from the users of International Bibliography of the Social Sciences: Sociology. But until there is some better theoretical and experimental basis on which to plan these services, we can hardly blame their planners.

In one sense, however, we can blame them. Since no one knows whether one type of arrangement is better than another, there is a good case for rather more standardization, on the grounds that a variety of arrangements of unknown utility is much more confusing to the user than one arrangement of unknown utility. Even when an indexing tool uses the same structure consistently, index terms for the same thing tend to differ from volume to volume. There may be good reasons for this, but the utility of improved subject entries should be weighed against the utility of consistency from volume to volume.

The physical design, layout, density, typography and so on, of secondary tools could well receive more attention. Presumably some arrangements are clearer, and quicker to use, than others. It would not require tremendous effort to study this, and indeed some work has already been done in this area, for example by Drage[13] on user preferences in the layout of indexes, and by Slater and Keenan[14] into the arrangement and format of Current Papers in Physics.

A more general problem concerns the sheer proliferation of secondary tools. The number of indexing and abstracting journals, or journals containing index or abstract sections, is now about 3,000--this was the number of primary journals 100 years ago. It is easy to see how this has happened. The expansion of recorded knowledge on the one hand, and increasing pressures on the time of users on the other, have stimulated the growth of secondary tools--an almost totally unplanned, unco-ordinated and piecemeal growth, which institutions and governments have fostered for the best of reasons, and publishers for less altruistic reasons. This growth of secondary tools has solved nothing at all, except in the short term for small bodies of people. In the first place, they do not, except in very rare cases, even attempt to supersede, or compete with, previous systems; the situation is quite different from that of the new washing powder which competes with old washing powders. They therefore add to the number of systems to be used by the individual. But if he uses several, he will find a lot of the same references cropping up in them all, so that each additional one he uses brings less reward for his effort. Moreover, even if he uses ten or even twenty, he will still miss something. On the other hand, if he acts as if the new system does supersede others, he will miss a great deal--perhaps more than 50 per cent of relevant material.

In recent years, the printed "current awareness" services that have begun to proliferate are not so much arranged as strung together, and usually have to be read right through to make sure you are not missing anything. If you get a month or two behind, catching up is very laborious. If your field is interdisciplinary, you may have to use two or three of these current contents journals.

So the computer has been brought in to help. The ways in which it does this do not need stating here. If it is used to speed up publication of indexing journals, the choice lies between manual indexing and computer indexing on the one hand, and computer typesetting and direct computer printout on the other, the combination of manual indexing and computer typesetting being the most expensive of the four alternatives thus offered, and computer indexing and computer printout the cheapest.

Whether a computer-based system offers a current awareness service or retrospective searching, numerous problems arise; not merely the well-known problems of profile-construction and recall/relevance, but problems of overload. The retrospective search in particular corresponds to nothing a researcher would ever do naturally, except perhaps a Ph.D. student starting on his work, or an experienced man writing a comprehensive literature review. Normally, a researcher searches a bit, reads a bit, thinks a bit, experiments a bit, writes a bit, searches a bit more, and so on; he wants his references in drips rather than lumps, which tend to clog up his intellectual works.

The poor researcher is then faced with a large number of different published indexing systems; to use any of these effectively is not easy, to use them all effectively impossible. If he does attempt to do so, he will have little time left to spend actually doing research. Alternatively, he can go in for a computer retrieval system. He will soon be faced with a fair range of these too, and it is a good bet that these too will overlap, leave gaps, require different approaches, and be difficult to use. When he does use any of these systems, they will lead him to a far wider range of primary literature than he has been accustomed to using, scattered through anything up to 1,000 journals (not to mention conferences, reports, etc.).

This system is not one it would have been thought necessary to invent if it did not exist already. It combines some of the worst elements of Utopian planning--in attempting to achieve comprehensiveness, for example--with some of the worst elements of short-term expediency.

Developments in the secondary system have been paralleled by developments in storage of primary material. Prophecies have been made for at least thirty or forty years that microfilm will supersede ordinary print to a large extent. Its advantages are of course well known; many of these are still greater with ultrafiche. There is only one snag: <u>people simply do not like using microfilm.</u> A recent user survey of microfiche15 records some illuminating comments from users, most of whom were either positively antagonistic or apathetic:

> Anybody who strikes a blow against microfiche can't be all bad.
>
> Everything about microfiche is marvellous...except using it.
>
> Microfiche is an information burial system.

The writer of the survey, Harold Wooster, comments:

The 47 per cent of individual users who disliked detested and despised microfiche did so for the following reasons, ranked in descending frequency:

1. Unavailability of, or difficult access to, readers for their own use.

2. Inability to make notes on fiche.

3. Poor optical and mechanical quality of readers.

4. Can't read fiche at home, on airplanes, etc.

5. Can't flip pages, refer back and forth from appendix to text.

6. True cost of blow-backs is probably greater than 25¢ a page, especially when scientists or engineers must operate the reader-printer themselves, as is frequently the case.

7. Print-outs after you get them are unwieldy, thick, curl up into Dead Sea scrolls.

8. Personal reading rates are slower.

9. Can't read and work with graphs, tables and continuous tone photographs, especially with negatives when they're accustomed to reading positives.

10. Can't identify fiche by color and physical location. Can't scan quickly.
Poor indexes to what's available on fiche.
Hard to store.
Can't read titles without readers.
Lack of standardization in fiche size (e.g. COSATI vs. Industry vs. IBM standards.)

To these disadvantages I would add one other: that microfilm does not <u>invite</u> use, you are not exposed to it in the same way as you are to books. Microfilm is however at least something you can see and handle. Some solutions to the book storage problem involve the storage of information in computers, or at long range in computer-controlled stores, accessible by facsimile transmission. The remoteness and intangibility inherent in such systems are somehow vaguely alarming: how can you control and use something that can't

be seen, and that has to be approached in very special ways? I suspect there is something more in this than a threat to one's security. After all, we have all been brought up in an environment where we have been exposed to information visually over long periods. We have thus acquired a personal internal store of information; much of this store may be little used, but from it we draw the words, symbols and ideas by which we may obtain access to other, external stores of information. Now imagine, if you can, someone who has been brought up without such visual exposure to information; who has not been able to browse or pick up snippets of knowledge from books. How can he obtain access as an adult to a computer-stored information system? The store from which he must draw his access points must be a very impoverished one. This is an extreme case, and I do not for one moment imagine it will come about; but I do believe there is a serious danger that prolonged use of a computer system could narrow one's horizons and range of interest in a way that could be very damaging to the progress of science, the major advances in which are made by the imaginative leap, the seeing of similarity in two apparently disparate areas, not in "crawling along the frontiers of knowledge with a hand lens," as Sir Eric Ashby has neatly put it. It is interesting that at MIT, where TIP, the fairly sophisticated on-line computer retrieval system in physics, has been in operation for three or four years now, some physicists still prefer browsing in the library.[16] It will be even more interesting to see how experimental interactive systems, by which the computer can actually provide some browsing facilities, work in practice. I suspect that, for at least a long time ahead, the sheer complexity of operating the system will present a very formidable barrier. The user will probably have to choose between using a highly structured language which the computer can handle tolerably easily, and using natural language, which will require very much more elaborate and expensive systems, which in turn may require a more complex mode of working--by the time an interactive system has got round to understanding exactly what its innocent user really wants, he may have been infuriated to a point where he reverts to his old habits of asking Charlie or looking through a few selected journals.
Some current experimental on-line systems demand a high degree of accuracy and persistance from the user, not to mention practice and familiarity. At present, one writer claims that 'Existing machine searching systems have physically and psychologically enlarged the gap between the reader and the information store.'[17]

Miller[18] has posed another objection to the invisible store of information: that it lacks any spatial frame of reference. Unless information can be <u>located</u> somewhere, unless the user can visualize its place <u>within</u> a book, or a library, or whatever, its accessibility is greatly reduced.
We are all familiar with this phenomenon in the form of the angry user who asks where his books have been moved to now; if they have been reclassified, it is far worse for him than if they have simply been moved, since the spatial frame of reference is totally lost in the first case. This may account for some of TIP's non-users. There is, as Miller points out, no particular reason why libraries and information systems of the future should not take account of this factor; the fact is that up to now there is little sign that system designers are aware of it.

Let us have a closer look at our user. Users are not, I would remind you, some special kind of animal, but ordinary human beings, exhibiting the infinite variety of human nature. In certain environments--research establishments, for example--it is true that users may have some characteristics in common, such as (presumably) reasonable intelligence and a concern with the same subject areas; but there will inevitably be a wide range of personalities and behavioural patterns.

By now, a great deal is known about individual human psychology and the behaviour of human groups. Unfortunately, there has as yet been little serious attempt to apply this knowledge to information use and transfer, although they are clearly matters both of individual psychology and group behaviour, and one would expect such a study to be potentially very fruitful. It is true that we have, thanks especially to the American Psychological Association's studies of the last few years,[19] a collection of data on patterns of information transfer, ranging from informal communication at conferences to the process by which research gets published and what happens to it then. This is very useful background material concerning what actually happens, and it provides a useful check on hypotheses as to what sort of system would be acceptable in practice. However, large-scale studies of this kind cannot provide the psychological and sociological data required for the sort of study I am suggesting.

More directly to the point at issue is Allen's[20] work on information flow in R and D laboratories, which uses sociometric techniques, and demonstrates the extreme complexity of transfer. Also relevant is the work of Rosenberg[5] on factors which affect the preference of industrial personnel for information-gathering methods.

All these studies are valuable, starting as they do at the operational end, as it were, and more are needed. However, parallel with this research, I would like to see work starting at the theoretical end, testing hypotheses derived from sociological and psychological theory in different situations and environments. Most studies have up to now been carried out by persons without special training in sociology or psychology, and consequently have severe limitations. They have the further limitation that what people do is inevitably constrained by what there is; the present range of choices is limited, and we cannot tell from user studies what users might do given new choices or possibilities. User studies are of little predictive value.

A useful programme of work would include the identification of potentially relevant findings and theories from sociology and psychology; a review of what is already known about user behaviour; a bringing together of the two, leading hopefully to the development of specific theories and hypotheses concerned with information use, and the refinement of techniques of testing them; and the design of a series of studies.

Such a programme of research is not merely an interesting exercise: it is essential if we are to find out enough about users to build systems suited to them, instead of designing systems (or making them up as we go along) and then hoping to goodness they can be used. As I have suggested, even on a commonsense level the present system makes very little sense, even less sense when one considers the little knowledge we do have already about users and their information habits.

First, it appears that a very high proportion of all information, even at a research level, is not acquired directly from documents at all, but informally--through correspondence, meetings, and ordinary conversation. This fact surprises most researchers until they observe their own behaviour; the seeking out and perusal of a document are more positive acts than a casual conversation, and thus assume a prominence in the user's mind which is not justified by the facts. There are fairly obvious reasons for preferring informal communication. It is usually easier and pleas-

Technical Services 227

anter. It gives a rapid feedback, so that if one does not start quite on the right wave-length it does not matter much-- contrast formal systems, whether computer-based or printed, where a wrong initial approach yields no results at all. It brings added dividends, in the form of additional information which the person contacted believes will be of interest. It may lead to further contacts. It has a stimulus value lacking in much formal documentation. All these rewards are immediate, and although formal documentary systems have their own advantages, the fact that the rewards are less immediate is alone a sufficient reason why informal systems are preferred: given an immediate reward, however small, most people will prefer it to the possible long-term reward. I would incidentally expect learning theory in general, and in particular the role of rewards and reinforcement, to be capable of a number of fruitful applications in the study of information transfer. (The offer a year or two ago by the Librarian of Cambridge University of prizes for successful catalogue searches may perhaps be regarded as a primitive attempt to apply learning theory to library use.)

The main reason, however, why informal systems are preferred is the second fact that can be regarded as reasonably well established: most researchers suffer from (or perhaps enjoy) an astonishing degree of inertia. This is not quite the same thing as saying that short-term rewards are preferred to long-term rewards. It is more like Zipf's law of least effort. It has been shown that, given a choice of going next door with a small probability of obtaining relevant information, or indeed much information at all, and walking a hundred yards with a much higher probability of success and quantity, people go next door.[5,6] They may never go beyond next door, and if they do they generally go next door but one. They may eventually go the hundred yards to the good source of information, but only after exhausting all the closer sources on the way. Expected ease of use, as well as physical accessibility, has a much higher priority than the expected quantity and quality of information. This should not incidentally surprise us: on a more mundane level, I sometimes go into extraordinary contortions to reach something nearby without getting out of my chair, when it would be much more sensible to walk a yard or two.

Among the reasons why informal systems are preferred, stimulus and enjoyment were suggested. Human beings have a great need for both, but here we have a dilemma. For vast amounts of relevant information to be transferred at all, some condensation is required; but condensation usually makes information neither acceptable nor memorable. Protein tablets and other packaged forms of food may give you as much nourishment as a good meal, and they certainly take much less time to eat, but they are hardly as satisfying; nor will you return to them again until you are really hungry. Information as a stimulus can be considered from two aspects: if information is not inherently stimulating, people are less likely to use it at all; and the process of stimulating thoughts and ideas is one of the most valuable properties of information. We must at all costs avoid the concept of information as mere lumps of facts and data.

The preference for informal systems has several practical implications. Is it possible, for example, that informal information transfer could be organized in such a way as to enable it to partake of some of the advantages of the formal system? Or can the formal system be so re-designed as to have some of the important properties of informal transfer?

What has been discovered about informal transfer has other interesting aspects. De Solla Price has written a good deal about the 'invisible college,' the group of individuals, often scattered quite widely, with a specific common interest, exchanging correspondence and previews of forthcoming articles and quoting each other's works; with a membership which is flexible but not easy to break into, while the penalty for remaining outside is to be out of touch with the latest work in the subject.

The preference for informal communication also means that the isolated worker, or a team composed of as few as two or three individuals, is at a great disadvantage compared with the team of five or six. The chances of stimulus and new ideas are greatly reduced with small numbers. Very large teams create their own problems of communication: there seems to be a fairly narrow band of numbers which is the optimum size. Teams also seem to throw up regularly one member who acts as chief communicator, both from the inside going out and from the outside coming in; it is he who has most contacts, and he is the person to whom members of the team turn automatically for information.[20] Whether groups tend to recruit these "gatekeepers," or grow them at home, as it were, is not known; it is evident that they have certain characteristics of personality that distinguish them from other members. Any formalization of an informal system would clearly have to make use of gatekeepers, as well as of invisible colleges.

At present even the formal system--of documents, libraries, and secondary tools--receives a great deal of informal use. A study carried out at Johns Hopkins University some years ago indicated that 18 per cent of books borrowed from the University Library by scientists were items that they did not go there specifically to find.[21] I have been told of a university researcher who, on parking his car each morning, noted down the numbers of adjacent cars and then went to the Library to look at the corresponding Dewey numbers, rarely failing to find something of interest. Purposeful browsing and, especially, serendipity both benefit from a certain element of randomness. I know that in my own work I would like to have everything--yes, absolutely everything--in a very narrow area, a careful selection from peripheral areas, and random exposure to other areas. From the last comes at least occasional entertainment, often stimulus, and sometimes a real shaft of light on my immediate work--the perception of a link between two apparently different fields, a striking analogue, a technique developed originally for other purposes but potentially useful to me. The point of this is that computer retrieval systems aim to eliminate randomness, whereas they are almost uniquely suited to providing a random element in addition to specificity. It is interesting that, with the increasing specialization of periodicals, the random element is now being catered for by such journals as New Society and, increasingly, by newspapers such as The Times and The Sunday Times, which have semi-popular scientific snippers or even full-page articles of a kind that was very unusual a few years ago.

Over the years people have developed ways of using libraries and information that, viewed rationally, appear rather clumsy. What is not known, and what must somehow be ascertained, is how far these habits are the products of basic psychological characteristics which are not subject to change, and how far they can be modified by a different system. As pointed out earlier, human beings are certainly immensely flexible, but they have a way of appearing more flexible than they are; many radical innovations have after a few years turned into something remarkably like what would have evolved anyway from the previous system. One implication of this phenomenon is of course that no system can be properly evaluated until several years have passed and all novelty has worn off.

There must be individual limitations which cannot be trangressed. For example, there must be limits beyond which individuals can no longer take in information. Some research has been carried out into how many articles the average scientist reads a week, but not into how many pages of solid matter he could read in an average working week. Obviously there must be huge variations here, not only between but within individuals (according to their health, motivation, etc.); but within the variations there must be a band within which most researchers fall, and if an information system consistently exceeds the upper limit of this band it is failing to meet a basic criterion.

Actually, one wants to know of the newer methods of transferring information, particularly those using computers, not merely whether they will demand changes of such a nature or magnitude as to be unacceptable (except in the short term when they are fun to try out), but whether the changes they may induce will be such as to do damage, for example by reducing stimulus and browsing possibilities. Undoubtedly some very large changes are possible in information use: consider, for example, the medieval monk working in solitude, and compare him with the gregarious conference-goer of today. There are of course excellent social reasons why this particular change has occurred, and in any case the Middle Ages were hardly notable for intellectual progress and creativity, but the point I want to stress is that it has been possible. How much change is possible <u>within</u> a society, rather than between societies, is another <u>matter</u>.

It is interesting in this context to consider the technological advances that have brought about significant changes in behaviour, and those that have not. The invention of printing is perhaps the most significant invention of this millennium in its impact on human beings, individually and in groups. More recently, the invention of electrostatic copying has had an effect on information habits: whereas previously users would read an article in the library, or borrow and return it, in either case making an abstract if it proved useful, now they tend to make a copy (at someone else's expense usually), and after a quick scan file it away, thus building up their own selective personal libraries, half-read. They probably read rather less and scan rather more. The growth of paperback publishing may have had a rather similar effect. If I am right about this, the explanation may be partly that it is one means of coming to terms with an increasing volume of literature, so that an interaction is occurring: the growth of literature stimulates use of new technology, which therefore accelerates, changing in turn the use of literature.

Developments which have not (yet, at any rate) altered significantly information use or habits include microfilm and programmed learning. I suspect several of the newer media will never catch on, not because of any technical deficiencies but because, for reasons which may not always be easy to specify, people do not use them.

There are obvious limitations to the study I am advocating of the psychology and sociology of information use. I pointed out earlier that users are simply human beings; and information use is a very personal matter. It might well be established that there was a clear relationship between certain psychological characteristics and information use[22]--for example, that extraverts showed important differences from introverts, or convergers from divergers, or stable personalities from neurotic ones, or even men from women. This would be fascinating to find out, but of no conceivable use to anyone: I cannot imagine a special abstracting service for neurotic extravert women, or special libraries for stable convergent men. Nor would investigations into, for example, the eyeblink rates or galvanic skin responses of individuals confronted with the Science Citation Index be of great value. What should be looked for is the characteristic or reaction that is universal or extremely common; for example, it might be shown that 70 per cent of users preferred one form of layout of an index to another. One possible practical solution to the growth of literature is an increase in reading speed that newspaper-style printing would offer: given a careful layout, it might be possible to absorb information, at least in a superficial way, much faster from a newspaper page (containing the equivalent of perhaps twelve normal pages) than from twelve separate pages, and in peripheral areas this could be valuable. (It could incidentally also cut publishing costs, particularly if the originals were stored centrally and the "newspapers" printed on ordinary newsprint paper.)

At a more fundamental level, little is known about the effect of different kinds of media on the learning process. It is possible that in the next few years books will give way partly to various audio and visual devices. One would expect this to benefit those who take in information readily through the ear or in pictorial or semi-pictorial form, but the prolonged visual exposure permitted by the book may have great advantages, e.g. in "imprinting" something to be memorized on the brain, which should not be lost. In fact, it is probable that different sorts of information are best suited to different media, and future developments should take account of this.

Obviously, in the last resort, when we have found out all we can about users, no information system can be designed entirely around them, since it is inevitably bound by practical constraints, chiefly (but not entirely) economic, technical and physical. However, unless users are fully considered, a system may fall well short of full utilization: it will be used if it is the only alternative, but even on strict economic grounds it would make sense to ensure that it was as fully used as possible (particularly in the case of libraries, which represent expensive capital resources.)

It may be that at the end of prolonged (or perhaps not so prolonged) study there proves to be an irreconcilable conflict: a system, to be fully effective in retrieving information, may require a very high level of sophistication, which makes it unusable by most people, while a system to be fully usable must remain at a primitive level of development. I suspect this may indeed be so, but it is no cause for despair; indeed, if we know it to be so, we could probably make much faster progress, on the understanding that there must always be a human intermediary--the information officer--between the system and the user.[23] The system could then be developed to any pitch of sophistication, without any breach of the rules about accessibility and usability.

I am aware that I have ranged over a very wide area in a very superficial way. The points I have made are not new. Rees and Schultz[24] said a few years ago: "If we are really concerned with facilitating information transfer in order to improve the research productivity of scientists and engineers, then it is profitable to turn at least some of our attention from the fashionable pursuits of debating the respective merits of classification schemes, subject headings, thesauri, links and roles, and the like, and to consider the psychological and environmental variables which determine the need for, and processing of, information." Cavanagh[25] too has discussed some of the issues I have raised. I would like to emphasize my main points. The first is a general principle, that information systems should as far as possible be built around users. The second is that systems inevitably affect use and users, and we should ensure that the effects of changes are desirable ones. The third is that the application of psychological and sociological theory and methods to information systems could help to guide us as to their development.

Dr Urquhart has his own favourite psychological theory, of the "manurial value of pure rubbish." The really bad article or paper stimulates the production of adrenalin in the reader or hearer, and hence provokes him to ideas and arguments that would otherwise never have entered his head. May I hope you have found this paper profitable on these grounds, if on no others?

References

1. Armytage, W. H. G. Heavens below. London, Routledge, 1961.
2. Morris, Desmond. The naked ape. London, Cape, 1967.
3. Licklider, J. C. R. Libraries of the future. Cambridge, Mass., MIT Press, 1965.
4. Academy for Educational Development, Inc. The use of libraries and the conditions that promote their use. 1967 (ED 022 489).
5. Rosenberg, Victor. Factors affecting the preferences of industrial personnel for information gathering methods. Information Storage and Retrieval, 3, 3, July 1967, 119-27.
6. Allen, Thomas J. and Gerstberger, Peter G. Criteria for selection of an information source. Cambridge, Mass., MIT, September 1967. (Working Paper, Alfred P. Sloan School of Management.)
7. Sommer, Robert. The ecology of privacy. Library Quarterly, 36, 3, July 1966, p. 234-48.
8. Gifford, Robert and Sommer, Robert. The desk or the bed? Personnel and Guidance Journal, 46, 9, May 1969, p. 876-8.
9. Line, Maurice B. and Bryant, Philip. How golden is your retriever? Thoughts on library classification. Library Association Record, 71, 5, May 1969, p. 135-8.
10. Norman, Donald A. The library and human memory. Part 13 of: California. University (Los Angeles). Institute of Library Research. Mechanised information services in the University library: Phase I--

Planning. Final report. 1967 (PB 178 441).
11. Ayres, F.H., German, Janice, Loukes, N. and Searle, R.H. Author versus title: a comparative study of the information which the user brings to the library catalogue. Journal of Documentation, 24, 4, December 1968, p. 266-72.
12. Chicago University. Graduate Library School. Requirements study for future catalogues. Progress report no. 2. March 1968.
13. Drage, John F. User preferences in technical indexes: a preliminary test. The Information Scientist, 2, 3, November 1968, p. 111-14; reprinted in The Indexer, 6, 4, Autumn 1969, p. 151-5.
14. Slater, Margaret and Keenan, Stella. Current Papers in Physics user study: coverage, arrangement and format. London, Institution of Electrical Engineering, 1968 (INSPEC/2, AIP/CPP 2).
15. Wooster, Harold. Microfiche 1969--a user survey. 1969 (AD 695-049).
16. Kessler, M.M. Search strategies of the MIT Technical Information Program. In: Simonton, Wesley and Mason, Charlene. Information retrieval with special reference to the biomedical sciences. Minneapolis, Minn., University of Minnesota, 1966, p. 23-33.
17. Doyle, L.B. Semantic road maps for literature searchers. Journal of the Association for Computing Machinery, 8, 4, October 1961, p. 553-78.
18. Miller, George A. Psychology and information. American Documentation, 19, 3, July 1968, p. 286-9.
19. American Psychological Association. Project on scientific information exchange in psychology. Reports. Washington, DC, APA, 1963--.
20. Allen, Thomas J. Organisational aspects of information flow in technology. Aslib Proceedings, 20, 11, November 1968, p. 433-54.
21. Johns Hopkins University. Progress report on an operations research and systems engineering study of a university library. Baltimore, Md, Johns Hopkins University, April 1963.
22. Line, Maurice B. Information requirements in the social sciences: some preliminary considerations. Journal of Librarianship, 1, 1, January 1969, p. 1-19.
23. Line, Maurice B. Information services in university libraries. Journal of Librarianship, 1, 4, October 1969, p. 211-24.
24. Rees, Alan M. and Schultz, Douglas G. Psychology

and information retrieval. In: Schecter, G. (ed.). Information retrieval: a critical view. New York, Academic Press, 1967, p. 143-50.
25. Cavanagh, J.M.A. Some considerations relating to user-system interaction in information retrieval systems. In: Tonik, Albert B. (ed.). Information retrieval: the user's viewpoint on aid to design. Philadelphia, International Informatics Inc., 1967, p. 119-25.

PART III:

COMMUNICATION AND EDUCATION

Book Publishing's Hidden Bonanza

by Curtis G. Benjamin

Reprinted by permission from the April 18, 1970 issue of Saturday Review (53:14), p. 19-21, 81-82. Copyright 1970 by Saturday Review, Inc.

The division of the book world most readily recognized by the general public is between textbook publishing and general (or "trade") book publishing. Indeed, the U.S. book industry has for many years divided itself in this way by maintaining two trade associations: the American Book Publishers Council for producers of general books, and the American Educational Publishers Institute for producers of textbooks and related teaching materials. But this dichotomy loses validity every year as educators continue to move sharply away from the traditional one-subject-one-book teaching practice. In fact, most publishers today, foreseeing a sure meeting of the twain, think their two trade associations should be merged; this move seems imminent.

Another division, and a more natural one, is between what are known within the industry as literary books and nonliterary books. The first category includes fiction, biography, poetry, drama, and general literature. The second encompasses several classifications of practical and professional works in such subject areas as agriculture, business, economics, education, law, medicine, science, and technology; and it includes a multitude of handbooks, manuals, directories, statistical reports, sets of numerical tables and data, and "how-to" guides. Most textbooks, by nature as well as subject matter, fall into this second category. The classifications of the respective categories have been used since the turn of the century by the Publishers' Weekly annual statistical reports.

This division represents two worlds of publishing, each quite different and separate, and sufficient unto itself. There is, in fact, a far greater distinction between literary and nonliterary houses than between textbook and nontextbook houses.

During the 1960s, there occurred an astonishing explosion of nonliterary books. This unexpected development was doubly astonishing in that it was within the hardcover realm, and it came at the end of a long and little noticed sea change that began some forty years earlier. Although the explosion was a big one, not many people heard it, or even heard about it. This was because it occurred in the hidden part of the book-industry iceberg, the much larger part that is all but invisible to the general public, and that is not much celebrated within the industry itself.

In the early years of the century, newly published literary works outnumbered nonliterary works by two to one. Then, starting with the 1930s, there came a change in this imbalance; the production of literary works declined, while that of nonliterary works increased in proportion. The decline of the former was caused presumably by restricted spending for nonessentials during the Depression.

In the following decade, the 1940s, literary works declined a little more, while nonliterary works climbed a little higher. Then both categories climbed sharply through the 1950s, and by the end of that decade the two were almost even. Happy days were here again for all kinds of literary books, and for fiction especially. Income from sales of reprint, book-club, and motion-picture rights gave novels a new lease on life, and restored their production to an interesting level of profitability.

Then came the 1960s and the spectacular leap ahead in the production of nonliterary works. In that decade alone, the number of such works produced annually increased by 164 per cent, while literary titles increased by only 29 per cent. The imbalance of the earlier years was completely reversed, and by 1969 new nonliterary works outnumbered new literary works by more than two to one.

The long-range change over this forty-year period was even more striking: Annual nonliterary book production increased by some 380 per cent, while literary production increased by only 40 per cent.

The story is dramatically revealed in Chart I. What cannot be revealed as simply are the more subtle mutations in the health and behavior of the book industry that came with the change. Certainly, the industry as a whole became more stable, more vigorous, more venturesome, and more prosperous. Also, it grew enough in size and affluence to be recognized nationally as a moderately important area of commercial enterprise and financial speculation.

How much each of the subject-matter components contributed to the nonliterary explosion can be seen in Table I, which shows the historical thrust as well as the total surge of the category. Note in particular the astonishing records of books in the social sciences and in the natural sciences and technology.

It is amusing to note the aloofness of certain lofty-minded literary publishers and commentators who like to describe many kinds of nonliterary works as "nonbooks." The publishers of these books laugh all the way to the bank over this disdainful characterization. They know that these "nonbooks" are in great demand, that they have high societal value, and that they are of large importance to the overall resources and economy of the book industry. They know, too, that in many a large, multi-interest publishing firm, the profit earned by nonliterary titles bankrolls the whole house; that more often than not this profit provides large sums for investments in glamorous but uncertain literary ventures of great worth and prestige--ventures of the very kind that always are warmly applauded by the literary buffs.

Another possible division of the book publishing world is the paperback/hardcover bisection. This division actually is not as sharp or as meaningful within the industry as it is in the public's mind. Strangely, one of the most persistent of current myths about book publishing is that the two kinds of books are locked in a battle for survival. Indeed, many people on the fringes of the publishing world now believe firmly that paperbacks are in and hardcovers are out. This belief has gone so far that many students today suspect the value of any book that has not been reprinted in somebody's paperback series. I, myself, often have to suffer the pity of certain of my young friends when I insist that hardcover books are here to stay. To them paperbacks have a high public visibility--at bookstores, newsstands, drugstores, supermarkets, railroad stations, bus terminals, and airports everywhere. Besides, they have had the truth of the matter from their teachers and from numerous reporters, columnists, lecturers, TV commentators, and book reviewers.

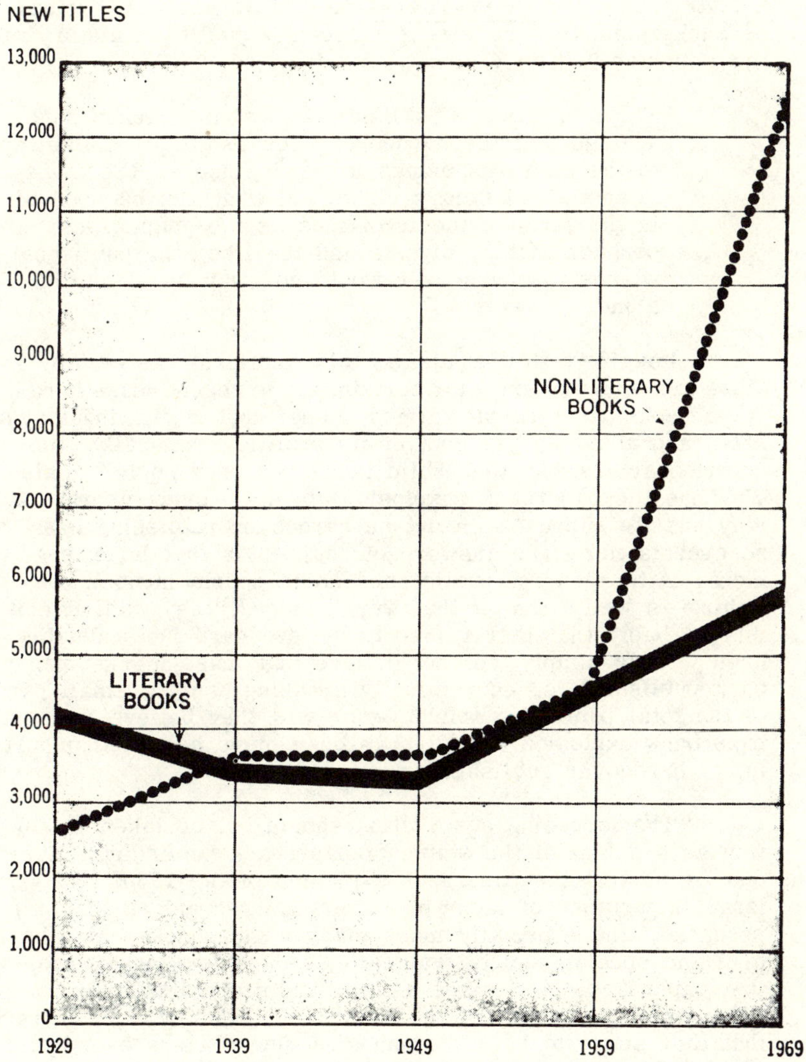
NEW TITLES
13,000
12,000
11,000
10,000
9,000
8,000
7,000
6,000
5,000
4,000
3,000
2,000
1,000
0
NONLITERARY BOOKS
LITERARY BOOKS
1929
1939
1949
1959
1969

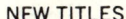

As an example of how the public can be misinformed about the fortune of paperbacks and the fate of hardcovers, a statement in The New York Times of January 31, written as background to a review of a recently published history of the Houghton Mifflin Company, read:

> The economics of publishing today has reached such a stage that the hardcover book is almost a liability to the man who brings it out. Since all the money is in the subsidiary rights, in what can be spun off in the form of movie options, stage adaptations, paperback rights, digests and the like, the publisher wishes the hardcover would go away and leave him alone.

Imagine with what dismay this statement was read by those insiders who know for certain that in recent years hardcover books have provided almost 90 per cent of our industry's sales and about 95 per cent of its profits. Naturally, the question arises why the public fancy has been so far misled. Why has the paperback "explosion" been so overcelebrated? Why has its supposed impact on hardcover publishing been so overstated? The answer, of course, is that large segments of the general public, and some people in book publishing as well, want it that way. Indeed, they want it that way so badly that they refuse to believe hard facts and figures. They simply will not believe that mass-market paperback publishing is, economically speaking, only a small part of the total publishing world. Nor will they believe that the paperback explosion actually has been more helpful than hurtful to hardcover publishing.

The foregoing observation should not be taken in any way as a denial of the status of paperback publishing. Everyone knows that the paperback explosion of the 1950s had large importance of its own. Everyone recognizes that paperbacks, and especially mass-market paperbacks, also have high and special societal values. The insider knows, too, that paperbacks have made a large indirect contribution to the overall prosperity of the U.S. book industry. He sees that they serve to hook thousands of new readers every year who would never have started on the hardcover stuff. Thus, he knows that the importance of the many millions of paperbacks sold each year is far greater than the dollar income and profit derived from their sale.

In this light, it is especially regrettable that paperback publishing had several difficult years in the second half of the 1960s. Although between 300 million and 350 million copies of mass-market paperbacks were sold annually, some of their major producers had rather rough going. The trouble came not from a lack of buyers, but rather from excessive payments for reprint rights and from costly competition for market outlets. Some of this trouble was offset by newfound success with what have been dubbed "instant paperbacks"--meaning quick reprints in large quantities of certain public documents of wide popular appeal, such as the report of the Warren Commission. These quick reprints, in some instances, have put paperback books into fairly direct competition with the news media, and thus have given a "new dimension" to the book industry.

In fairness, the quotation from the Times is true of fiction; still, fiction represents less than 10 per cent of the present annual output of new books. In any case, it appears that the Times reviewer, like most other outside observers of the publishing scene, was totally unaware of the great hardcover explosion that had occurred on the nether side of his world.

The striking aspect of the book market as a total aggregate is that, while the annual production of new books of all kinds increased by only 40 per cent in the three decades that ended in 1959, the increase in the subsequent ten years was over 100 per cent. It was inevitable, of course, that there would come with this sharp increase an intensification of the perennial cry that too many books are being produced. Unfortunately, this cry has been repeated through even the years of the book industry's greatest and soundest growth. It comes from certain breast-beating publishers who loftily call for "fewer and better books." What they plainly want, of course, is to cut out the other fellow's trash. Often they want also to eliminate all those dull "nonbooks" that no one ever sees.

Nearly all these advocates of fewer and better books are literary buffs. Observing the publishing scene narrowly, they look no deeper than the rising total numbers of books produced annually, and then declare positively that the market cannot possibly absorb so many new titles. Often they wail, correlatively, that quality is being sacrificed for quantity, that bad books are driving out good books, and that the book industry is going to hell in a crassly overloaded handbasket. Such talk has always been popular with literary audiences and with reporters looking for stories about the charismatic world of publishing. Yet, it has never made sense, and it never made less sense than in the 1960s. For example, how could the great increase in scientific and technical books have anything whatever to do with the quality of the new fiction of the decade? And did the slowdown in published general literature really improve its quality? No, the postulate of fewer and better books patently has no general value as a working principle for the industry.

Far from being choked up in recent years, book markets have actually been expanding rapidly in size and receptivity. In fact, sales of almost all kinds of books climbed sharply through the 1960s. In that decade, total dollar volume of industry sales increased by almost 150 per cent, from $1.106-billion to $2.760-billion. Much of this gain came, to be sure, from higher prices and inflated dollars-- about a fourth of it, roughly. With an adjustment for this inflation factor, the real ten-year gain was about 110 per cent. In the same period, the country's Gross National Product, after application of the same kind of implicit deflators, grew by only 50 per cent. It is clear, then, that the book industry's growth was far greater than that of the nation's economy as a whole.

In the longer view, looking back through the earlier years of sea change, the book industry as a whole in a way scored a truly remarkable long-term growth record, but in another way it seemed not to keep up with its true potential. Some interesting comparative figures on forty-year growth trends appear in Table II. According to these figures, the book industry in sales growth again far exceeded the long-term growth of the national economy. (The dollar figures for both book sales and GNP are adjusted to 1929 values-- and who won't be shocked to see that the 2.760-billion of 1969 sales dollars converts to only 1.290-billion of 1929 sales dollars?)

On the other hand, looking at the long-term growth in the nation's population of college graduates, one can ask whether the book industry has not failed to make the most of its growing opportunity. Assuming that college graduates represent the country's hard core of book buyers, it appears that publishers have not kept up with the natural growth of their markets. (In the forty-year period, the college graduate population increased only sixfold.) Indeed, it can be fairly said that the industry as a whole has been riding rather than making the long wave of its good fortune.

The publishers of educational and reference books rode high on the wave through the 1960s. The injection of massive federal funds into education and library budgets caused a soaring of sales that reached a truly dizzying height in 1966: In that year, an aberration in government disbursement practice caused most of the funds for two federal fiscal years to be spent in the one calendar year. In the following three years, there was a disappointing slackening in the sale of textbooks and related instructional materials, and of encyclopedias, dictionaries, atlases, etc. Still the publishers of such works, always more prosperous than general book publishers, never had it better. In the decade, their sales increased by 156 per cent. Their net profits failed to soar proportionately, largely because the costs of intensified competition exacted a heavy toll as more and more firms rushed to what was for them a newfound and unfamiliar mother lode.

Many inside observers were bemused by one particular behavioral response of educational publishers in the 1960s. This was the alacrity and enthusiasm with which many reputedly turgid textbook firms answered the call of educators for more and larger multi-unit instructional packages. When teachers began some years ago to move away from the conventional textbook as a monolithic instructional instrument, many textbook publishers pushed to the head of the parade. Sure, they could supply rather quickly the needed multiunit packages containing core text materials, supplementary readers, laboratory manuals, workbooks, tests, and whatever else was wanted. Some could, and did, supply even larger and more costly multimedia packages (including films and tapes), which were scooped up by the more affluent school systems and certain government-financed special programs. All this explains in part the juiced-up growth in the educational publishers' sales volume. It also explains how many an old-line textbook firm quickly acquired a refreshing stimulant and a higher sense of professional responsibility. Thus again did progress and prosperity go hand in hand.

The curious phenomenon that helped to produce in the 1960s an inordinate increase of scientific and technical books had a powerful effect on publishing through many years; I have called this, by analogy, the "twigging phenomenon." It can best be described as the continual furcation and fractionation of scientific and technical knowledge, and, hence, of the subject matter of books in these fields. Naturally, this endless fractionation has resulted in the publication each year of hundreds of highly specialized books for groups or readers that are no larger today than they were ten or twenty years ago, despite the fact that our total population of scientists and engineers has almost quadrupled in the past two decades. The specialists need and write books on proliferated and refined subjects; the technical publisher who properly serves his clientele must, of course, publish them in proliferated numbers.

In my analogy, the subjects of such books represent the twigs on the tree of scientific and technical knowledge. Although the tree itself is perhaps five times as big as it was twenty years ago, the twigs are still the same size-- and so are the markets for the specialized books. This phenomenon explains in large part why publishers of scientific and technical books have had to scramble to keep up with their markets, and why these particular markets have so readily absorbed the greatly escalated numbers of new titles published in the past decade.

Finally, another, but not so subtle, phenomenon that worked with force on the book industry in the 1960s was the wide impulse for corporate mergers and for related marriages, in some instances, between the electronics industry and book publishing. Many of the mergers were impelled by "cross-media" marriages, and all the latter were inspired by rationalized dreams of synergistically induced extra-dividend happiness. The industrial giants (hardware grooms) happily took to wife many carefully selected bedmates among the available book firms (software brides). "We have the hardware, they have the software," General Sarnoff is reported to have said when RCA acquired Random House in 1965.

Then what happened? It is, of course, too early to say for sure, but two things now seem quite obvious to insiders.

First, the hardware-software marriages, though widely celebrated in the press and greatly feared by many in the book industry, have been tried and found wanting. The synergistic effect has not come off as expected; to date, the unions have been disappointingly unproductive of profitable hybrids. Clearly, computers and books have not mixed so readily and effectively as many people believed they would.

Communication and Education

Table I: Books Published Annually--by Subject

Literary Books	1929	1939	1949	1959	1969
Biography	738	628	595	776	1,161
Fiction	2,142	1,547	1,644	2,437	2,717
General Literature	572	584	535	836	724
Poetry & Drama	727	657	574	499	1,254
	4,179	3,416	3,348	4,548	5,856

(Increase 1969 over 1929: 1,677 titles, or 40.1 percent.)

Nonliterary Books					
Agriculture	82	129	191	129	260
Business	213	357	306	422	683
Education	317	315	254	417	842
Sports & Games	130	219	235	259	734
Home Economics	53	148	263	181	314
Law	116	160	267	302	525
Medicine	402	431	450	590	1,190
Sociology & Economics	484	854	548	625	4,462
Science	424	523	676	1,033	2,353
Technology	359	461	455	736	1,035
	2,580	3,597	3,645	4,694	12,398

(Increase 1969 over 1929: 9,818 titles, or 380.5 per cent.)

Table II: Comparative Growth Figures

	Number of Titles Published Annually	Value of Book Sales* ($Million)	Value of U.S. GNP* ($ Billion)	Number of College Graduates (Million)
1929	10,187	$ 199	$ 104.4	1.7
1939	10,640	178	108.7	3.4
1949	10,892	NA	167.9	5.3
1959	14,876	675	244.3	8.3
1969	29,579	1,290	368.3	13.8
1969 over 1929 Actual	190 percent			712 percent
1969 over 1929 Adjusted		548 percent.	253 percent	

*Stated in 1929 dollars

Consequently, some high-powered grooms already have been heard to grumble about their brides, many of which were bought at quite fancy prices. At the same time, many relatively low-powered book publishers have unexpectedly been enjoying life as millionaires. Thus, by the end of the decade, the miscegenetic marriages were rapidly going out of style. Maybe we shall see some annulments or spin-off divorces in the 1970s. Even so, many publishing houses will have been provided, meanwhile, with more adequate working capital and more progressive management.

Second, the many mergers and cross-media marriages have not resulted, as widely supposed, in a baneful concentration of book publishing in the hands of a few large and powerful corporate complexes and conglomerates. To be sure, many independent houses, both large and small, have become operating units in a wide variety of much larger corporate structures. But, at the same time, many new and growing firms have come along to take their places in the ranks of the independents. In fact, contrary to popular belief, these ranks have been more than filled every year. Actually, there were more independent book houses in the United States at the end than at the beginning of the 1960s, just as there were more at the end than at the beginning of the 1950s. Anyone who doubts this statement can be self-convinced by counting the number of independent firms listed in Literary Market Place (Bowker's annual guide to book publishing) for certain years. He will find that there were 508 in 1949; 638 in 1959; and 675 in 1969.

No, the book industry is not about to be gobbled up or monopolized by a few large and sinister industrial octopuses--not, at least, for some time to come.

Collecting Modern Imprints

by G. Thomas Tanselle

Reprinted by permission from the Summer 1970 issue of The Book Collector (19:2), p. 203-213.

Some bookshop proprietors have the habit of trying to guess their customers' interests, by looking over the books the customers select, so that they can mention other related books currently in stock. Although I have encountered many such dealers, I have never yet found one who correctly guessed my reason for choosing whatever books I picked out; and when I have finally confessed the motive for my selection, some of the dealers have not been able to conceal their incredulity, occasionally tinged with ridicule. In one shop where I found a copy of Vincent Fuller's The Long Green Gaze, 1925, the clerk assumed that I was interested in mystery stories and mentioned a particularly good one which he had just purchased as part of a private library. When I replied that I was not looking for mystery stories at the moment, he concluded that I must be a devotee of crossword puzzles, for he was acquainted enough with the Fuller book to know that in it the resolution of the plot turns on the solution of a crossword puzzle. He therefore directed me to his understandably meagre supply of used crossword puzzle books, and I was forced to reveal that I was buying the book not because it was a mystery about crossword puzzles but because it was published by B.W. Huebsch. This statement left him at a loss, since he could not immediately lay his hands on another book published by Huebsch.

I do not mean to imply that the majority of dealers have never heard of imprint-collecting, for even the most unscholarly and provincial bookshop owner would not find anything unusual in an interest in Elzeviers, or Baskervilles, or Kelmscotts, or even Stone & Kimballs. Indeed, such dealers often have a shelf reserved for private press books or "gift editions" (invariably, in the United States, those of the Heritage Press); and they recognize that a major aspect of collecting has always been the search for books bearing the names of printers or publishers who played a significant role in the history of printing or book production. Bibliographies, like Philip Gaskell's of Baskerville and Sidney Kramer's of Stone & Kimball, have served to emphasize the importance of certain imprints and have caused dealers to be on the lookout for them; it is not uncommon, for example, to find--even in the average bookshop--the phrase "Stone imprint" pencilled into a book as a justification for its higher price. Bookdealers, in other words, are well aware of imprint-collecting because particular imprints have been publicized by collectors and scholars.

What came as a surprise to the dealer I have mentioned is that anyone would collect the output of a modern commercial publisher--not a printer, or a designer, or a private press, but an "ordinary" trade publisher. If many people collected such imprints, the idea would not have appeared novel to him, so his reaction is indicative less of ignorance on his part than of general indifference on the part of collectors. The interests of collectors have usually centred on particular authors or subjects; when collectors have sought books for their imprints, they have normally been concerned more with printing than with publishing, more with the work of fine (or historic) printers than with the products of important (or interesting) publishers. Although the uses of a publisher-collection are obvious, the traditions of bibliophily have not encouraged such collections, just as the emphasis on first impressions has tended, until quite recently, to turn attention away from many textually significant later impressions.

Even if the value of a publisher-collection as a research tool seems obvious, so few such collections exist-- either in private hands or in institutions--that some comment on this approach to collecting is perhaps in order. For the private collector, the attractions of collecting publishers' imprints are both financial and scholarly: in this area an individual need not spend much money to bring together a collection which makes a contribution to learning. For the institutional collector, the same advantages of course still obtain, since a relatively small outlay will procure a collection which can bring increased prestige to the institution as a research centre; the difficulty, however, from the rare-book custodian's point of view, is that the process of forming this sort of collection is extremely time-consuming, since the antiquarian book trade is not organized in such a way as to make an efficient procedure of the search for books by imprint. That is to say, one cannot quickly check a dealer's catalogue (except in rare cases) to see whether any books with a given imprint are listed, since there is usually no imprint index; and one generally does not have much success in presenting a dealer with a blanket request for a particular imprint, for his stock is not arranged by imprint and he cannot keep many such requests constantly in mind. Instead, one must perform the research necessary to construct a check-list of the imprint and then request the specific titles in the usual fashion; and institutional purchasers rarely have the time for this kind of research on any significant scale. Imprint-collecting is therefore a peculiarly appropriate form of collecting for the private individual: in pursuing it, he is not duplicating (or attempting to duplicate) the collections formed by institutions with considerably more money at their disposal, but he is performing a valuable service which institutions are not so well equipped to perform; indeed, one may predict that institutional libraries will look to individual collectors as the source for this kind of collection, ready-formed, to complement their author collections.

Of the two basic attractions which imprint-collecting has for the individual, the monetary perhaps requires less comment than the scholarly, since it is even more self-evident. In the case of publishers' imprints, a large part of the output of any given publisher is likely to be of little intrinsic interest--and therefore, at least for 19th- and 20th-century publishers, inexpensive. If one has decided to collect Mitchell Kennerley imprints, for example--because of Kennerley's distinguished typography as well as his willingness to experiment with the 'new' literature and to give a hearing to unknown writers who later became famous--one would have to purchase such works as E. Temple Thurston's The Garden of Resurrection: Being the Love Story of an Ugly Man, 1911, and Elsa Barker's Letters from a Living Dead Man, 1914. If one chose B.W. Huebsch--an ideal example of the one-man experimental firm which had a great impact on modern literature--one would be forced to procure Emily M. Bishop's Daily Ways to Health, 1910. All these books are quite cheap--and rightly so--when one finds them (they are not easy to locate); but they are essential for understanding the range of interests of these two publishers and the context out of which the more important books emerged. Thus a great number of books which are cheap, regardless of their scarcity, because they are of almost no interest in themselves, take on value when they are placed in a collection of other books bearing identical imprints.

At the same time, it goes without saying that the collector of modern publishers' imprints will not find all his desiderata so inexpensive. As collectors have always recognized, when one's own interests converge with another's on a particular item, prices must inevitably rise. Since Kennerley published work by Edna St Vincent Millay, Vachel Lindsay, Van Wyck Brooks, D. H. Lawrence and Joseph Hergesheimer, and Huebsch brought out early volumes by Sherwood Anderson and James Joyce, a collector of Kennerley and Huebsch imprints finds himself in competition with many other persons for books by these authors, and he must accordingly be prepared to encounter high prices (high, that is, in comparison to those asked for the average books of these publishers). H. G. Wells's The Door in the Wall (Kennerley, 1911) is sought by both Wells and Goudy collectors; Philip Dru, Administrator (Huebsch, 1912) is in demand by those interested either in its anonymous author, Colonel E. M. House, or in Woodrow Wilson's administration in general. A number of books bearing any given imprint, in other words, will be comparatively expensive; but the difference between imprint- and author-collecting is that, with imprints, the lesser (and often scarcer) items are not likely to be costly, whereas with authors--at least important or "collected" authors--the scarcer (and often lesser) works are decidedly expensive. In the case of printers' imprints this difference may not always be so great, for the quality of the typography and design of books printed by the Goudys or the Grabhorns, for instance, may have attracted enough attention for their prices to be high regardless of the merit of their contents. But this observation only reinforces the basic point: collecting imprints involves picking up many books which are of little interest except for their imprints, and, since relatively few imprints (both publishers' and printers') have been of interest to collectors, it follows that such books will generally be cheap.

If it is true that a large part of the output of any publisher is insignificant, or at least dull, what is the reason, one may ask, for going to the trouble of assembling all the volumes bearing that publisher's imprint? The fact that most of them are cheap is of course not a sufficient justification, though it is related to a quite important reason: for the lack of general interest in a book (with its resulting low price) does not necessarily mean that the book is useless but may instead indicate that the uses to which it can be put have previously been overlooked (or not widely recognized). If one grants that the history of publishing and printing is a legitimate field of inquiry, then complete collections of the output of individual publishers and printers, the raw material for such study, become desirable from a scholarly point of view, and in those collections each book, however trivial, plays its role. That collections of this sort have not been frequently formed in the past is no sign that they do not have purpose or value; and, for the very reason that they have not been formed so often as other types of collection, the person who turns his attention to them and builds up an integrated one can make an especially significant contribution to knowledge.

    When a number of related books are physically brought together, connections between them and generalizations about them often become apparent which would have escaped notice if the volumes were examined separately. In any case, drawing all the books issued by one publisher from an ordinary library stack requires previous knowledge of what titles to request--information which can sometimes, but not always, be extracted from the standard reference works of the book trade or from the publishers themselves. Some publishers, whose records no longer exist, were negligent in sending copies of their books to the Publishers' Circular or Publishers' Weekly offices for listing and prepared no catalogues or comprehensive advertisements. In such cases, a separate assemblage of the actual books is the only source for writing a history of the firm or for reconstructing its list; and, even when some form of external information is available, a collector constantly on the alert for a particular imprint often turns up titles (or editions) not otherwise recorded for that firm. There is no substitute, in other words, as far as the study of publishing history is concerned, for collections of books arranged by imprint and consciously formed with that purpose in mind.

    Such collections also serve useful purposes in the historical, textual and bibliographical study of the authors involved. In the same way that accurate literary history demands extensive knowledge of the minor literature of a period, against which the major works can be viewed in perspective, an acquaintance with the entire output of a publisher enables the student of a particular author to see more clearly the contemporary position which that author's writings occupied. Thus John Murray's predilection for nonfiction, particularly in his "Home and Colonial Library," helps account for the changes he requested in Melville's Typee, 1846. Similarly, textual work on Typee would be facilitated by a collection of the "Home and Colonial Library," if not indeed of all Murray's publications from the late 1840s, so that one could more reliably ascertain the degree to which a uniform house style existed and was imposed upon Typee. And, bibliographically, this collection would illustrate Murray's customary practices in regard to binding and the general physical appearance of his books, helpful collateral evidence for classifying various issues or states of Typee and perhaps for dating changes in binding designs, endpaper styles, and the like. There is no question but that modern textual and bibliographical scholarship would greatly benefit from readily accessible publisher-collections of this sort, for bibliographers are increasingly more aware of the fact that whatever book they are examining was not the only one with which its publisher (or printer) was concerned and that it must be examined in the context of the other books which he was producing at the same time.

The historical value of an imprint collection can be increased in various ways, by extending it both in breadth and in depth; and an individual who has nearly completed a collection of one publisher or a group of publishers has a number of options open to him for considerably enhancing the significance of his library. If I may turn to my own collection for a moment as an illustration, I can suggest a few of these directions. In the belief that there was a clearly defined group of American publishers, in the first three decades of this century, who were willing to take risks on new and experimental young writers and who thus bore the same relation to the large established houses as the "little magazines" and "little theatres" did to the popular commercial magazines and the Broadway theatre, I have been attempting to assemble the total output of these "little publishers" as one way of illuminating the literary milieu of a major period in American literary history. My principal attention has therefore been given to five imprints--Boni & Liveright, Huebsch, Kennerley, Knopf (pre-1930) and Seltzer-- but not to the exclusion of many lesser ones that served a similar function, such as Egmont Arens, N. L. Brown, Laurence Gomme, Lieber & Lewis and Frank Shay.

A list of the authors published by these firms reads like a rollcall of the leading figures in early 20th-century literature. Boni & Liveright could boast of T.S. Eliot, e.e.

cummings, Theodore Dreiser, Eugene O'Neill, Conrad Aiken, Hart Crane, William Faulkner, Robinson Jeffers, Edgar Lee Masters, Waldo Frank, and H. D. Knopf in the early years published H. L. Mencken, Willa Cather, George Jean Nathan, Wallace Stevens, T. S. Eliot, Conrad Aiken, Carl Van Vechten, Adelaide Crapsey, Floyd Dell, Arthur Davison Ficke, Witter Bynner and Arthur Waley, and he was the American publisher for the Sitwells, Dorothy Richardson and Katherine Mansfield. Huebsch's list included Sherwood Anderson, Van Wyck Brooks, D. H. Lawrence and James Joyce, while Kennerley was the first publisher of Edna St. Vincent Millay and Vachel Lindsay, and Seltzer brought out many of D. H. Lawrence's works (in some cases before they appeared in England) and the Scott Moncrieff translation of Proust. Although these publishers were essentially similar--in their interest not only in whatever was new in literature but also in liberal approaches to political and social issues--they nevertheless had distinctive characteristics. Kennerley and Knopf, for example, devoted considerable attention to typography and produced the most handsome volumes physically; Huebsch expressed his concern with economic and political questions by publishing the work of Thorstein Veblen and many books on India; Knopf--to an even greater extent than Seltzer and Huebsch--made European fiction known in the United States; and Boni & Liveright--even more than Seltzer and Kennerley--issued great quantities of fiction, often with sensational titles, to help offset the small sales of their poetry, drama and essays. The related smaller publishers reflected the same interests on a lesser scale: N. L. Brown and Lieber & Lewis were particularly drawn to foreign writers, while both Shay and Arens published plays performed in the little theatres of New York, and Gomme (who was associated with Kennerley in the Little Book-Shop Around the Corner) issued poetry (Joyce Kilmer, Braithwaite's annual anthologies, <u>Eight Harvard Poets</u>) and essays by John Jay Chapman.

Since all the publishers in this basic group had their headquarters in New York, one way to expand the collection in breadth was to represent other sections of the country. Accordingly, I have added to the list certain publishers of Chicago (Covici-McGee and R. F. Seymour, who, despite frequent lapses in taste, served as outlets for writers of the area, such as Harriet Monroe, A. D. Ficke, Alice Corbin, Ben Hecht and Maxwell Bodenheim), San Francisco (A. M. Robertson and Paul Elder, both interested in book design and in local writers), and Boston (John W. Luce--influential promoter of foreign literature--and Badger and Four Seas--

early and illustrious examples of the "vanity" publisher, whose lists included E.A. Robinson, William Faulkner, Conrad Aiken and Gertrude Stein). Indeed, the geographical extension could well proceed abroad, for a characteristic of most of these publishers was their effort to promote the "new" writers of England and Europe, as well as of the United States; copies of the overseas editions of the works they published, therefore, would form a useful adjunct to the collection, valuable both for an investigation of their relations with other publishers and for textual study.

Another principle of expansion, besides the geographical, is the chronological. In order to illustrate the American publishing scene in the years just preceding my main period of concentration, I have selected for extensive collection several of the most interesting publishers of the 1890s: Stone & Kimball and Way & Williams of Chicago, William Doxey of San Francisco, R.H. Russell of New York, and Copeland & Day and Lamson Wolffe of Boston--publishers whose names often appeared in joint imprints with such English firms as John Lane and who illustrate (in both the content and the design of their books) most aspects of the fin de siècle. Then, to place all these publishers of the 1890-1930 period in the context of the whole development of American publishing (and printing), I am trying to put together a selection of books which will represent every year from about 1775 to the present and every part of the country. Such a group of books, if carefully limited and controlled, can sometimes reveal basic patterns and trends more effectively than can a large library, where those patterns may be obscured by the exigencies of housing and classification. All forms of publication should ideally be included (such as the literary annuals, the cheap reprints in elaborate bindings, the paper-covered series of the 1890s, the paperbacks of the 1940s); and even the years covered by the main collections (that is, 1890-1930) are to be represented, so that there will be at hand a sampling of the output of the major established firms against which to view the work of the newer, more experimental publishers. A card catalogue of the entire collection, indexing the books not simply by author and title but by imprint, place and year as well, can be developed into a useful tool for research, particularly since few library catalogues are organized in this fashion for 19th- and 20th-century books.

If techniques such as these broaden the range of an imprint collection, there are other ways of increasing its depth--particularly by giving attention to later printings, dust-jackets, ephemera and manuscripts. Thus, for my main publisher-collections, I am concerned with obtaining not simply the first impression of each book but every impression. To have all the successive printings of a work together is naturally of inestimable value for textual study and descriptive bibliography; in addition, many of these publishers carefully identified and dated each impression on the verso of the title-page, and sometimes--when a publisher's records do not survive or are inaccessible--the only way to establish the printing history of a work is to examine these dates in the books themselves. In any case, one would expect a collection organized around publishers to contain material illustrating those publishers' practices in handling later printings and showing the relative popularity of their books in terms of the numbers and dates of new impressions. Because copies of later printings have not been sought after so assiduously as those of first impressions, they are generally much cheaper; but for that reason they have often been discarded and are sometimes scarcer than the firsts. This part of a publisher-collection can therefore be built up at a moderate cost and at the same time be extremely valuable for historical and bibliographical research.

The same points could be made about the other ways of strengthening a collection in depth. Like later printings, dust-jackets are frequently disregarded and difficult to locate but sometimes contain material not elsewhere available (such as the texts of comments by well-known persons) and are essential for descriptive bibliography and for understanding a publisher's style of advertising and design. Similarly, any kind of ephemera--advertising leaflets, broadsides, promotional pamphlets, catalogues, bookmarks, subscription blanks, and so on--reflect the character of the publisher, sometimes preserve information that would otherwise be lost, and often are desirable items in their own right. Among my Boni & Liveright material is a brochure issued in 1925 to promote Dreiser's books, containing essays by Sherwood Anderson, Edgar Lee Masters, and H. L. Mencken; my Kennerley collection includes one of Kennerley's blue shipping labels, which is also an example of Goudy typography. Finally, it goes without saying that any sort of manuscript material-- even seemingly routine letters or inscriptions to or from a publisher--may shed light on that publisher's relations with his authors or on his general method of operation.

All this is obvious, but not many collectors over the

years have formed collections of this sort. In a day when the kinds of books which have traditionally been collected are fetching extremely high prices and are rapidly disappearing into institutional collections, the private collector--or even the librarian of a young institution--may find himself turning into less familiar (and therefore, perhaps, more exciting) paths. I have described the collecting of modern publishers' imprints as one such direction--one in which an individual of limited means can have the satisfaction of manipulating a considerable quantity of books, sometimes insignificant in themselves, in such a way as to create (through imaginative selection, arrangement and cataloguing) a context that reveals their potential importance. Mitchell Kennerley in 1945, long after he had stopped his own publishing, wrote an article for the American Mercury (LX, 361-6) to explain the fascination of unusual imprints and the pleasure of finding them on the bargain tables of used-book stores. He was describing a casual approach to collecting, but he recognized the historical value which an imprint can lend to an otherwise dull book. And he would have agreed that, true to the highest traditions of bibliophily, much of the excitement comes from putting together and shaping an entity within which individual items take on significance, for only through this process can order and some degree of understanding be brought to the past.

Charles Bukowski
and the Little Mag/
Small Press Movement

by Sanford Dorbin

Reprinted by permission from the May 1970 issue of
Soundings (2:1), p. 17-32.

I

   Poetry in America today is a lot like jazz--joyful, sad, vital, vulgar, exalted, and full of that strange historical sense our situation squeezes like juice from a lemon out of those of us who don't know how to blink the facts.

   Anything that can be reasonably called "the poetry audience" in the United States at present probably consists of no more than four thousand people--in a country of two hundred million. It is likely half of these are poets. Unacknowledged legislators indeed!

   The poetry scene in the U.S. since the end of World War II has been incredibly rich and varied, yet no public exists for it. (Some say poetry stopped speaking publicly after Shakespeare. Some say Dryden, or Yeats. Doubtless the running warfare among poets today as to what poetry is has helped turn people off.) So for most people poetry is what the large, mostly New York-based trade publishers say it is. And mostly they say it is unsalable. Even so, their production does encompass enough titles each year to include a few actual poets as well as the latest song offerings of America's leading athletes and popular singers, and others of our spiritual leaders.

   A Controversy of Poets (Anchor Books, 1965), an anthology edited by Paris Leary and Robert Kelly, was put together with the intention of featuring the best poets of the principal "schools" of poetry--two ways of writing, really, and to permit each editor to polemicize in behalf of his own bias in an appended essay.

Aside from A Controversy of Poets, and Donald Allen's anthology The New American Poetry (Grove Press, 1960); aside from the late Alan Swallow of Denver and James Laughlin, whose New Directions imprint has done more than everyone else together to bring significant poetry to American audiences since the Spanish Civil War--aside from these and the occasional book whose publication is as welcome as it is inexplicable, American trade publishers have pretty much foreclosed on serious poetry.

Most of our poets, understandably, have tended to concentrate their interests and efforts in the so-called "Little" magazines and the small press movement.

II

The little magazine/small press movement as it exists today is peculiarly a twentieth century phenomenon. The nearest historical parallel that comes easily to mind is that stage of Rome when "publication" consisted of the public reading of a poet's latest work. (Next day someone stood out on the street and passed out papyrus or parchment sheets bearing the poem, or painted it on corner walls.) The little magazine is mostly a state of mind. It is inherently international, impecunious and avant-garde. (For avant-garde read politically and socially heterodox, literarily unfashionable by virtue of its experimental nature.) The post-World War II little magazines spring from a noble lineage. One thinks of publications like Egoist (London, 1914-19); Little Review (Chicago, 1914-29); Wyndham Lewis's Blast (London, 1914-15); T.S. Eliot's Criterion (London, 1922-39); Ezra Pound's Exile (Dijon, Chicago, 1927-28); Transition (Paris, Den Haag, 1927-38); Furioso (New Haven, 1939-53); Tiger's Eye (New York City, 1947-49); and Trace (London, Hollywood, 1952-to date). Transition One appeared in April 1927; its contributors included James Joyce, Gertrude Stein, Archibald MacLeish, Hart Crane, Philippe Soupault, Max Ernst and Georg Trakl.

Times have changed, but only somewhat. Fewer American writers live abroad. ("I am not the kind of rat that deserts a sinking ship," Robert Duncan once said.) And even though society is, as they say, more permissive in respect of literature, stuffiness and timidity still exist in the academic community. At least one important little magazine of recent times was born of institutional censorship; I refer to Big Table, whose first issue contained "the complete contents of the suppressed Winter 1969 Chicago Review." University of Chicago administrators desired that William Burroughs, Edward Dahlberg and others should appear in expurgated texts, or not at all. (See editor Irving Rosenthal's editorial in Big Table One, 1960). Big Table went only five issues but its pages were lively and noteworthy.

Like conversation in general, the format of little magazines is less formal nowadays; anyone with the inclination and enough bread for paper and the use of a mimeo machine may become a little magazine editor. He understands that just as corporations have unlimited, so little mags have (very) limited life.

The small press movement is clearly an outgrowth of the little mag scene, and symbiotic with it, thru (meager) advertising revenues and directory listings. The recent organization of an overall consortium, COSMEP (Congress of Small Magazine Editors and Publishers) may help, but just now the poet's situation in particular is so scandalous that even an "established" poet like Clayton Eshelman regards small press publication as no more than a species of vanity publication (see his "Open Letter to George Stanley" in Caterpillar 8/9). Our libraries seem to be the last outposts of that enlightened anarchy without which the more innovative manifestations of culture would simply not exist. The UCSB Library is a case in point: the holdings of the Department of Special Collections in new American poetry are as large and varied as those of any library in the world. And the presence there of the Charles Bukowski Archive seems as miraculous as the celebrated beerbottle of his that somersaulted off the edge of his table and landed upright on the floor with contents intact.

oct. 1966

THE ORIGINALS

hello Ann:
    night off but Frances left Marina with me, Bukowski the nursemaid, and hard to type because she keeps wanting the attention bit and you can't blame her and all that and ect. and ect.   etc., I mean.
    listen, on the poems, I only want the poems back if they decide not to print them. if they go with them I don't care what happens to the copies.
    on obscenity obscenity whatever, I don't know much about it, exept that it (the charge or talk about it) frightens and bothers so-called honest writers. to me there is nothing obscene about sex or bodily fuction (tho both become a mess sometimes); the only obscenity is bad writing on the subjects. good writing or pure Art is never obscene no matter what the subject, wordage, painted or sculped matter. I don't think a hell of a lot more than that can be said. I suppose then it is only up to us to decide what is good, what is Art or what is not. and that's where roads and swords cross--Artistic moralities. what may be Art to me may not be Art to you and therefore obscene, or the other way around. and the line of demarkation is different in each of us. in other words we are never going to agree-- you or I or anybody else, just what is obscene and what isn't. so no need for me to go on talking about it.
    rejects are part of the game for anybody who plays around in it like you and I, and since we've been on the giving end ourselves we know how much easier it is to give then to receive, as the old saying goes.
    Marina keeps doing things and I have to watch her or she'll set the place on fire or drown us, so this nervous short letter.... meanwhile, hang on in.

    love,

    Buk

III

I was born August 16th, 1920, Andernach, Germany ...something to do with the war. Old man American soldier. Brought his German wife and me over here in 1922 and the land was gifted with a hardmouth poet...I stood around a lot as a kid and I didn't learn much. I am still in the process. Went to Los Angeles City College for two years--journalism, art and diddling; only the latter has held water for me. I didn't go to the war.

In my 20s, I thought I was a short story writer and I starved in little rooms and wrote hundreds of short stories, 5 or 6 a week, sending them to the Atlantic Monthly and Harper's, and, naturally, they all came back running and punched in the mouth. I finally landed one in the old Story Magazine, the one with the orange cover. Then I said to hell with it and got drunk for ten years. Then I started writing again and this time poetry. Had luck. Five books of collected poetry...

The self-description is taken from the cover of Cold Dogs in the Courtyard (Literary Times-Cyfoeth, 1965), his seventh book. The words suggest a kind of life that hardly exists any longer for those over thirty.

In fact, Henry Charles Bukowski is the archetypal dropout; he was a dropout two decades before the phrase was invented--disaffiliated, disenfranchised by choice. But courageous and crazy enough to look at the world and himself just the way they were, and to report back. This is why, apart from the intrinsic power of his art, Bukowski is so important to us: there simply are no people left who can, or care to, bring us news of those particular precincts.

By his prodigious output Bukowski has practically defined the geographical boundaries of the little mag/small press movement: sixteen books and chapbooks, another dozen-and-a-half broadsides and pamphlets, some tape recordings, a phonograph record. Over six hundred periodical and anthology appearances in twenty-three states, the District of Columbia and six other countries. The names of some of these magazines and particularly their places of publication give some idea of the flavor of "the underground" and where it's at: Steppenwolf (Omaha); The Goodly Company (Kalamazoo); In/sert (Portland); South and West, Spectroscope, and Border (all of Fort Smith, Arkansas); Evidence (Toronto); Wanderlust (Metaire, Lousiana); Klactoveedsedsteen (Heidelberg); Inconolatre (West Hartlepool, Durham); Copkiller (New Orleans); Moonstones (Niagara Falls); Showcase (Barstow, California); Labris (Lier, Belgium); Jacaranda and Ferment (both of Canton, Missouri); El Corno Emplumado (Mexico D.F.); Scimitar and Song (Sanford, N.C.); Literary Artpress (Cheney, Washington); The Anagogic and Paideumic Review (San Francisco and Half Moon, California); The New Lantern Club Review (Houston); The Wormwood Review (Storrs, Connecticut, and Stockton, California) and Mica (Santa Barbara). These are just some of them. He's even had a poem in American Turf Monthly.

> get your name in LIGHTS
> get it up there in
> 8 1/2 x 11 mimeo

he said, making fun of himself as much as the others. It reminds us of Farrells's credo: "I'm looking for an audience, I aim to get famous." But Bukowski gets the last laugh too, because he has achieved a kind of fame, circumscribed but genuine, and, more importantly, based on a genuine achievement. In America particularly, that is

THE MIRACLE

> To work with an art form
> does not mean to
> screw off like a tape-worm
> with his belly full,
> nor does it justify grandeur
> or greed, nor at all times
> seriousness, but I would guess
> that it calls upon the best men
> at their best times,
> and when they die
> and something else does not,
> we have seen the miracle of immortality:
> men arrived as men,
> departed as gods--
> gods we knew were here,
> gods that now let us go on
> when all else says stop.

His books and chapbooks (etc.) cover much of the same uncharted territory--expeditions into the bibliographically obscure. E.V. Griffith, his first book publisher (<u>Flower, Fist and Bestial Wail,</u> 1960) is the editor and publisher of a necrophiliac combine out of Eureka, California. (E.V. edits <u>Hearse: A Vehicle Used to Convey the Dead</u>) which was resurrected last year after eight years of suspended animation. His brother, Jon, edited <u>Gallows</u>, which succumbed after two issues, 1959 and 1962.)

Bukowski's second chapbook was a special issue of <u>Epos</u>, a little mag out of Crescent City, Florida. Third was <u>Longshot Pomes For Broke Players</u>, brought out by the pre-Fugian cultural comic Carl Larsen, who in his spare time edited a little mag called <u>Rongwrong</u> in New York City. Others of Bukowski's publishers have mined for their modicums of immortality in Chicago, New Orleans, Bensenville, Illinois, Cleveland, Los Angeles, Glendale, North Hollywood, Madison, Wisconsin, Albuquerque, and Santa Barbara.

Of his many editors and publishers, Douglas Blazek particularly should be mentioned here. Blazek is himself a poet of power--see Gershon Legman's The False Revolt (Breaking Point, 1967) for praise from an unexpected source. As editor of Olé, Blazek published some of Bukowski's earlier poetry plus some of his correspondence and other prose (book reviews e.g.); as publisher of Mimeo and Open Skull Press, he brought out two of Bukowski's books of prose. Confessions of a Man Insane Enough to Live with Beasts appeared in 1965; it is the prototype of Bukowski's best known book, Notes of a Dirty Old Man. In 1966 Blazek brought out a chapbook entitled All the Assholes in the World and Mine, Bukowski's scatologico/autobiographical account of a hemmorrhoid operation received courtesy of the Los Angeles County's Bureau of Charities. Blazek moved to the Bay Area a few years ago and with Dust editor Len Fulton became one of the founders and tireless workers in behalf of COSMEP.

Another element of the little magazine/small press movement that should be mentioned is that of the graphic artist. Besides the mimeo and offset productions, a few really fine letterpress little magazines exist. Two that come immediately to mind are Jon and Louise Webbs' The Outsider (particularly the latest and, we are told, last issue--double number 4/5), out of Tucson; and Clifford Burke's Hollow Orange (San Francisco). Taken side by side, these two show how much two magazines can differ from each other in size, design concept, etc. and still both be examples of fine printing. (The Webbs also printed and published Bukowski's fifth and sixth books. These have been widely praised, and have won awards for graphic arts excellence. Some people--the present writer includes himself--feel that these books are self-consciously typographical; interesting, perhaps even fascinating at times in their various parts, but not really books, that is--vessels. But there can hardly be any dispute as to the accomplishment The Outsider 4/5 represents in little mag production.

Bukowski figures in this respect too. His second chapbook, the special issue of Epos, included three of his drawings. Since then a number of his books as well as some of his newspaper and magazine appearances have featured his own art work. In the realm of improbable formulations, one might write an essay on this theme called "The Poet as his own Book Illustrator."

IV

Given hostility and indifference to his work in the academic community, it must have taken a certain amount of courage for a university library to purchase the Charles Bukowski Archive. And beyond the fact that it gets a lot of student use, UCSB is an appropriate place for it, housed as it is in the Department of Special Collections, within burning distance of Morris Ernst's Banned Books Collection and the Collection on Marie Stopes, Sex and Birth Control.

We would expect the archive of a still-working writer to contain about the same materials as that of a dead writer. It should tell us much about the man and his work, and, finally, something about the time in which he lived--hopefully a great deal.

An inventory gives some idea to what extent the Charles Bukowski Archive fulfills these hopes. Together with the Library's previously acquired holdings of published materials, there are copies of all of Bukowski's books, chapbooks, pamphlets and broadsides, including half-a-dozen variants of different kinds--binding variants, extra-illustrated copies, and the like. There are copies of the one tape recording and the one phonodisc which were commercially released. The other segment of published material includes newspaper, magazine and anthology appearances, and various association items. Because of his amazing productivity there are over 500 items in this section, mostly little mags but including, too, a number of underground newspapers. (Bukowski was a contributing editor to Open City, and appeared in ninety of its ninety-four issues. These alone are roadmaps to what has become known, now that hippie fashions, language and music have been taken over by the great society, as "alternate culture.")

Among unpublished materials the Archive includes typescripts, galley proofs, holograph mss. material, notebooks, letters and memorabilia.

In the case of some authors, galley proofs of material about to be published and referred to him for final corrections and/or additions are of great importance. Bukowski rarely has patience to proofread or a desire to correct or add. He tends to trust editors until having a reason not to, and he has an almost heroic indifference to other people's errors.

Doubtless the most valid negative criticism of Bukowski is that he has published too much, i.e. too much bad stuff. (One is reminded of Eliot's observation about Byron and the wastebasket.) That being so, the amount of unpublished mss in the Archive is startling. The quality is uneven but there is the same great range of subject, method and mood as in the very best of his published poetry, and much of it is worthy of publication. Here is one such; it might be called "wine-haiku" but in fact its title is:

THE IMMORTAL BOMBS,
THE STINKING FEET OF GOD, BE QUIET

the white-grey
vanilla ash of a
cigartip resting

as the crickets
bring it on in
through the
window

A lot has been written in little magazines about Bukowski's correspondence. "The Bukowski-McNamara Letters," excerpts from the correspondence between Bukowski and editor Tom McNamara appeared in two issues of Down Here in 1966 and 1967. Certain others of his letters to various little magazine editors have appeared in their magazines. And references to and about his letters have appeared in the writings of certain of his confreres (Blazek, Steven Richmond, William Wantling, et al). The letters are amazing--again, one is staggered by the sheer number of them; it seems incredible that all this production, poems, stories, books of poems, letters and drawings were the production of a man working, and working the deadliest, most soul-destroying kind of work: stock boy, farm and casual labor, post office nightclerk. And Bukowski has been particularly conscientious in seeing to it that we realize how much of his time went into playing the ponies, courting the ladies, tossing booze and being bonged into and bailed out of the hoosegow.

He also found time to write letters which show, beyond the brusque images put forward by idolators and enemies alike, gentleness, intelligence and humility. I should like to quote two paragraphs from one of them. (Addressed to Ann Mennebroker of Sacramento, this letter might be considered an installment of that nineteenth century convention "a literary romance." See the Bukowski poem of that title.) The letter bears the heading "l.a. a Saturday night of radio screaming some opera; myself with cigar and beer. I'd guess it's 8 September, and, I'm told, 1966." in upper left-hand of page, with the printed holograph notation opposite "THIS ONE TOO LAYED AROUND A WEEK, B."

very odd thing happened today. I got a letter from a streetsweeper in Munich, Germany, and he showed a magazine (English-printed in Germany, the editor is a dishwasher) to a postcard seller on the street, an old man, and the old man read my long poem in the mag to a group of young people in the streets, translating from English to German as he went along. this is enough to chill hell out of me. I was originally born in Germany and once spoke the language as a child but now can no longer speak or understand it. and here was this old postcard seller reading one of my poems in GERMAN, in the streets of the land I was born in. who says we don't return? who says that miracles never happen? unfortunately, the long poem is printed with a couple of pages reversed (Vagabound 2 is the mag), but the message still seems to get through, so what the hell? you've got to write pretty strangely to have your poem printed in any order, but, since, in this one I was talking of the old mysteries of the soul plus the good fight, it read almost sensibly. good.

meanwhile, another German magazine Klacto has taken a couple of my poems. the editor of this one is also very poor. what are all these poor men doing? what crazy souls they possess! it is good to have your own courage but it is also good to take hope and courage from the ways of others. this I haven't been able to do until lately. some very very strange people are arising, Ann. but mostly they are not arising in America. there is something about this land and its ways that kills almost everybody. there doesn't seem room or reason for the truly living creature.

The remaining material in the Archive, unclassified and unclassifiable, certainly warrants use of the term memorabilia. It includes, besides the usual ephemera (adverts, announcement mailers, etc.) the likely trappings of a modern Archilochus: annotated racingforms, bail bondsman's contracts, form letter from Los Angeles County's Bureau of Charities stating the balance owed for the hemmorrhoid operation. There is also a large portfolio of drawings and paintings, most of them melted crayon drawings and those line drawings which have appeared in several of his books and with some of his magazine appearances. There are also drawings and paintings that go back to his LACC "journalism, art and diddling" days: cows at pasture, a rotting but still imposing Bunker Hill mansion, now demolished no doubt, like Bukowski, superannuated by the new--glass, concrete and plastic.

Apart from this, the unpublished materials in the Archive include 224 typescripts (mostly poems, published and unpublished), 138 TLS, 17 ALS and four spiral notebooks, all of which contain published and unpublished poems

270 Library Lit.

and prose, plus drawings and columns, rows and pages of figures that may pertain to either theories of composition or How To Beat The Horses, or possibly some unlikely synthesis of the two.

V

    Obviously what we have here is not the Great American Success Story. Or is it? It is surprising to find a man of fifty who believes he can live life on his own terms, say 80% of the way, and not go under. <u>Poetry</u> you say?

    No wonder young people feel such a strong affinity with him. Dropping-out may be the opposite of giving-up, but it's a difficult lifestyle: don't hold on to things, don't gather about you, let things happen and get with the happenings. Synchronicity, Huxley called it. Maybe it's not a matter of choice at all, but some beneficient (or malefic) thing inside people that just happens. The automobile down the road, 3:40 AM, incense burning hypnotically in the ashtray and a calm inward voice advising "Don't make plans, baby."

Bukowski decided early in the game to adopt the tough guy image. For one thing he was a tough guy (prize fighter, slaughter house worker, etc.). Also, coming on tough protected him somewhat from the praise of his friends at the same time it made him an easier target for detractors. (Detractors are a necessary counterbalance against the inclination to feel like a prince, one's inmost desires to believe one's friends and to coast. They force a man to stay inside and keep banging away.)

Of course the problem is that he was typed. No doubt there is such a thing as "the Bukowski poem." Never mind that Bukowski also writes other kinds of poems. Now he was defined, laboratory-tested, ready for packaging and market. So "the Bukowski poem" is direct, colloquial, and says pretty much what it seems to say--often with an abundance of those words Ladies Auxiliary ladies don't admit understanding the meaning of. It reminds us of Hugh Kenner on Archilochus, "the expletive function of language."

But the Bukowski image lends itself to ridicule, and the Bukowski poem lends itself to parody--precisely the way and for the same reasons a passionate priest's sermon does.

Mostly, Bukowski's critics have accused him of being monoblastic. The tough guy, without wit, tenderness, subtlety or any particular brains. The more hostile of these seem to be the less secure of the Black Mountain poets, and those of that particular persuasion. Their fulminations were especially acrid in the mid-1960s. Predictably, Bukowski and his own disciples responded in kind. Ho-hum, another literary war.

This particular war seems to have had its genesis in professional jealousy, dressed now in one of those artificial aesthetic arguments--in this case the one about "abstract" art being a "higher" form than gut-level realism. Bukowski's enduring popularity simply rankles. Therefore it is more amusing than anything else that A. Frederic Franklyn, who wrote the most destructive essay on Bukowski to date ("The Soi-Disant Plaintiffs," in the Fall 1964 issue of Grande Ronde Review), recently appeared in one of the porno mags that frequently features Bukowski.

As a matter of fact, Bukowski's latest book, The Days Run Away Like Wild Horses Over the Hills (Black Sparrow Press, 1969), encompassing fifteen years of his poetry, was intentionally conceived as a retrospective exhibit. In approximately three minutes one could compile an impressive-enough subject index to prove beyond a reasonable doubt the point about his range. For example, faithlessness (FREEDOM, SELF-DESTRUCTION, A DRAWER OF FISH); faithfulness (UAUGUAY OR HELL, MINE, NOTICE); fatherhood (BIRTH, KAA-KAA AND OTHER IMMOLATIONS); the spoof (WHAT A MAN I WAS, SCENE IN A TENT OUTSIDE THE COTTON FIELDS OF BAKERSFIELD); the parody (THE SEMINAR); the artist and his patron (THE GREAT ONE), and Daumier-like social commentary (POEM FOR PERSONNEL MANAGERS:, PEACE, DID I EVER TELL YOU?, EVEN THE SUN WAS AFRAID, YELLOW, THE UNDERGROUND, FINISH, ONE FOR GING, WITH KLUX TOP).

So much for the single-layered onion. Like any other writer of power, Bukowski is able to satirize a particular image of himself (in this case, the myth of his savagery) and still produce an authentic poem.

THE FLOWER LOVER

in the Valkerie Mountains
among the strutting peacocks..
I found a flower
as large as my
head
and when I reached in to smell
it
I lost an ear lobe
part of my nose
one eye
and half a pack of
cigarettes
I came back
the next day
to hack the damned thing
down
but found it so
beautiful I
killed a
peacock
instead.

VI

What makes Bukowski stand out now, in 1970, is that he hasn't folded up and died the middleclass death, hasn't copped out and gone straight. In fact, he's just kicked his eleven year habit (post office gig). For him this meant sticking letters on the swingshift; while those of us who live in and around our mailboxes drift to sleep at night thinking, among other automated fantasies, "By golly it can't <u>all</u> be bad, that mail is being whisked onto planes and heading toward me right now." But some whacked-out sap that comes in at four or five and works till midnight every night but Fridays and Saturdays is perched on a stool like a worn cape and shoving that mail whose voyage we rhapsodize into steel cases that bear coded numbers that become the streets where we live. Then home to write the rest of the night.

This is not an obit. Mr. Bukowski is still on De-Longpre and beer, alive and (reasonably) well. Regularly published in <u>Evergreen Review</u>, awaiting royalties from foreign translations, and so forth. But he hardly believes he has it made. Libraries and collectors may soon rebel against the slick gougings of those few of the small press people who are playing the limited editions game for all its worth. The general economic chaos we're all living in could wipe out this heady independence in the motion of a horse's hoof. He knows all this. Smokes, pops another top, listens. Writes.

"my poems are only bits of scratchings/on the floor of a/cage" he wrote in a modest moment. Most of them are more like the screw's wood across the cell bars. Surprisingly often a kind of music comes of this.

Feature Films in Your Library

by Paul Spehr

Reprinted by permission from the April 1970 issue of
Wilson Library Bulletin (44:8), p. 848-855. Copyright
1970 by the H.W. Wilson Company.

Do you have Fellini in your library? Bergman? Welles? Eisenstein? How about Georges Méliès, John Ford, or, for that matter, D.W. Griffith? You do? You have books by and about them...and even published copies of their film scripts? Why don't you have their movies? Not possible? Well, perhaps one can make it so. My point is that it is possible, desirable, and at some time in the future it will be mandatory for university and public libraries to serve movies to interested scholars.

The straws are already in the wind. In colleges and universities all over the United States (and in all the rest of the world, for that matter) students are taking up the study of film almost as fast as the courses can be added. In fact, the supply of teachers is far behind the demand. In 1969, the American Film Institute surveyed the situation in the United States and determined that there are now 219 institutions of higher learning offering some sort of film course and 51 offering degrees (5,300 students were working toward degrees). This may not seem to represent enough of a flood to cause you to remake your library collecting habits, but it does represent a significant trend. The American Film Institute estimates that this constitutes an increase of 85 percent in the past five years. High schools, too, are beginning to offer film courses.

Course changes and student enthusiasms do not constitute just cause for revising long-range growth programs and changing next year's budget. The factor which makes this a development of uncommon importance is the intrusion of cinema into the exclusive world of art, culture, and intelligence.

The young people flocking to cinema courses in college, struggling to express themselves with camera and splicing cement, are convinced that the film is an integral part of cultural expression. To those in the embattled older generations, this may not appear as a truism and may require some justification. The American cinema developed as a part of cheap, popular entertainment and it continues to maintain this tradition. Sometimes lost in the midst of this flood of popular diversion are unique examples of a new, contemporary art form, one that is so new that it is still trying to define itself and is frequently far too apologetic for its existence. Anyone who regularly attended the films of the sixties or is going to film society screenings of older "classics" knows that there is little to be apologetic about. The increasing number of "serious" film makers are creating art, culture, and intellectual communication of the most vigorous and far-reaching sort.

The ever-increasing tide of students is now searching for film material to study in the traditional way that they have learned to study other intellectual disciplines. They find that films are difficult or impossible to find without expensive trips to Washington, New York, Rochester, or even to London or Paris. The alternative is to persuade some film society to book the desired film or take the chance that a shrivelled and chopped version will appear on the local TV tube.

It is not that public and university libraries have no film programs. Of course these programs exist and in some cases have been very active for years. The scholar's problem is that the program is not really oriented to the film as film (or cinema, or art, or whatever term you prefer). The basic emphasis of such programs is on the film as an auxiliary material--on the film as supplementary matter to biology, physics, community relations programs, etc. Public library (or State educational system) films are selected because they are good films about something or because they are good for somebody (children, old people, poor people, black people, or all people). This is not an evil situation in itself. The audiovisual programs have a place within the institution, but it is sad that selection of films of cinematic merit is given such perfunctory treatment within the selection system.

A shift in emphasis in your film program will inevitably bring you face-to-face with two problems which I am sure have already occurred to you. The first is the high costs of such a program and the second is the extreme difficulty of purchasing the films.

Money Matters

Costs are inevitable in the motion picture field. Even if it is possible to purchase films at the minimum laboratory costs, a half hour of 16mm film will cost at least $40 for a black-and-white sound film and about $80 for color. A feature-length film will cost from $120 to $500. The costs for 35mm film run much higher (it may comfort you to learn that for a public library 35mm film is probably impractical). If there are even minimum profits involved, the cost of purchasing films reaches levels which panic administrative officers and other executives of the exchequer. If you add the cost of projectors ($500 for the bottom of the line), film cans, film handling, and inspection equipment, it is no wonder that the salaries of audiovisual librarians remain low. Money has to be saved somewhere along the line!

Costs of this nature must be carefully planned for and realistically met. Far too often, planners avoid the total required and begin from half-way. This results in halfway growth by a process of attrition, a system which punishes both user and librarian. If the full costs are recognized, it will become obvious that the costs will have to be shared by large, interlibrary programs (metropolitan, regional, etc.). Such programs, carefully considered, can seek additional funds from foundations or government, and provide full, rather than partial service.

Unavailability, or, the Film Flam Game

The matter of obtaining films is an equally thorny problem. At present, practically no "theatrical" films are available for sale to public libraries. There appear to be two factors responsible for this situation. First is the limited demand on the part of libraries, which means that the potential for sales is small. Second, and far more basic, is the tradition of exclusive ownership which has been the keystone of the marketing system of the American motion picture industry. Screening copies of theatrical films are very rarely sold on the open market. Distribution depends on lease and rental to the exhibitor, and reissue for purposes other than theatrical showing usually is done by very restrictive contract--the owner of television rights may not rent for 16mm exhibition and the owner of 16mm rights may not display on television. Such contracts ordinarily prohibit resale. Therefore, no matter how desirable it might be to own Citizen Kane, Persona, Dr. Strangelove, 8 1/2, On the Waterfront, La Chinoise, or some other contemporary cinema gem, they just don't appear on the market.

It appears unlikely that this situation will change immediately, but there are some factors which offer hope for increased film availability. The well known Hollywood companies had been owned by the same management since the time they were founded, usually fifty or more years ago. In recent years, these companies, one after another, have been passing into the hands of large investment corporations. New management and new competition from TV and foreign sources have forced the industry to search for new ways of sustaining itself. It seems likely that the management must inevitably respond to new market demands.

Evidence of response to new demands appears in the form of the growth and expansion of distribution companies renting 16mm films to students and to film societies. Several major Hollywood companies have founded 16mm subsidiaries or have expanded existing operations. Two pioneer companies in this field, Brandon Films and Contemporary Films, have been purchased by larger corporations that promise more expanded operation.

This response to new demands comes despite a particularly sensitive reaction on the part of the nation's theater owners who have, for the past twenty-five years, faced perplexing problems of deteriorating theaters, increasing competition from television and foreign films, increasing costs, and the by no means crucial but rather frustrating demands from film enthusiasts who desire older films but cannot agree which ones they want to see. These exhibitors, always the most conservative part of the industry, became more protective as they felt more vulnerable. They had a particularly strong reaction to what some exhibitors felt was undue competition from the student and film society movement, and the reaction came at a time when these groups were beginning a period of significant growth. This has meant that the past fifteen to twenty years have seen rather strong pressures to inhibit the availability of films desired by the small groups of cinema enthusiasts and by students.

The new 16mm film distribution companies offer more

films than ever before; however, rental films have specific
and stringent restrictions placed upon their use, and rental
rates have risen sharply. More significant to the librarian
is the confusion which confronts the potential film user who
is finding it more and more difficult to locate the film he
wants.

Library Service to Film Enthusiasts

As an immediate improvement in library service to
film scholars and enthusiasts, information about film sources
needs to be expanded in almost every library. An excellent
basic reference tool is James Limbacher's Feature Films on
8 and 16 Mm (New York, Educational Film Library Association), a book all too often missing from library shelves.
This should be supplemented by catalogs from the major theatrical distributors and film periodicals serving both film
enthusiast and film scholar. A list of some of these catalogs and journals is appended.

There are two things which can bring the library directly to the scholar's service. First is an effort on the
part of the professional organizations in the library field to
reach the organizations of the commercial movie industry--
the producers, distributors, and exhibitors--to develop a
precedent and program for library service in films. This
has never existed before, with the exception of films made
for educational or promotional purposes. The librarians
should approach the industry with a proposal to use the feature film as a scholarly reference tool, serviced to individual film scholars, in a program quite devoid of any other
use, particularly exhibition of the films. It should be
stressed that such a proposal would be unique in the film
field. Proposals for public screenings always raise the fear,
however remote, of commercial competition. The appeal
made by the librarians to the film industry should be one
which would raise the industry from showmanship to scholarship. This is exactly what the young film students feel is
necessary.

Regional depository collections of film classics might
be developed and made available to member libraries, where
scholars could view the films on small screen viewing machines such as the Moviola Library-Reader, or adapted film
editing machines such as the German Steenbeck machine.
These machines permit the scholar to control the viewing of
films himself--stopping and starting at will and re-running

if desired--while assuring privacy of viewing and a minimum of wear and tear on the films.

Separate programs geared to audience viewing might be developed, so long as it was clear that they had nothing to do with the service being provided to the film scholar.

A proposal for regional libraries providing this service was made at the time the American Film Institute was founded in 1967. At the present writing, no specific proposal has been forthcoming from them, but they do have a program for promotion of educational activities. It would seem most logical that this program, if it is developed, should find a home in the institutions best geared to serving the multiple needs of the scholar--the university and public libraries. Otherwise, the programs will come about but will develop as separate libraries, unrelated to collections of books, periodicals, and manuscripts which the scholar has a right to find in one location.

The second factor which can improve library service to film scholars is the training of film librarians. At the present time, film training and library science are separate disciplines, frequently unavailable at the same school. Only students with individual initiative can obtain training in both fields and almost no effort is made to relate the two. Furthermore, should the library science student prepare himself for work with films, there is little or no possibility that there are jobs waiting for him. It seems axiomatic that if any program to provide the film scholar with library service is developed, it must be done by well trained professionals who have a background in the history, aesthetics, and some of the technology of the motion picture field.

Trained film librarians, given a well planned and carefully developed program, can answer the needs of the generation of students who are now coming to the libraries in search of their world of knowledge, their new dimension of communication. They have a right to expect that their intellectual demands will be met with intellectual resources.

Motion Picture Distributors

Catalogs may be obtained from the following companies or organizations that sell, rent, or lease feature-length motion pictures. Some distribute interesting short films, too. I have also included some distributors of experimental or underground films.

Audio Film Center, 34 MacQuesten Parkway South, Mount Vernon, N.Y. 10550.

Blackhawk Films, Eastin-Phelan Corp., Davenport, Iowa 52808.

Brandon Films, Inc., a subsidiary of Crowell Collier and Macmillan, Inc., 221 West 57th Street, New York, N.Y. 10019.

Canyon Cinema Co-operative, Room 220, Industrial Center Building, Sausalito, Calif. 94965.

Center Cinema Co-op, 540 North Lake Shore Drive, Chicago, Ill. 60611.

Cinema 16/Grove Press, Cinema 16 Film Library, Inc., 80 University Place, New York, N.Y. 10003.

Columbia Cinematheque, Columbia Pictures Corp., 711 Fifth Avenue, New York, N.Y. 10022.

Contemporary Films/McGraw-Hill, 330 West 42nd Street, New York, N.Y. 10036.

Continental 16, a division of the Walter Reade Organization, Inc., 241 East 34th Street, New York, N.Y. 10016.

Walt Disney Productions, 800 Sonora Avenue, Glendale, Calif. 91201.

Em Gee Film Library, 4931 Gloria Avenue, Encino, Calif. 91316.

Embassy Pictures Corp., 1301 Avenue of the Americas, New York, N.Y. 10019.

Film Classic Exchange, 1926 South Vermont Avenue, Los Angeles, Calif. 90007.

Film-Makers' Cooperative, 175 Lexington Avenue, New York, N.Y. 10016.

Films Incorporated, 4420 Oakton Street, Skokie, Ill. 60076.

Fleetwood Films, 34 MacQuesten Parkway South, Mount Vernon, N.Y. 10550.

Ideal Pictures, 34 MacQuesten Parkway South, Mount Vernon, N.Y. 10550.

International Film Bureau, 332 South Michigan Avenue, Chicago, Ill. 60604.

Janus Films, 24 West 58th Street, New York, N.Y. 10023.

Mogull's, 112 West 48th Street, New York, N.Y. 10019.

The Museum of Modern Art, Department of Film, 11 East 53rd Street, New York, N.Y. 10019.

The Newsreel, Box 302, Canal Street Station, New York, N.Y. 10013.

Radim Films, 220 West 42nd Street, New York, N.Y. 10036.

Rogosin Films, 144 Bleeker Street, New York, N.Y. 10012.

Trans-World Films, 332 South Michigan Avenue, Chicago, Ill. 60704.

United Artists 16, 729 Seventh Avenue, New York, N.Y. 10019.

Universal 16, a division of Universal City Studios, 221 Park Avenue South, New York, N.Y. 10003.

Warner Brothers-Seven Arts, Inc., 16mm Non-Theatrical Division, 666 Fifth Avenue, New York, N.Y. 10019.

Cinema Periodicals, a selected list

The periodicals listed here include a variety of approaches to the cinema. Some deal with film as an art form, others as leisure, education, trade, or commerce. All of them, with the exception of Cahiers du Cinéma, are English-language publications.

AFI Education Membership Newsletter. The American Film Institute, Education Department, 1815 H. Street, N.W., Washington, D.C. 20006.

The American Cinematographer. 1782 North Orange Drive, Hollywood, Calif. 90028. (Monthly.)

Box Office. 825 Van Brunt Boulevard, Kansas City, Mo. 64124. (Weekly.)

Cahiers du Cinéma. 63 Avenue des Champs-Elysées, Paris-8, France. (Monthly.)

Canyon Cinema News. 5313 Rosalind Avenue, Richmond, Calif. 94805.

Cinéaste. 27 West 11th Street, New York, N.Y. 10011.

Cinema. 9667 Wilshire Boulevard, Beverly Hills, Calif. 90212. (Quarterly.)

Cinema Journal (Journal of the Society of Cinematologists). Radio-TV-Film Department, William Allen White School of Journalism, University of Kansas, Lawrence, Kans. 66044 (attn. Richard D. MacCann).

Classic Film Collector (formerly 8mm Collector). 734 Philadelphia Street, Indiana, Pa. (Quarterly.)

Daily Variety. 6404 Sunset Boulevard, Hollywood, Calif. 90028. (Daily except Saturdays, Sundays and holidays.)

Film Comment. 100 Walnut Place, Brookline, Mass. 02146. (Quarterly.)

Film Culture. G.P.O. Box 1499, New York, N.Y. 10001. (Quarterly.)

The Film Daily. 1600 Broadway, New York, N.Y. 10019. Also publishes Film Daily Yearbook. (Daily except Saturdays, Sundays and holidays.)

Filmfacts. Box 213, Village Station, New York, N.Y. 10014. (Semimonthly.)

Film Heritage. Box 42, University of Dayton, Dayton, Ohio 45409.

Film Library Quarterly. 101 West Putnam Avenue, Greenwich, Conn. 06830.

Communication and Education 283

Film News. 250 West 57th Street, New York, N.Y. 10019.
(Six times per year.)

Film Quarterly. University of California Press, Berkeley,
Calif. 94720.

Film Society Review. 144 Bleeker Street, New York, N.Y.
10012. (Monthly, Sept. through May.)

Film World and AV Newsmagazine. 672 South Lafayette
Park Place, Los Angeles, Calif. 90057.

Films and Filming. 75 Victoria Street, London SW1, England. (Monthly.)

Films in Review. 31 Union Square, New York, N.Y. 10003.
(Monthly except summer, when published bimonthly.)

Filmmaker's Newsletter. 80 Wooster Street, New York,
N.Y. 10012. (Monthly, except summer.)

The Hollywood Reporter. 6715 Sunset Boulevard, Hollywood,
Calif. 90028. (Daily, except Saturdays, Sundays and
holidays.)

The Independent Film Journal. 165 West 46th Street, New
York, N.Y. 10036. (Biweekly.)

Journal of the Society of Motion Picture and Television Engineers (SMPTE). 9 East 41st Street, New York, N.Y.
10017. (Monthly.)

Journal of the University Film Association. c/o Mr. Robert
W. Wagner, ed., Motion Picture Division, Department of
Photography, 156 West 19th Avenue, Ohio State University,
Columbus, Ohio 43210.

Motion Picture Daily. Quigley Publishing Co., Rockefeller
Center, 1270 Sixth Avenue, New York, N.Y. 10020.
(Daily except Saturdays and Sundays.)

Motion Picture Exhibitor. Jay Emanuel Publications, 317
North Broad Street, Philadelphia, Pa. 19107. (Weekly.)

Motion Picture Herald. Quigley Publishing Co., Rockefeller
Center, 1270 Sixth Avenue, New York, N.Y. 10020.
(Biweekly.)

Sightlines. Educational Film Library Association, 17 West 60th Street, New York, N.Y. 10023.

Take One. P.O. Box 1778, Station B, Montreal 2, Canada

Variety. 154 West 46th Street, New York, N.Y. 10036. (Weekly.)

List of Feature Films

The list of feature films which follows is not intended to be a list of "all-time-great-classics." Several standards have been applied to determine appropriate titles. Among these standards are: artistic merit, historical importance, popularity, and critical acclaim. A few are personal favorites. Several are films which I do not really like, but others are ones I am enthusiastic about. A number of titles are included because they represent types or important trends, and if your mind says to you that another related title is better than the one I have included, please feel free to mentally substitute it. The list is terminated in the early 1960s.

A Trip to the Moon. Georges Méliès, Star Films, 1902.

The Great Train Robbery. Thomas A. Edison, 1903.

His Trust and His Trust Fulfilled. Biograph Co., 1911. (director, D.W. Griffith)

The Birth of a Nation. D.W. Griffith and Epoch Producing Corp., 1915.

Intolerance; a Sun-Play of the Ages. D.W. Griffith, 1916.

Shoulder Arms. Charles Chaplin, 1918.

The Cabinet of Dr. Caligari. Ufa-Decla Bioscop, 1919. Released in the U.S. by Goldwyn Pictures Corp., 1921.

The Toll Gate. William S. Hart Co., 1920. Paramount-Artcraft.

The Last Laugh. Ufa Films. Released in the U.S. by Universal, 1925.

Nanook of the North. Robert J. Flaherty and Pathé Ex-

Communication and Education 285

change, Inc., 1922.

Battleship Potemkin. First Studio of Goskino, 1925. Released in the U.S. by Amkino, 1926.

The Freshman. Pathé Exchange, 1925.

Greed. Metro-Goldwyn-Mayer Pictures, 1925.

The Gold Rush. Charles Chaplin, 1925. Released by United Artists.

The General. Joseph M. Schenk, 1926. Released by United Artists.

Sunrise. Fox Film Corp., 1927.

Secrets of a Soul (Geheimisse der Seele). Ufa, 1926.

The End of St. Petersburg. Mezhrabpom-Russ, 1927. Released in the U.S. by Arthur Hammerstein Enterprises, 1928.

October (The Ten Days that Shook the World). Sovkino, 1927. Released in the U.S. by Amkino, 1928.

Storm Over Asia. Mezhrabpomfilm, 1928. Released in the U.S. by Amkino, 1930.

The Passion of Joan of Arc. Société Générale des Films, 1928.

The Wedding March. Paramount Famous Lasky Corp., 1928.

Variety. Produced by Ufa, 1926. Released in the U.S. by Famous Players-Lasky Corp.

The Jazz Singer. Warner Bros. Pictures, Inc., 1927.

All Quiet on the Western Front. Universal Pictures Corp., 1930.

The Blue Angel. Ufa and Paramount-Publix Corp., 1931.

Frankenstein. Universal Pictures Corp., 1931.

Kameradschaft. Nero Film A.G., 1931.

Scarface. Howard Hughes, 1932. Released by United Artists.

King Kong. RKO Radio Pictures, Inc., 1933.

Gold Diggers of 1933. Warner Bros. Pictures, 1933.

Queen Christina. Metro-Goldwyn-Mayer Corp., 1934.

Top Hat. RKO Radio Pictures, Inc., 1935.

Modern Times. Charles Chaplin, 1936. Released by United Artists.

The Spanish Earth. Contemporary Historians, 1937.

Snow White and the Seven Dwarfs. Walt Disney Productions, 1937.

Grand Illusion. Realization d'Art Cinématographique, 1937. World Pictures Corp.

Ninotchka. Metro-Goldwyn-Mayer, 1939.

The Wizard of Oz. Metro-Goldwyn-Mayer, 1939.

Stagecoach. Walter Wanger Productions, 1939. Released through United Artists.

Gone With the Wind. Selznick International and Metro-Goldwyn-Mayer, 1940.

The Grapes of Wrath. Twentieth Century-Fox, 1940.

Citizen Kane. Mercury Productions, 1940. Released by RKO Radio Pictures.

Shadow of a Doubt. Universal Pictures Co., 1942.

The Magnificent Ambersons. A Mercury production. Released by RKO Radio Pictures.

Desert Victory. British Ministry of Information, 1943.

The Miracle of Morgan's Creek. Paramount Pictures, 1944.

Open City (Roma, Città Aperta). Excelsa Films, 1945-6.

To Have and Have Not. Warner Bros. Pictures, Inc., 1945.

La Belle et la Bête. Andre Palvé, 1946. Released in the U.S. by Lopert.

Les Enfants du Paradis (Children of Paradise). Tri-color Films, 1946.

Shoeshine (Sciuscià). A.L.F.A. Cinematographica. Released in the U.S. by Lopert, 1946.

The Postman Always Rings Twice. Metro-Goldwyn-Mayer, 1946.

Great Expectations. Cineguild. General Film Distributors, 1947.

Home of the Brave. Screenplays II Corp., 1947. Released by United Artists.

Monsieur Verdoux. Chaplin Studios, 1947. Released by United Artists.

Paisan (Paisà). Organization Films, 1947. Released in the U.S. by Mayer-Burstyn.

Odd Man Out. J. Arthur Rank. A Two Cities Film. General Film Distributors, 1947.

Symphonie Pastorale. Gibe Film for Pathé Cinema, 1948.

Hamlet. Two Cities Films, 1948. Released in the U.S. by Universal-International.

Key Largo. Warner Bros. Pictures, Inc., 1948.

Louisiana Story. Robert J. Flaherty, 1948. Released through Lopert.

Yellow Sky. Twentieth Century-Fox, 1948.

The Heiress. Paramount Pictures, Inc., 1949.

The Bicycle Thief (Ladri di Biciclette). DeSica Productions; S.A.F.A. Studios. Released in the U.S. by Mayer-Burstyn, 1949.

The Third Man. London Films, 1949.

The Treasure of the Sierra Madre. Warner Bros. Pictures, Inc., 1948.

Sunset Boulevard. Paramount Pictures Corp., 1950.

Lavender Hill Mob. Ealing Studios, 1951. Released in the U.S. by Universal Pictures.

Tales of Hoffmann. London Films, British Lion, 1951.

High Noon. Stanley Kramer Co. Released by United Artists Corp., 1952.

Rashomon. Daiei Kabushiki Kaisha. Released in the U.S. by RKO Radio Pictures.

The Robe. Twentieth Century-Fox, 1953.

From Here to Eternity. Columbia Pictures, 1953.

Marty. Hecht-Lancaster Productions. Released by United Artists, 1954.

On the Waterfront. Horizon Pictures, 1954. Released by Columbia Pictures Corp.

La Strada. Ponti-deLaurentis. Released in the U.S. by Paramount Pictures Corp.

Around the World in Eighty Days. Michael Todd Co., 1956. Released by United Artists.

Pather Panchali. Presented by Edward Harrison, 1958.

The Seventh Seal (Det Sjunde Inseglet). Svensk Film Industri, 1957. Released in the U.S. by Janus Films.

Paths of Glory. Bryna Pictures, 1957. Released by United Artists.

The Defiant Ones. Lomitas Productions, Inc. & Curtleigh Productions, Inc., 1958. Released by United Artists.

Breathless. Produced by Georges de Beauregarde. Released in the U.S. by Films-Around-the-World, 1961.

The 400 Blows (Les Quatre Cents Coups). Les Films du
 Carosse et Sedif. Presented by Zenith International, 1959.

Ballad of a Soldier. Mosfilm. Released in the U.S. by
 M.J.P. Enterprises and Kingsley International, 1960.

L'Avventura. Cino del Duca. Released in the U.S. by Janus
 Films, 1961.

My Life to Live (Vivre sa Va). Union Films release presented by Pathé Cinema Corp., 1963.

Hiroshima Mon Amour. Argos-Daiei-Pathé Overseas Production. Released in the U.S. by Zenith International, 1960.

Out on a Limb with the Critics:
Some Random Thoughts on the Present State
of the Criticism of Children's Literature

by Paul Heins

Reprinted by permission from the June 1970 issue of
The Horn Book Magazine (46:3), p. 264-273. Copyright 1970 by The Horn Book, Inc.

To be a critic -- a literary critic -- is almost by definition, to be out on a limb. In addition to being in a precarious position, one never knows whether one will be top-heavy and crack the limb because of his weight or whether somebody will come along with a saw. Either way, the position is fraught with danger. Yet, since critics rush in where angels fear to tread, there must be some justification or explanation for their existence.

I do not think we have to be concerned about the criticism of what might be called adult literature. Aristotle started the business long ago, and it is enough to mention Coleridge and Goethe, Dr. Johnson and Matthew Arnold, I.A. Richards and Allen Tate, to show that whenever literature is produced, critics are sure to follow. What does concern us, however, is the criticism of children's literature -- a formidable task, and much more difficult than the criticism of adult literature.

Children's literature -- for good or for bad -- is not the concern of children alone. Parents, teachers, and librarians as well as authors, illustrators, and publishers are potential judges of books for children. Questions of suitability and vocabulary jostle with personal likes and dislikes, and there is always the question of whether a particular book written for children will appeal to children. We have also been made painfully aware of the fact that we are dealing with a generation conditioned by television; and we are being told that children's literature should be realistic and should absorb, in some form or other, the social and psychological problems of the day.

Even a philosopher can say something -- at times --
that has a bearing on children's literature. In 1957, Suzanne K. Langer, in Problems of Art: Ten Philosophical Lectures, made a number of statements worth considering:

> Every generation has its styles of feeling. One age shudders and blushes and faints, another swaggers, still another is godlike in a universal indifference. These styles in actual emotion are not insincere. They are largely unconscious -- determined by many social causes, but shaped by artists, usually popular artists of the screen, the jukebox, the shop window, and the picture magazine. (That, rather than incitement to crime, is my objection to the comics.)

Furthermore, she comes to a rather stringent conclusion about what she calls "art education"; and if we think about children's literature at all, it does not seem too farfetched to consider it in the category of the arts.

According to Mrs. Langer, "Art education is the education of the feeling, and a society that neglects it gives itself up to a formless emotion. Bad art is corruption of feeling." How many of us are willing to say that the moving-picture versions of Mary Poppins and Dr. Dolittle were bad art? Some of us will, because we believe that each picture version failed to capture the spirit of the book on which it was based. How many of us would go so far as to say these cinematic productions were not only bad art, but -- because they were bad art -- were corrupt in feeling? I, for one, am willing to say so.

Incidentally, critics of children's literature have frequently spoken up against shoddy methods and shoddy productions. Perhaps three of the most famous Horn Book articles represented this kind of frontal attack on mediocrity: "Walt Disney Accused" (Frances Clarke Sayers, Horn Book, December 1965), "Not Recommended" (Ruth Hill Viguers, Horn Book, February 1963), and "An Imaginary Correspondence" (Rumer Godden, Horn Book, August 1963), which delightfully accomplished its aim indirectly -- by satire, humor, and irony. The chief value of this kind of criticism -- of debased classics, of vocabularized texts -- consists of clearing the decks for a more positive kind of criticism.

It has been said that people who insist that they have no philosophy or no religion will ultimately, in the course of conversation or discussion, reveal their explanation of the universe or of the beliefs which guide their lives. We are all critics whether we know it or not; and every time we pass judgment on a book or express enthusiasm for it, we are engaging in a critical act.

In her recent amusing book The Girl on the Floor Will Help You, Lavinia Russ speaks of "that crashing bore of a question which inevitably totters into any discussion of children's books, 'Are they written for children or for adults?'" Now, Mrs. Russ is naturally entitled to her opinion, not to say to her emotions; but she immediately follows up her condemnation by adding two statements: "She [E. Nesbit] didn't write for adults; she didn't write for children; she wrote for herself. Not her adult self, but to please and delight the child in herself -- the child she remembered with fondness." In spite of her boredom, in spite of her initial outburst, Mrs. Russ was drawn into an act of criticism; and although she did not develop a point of view at length -- as did Eleanor Cameron in her article "Why Not for Children?" (Horn Book, February 1966) -- Mrs. Russ was actually delivering herself of an opinion on a topic which -- as she herself states -- unavoidably crops up in many discussions concerning children's literature. Mrs. Russ is a critic in spite of herself.

Children's books and authors, naturally, are not exempt from the random impressions and evaluations of readers. Perhaps the time has come for the criticism of children's literature to be more conscious than ever before of its existence -- and better still, of its function. It should learn to speak with precision and to qualify its enthusiasms. There is certainly available a large body of worthwhile children's books that invites critical consideration. As a matter of fact, because of the proliferation of good books for children during the last fifty years, the era has been termed a "golden age."

Incidentally, the term "golden age" is not without its difficulties. It can be a confusing term, for it seems that there are two golden ages. Both of them are mentioned in John Rowe Townsend's brief but excellent literary history, Written for Children: An outline of English children's literature. In it we find an interesting summary of the last years of the first golden age:

> In children's literature at least, the opening years
> of the century were the last of a golden age.... the
> shortest of short lists... must include nearly all of
> E. Nesbit's work and much of Kipling; the play of
> Peter Pan; The Wind in the Willows; The Secret
> Garden; and -- Beatrix Potter's splendid little books
> for small children.
>
> The Victorian-Edwardian era ended gloriously.

Elsewhere in Townsend's book, the two golden ages are brought into focus:

> The half century before 1914 was the first golden
> age of children's literature. The second golden age
> is now.

In A Critical History of Children's Literature, Part Four is entitled The Golden Age 1920-1950. (In the Revised Edition of A Critical History of Children's Literature (1969) this section is entitled Golden Years and Time of Tumult 1920-1967.) In this book, the term is applied to children's literature in both the United States and England, and Ruth Hill Viguers naturally discusses both American and English books. In "The Book and the Person" (Horn Book, December 1968), Mrs. Viguers names more than two dozen men and women who during the twentieth century have written outstanding books that "give pleasure to children"; and in her list of "...Twentieth-century Children's Books Every Adult Should Know" she supplies titles by thirty authors. Although voices are occasionally raised deploring what the uninitiated call the inadequacy of children's literature, students of children's literature and people working with books and children know that there is almost an embarrassment of riches.

Along with the growth in the number of outstanding books for children, there has crystallized a feeling -- to use Eleanor Cameron's words -- that "children's literature does not exist in a narrow world of its own, but is enmeshed in a larger world of literature...." Moreover, this perception of the locus of children's literature carries with it a further consequence. To quote again from Mrs. Cameron: "the highest standards of the one hold good for the other." And more than twenty years ago Bertha Mahony Miller wrote in a Horn Book editorial (May-June 1946):

> Arts flourish where there is sound critical judgment

to examine and appraise. The critic must, first of all, have a real point of view about his subject. The essential point of view grows out of acquaintance with the best children's books past and present, and also with the world's best literature for everyone.

This high standard for the criticism of children's literature may be seen exemplified in such works as Books, Children and Men and The Unreluctant Years. It continues with unabated significance in Mrs. Cameron's recent volume The Green and Burning Tree.

About the relationship between children's literature and literature in general, John Rowe Townsend also has made some clear and definite statements:

> I believe that children's books must be judged by much the same standards as adult literature. A good children's book must not only be pleasing to children: it must be a good book in its own right.
>
> Where the works of the past are concerned, I have much faith in the sifting process of time -- 'time' being the shorthand for the collective wisdom of a great many people over a long period of time.... Survival is a good test of a book.... With present-day books, the sifting process is incomplete and judgments [Townsend is modestly referring to his own] are provisional.

But what of reviewing? Is reviewing criticism, or should it be criticism? Actually, criticism cannot be kept out of reviewing. Even the short capsulelike review cannot avoid making some critical comment, and a long review tends to become a critical essay.

What is the function of reviewing? I know of no better discussion of the subject than is found in a pamphlet published by the Hogarth Press in England in 1939. Entitled Reviewing, it was written by Virginia Woolf, some of whose previously unsigned reviews have recently been identified and republished in the London Times Literary Supplement. She states her observations in a definitive manner. When reviewing rose in importance at the beginning of the nineteenth century, "Its complex task was partly to inform the public, partly to criticize the book and partly to advertise its existence." During the present century, "The critic is separate from the reviewer; the function of the reviewer is partly to sort current literature; partly to advertise the author; partly to inform the public." Present-day authors will doubtless acquiesce in her opinion that "it is a matter of very great interest to a writer to know what an honest and intelligent reader thinks about his work." And when Virginia Woolf states that "It is impossible for the living to judge the works of the living," one recognizes the confession of an honest reviewer, who was also a critic in her own right.

Although a review serves the practical purpose of giving information and of advertising -- using the word in its Woolfian sense -- it cannot avoid making certain critical gestures. To consider only children's books: Of the thousands published yearly, how many of them is it physically possible to review? If a journal, like The Horn Book Magazine, reviews only books considered worthy of mention, the very task of selection is, by its very nature, a task of criticism -- of judgment. Any form of literary classification, comparison, or evaluation must also be considered a form of criticism. Actual -- one should even dare to say serious -- criticism will occur only when judgments are being made in a context of literary knowledge and of literary standards. If a reviewer perceives clearly the intention of the author and states it, the author will surely appreciate the intelligence -- that is, the critical acumen of the reviewer. If the reviewer tries to indicate how well the author has succeeded in accomplishing his intention, the reviewer -- once again -- assumes the role of the critic.

Reviewing, however, is only concerned with what is imminent in publishing, with what is being produced at the present time; and does its job well by selecting, classifying, and evaluating -- evaluating for the time being. Criticism deals with literature in perspective and places a book in a larger context -- be it historical, aesthetic, psychological, or what you will. I deliberately say "what you will" for there are -- as we all well know -- Marxian critics, Thomistic critics, and psychoanalytical critics, who concern themselves with evaluations which are not always purely literary.

As I have suggested before, the reviewing and criticism of children's literature is more complex and more fraught with misconceptions than any other kind of reviewing and criticism. If children's literature -- at its best -- is worthy of consideration with the rest of literature, if the understanding and appreciation of children's literature is to lead to the development of relevant and reliable criticism, one must never forget that the term children's remains a specifying term and, willy-nilly, must be respected.

It is certainly important and necessary at times to consider children's literature purely as literature. Questions of style, structure, and technical subtlety are as applicable to children's literature as to any of the other branches of literature. Julia Cunningham's Dorp Dead (Pantheon) may be considered as an exemplar of the Gothic novel; and one could learn much by comparing the structure of her story with that of Jane Eyre. Incidentally, a good reviewer's critical apparatus should obviously include a wide knowledge of universal literature. The reviewer of Scott O'Dell's The Dark Canoe (Houghton) who confessed to an ignorance of -- that is, of having never read -- Moby Dick could scarcely begin to do justice to Mr. O'Dell's book, whatever its ultimate literary significance or value may be.

However, even if children's literature should be considered as literature, it does not cease to be children's literature. But, unfortunately, there is no simple, or clear and easy way by which to determine the proper relationship between the term children's and the term literature. The most one can do is to consider a few varying points of view.

To ask a child invites defeat. Often his response is primitive or rudimentary; a child's enthusiasm for a book is much better indication of what the book means to him and does for him than any direct answer to a question posed at him. Jean Karl, editor of children's books, Atheneum, has stated the child's case with great common sense:

> No book is for every child and no book should be made to appeal to every child. A book is made to be loved and cherished by the child it is right for and rejected by those who prefer others.

Or one may consider the point of view of the literary purist, as in Brian Alderson's article "The Irrelevance of Children to the Children's Book Reviewer" (Children's Book News, London, January-February 1969). One may agree with Mr. Alderson that such remarks as "My Euphemia loved the tasteful blue and yellows" does not get one very far; but when he states that

It may be objected that to assess children's books without reference to children is to erect some absolute critical standard relating neither to the author's purpose or the reader's enjoyment. To do much less, however, is to follow a road that leads to a morass of contradictions and subjective responses, the most serious result of which will be the confusion of what we are trying to do in encouraging children to read.

I wonder whether Mr. Alderson has not sidetracked one of the chief problems in the consideration of children's literature -- literary merit -- by speaking of "encouraging children to read," which is a pedagogical point of view and therefore should also be irrelevant to the children's book reviewer.

Interestingly enough, John Rowe Townsend looks upon "acceptability to a child as a preliminary hurdle rather than a final test." Personally, I question whether Mr. Townsend has not put the cart before the horse. In discussions of recently published children's books, generally after a discussion of a book of rare value, one often hears the voice of the devil's advocate: "But, will children like it?" or more pessimistically, "What child will read it?" Surely the question of acceptability to a child is a question concerning book selection and not a fundamental critical question -- not a question of literary criticism.

A conciliatory point of view is found in the editorial by Bertha Mahony Miller previously referred to. In it, she modified her statement about the criticism of children's literature by adding an important qualification. "This point of view -- this measuring stick --" (by which she meant literary standards) "must also bear some relation to children themselves and their reaction to books today." The word "some" is significant. Mrs. Miller's chief accomplishment was to have considered the child and the book together, not in an intellectually critical way, but appreciatively -- one may say, intuitively. Some of her intuitions still bear repeating:

> Who can say what is the right book for the right child? That, thank God, is the child's own adventure (<u>Horn Book</u> editorial, November 1933).

> ...it is foolish to say 'we ought only to give the

child conceptions it can understand.' His soul
grows by wonder over things it cannot understand
(Horn Book editorial, January 1934).

These statements may seem both inspirational and idealistic
in form and utterance, but in essence they show a deep respect for the child as a person.

Except by taking polls and by compiling statistics,
one could not determine the frequency of appeal of William
Mayne's Earthfasts (Dutton) or Alan Garner's The Owl Service (Walck) among children. But popularity is only a descriptive, not a critical term. Among mature readers, how
many are there who read Paradise Lost or Finnegans Wake
for the sheer pleasure of it? There are some, of course,
who do; and if children's literature has so developed in richness and scope as to have produced a number of recondite
masterpieces, these works should first be respected and
treated as works of literature before one goes through the
agony of deciding: To how many, to what kinds of children
will these works appeal?

Finally, reviewers and critics are but readers; and if
they function properly, should simply be better readers than
most. Perhaps they should try to be humble rather than
clever. Lewis Carroll once managed to be both in a letter
that was disarmingly simple and devastatingly logical:

> As to the meaning of the Snark (he wrote to a friend
> in America), I'm very much afraid that I didn't mean
> anything but nonsense. Still, you know, words mean
> more than we mean to express when we use them;
> so a whole book ought to mean a great deal more
> than the writer means. So whatever good meanings
> are in the book, I'm glad to accept as the meaning
> of the book. The best that I've seen is by a lady
> (she published it in a letter to a newspaper), that the
> book is an allegory on the search after happiness.
> I think this fits in beautifully in many ways -- particularly about the bathing machines:[1] when people
> get weary of life, and can't find happiness in towns
> or in books, then they rush off to the seaside to see
> what bathing machines will do for them.[2]

One of Carroll's statements -- "whatever good meanings
are in the book, I am glad to accept as the meaning of the
book" -- invites speculation. He does not consider a possi-

ble logical loophole -- the possible bad meanings. I am sure that Freudian critics have already taken care of the loophole. As for the lady's idea that "the book is an allegory on the search after happiness," Carroll delightfully and logically destroys her interpretation by pursuing it to its absurd extreme. And yet, Maurice Sendak was to give creative vitality to a very similar bizarre situation in Higglety-Pigglety Pop! by transforming nonsense into allegory. During the past year, the editor of The Horn Book Magazine received a letter from a student of children's literature who was planning to investigate symbolism in Beatrix Potter. She was -- unfortunately -- unacquainted with Lewis Carroll's letter.

In Notes Towards the Definition of Culture, T.S. Eliot stated what he considered to be "the three permanent reasons for reading: the acquisition of wisdom, the enjoyment of art, and the pleasure of entertainment." It is certainly the third of these reasons which is the most nearly universal. Most children become aware of words at an early age and advance naturally to the more complicated pleasure of listening to stories. If conditions are favorable, children will discover that the world of books can still further augment their verbal pleasures. The prime function, then, of the reviewer and even of the critic of children's books is to signalize those books which appealing at present to children will seem even better when they are reread by those same children in their adulthood.

Notes

1. Bathing machine -- a small bathhouse on wheels, to be driven into the water, for bathers to undress, bathe, and dress in (Webster's New International Dictionary of the English Language, Second Edition, Unabridged, 1943).
2. Quoted by Bertha Mahony Miller from The Life and Letters of Lewis Carroll by Stuart Dodgson Collingwood in a Horn Book editorial, February 1932.

Bibliography

ALDERSON, BRIAN W., "The Irrelevance of Children to the Children's Book Reviewer." Children's Book News (Jan.-Feb. 1969), p. 10-11.

ALLEN, ARTHUR T., "Literature for Children: An Engagement with Life." The Horn Book Magazine, Vol. XLIII (Dec. 1967), p. 732-737.

CAMERON, ELEANOR, The Green and Burning Tree: On the Writing and Enjoyment of Children's Books. Boston, Little, Brown and Company, 1966.

―――――, "Why Not for Children?" The Horn Book Magazine, Vol. XLII (Feb. 1966), p. 21-33.

COLLINGWOOD, STUART DODGSON, The Life and Letters of Lewis Carroll. Detroit, Gale Research Company, 1898.

ELIOT, T.S., Notes towards the Definition of Culture. New York, Harcourt, Brace and World, 1949.

GODDEN, RUMER, "An Imaginary Correspondence." The Horn Book Magazine, Vol. XXXIX (Aug. 1963), p. 369-375.

KARL, JEAN, "The Real and the Unreal." Wilson Library Bulletin (Oct. 1966). Based on an address made at a meeting of The School and Children's Section, Michigan Library Association, Oct. 13, 1965.

LANGER, SUZANNE K., Problems of Art: Ten Philosophical Lectures. New York, Charles Scribner's Sons, 1957.

MARTIN, BILL, JR., "Helping Children Claim Language Through Literature." Elementary English, Vol. XLV (May 1968), p. 583-591.

MEIGS, CORNELIA et al., A Critical History of Children's Literature. New York, Macmillan, 1953.

MILLER, BERTHA MAHONY, Editorials. The Horn Book Magazine (Feb. 1932); (Nov. 1933); (Jan. 1934); (May-June 1946).

RUSS, LAVINIA, The Girl on the Floor Will Help You. New York, Doubleday & Company, 1969.

SAYERS, FRANCES CLARKE, "Walt Disney Accused." The Horn Book Magazine, Vol. XLI (Dec. 1965), p. 602-611.

TOWNSEND, JOHN ROWE, Written for Children: An outline of English children's literature. New York, Lothrop, Lee & Shepard Co., Inc., 1967.

TUNIS, JOHN R., "What Is a Juvenile Book?" The Horn Book Magazine, Vol. XLIV (June 1968), p. 307-312.

VIGUERS, RUTH HILL, "Not Recommended." The Horn Book Magazine, Vol. XXXIX (Feb. 1963), p. 76-78.

―――――, "The Book and the Person." The Horn Book Magazine, Vol. XLIV (Dec. 1968), p. 657-665.

WOOLF, VIRGINIA, Reviewing (With a Note by Leonard Woolf). Hogarth Sixpenny Pamphlets, No. 4, London, 1939.

Identifications and Identities

by Lloyd Alexander

Reprinted by permission from the October 1970 issue of Wilson Library Bulletin (45:2), p. 144-148. Copyright 1970 by the H.W. Wilson Company.

While our once-affluent society may be running a little short in some areas, we can certainly never complain about a lack of identifying documents. Those we have in abundance: draft cards, driver's licenses, birth certificates, death certificates; it seems easier to prove membership in the Diner's Club than membership in the human race.

But these are identifications, not identity. Though our parents give us whatever name suits their fancy, we are nevertheless all born Anonymous. Identity isn't given as a birthday present, but grows gradually in that special, personal area where we are most alone but most ourselves. We have to acquire it bit by bit, as we learn how to be people.

We're not alone in this endeavor. Even chimpanzees have to learn how to behave like apes. In nature, a sense of identity is a survival mechanism. For example, wolves --actually gentlehearted, though suffering a bad public image since that confrontation with Red Riding Hood--find their identity through their relationship to the pack and pack-leader. If, for some reason, this doesn't happen, the result is a very disoriented and desperately unhappy lone wolf. In geese, there takes place the mysterious, fascinating process of "imprinting." A new-hatched gosling tends to identify with just about the first thing he sees. Fortunately, it's usually another goose. But goslings have been imprinted by human beings and have grown deeply attached to them; although in such cases it's not that the gosling believes himself a human being, but takes the human being for some kind of enormous goose.[1]

Our own cultural equivalents have become something less than satisfactory. Blind allegiance to human-style pack-leaders usually results in disaster. Finding identity through parental models has been one of the most traditional ways, but seems to become less acceptable to more and more young people. Finding identity through one's labor hardly seems even possible. Industrial technology continues rapidly to separate executives, managers, and workmen from finished product, just as the nineteenth-century factory system separated the craftsman from his craft. The consequences are bound to be still greater loss of identity, as well as loss of the satisfactions that come from creating a whole product with one's own hands.

But many channels are still open. Social action, political action, still offer chances for strong group identity. Developing identity is a powerful force in civil rights militancy and women's liberation.

In addition to these large-scale social movements, we also have more individual and intimate ways. Hair styles, clothes, fashions reflect a kind of trying out of identities and roles to find out which suits us best. To find out whether, somewhere in our secret hearts, we're really cowboys, or pirates, or gurus; or even whether we're men and women or totally aseptic modules, as such high-fashion images as Jane Forth might suggest. [2]

The serious matter of identity is also a matter of child's play. In Children's Games in Street and Playground, Iona and Peter Opie show how such games, very ancient ones, are a little like auditioning for real life; an acting out of roles in situations where the stakes aren't so high as to be harmful. [3]

And, of course, there's one of the greatest games of all: the game of let's pretend, in one of its many forms-- literature. The let's pretend of literature can have both an immediate and a long-range impact on our lives, collectively and individually. Certain books, like certain works of art or music, have been able to crystallize the attitudes and outlooks, even the self-image, of a whole society; to define and set the tone for a generation or an era; and sometimes to be instrumental in creating such a tone. If life sets its stamp on art, art also sets its stamp on life.

Sartre and Camus, for example, have had this kind of

tone-setting influence. Perhaps, too, Hemingway, Fitzgerald, and Salinger. Not forgetting Charles Dickens, who practically re-invented Christmas--or at least our ideal of an "old fashioned" Christmas. More than that, Dickens gave the English the sort of self-image they never had before; they realized how Dickensian they were, which they might not have known if he hadn't shown them.

Whether its effects are obvious or subtle, immediate or long range, literature influences our view of society and raises questions about it. It can ask us to accept our condition as good; or to change it.

It can also help us shape a view of ourselves. The deepest and most durable works of art go beyond a specific social unit, beyond a specific area, and become explorations of the world, not only of the neighborhood; journeys not only to another country, but into the cosmos of human personality.

We can clearly see the immediate, real values of biography and history, as well as historical fiction. History is not merely an antiquarian's amusement. Like it or not, we are creatures with a past. Instead of ignoring it, we can use it as a means of finding ourselves. The many excellent books of black history in particular are important to blacks and whites alike.

Topical novels, the new realism in young people's books, no longer have to observe many of the nonsensical taboos of a few years ago. Children's writers now have a much better artistic climate in which to deal with urgent, current situations. This new freedom, unfortunately, is no guarantee of excellence. Or identity. Too many writers are content merely to update the furniture without updating their ideas; their sense of the contemporary scene has all the depth of a painted backdrop against which the same trite and tired drama is played out.

The main thing, I think, is to differentiate between the superficially topical and the deeply relevant; between what stimulates the nerves of the epidermis and what reaches the bone. The novel using contemporary material gains stature to the degree that it can still speak to us long after the specific, current problem has been resolved; to the degree that it continues to move us beyond our immediate interest in the subject matter. War and Peace is rather more than an account of Napoleon's Russian campaign. Moby Dick tells a huge amount about the New England whaling industry, but it's hardly a fish story.

Paradoxically, many books that give us the strongest impression of being "real"--in the sense of a convincing psychic, emotional reality--seem, on the surface, to have nothing whatever to do with our immediate concerns. They deal with nothing we could possibly know about in real life, and with characters the like of which we shall never meet.

I mean, of course, books of myth, fairy tales, and folk tales, in all their worldwide variations. We should have to be very jaded indeed if we could recall them without some quickening of the heart.

Our response to them is emotional, not intellectual. They touch some deep, non-rational level, and we sense that there is more to them than meets the eye.

Whether we can discover precisely what that something is--is unlikely. The question has absorbed a good many brilliant minds: psychologists and psychoanalysts like Freud, Jung, Roheim, Karl Abraham; scholars like Lord Raglan; structural anthropologists like Levi-Strauss; poets like Robert Graves. Naturally, in the honored traditions of scholarship, nobody quite agrees with anybody else.

Yet, putting all their insights and speculations together, we do glimpse a picture, multifaceted and ambiguous, nevertheless with a certain general consistency.

Patterns begin to emerge--and merge--into what James Joyce calls the "monomyth." A world, as Northrop Frye describes it, of heroes, gods, and titans; a world of powers and passions, and moments of ecstasy far greater than anything we meet outside the imagination. [4]

The basic movements of the figures in this world--centrally, the figure of the hero--are threefold: a separation, an initiation, and a return. The hero typically leaves the common world, as Joseph Campbell points out, for a region of supernatural wonder; he wins a decisive victory or undergoes some ordeal reflecting initiation, enlightenment, or personality change; he returns with the power to bestow boons on his fellow men. At the end, like all of us in our commonplace world, he must accept death. [5]

This very simple pattern is subject to endless permutations, combinations, and elaborations. Sometimes only small fragments of the larger tale appear. In embroidered detail, the hero may encounter natural or supernatural obstacles; he may love, suffer harrowing ordeals, be confronted with terrible choices, experience fear and despair.

We can begin to see that the stuff of the monomyth, on a symbolic, dreamlike level, is not too different from the raw material of human experience in general. If, as Joseph Campbell says, myths are metaphors of the destiny of man, man's hope, man's faith, and man's dark mystery, I think they can apply not to just a few of us in one limited area, but to all of us everywhere. The hero has many more than a thousand faces, and all of them ours.

Although folk tales grow from the same myth-making process as the hero tales, their subject matter and tonality are often quite different. Nevertheless, they offer us the same points of identity. Jung points out that many of the traditional characters fall into certain basic categories. The most familiar archetypes include the young man (prince or peasant); the young girl; the wise old man; the wicked stepmother; the good godmother, and so on.

These archetypes are the common property of cultures throughout the world. They come, according to Jung, from an ancient reservoir of memory; not peculiar to any one people or society, but a memory shared by the human race.[6] Through them, we can sense a universal personality, a universal identity. As Pablo Casals says, "We are all leaves on the same tree."

Rudyard Kipling, a writer usually associated with quite a different attitude, says much the same. Everyone knows his famous "East is East and West is West, and never the twain shall meet." But the closing verses state the exact opposite: "There is neither East nor West, border, nor breed, nor birth, when two strong men stand face to face, though they come from the ends of the earth."[7]

There is, in this matter of identity, a fascinating dialectic, an intrinsic paradox and contradiction. On one hand, every human being, every human personality is different, altogether unique. Each human life is the first and last of its kind; it can never be duplicated. Our individual autobiographies are limited editions: one only. But, simultaneously, we are both ourselves and everyone else. On the broadest human scale we measure the same.

This paradox, this duality of the unique and universal, is a very dynamic and creative one. It becomes destructive when we accept one aspect only and exclude the other. If we see our differences only, we can tend to become Ishmaels --our hand against every man and every man's hand against us. If we see our similarities only, life can turn into bland conformity. Balance and tension between the two, however, gives our personalities and interrelations variety and richness.

Literature has the ability to play back and forth between the two; sometimes emphasizing one aspect, sometimes the other, sometimes both together. I wonder if this might not be one of the mechanisms allowing us to identify with so many different sorts of literary characters. Or it might be that the fabric of individual personality is woven from so many different strands; that we are, in effect, a whole cast of characters in ourselves. So it might be more accurate to say that we have not one identity but a multitude.

And so we can, to our great enrichment, identify and find identity through every type of literature. But the writer who uses fantasy as a literary mode may have a somewhat easier task. Without concerning himself with historical accuracy or factual detail, as the biographer must, he can create the facts of his imagined world. Unlike the novelist who deals with the "now" at point blank range, he benefits from a longer perspective. He has greater freedom to work with the universals of life rather than its specifics. In fact, he must work in terms of universals or his fantasy will end as cleverness minus content.

But I'd like to distinguish between universals and generalities. The more concrete a fantasy is, the more convincing and universal it becomes. The more realistic the dream, the stronger its impact. The archetypes of mythology are featureless and voiceless. The writer must give them faces and make them speak. He must combine the two poles of human personality, the unique and the universal. If he does this successfully, the reader can identify with the personae of fantasy as easily and strongly as with a contemporary, realistic character.

Fantasy, like all forms of art, tries to get at the

truth of the matter. The search for truth is always relevant. And to the degree that fantasy illuminates some aspect of the truth, it, too, is relevant; always new, and always "now."

And so the hero's quest turns out to be our own. The long voyage of Odysseus is a voyage each of us makes, and at the end of it there are no distinctions between tourist and first-class.

We talk of an identity crisis; and in fact we are in the midst of one. Though I use the word in one of its original and literal meanings: i.e., a decision. Hopefully, we will decide that we're human beings. I think we will because it seems to me that anyone seeking identity is, by the very seeking, already halfway toward finding it.

There is a frightening contrast between John Donne's "No man is an island"[8] and Jean-Paul Sartre's "Hell is other people."[9] But I'd much rather compare two other quotations, one by the Roman poet Terence, who wrote, in the second century B.C., "I am a man; nothing human is alien or indifferent to me."[10] And the other, a statement by an anonymous button-maker in the late twentieth century A.D., "I am a human being; do not fold, spindle, or mutilate."

As TV likes to remind us, we've come a long way, baby. But, between Terence and the button-maker, perhaps the distance isn't so great after all.

References

1. Konrad Z. Lorenz. King Solomon's Ring. Crowell, 1952.
2. Life, LXIX (July 4, 1970) p. 54 (photo).
3. Iona and Peter Opie. Children's Games in Street and Playground. Oxford, 1969.
4. Northrop Frye. The Educated Imagination. Indiana, 1964.
5. Joseph Campbell. The Hero with a Thousand Faces. Meridian, 1969.
6. C.G. Jung. Psychology and Religion. Yale, 1938.
7. Rudyard Kipling. The Ballad of East and West.
8. John Donne. The Tolling Bell: A Devotion.
9. Jean-Paul Sarte. Huis Clos (No Exit).
10. Terence. Heauton Timoroumenos.

Implementing Educational Change

by Henry M. Brickell

Reprinted by permission from the Summer 1970 issue of School Libraries (19:4), p. 17-23.

When I first read the ALA standards back in 1960, and the audiovisual standards in 1965, I thought that they were ambitious, maybe overly ambitious, that they might have been presented in graduated steps because for many schools it would take a long time to arrive at the point that they would be able to adopt those changes. But when I read the new guidelines, my reaction was quite different. Rather than thinking it was ambitious, hopeful, maybe beyond the reach of many schools for a long time to come, I got the impression that you librarians and media people are seriously intending to change the school. You say things such as these:

> Media convey the information, affect the message, control what is learned, establish the learning environment.... Therefore the media specialist ought to participate actively in shaping the design of instruction. Audiovisual departments and libraries should be combined, administratively and organizationally. The focus of the media program is on the learner, on ideas and concepts rather than isolated facts, on inquiry rather than rote memorization. Media specialists have as their goal the guidance of students in an enthusiasm for exploration and research. Other media specialists work with teachers, helping them clarify objectives of student performance, and in developing the means to reach those objectives, and in evaluating the results.... The media specialist is knowledgeable about the learning process, child and adolescent growth, curriculum development; works closely with teachers.... The media program provides consultant services; direct instruction; information on new developments; tailor-made materials produced in the school building--materials for class use

Communication and Education

and individual use; working areas for students and faculty; equipment, of course.... The media specialist is expected to know about new materials, make them easily and quickly available, produce what is needed if it is not on the market, keep the faculty informed about recent developments in their subject areas, channel information to them regarding students' progress and problems, organize and conduct inservice courses for the full spectrum of media and their uses, teach students how to use the media center, and assist with the analysis of instructional needs and the design of learning activities.

If you are serious about that, you have to know that the school is a very complex system (that badly overused word is the only one to describe this enterprise) in which you are trying to intervene. Because you do not describe yourselves as being in the materials export business, you do not settle for just equipping-up the school and getting materials deposited in the library. You intend some new kind of relationship between the students and the media center, between the media specialist and the faculty. That is a deep intervention, a change. Not many media specialists perform that way today (I think); not many play such a role. And if you are serious about it: you are reaching into a piece of machinery that, while not engineered, is composed of interlocking, self-sustaining parts that fit together in a very intricate way. And you would change that.

Like any system, the school has considerable ability to resist that kind of intervention. If you would intervene, you ought to understand that. You can picture it as made up of components, which could be replaced by other components and, in effect, you are offering an alternative component--or, more accurately, I think, an alternative subsystem to fit into the school. The present components of the school are so interconnected that if you do that you will dislocate the other components, change their relationship with each other. If we went this route, mass instruction might have a bad time up ahead, for example, and the institution is engaged in mass instruction, for the most part. You would change that. Well, you do not undertake that lightly, and you do not reach into a piece of machinery and put in a new part without knowing what the rest of it is like.

Moreover, the component that you would install, the alternative that you would offer, has competition. During a

period of fairly energetic change, such as schools have been
moving through for the past ten years or more, you are in
competition with other people who have other ways of how to
spend money, and other things to do with teacher time.
They are competing for a place in the program. You may
think that what you would do is instrumental to everybody
else's motives and desires, but they probably do not think
so. It probably is a condition of competition. The school
has to look over what you are offering and assess it against
other components that are being purveyed.

Again, they interlock--the various pieces of the system; you cannot deal with them singly, each in its own
terms. Certainly, the way you describe this media program,
it is indeed the heart of the school and it has no end to its
reach. It touches every piece of the program. It touches
the behavior of every teacher and every child, every administrator. And you would change the whole school. All right:
you cannot deal with that singly. You will affect the working
of the others; in fact you deliberately intend to affect the
working of the rest of the school as a system.

Some changes in schools are relatively simple and do
not demand much of the system. A change in textbooks lets
the teacher continue with the pattern of assign, hear recitations, test, and reassign; not much change there. But some
modification--say, computer-assisted or computer-delivered
instruction--is quite different. It may, for example, take
the teacher out of his accustomed role as a presenter of information. If the teacher thinks that presenting information
is the supreme teaching act, the introduction of the computer
can disturb him seriously, cut his productivity, and perhaps
drive him to strong resistance.

As I read you, you would change the teacher's role
as a presenter of information. You would change that, if
you would have information presented through media, or directly to the student without teacher intervention. You are
going to dislocate the man, the woman, and ask him to do
new things. That is the rest of the system I am addressing
your attention to now--the teachers, who must adapt themselves to this type of media program (not to mention the media specialist and the changes you would demand in his behavior).

This kind of intervention, this innovation, is so big,
and runs so deep, and touches so much of the program that

Communication and Education 311

it is not like small-scale changes that teachers can accommodate to with skills they already have in their possession.

When you propose a new component for any system, you have to be able to answer a lot of questions about it. In general, an innovation can be more readily added to an existing system if it is:

> Small in magnitude (Does it have a low degree of interaction with the rest of the school?)
>
> Complete in conception (Is it complete in conception, in operating procedures--media center and classroom procedures, and in supporting materials?)
>
> Relatively simple (Is the operation straightforward and unembellished; or does it depend upon an intricate series of steps that the media personnel must take?)
>
> Convenient for teachers (An innovation may be complex, as the new media program seems to be, and yet be convenient for teachers. Will the new unified media program be simpler for teachers to use than the separate services available previously?)
>
> Flexible (Does the innovation depend for its success on the media specialists and the teachers following certain prescriptions quite closely, or can they deviate substantially and still succeed? It would seem that the media program you envision is highly flexible. If so, this should be pointed out to the school.)
>
> Distinctive (Is the innovation recognizably different from standard programs?)
>
> Replicable (Is it possible to copy it authentically in ordinary schools?)
>
> Ready for use (Is the media program you recommend now ready to go? Can it be taken elsewhere immediately and used, or are further developments and testing in the original settings essential?)

Staff roles and training requirements must be considered. Most local schools do not have a strong tradition of inservice training. Media specialists, like teachers, ordinarily get reeducated by using their own initiative. Many innovations depend for their success on a retrained faculty; this one might. If it does, the amount of retraining that might be necessary, both for present faculty and newcomers arriving in later years--training in the technical equipment, in some of the content, in the instructional procedures, in new behavior for the classroom teacher--may be so out of keeping with local traditions that the innovation cannot be successfully installed. But unless the training conditions can be met it is unlikely that the innovation ever could become a part of the local school.

So far we have talked about the school as a very tightly knit, resistant system. You cannot push around a piece without pushing around the whole thing, and you are very daring here. You do not pull any punches about it. You seem to be proposing to change the whole scheme--not just the media center, but the whole instructional pattern.

I think you are very well situated to achieve it. I am for it. But it will be very hard; if it was hard to get a book room in every elementary building, this will be harder. The school is a very stable organization, quite able to defeat all manner of innovation.

It is not entirely clear whether you feel that media centers of the kind that you envision in the Standards have been invented as yet. If not, the local schools cannot adopt unified media programs by copying those available elsewhere but must instead invent their own, using the Standards as guidelines. The school is not typically well situated for invention. A school which seriously intends to develop its own innovation must deliberately create a special invention setting.

Conditions that are necessary for invention appear to be these: (1) a group of highly intelligent people with differentiated roles; (2) a limited (narrowed) problem; (3) available time; (4) a special place in which to work; (5) an expected product; (6) knowledge of human behavior (what motivates students, teachers, the community); (7) proper equipment and materials; (8) a knowledge of parallel efforts; (9) freedom to design almost any promising approach; (10) tryout situations; (11) the likelihood that the invention will be used; and (12) the prospect of personal recognition if the innovation is successful.

Did the Standards arise from such conditions? Are the human behaviors described in the Standards fully invented? Or does the local school have to invent them or complete the invention? I suspect that there is a good bit of inventing yet to be done. Most local schools cannot create the invention conditions required. If the Standards do not represent a complete invention, you must be prepared to sponsor invention settings in your states.

Perhaps you believe that the kind of media program you envision in the Standards has already been invented and that the role of a local school is one of adoption rather than invention. In that case you would be acting as disseminators.

Probably there is no better way to think about dissemination than to start with the obverse of dissemination, which is adoption. Dissemination is sending; adoption is receiving. The new media programs we disseminate must be adopted by somebody else. By examining carefully the problems faced by the prospective adopter, we can draw implications for dissemination techniques. What are the conditions necessary for export of an innovation, for adoption of a new program?

The first condition for adoption is an identifiable innovation. It is not enough to have profound principles, high resolve, a great guiding spirit. There must be a body of professional behavior, a set of practices that the school can take on. It must be in a form such that if the school adopts the behaviors, it will get the results. The greatest problem in completing the invention, finishing the development, is to cut the umbilical cord between the developer and the development. We talk at the university about professors making exportable packages and we worry about how to get the package out of the professor. The real trick is how to get the professor out of the package, how to make it so that he can let go of it, so it can travel without him. You have to complete the development, get it out of the heads of the men who thought it up, and get it into a form that can go anywhere, across the country, without their having to take it with them. That is not easy.

Now: I doubt that the description of the media program is adequate as a description. I do not think the user can picture what you mean. He can picture the equipment and books, I suppose, but I do not think he can picture the human behaviors that you are calling for. There is a serious question in my mind as to whether you can stick to one

medium in communicating this very important message. It
may be that for the human behaviors you would like to describe, print is not a very good medium. The user cannot
adopt what he cannot picture. He literally cannot know whether he has it or not.

The second condition for adoption is public acceptance.
While neutrality is harmless, opposition is devastating. The
limited information needed to prevent opposition can be carried in the standard channels such as newspaper reports,
letters from the schools, PTA meetings, and so on.

Condition three: strong administrative endorsement.
If any principle is well-established, it is that a positive desire for the change--not merely a neutral acceptance--must
be displayed by the administrative staff. The administrator
is probably the key member of your audience (rather than
the media specialist), because the innovation demands new
behavior of many teachers that cannot be brought about without administrative intervention and strong drive.

Four: balanced attention to the novel and to the familiar elements of the new program.

Five: the convergence of outside reference group
norms. Staff members belong to professional associations
outside the local school system and to other outside groups
that can grant them status and prestige, and they look for
approval to these outsiders. If this program is endorsed by,
fits the values of, professional associations and valued outside colleagues, it will have a better chance of being adopted.

Six: early staff awareness and interest. Diffusion
studies suggest that practitioners go through a series of steps
in adopting a new program: they become aware, develop an
interest, decide to try it, experiment, and finally adopt it.
They probably need different information at each step. The
medium to make you aware is probably different from the
medium to get you interested, and that is not the same as
the medium for getting you persuaded. Simple awareness
can be handled by printed material and speeches at meetings.
To convert awareness into interest, what you want to be able
to say is, "This solution fits a problem you have been having lately," and you want them to recognize that. To do
that, it looks as though you have to go beyond print. It
looks as though the practitioner needs a kind of "artificial

visit." Longer printed or maybe film descriptions can be used for this "artificial visit." The ideal form makes further inquiry easier; that is, correspondence is better and conversations are better still. Speakers and consultants need to be made available, preferably people who have used the program in their own schools.

Seven: the decision to try the innovation. The chief questions in the practitioner's mind are likely to be: "Is it designed for a setting like my own?" and "Can I make it work?" It seems fairly clear that the best way to answer those two questions is to have the prospective adopter actually visit a site where the innovation is in use. Certain conditions are desirable if the visit is going to work: there should be a minimum of artificiality and showmanship in the program being demonstrated; the school he visits ought to be like the one he comes from; there should be no special (expensive or unmanageable) features of the program which the visitor will regard as essential but unreproducible. He needs to talk to teachers and students and administrators, as well as media personnel--to get the perceptions of those who have to live with this day by day.

Eight: prohibitive regulations removed, from state departments of education, individual school systems, or even buildings. I do not know whether having to get a hall pass every time you want to leave the classroom is an inhibiting regulation or not; it probably is, for independent learning. Such prohibitive regulations, including the "little" things as well as the bigger things like certification of media personnel, may prevent adoption. Also, the perception of nonexistent regulations is common, and these perceptions are just as inhibiting as the real regulations.

Nine: physical facilities may need to be modified.

Ten: time schedules may need to be modified.

Eleven: the materials and equipment have to be provided. One of my strong curiosities is whether this program, this set of human behaviors, can work at any level of equipment and materials supply. Is the media center an adoptable concept at some lesser level of equipment and materials than you call for in the Standards?

Twelve: initial staff training. Of all the steps in disseminating an innovation, the most consequential one is training the staff to conduct it. Training the staff is the key to success, an inescapable requirement of an authentic adoption. "Guided practice over time" describes the fundamental character of the training program.

Thirteen: continuing staff training. Turnover in school faculties is so high that you must arrange to train the newcomers continuously as they arrive.

This presentation was intended to make one major point: new media standards cannot simply be mailed out to the practitioners. You will need to invent the behaviors, as well as the equipment list, or sponsor the local schools in inventing it. Or, if it has been invented already, and you are in the diffusion business, you still cannot just mail out the standards. You will not get the results. You may get the equipment bought, but you will not get the new behavior that you are set on producing. The dissemination of new forms of practice into elementary and secondary schools is a massive job--expensive, complex, and long.

Some time ago I joined a group of people who were hunting for the School of 1980. We were working under the notion that the School of 1980 would not appear on January 1 of that year, but gradually, in pieces, all over the place. Some of it emerged by 1960, some of it earlier, and if you knew what to hunt for you could find it now, in bits and pieces and fragments lying around the landscape. A team of us went out, looking for the individualized instruction that we felt certain would be universal by 1980. We went to the very likely places: classes with fewer than twenty pupils in well-supported schools in wealthy suburbs. I used a simple rule of thumb upon entering a classroom: were all the children doing the same thing at the same time? If so, I would close the door and move on.

When the team gathered afterward to search its observations for generalizations, it reported some examples of individualized teaching. We had found it in kindergartens, and sometimes in grades 1 and 2, but noted that it became rarer in successively higher grades--except in art rooms at all grade levels, where it took the worst imaginable teaching to crush it out, and in industrial arts shops, in home economics rooms, in instrumental music groups, in bookkeeping classes, and in a few other places. Individualized teaching was notably absent in the "academic" subjects--English, social studies, mathematics, science, and foreign languages--

except in the teaching of reading and in the teaching of science in the occasional well-equipped laboratory.

What struck me most forcibly, and I was not prepared for it, was the fact that we almost never found individual instruction--and its corollary, independent learning--except in the presence of ample space and ample teaching materials. Space and materials--room for the child to do something besides sit, and things for him to pay attention to besides the teacher's voice.

It generated considerable enthusiasm in me for space and materials and the kind of media program that your new guidelines call for. So--I'm for it. You have to realize what is involved in changing school behavior; but, in your aspirations and your hopes, in what this would do to learning, if you are serious about it, I am with you 100 percent.

PART IV:

THE SOCIAL PREROGATIVE

Libraries and the Climate of Opinion

by Ervin J. Gaines

Reprinted by permission from the July 1970 issue of Library Trends (19:1), p. 39-46. Copyright 1970 by University of Illinois Press.

In any social setting, censorship is a weapon of the dominant group. It is the means of exercising social control in favor of prevailing doctrines, whether political, economic, theological, moral--or any combination of them. Censorship is effectively exercised only with the participation of the executive, legislative and judicial processes of government, for through enforcement of laws and the punishment of those who offend those laws the purpose of censorship is achieved. In the absence of repressive measures by the constituted authorities, censorship is rendered ineffectual and freedom is maintained for society. Voluntary censorship within, for example, a religious sect or any other tightly knit subcultural group whose members have by common consent decreed a set of exclusionary doctrines, is an entirely private matter and need not concern us, because it is a legitimate exercise of free choice, which is the essential ingredient of liberty. The right not to read is the obverse of the right to read, and both are defensible.

Conflict within democracy arises when any group attempts to impose its definition of acceptable communication upon the entire society by enacting laws which the enforcing arms of government--police and the courts--are obliged to inflict on those who do not conform. It is important to focus on the distinction between the proselytizing by individuals or organizations who are committed to limited expression on the one hand, and officially condoned censorship imposed by the state on the other. The first is acceptable, the second is not.

Some perspective on the history of censorship is helpful in understanding our present circumstances. Ralph E.

The Social Prerogative 321

McCoy's splendid bibliography[1] is the most nearly complete guide to writings about censorship ever assembled in the English-speaking world. Containing about 8,000 entries, it spans several hundred years, and it enables us to detect the rhythms of censorship in modern times. What anyone could have inferred is clearly demonstrable in McCoy: official censorship fluctuates with social tensions. As fears of social danger rise, censorship activity rises with it; when the one subsides, so does the other.

The first great wave of censorship swept the Western world in the sixteenth century after the printed book helped to precipitate the Reformation and Counter-Reformation movements within the Christian Church. The Catholic Index Librorum Prohibitorum was an invention to blunt the thrust of the Protestant revolt. It ramained a viable instrument as long as the internecine struggle continued and it faded only when the institutionalized forces of Christianity decided to terminate their 500-year contest for domination.

In England, after the Reformation, three distinct epidemics of censorship controversy raged. The first, during the seventeenth century Puritan attempt to consolidate control of the government, inspired the most eloquent of all works on the subject, Milton's Areopagitica. Although the debate over the right of the state to impose its will on free expression did not by any means disappear during the eighteenth century, it was conducted at a much lower pitch until it intensified again during the French Revolution and the Napoleonic period. So passionate was the struggle from 1790 to 1820 that notable authors like Byron and Shelley exiled themselves rather than endure what they regarded as the harsh and repressive climate of English society, while many lesser authors who remained behind suffered imprisonment and other forms of harassment for refusing to conform to the prevailing wisdom. The hundred years between Waterloo and the outbreak of World War I were relatively calm, and even though from today's vantage point Victorianism is regarded as especially repressive in sexual matters, there was a widespread social acceptance of the prevailing sexual mores, and authors displayed almost no rebelliousness at the constraints precisely because they felt none. Hence, Englishmen showed small disposition to joust with the authorities. Flurries of discontent, especially during the last decade of the nineteenth century, were quickly snuffed out. But after World War I, when literary giants like D.H. Lawrence and James Joyce (both of whom had exiled themselves for rea-

sons that recalled those of Byron and Shelley) clashed with
officially acceptable literary conventions, the censorship battles took on a renewed seriousness that has continued until
today. Upon reflection, one is moved to suggest that we are
at the tag-end of the sexual revolution, and that what Joyce
and Lawrence stood for has been established, if not yet completely accepted.

   The American experience parallels the British. The
most eloquent statements about freedom of the press tended
to occur immediately following the onset of the American
Revolution and, in some ways, were probably a reflection of
the European ferment; the issue of a free press in the United
States was most fiercely contested around 1800, focusing especially on the Alien and Sedition Acts. Generally, the nineteenth century was so calm on the pivotal question of censorship, that the quixotic Anthony Comstock operated virtually
without demur from the authors who towered over the literary
scene in the years after the Civil War. As in Great Britain,
World War I was the watershed experience that precipitated
new attitudes and a renewed dedication to the principle that
authors must be free of governmental intervention. The
1920's proved a lively time, leading inexorably to the importation of Joyce's Ulysses followed by the censorship battles
that have embroiled the Supreme Court over the last fifteen
years. Now the United States seems almost ready to yield
the point that sexual writings cannot be interdicted by the
state. We know that Denmark has already crossed the last
barrier, and it is likely that the United States will soon follow.

   It may be useful to ponder for a moment the meaning
of Anthony Comstock in the long warfare over intellectual
freedom. After the distractions of the Civil War, the United
States became intensely preoccupied with industrial and territorial expansion, possibly as a reaction to the emotional
excesses that had accompanied the great struggle to end
slavery and to save the Union. The finer points about human rights were dulled in the coarser dialog of the market
place. A zealot like Comstock could move freely in such an
environment, both because few thoughtful men particularly
cared and because they construed his efforts as harmonious
with the interests of those who labored in the industrial and
business communities. Questions of civil rights, in all their
prickly ramifications, had their renaissance after the sour
and disillusioning experience of the First World War, and the
special issues arising from censorship were deeply interwo-

ven with them. The collapse of Comstockery coincides exactly with the fierce struggles that occurred over the infamous Palmer raids, the Sacco-Vanzetti trial and other manifestations of American dissatisfaction with the status quo. The arguments about censorship are perennial, and the current issues are not critically different from those which arose during the early days of the republic. The safety of the state as achieved through "right thinking" is the rationale for censorship, and the freedom of the individual to dissent is the rationale for a free press. While it is hard to imagine Thomas Jefferson in the same milieu as Philip Roth or Eldridge Cleaver, the axial concept on which those minds turn is identical.

American thinking just now is modified by special circumstances--some of which are probably temporary and will have no lasting influence; others permanent and of increasingly cumulative force. These circumstances might be sorted out and the ephemeral ones disposed of first, both because they are superficial and because they are more prominent in the popular eye. Since the advent of the Soviet Revolution, which coincided with World War I, the United States has been under powerful psychological pressure to compete with another system. America's manifest destiny to bring light to the world has never been quite the same since the Russian Bear got on to the highway in front of us, which has caused us to push to "prove" our superiority. Although historical analogy suggests that this combative competition between Communism and democracy will eventually subside, its existence here and now heightens tensions and leads to some extraordinary inner conflicts in American society. Because a great deal of the censorship debate in recent decades has related to the international conflict, authors and institutions have suffered popular and even official opprobrium for allying themselves with causes that apparently or actually support the "enemy." The combined stimuli of fear and patriotism have prompted attacks on internal traitors or deceived innocents, and the United States has developed a rather extensive rhetoric of vilification to hold dissenters in line. The peak time for this censorship activity was about 1950, when Senator Joseph McCarthy led the American purge campaign. Although this effort is not as intense as it was, it has never been wholly absent from our society in the last half century, nor is it likely to disappear until some permanent accommodation is made with the Soviet Union.

The ideological campaign against Communism in many

ways resembles the earlier conflict within the Christian Church, and it often results in strange paradoxes. Political conservatism allied to anti-Communism seems to inspire a rather intense puritanism against sexual writings, as though there were some moral imperative to relate personal behavior to political beliefs. The tortuous thinking that causes John Birch Society adherents to equate juvenile sex education programs with Communist plots has a kind of mad logic to it that is difficult to deal with on a rational basis. Were it not so painful in its consequences, let us say, to teachers who would like their students to read Catcher in the Rye, it would be comic, for the rabid conservative neglects to observe that the Communist ideology is equally concerned with purity in personal behavior. Sexual puritanism is not a monopoly of Western democracy, and we may recall that many a Soviet writer has felt the iron hand of official disapproval for daring to contravene the older sexual codes. Hence, American conservative disapproval on political grounds of free sexual expression in literature is not valid, although we may expect it to continue simply because patriotic appeal is often the readiest way to quell dissent.

This anomaly in the American censorship movement may be illogical, but it is prevalent and troublesome because it aligns powerful social forces against the individual's assertion of his own dignity. Similarly, the revolt of the Blacks and the young evoke excited responses pointing to repression of their means of communication--the Berkeley Barb for example. America is particularly troubled at this moment by student restlessness and rebelliousness. As the nation goes through a transition from older conventions and relationships among the various races and between adults and the juveniles, literature not unexpectedly is often cited as the culprit. Concerns and anxieties that have been aroused while the social foundations move and shake have provoked extravagant claims about the evil effects of license in literature. If pornography is not at the root of our troubles, the argument runs, it must be at least a causative factor, and if the older literary conventions can be restored, then the revolutionary upheavals may cease. A boy who has ready access to dirty pictures is more likely to be corrupted than one who does not; ergo, forbid them.

But, if my premise that the Communist threat and the Black and youthful revolts will in time subside is correct, we expect that the pressures for censorship will subside with them. Past experience and a reading of the history of censorship lends confidence to this prediction. Aside from such speculation, however, there remain other and more difficult accommodations to be made, and these seem to relate to technology. Again, taking our point of departure from World War I, we observe that what has happened since then to cause turmoil and conflict over the permissive limits of expression may have less to do with politics and sex and much more to do with the invasion of our thought processes by newer means of communication. The strategy for dealing with communications in our legal codes is based on the printed word. The advent of the motion picture may have posed the first problem to us. It is instructive, for example, that earlier in the century the motion picture was regarded as lying beyond the protection of the First Amendment to the Constitution. In 1915, the Supreme Court held that films were "entertainment," and not until the Jacobellis case of 1964 did the Court accept fully the analogy between print and film by providing the legal basis upon which film-makers could assert their claims for protection at least equal to those of publishers and authors. The time lag between the popularization of the motion picture and the acceptance of it on the same legal footing as the printed word was not very great in historical terms, but when the forty-nine years are considered against the rate of change in our technology, the lag is quite serious. The motion picture was not accepted until after television had already made its first smashing impact upon our world. What we now face is a further struggle to assimilate this newer means of communication into our social institutions even though television's effect upon us is barely understood. Technology has created a communications revolution with which we do not know how to cope. It is evident from the tenor of popular discussion that awareness of the deep significance of the change is lacking in our manner of communicating.

In a recent symposium of historians, as reported in Daedalus,[2] discussion was given to the perplexity of historians in securing the documentation which traditionally has provided the basis for understanding historical developments. The use of the telephone and the increasing tendency to destroy records created during the formulation of important policy decisions are making problems for scholars. For librarians, the implications of verbal and visual displacement of the printed word are enormous. Not only are we faced with the diminution of certain kinds of documents, but we are increasingly baffled by our inability to identify the sources of the messages. One does not have to accept or reject the histrionics of Marshall McLuhan; it is enough to acknowledge that he has invited attention to a phenomenon of incalculable dimensions. We no longer have time to deliberate on our circumstances and to forge the instruments for dealing with the perplexities that beset us. Events outrun our institutional constructs for dealing with them. It is no wonder that rumblings of a social earthquake can be heard. Technology is ahead of us and is likely to remain there. By the time we have learned to live with television, personally, legally, politically and socially, we will find ourselves beset by still newer means of communicating across the barriers of political boundaries and social taboos.

Against this quickly sketched background, where is the place of the library and the librarian? It has occurred to me, as I am sure it has to others, that the pressures upon libraries are greatest at those points where public tax money is involved. Private libraries are virtually unassailed. Even in the heyday of the Watch and Ward Society in Boston, when the Boston Public Library was most circumspect in its dealings with the community, Harvard University remained apart from conflict because it lay outside the sphere of public control. State-supported institutions have not always been so fortunate.

Public and school libraries are in the most exposed position of all because they are most accessible to democratic control and because they are closely involved with children. Accountability and social responsibility weigh most heavily upon these libraries. Vulnerability to criticism is also one of their outstanding characteristics. One noisy citizen has the power to upset the functioning of a school or public library in a way not accessible to him if he reaches toward the better-protected university which is surrounded by moats of tradition and respectability that the newer libraries do not have available for their defense.

In saying this I do not mean to express regret for the absence of more effective shields. In a democratic society, the very openness of the institutions is of high value in promoting egalitarian aspirations. The public and school libraries are sensitized to the dangers and the opportunities presented by democratic control and are less likely to fall into somnolent disregard of human need. If all the casualties in the fight for intellectual freedom are in the public libraries, they only tell us where the fight is. The sense of danger adds excitement to the enterprise, and we might suggest what

The Social Prerogative   327

Henry V said before the battle of Agincourt:

> Gentlemen in England now abed
> Shall think themselves accurs'd they were not here,
> And hold their manhoods cheap while any speaks
> That fought with us upon St. Crispin's day.

It is certainly in the interest of intellectual freedom to go through the daily grinding battles, to knock the shackles off men's minds and help the individual citizen through the miasma of his fears and anxieties to the higher ground of reconciliation and acceptance. The library that has not experienced a battle is quite likely a library that has not attempted to challenge the conservative mores of a community by making available new and daring material.

The climate of librarianship is probably better than it was even as recently as the late 1950s when Marjorie Fiske's Book Selection and Censorship[3] revealed the timidity of librarians. There seem to be more librarians ready to risk their jobs in behalf of a more viable intellectual atmosphere within their institutions, and they are having more success. The American Library Association is bolder than it was and it seems now to be taking more seriously than ever before its responsibility not only to advocate but also to fight. These are good signs, and they should not be overlooked.

The most conservative area of librarianship now seems to be in children's work, both in public and in school libraries. The older traditions are still dominant, and the reluctance of school librarians to adopt a code equal to the Library Bill of Rights is a sign of the laggardly development of freedom for children within the context of the school library. True, the problems of intellectual freedom in children's services are intertwined with questions of responsibility for protecting the young in their tender periods of growth; nevertheless, it seems possible to make greater efforts than many librarians are willing to put forth to expand intellectual horizons at an earlier age.

In public libraries there is still a tendency for juvenile book selection to be less inventive than adult, and the hoary practice of marking children with special library cards that restrict their access to vast collections and services of the library not only diminishes the dignity of children but also inhibits their growth into the adult community.

In these areas of librarianship lies the greatest opportunity for the expansion of intellectual freedom in the next decade.

References

1. McCoy, Ralph E. Freedom of the Press. Carbondale, Southern Illinois University Press, 1968.
2. "New Trends in History," Daedalus, 98:888-976, Fall 1961.
3. Fiske, Marjorie. Book Selection and Censorship: A Study of School and Public Libraries in California. Berkeley, Calif., University of California Press, 1959.

How Mexican-Americans View Libraries:
A One-Man Survey

by Robert P. Haro

Reprinted by permission from the March 1970 issue of Wilson Library Bulletin (44:7), p. 736-742. Copyright 1970 by The H.W. Wilson Company.

During the 1960s, American librarians have demonstrated a growing awareness of the problems of poverty, minority group estrangement, and civil disorder. Librarians have become involved in programs not only to provide service to blacks in urban slums, but also to hire and train them as library users and workers. Recently, a few library schools have initiated recruitment drives to enroll blacks for training as librarians. The poor black neighborhoods have also been the target for business- and government-sponsored programs for new educational plants and methods, increased recreational facilities, improved housing, and a host of other local assistance projects. Unfortunate as they may seem, riots in cities throughout the country were a major stimulus for various action programs and projects.

Unfortunately, Mexican-Americans, whether in rural or urban setting, have been largely overlooked by librarians attempting to improve library service to the disadvantaged. As the second largest minority group in the United States, they should be of major interest to librarians in the Southwestern States and of concern to those in the rest of the nation.

In 1959, nearly 35 percent of the nation's Mexican-American families had annual incomes of less than $3,000.[1] To the extent that libraries and librarians have made a commitment to the war on poverty, the Mexican-Americans should represent an important challenge to their programs. It would be a serious mistake to treat the poor in the United States as a homogeneous mass. The concept of democratic library service seems as relevant to the disadvantaged as to the affluent. In this respect, librarians should carefully examine their libraries and service programs to the disadvantaged so that all the poor--Negroes, American Indians, Asian-Americans, etc.--are treated uniquely. Attitudes of the dominant society toward different groups certainly vary, as do the cultural and historical experiences of the various racial and ethnic minority groups. Therefore, librarians, if they are to deal effectively with Mexican-Americans, must understand the behavior and needs of this large minority group. Such an understanding is essential if sophisticated plans and programs for library service to this minority group are to be successfully formulated and implemented.

The metropolitan areas of Los Angeles and Sacramento, California, represent two significant types of Mexican-American communities in the United States. The Mexican-American community in East Los Angeles contains the largest urban concentration of these people in this country. The community in Sacramento, on the other hand, is smaller, but best represents the transition of a Mexican-American community from a rural to an urban setting. The Barrio in Los Angeles is concentrated in an area called East Los Angeles, two miles east of downtown and encompassing an area of about six square miles. In Sacramento, the Colonia is scattered geographically because of the transition from a rural to an urban setting, because of a continuing influx of poor Mexican-American families and Mexican immigrants, and the movement of people from farm labor jobs to laboring and unskilled jobs available in the city. Although the Sacramento Colonia is not centrally located, it is fairly well unified socio-economically, culturally, and politically. East Los Angeles now accounts for more than 75 percent of California's Spanish-speaking residents.[2] This area has serious economic difficulties with the unemployment rate in 1965 at 7.7 percent.[3] The Sacramento region, on the other hand, has an unemployment rate that varies seasonally between 6 and 11 percent.[4]

During late 1967, 1968, and early 1969, approximately six hundred Mexican-Americans in East Los Angeles and Sacramento were interviewed and questioned in an effort to answer three questions about libraries and library service:

1. What are the library attitudes of Mexican-Americans from various age groups?

Mexican-Americans and Libraries in Two Communities*

I. Use of Libraries (percentage):

	Children age 10-15	Young Adults age 16-25	Women age 26+	Men age 26+
Public Library (Main)	2	9	0	23
Public Library (Branch)	41	14	6	21
College Libraries	0	26	1	3
School Libraries	89	61	0	0

II. Respondents who have:

	Number	Percentage
Never been in a library	209	35
Only used school libraries	391	65
Used college libraries	55	9

III. Respondents who were:

	Number	Percentage
Dissatisfied with library service	102	17
Satisfied with library service	36	6
Did not care, or had no opinion	462	77

*Total number of persons interviewed was approximately 600 in East Los Angeles and Sacramento, California.

2. What are the attitudes and practices of librarians serving these people?

3. What challenges and opportunities face librarians and libraries in providing more effective service to the Mexican-American people?

The most disadvantaged segment of these two communities served as the principal targets for investigation. In fact, most of the interviews were conducted in Spanish. The median years of education in these two communities averaged less than eight years. Twenty-one percent of the people interviewed were foreign born and 41 percent had changed residence within the last year.

The methodology of the survey was as unstructured as it could be. Although the record-keeping was scrupulous, the interviewer sometimes had to resort to such devices as false moustaches and grubby street clothes to win the confidence of respondents encountered casually on the streets. Otherwise, arrangements for interviews were made through clubs, local press personnel, schools, and churches. Many nights and weekends were spent on this project over the two-year period, and some four hundred respondents were disqualified in order that as accurate and representative a sampling as possible could be established.

Library Attitudes of Mexican-Americans

Mexican-Americans evidence behavior that distinguishes them from other library users in the United States, including other disadvantaged groups. That which most distinguishes them from other segments of society is their need for cultural reinforcement in literature and library service. In spite of certain advantages to be gained from using larger centralized libraries, Mexican-Americans generally prefer to use libraries where Spanish is spoken and where Hispanic materials may be available to them. In fact, Mexican-Americans may often travel great distances to use libraries or book stores where Spanish is spoken or Spanish-language materials are available.

Although it may be thought that Mexican-Americans in East Los Angeles and Sacramento are library users, their language problems and mistrust of libraries have a different result. Of those interviewed in these two areas, 59 percent had a sufficient command of the English language to be able

The Social Prerogative 333

to utilize English-language library materials. Sixty-five percent had never used anything but a school library. In fact, a number of persons interviewed who lived close to libraries (public, school, or college) seldom frequented them. Eighty-nine percent of those interviewed would utilize their neighborhood libraries if Spanish were spoken and Spanish-language materials, especially those dealing with Mexican-American and Hispanic themes, were available. It came as something of a surprise to learn that various libraries and librarians were unaware of how large the Mexican-American communities were in their areas of service and how few of them frequented their libraries.

Table I reveals the extent to which respondents used libraries. The pattern of local use is significant. Young adults and children were the greatest library users, and adult men more often frequented libraries than did women in the same age group. This latter condition can best be explained by the role of women in the Mexican-American family. Basically, the woman functions as a housewife and homebody, with little mobility and very often a large family of children to shop for, clothe, feed, and attend. This pattern of home life provides little or no contact with outside influences and the dominant culture of the United States. Coupled to this is usually a language prejudice which makes these women more dependent upon stores and service agencies where Spanish is spoken.

Aside from the need for cultural reinforcement, perhaps the next most interesting characteristic of Mexican-Americans is their high degree of apathy concerning libraries. Only seventeen percent of the respondents complained about the various libraries and their service. The most vocal and bitter complaints came from teenagers and young adults. In some respects this pattern is quite similar to that of Anglo teenagers and young adults, who are critical of both library service and the types of library materials that are available. However, Mexican-American youths criticized the lack of Chicano materials and writers, Raza literature, and information by and about youth groups, especially the Brown Berets. On the whole, young Mexican-Americans wanted libraries to carry more activist literature about Mexican-American political movements, Brown power, and material on what makes Chicanos tick. Complaints by older Mexican-Americans ranged from a desire to see more Spanish-language materials available, including newspapers, periodicals, handbooks, and manuals, to a need for libraries to hire more Spanish-speaking clerks and librarians. To summarize, while most disadvantaged Mexican-Americans generally perceive libraries indifferently and seldom frequent them, those that do, especially the young, harbor an uneasiness and a resentment toward them.

School Libraries

The generally apathetic attitudes of Mexican-Americans toward libraries reflect that people of the Barrios and Colonias have limited access to information, have no voice in the types of library materials secured, and receive poor service for their children in school libraries. School librarians, teachers, and Mexican-American parents themselves are all partially at fault. School systems are only as responsive to the needs of a particular community as that community's interest and ability to participate in bettering education for their children. While Mexican-American parents may seem indifferent about their neighborhood schools and their libraries, this results not from a lack of interest but from their uneasiness and misunderstanding about how these institutions function and are administered. Anglo parents know how to deal with the schools and develop an understanding for the "system." Mexican-Americans, for a variety of reasons, do not understand the school systems and cannot relate with them in any sufficiently concerted manner as to effect changes to suit some of their needs. School libraries represent an institution that Mexican-Americans cannot deal with because they do not understand. Librarians and school administrators have not alleviated this situation, perhaps because they do not know the attitudes and lack of understanding by Mexican-American parents.

Concerning some of the actual problems that Mexican-American children have with reading and school libraries, school librarians usually can sense them. There are too few school librarians for so many children, however, and they gradually lapse into reliance upon marginal group programs and other limited methods of training Mexican-American children to use books and libraries. The approach used by one school was basically remedial and tended to group a variety of handicapped children, minority group children, and other "problem" children together. Such a program was not to be successful and as far as the Mexican-American children were concerned, it was a demeaning experience. These methods are of even more questionable value when problems with the English language slowly but surely develop

The Social Prerogative 335

into latent feelings of uncertainty, uneasiness, and mistrust of libraries. Various teachers and school librarians interviewed were unhappy about the lack of resources and facilities and constructive programs available to help disadvantaged Mexican-American children. What programs and facilities were available seemed destined for budget cuts and were unsupported either internally or externally. More than one librarian complained that in times of budgetary crisis the first cuts hit library personnel, materials, and programs.

Walking through the schools serving Mexican-American children in East Los Angeles and parts of Sacramento, one is struck by the age of the buildings and existing facilities. Most school libraries are housed in older structures and show few indications of repair or renovation. There are few signs that distinguish these school libraries from other urban ghetto libraries. An occasional display on Mexican literature or Spanish-Mexican heroes and explorers was offered up to these children as "Mexican" atmosphere and culture. Furthermore, conversation in Spanish, while not strictly forbidden, was discouraged in some school libraries. On a strictly comparative basis, newer high school libraries in predominantly white, middle-class suburbs of Los Angeles and Sacramento had highly flexible and innovative library-use classes and assignments, while their counterparts in the Mexican-American areas suffered from outmoded facilities, strict supervision of library use, and traditional approaches to the library as a study hall and place of silence.

Mexican-American high school students were among the most depressed and unhappy respondents. They felt cheated by the schools they attended and in the quality of education they received. As far as school libraries were concerned, they either refused to discuss them or had few kind words to say. It seems obvious that new programs to attract Mexican-American parents into participation in parent-teacher projects are desperately needed in Barrio and Colonia schools. Furthermore, these parents must be educated about the school systems, encouraged to work with teachers and librarians, and their fears or uncertainties about libraries and their children overcome. In addition, Spanish speaking volunteers and librarians must be utilized.

Public Libraries

There were too few Mexican-Americans that could understand the role of the public library and the services it could offer. Too many young, militant Chicanos purposely avoided public libraries because to them they represented a Gringo middle class institution. Older Mexican-Americans tended to use libraries mainly for reference purposes or to look at periodicals and newspapers. However, the variety of services that public libraries offer or can offer was completely unknown to many of these people.

Examining the remarks of younger Mexican-Americans first, one is impressed by the lack of understanding these youths have for the potentials of library service. To them, the public library is a complicated service agency. They are told, on the one hand, that it is present to serve them. When they demand certain services and materials, however, they are frequently things the library cannot or will not provide. A point in question is the demand for a meeting room in a branch library made by some Mexican-American teenagers. They needed a place to meet after school for discussions on educational topics of a political and social nature. The branch librarian was very receptive and prepared to make available the appropriate area. When it was learned that a controversial Chicano speaker might be addressing one of these meetings, permission to allow such a gathering was denied by the branch librarian's superiors. At another public library branch visited, Mexican-American teenagers had asked the library to carry certain newspapers and periodicals, mainly from activist Chicano organizations. After some investigations these publications were not secured because "they appeared irregularly, caused too much internal library problems in ordering and claiming missing issues, and their format might cause handling and preservation problems." At a subsequent date it was learned that a group of influential community leaders had become aware of the library's plans to order these activist Chicano publications. This group objected to the materials because they contained "foul language, called for political separatism, and condemned the behavior of the United States in a communistic and un-American manner." Rather than risk a confrontation with this group, the library decided not to order the materials in question, claiming procedural difficulties in securing and making available these items as justification for refusal.

The lack of adaptation by public libraries in affording meaningful service to all age groups of the Mexican-American communities in East Los Angeles and Sacramento was revealed in a number of ways. There are several excellent bibliographies on Mexican-Americans available to librarians who need purchasing guides. Seventy-nine percent of the respondents between the ages of 15 and 21 knew of the various bibliographies and had seen or used one or more of them. Of the leading bibliographies of library materials dealing with Mexican-Americans, only two public library branches out of the seven visited had two or more of them.[5] What also seemed like a failure was the inability of public libraries to "sell" their services to the Mexican-American community. Part of this failure was a lack of communication between librarians and Mexican-Americans. From various respondents, a general sense of mistrust and misunderstanding about librarians and libraries was quickly evident. Even user studies had not been initiated at several public libraries in an effort to determine successful or unsuccessful aspects of library service. In addition, the failure of libraries to utilize Spanish-speaking clerks, advertisements on Spanish-language radio and TV programs, audio tapes and records in Spanish dealing with topics of interest to this group, and advertisements in Spanish-language newspapers is highly suspect.

College Libraries

Perhaps no age group of Mexican-Americans was as willing to discuss libraries and library materials for Chicanos as college-age students. For these activist students, instant change in colleges and especially the schools seemed the only hope. In many respects Chicano college students are not too different from their Anglo counterparts in their impatience with the present situation. There are, of course, various elements in this grouping: militants, moderates, the timid, and the opinionless. The most articulate student respondents were adamant about the need for new methods and practices in college library collection and service policies as they affected Chicanos. Seventy-seven percent of the students interviewed believed that ordering more library materials was not the answer to their needs. Students cited the need for courses on library use as an important first step. There was also unanimous agreement on the need for new or additional reading centers, with the accumulation of related Chicano materials from various disciplines in central locations adjacent to conference rooms, duplicating facilities, and group study areas. More than one respondent complained about the lack of relevance between Mexican-American studies programs and the service policy of libraries. A few of the respondents suggested residential colleges be established with working collections of Chicano library materials located out side of the main library building. What was most impressive was the willingness of the Mexican-American students to talk about their problems and to offer suggestions. Many of them seemed overwhelmed by the fact that anyone, especially a librarian, might be interested in their suggestions for library service.

Professional Posture

As a professional, a librarian should be prepared to abandon the confines of the library, venture into the community, study and analyze its composition, determine its informational needs, and make appropriate plans to service those needs. Once formulated, these plans should be discussed with the articulate spokesmen of the community and other professionals to both criticize the plan and demonstrate to the community the librarian's interest and commitment. Once agreed upon, the plan or program should be implemented and reviewed periodically to ensure its success.

It would be unfortunate if the stimulus-response process in library service improvement waited for confrontations and possible violence before being set in motion. The ability of libraries to provide meaningful and effective service to Mexican-Americans will be greater if apathy, cynicism, and mistrust are not permitted to develop. The time for librarians to listen to and work with Chicanos is now. Wait too long and signs like "Abajo las Bibliotecas Racistas" and "Viva la Revolucion contra las Bibliotecas" may usher in a wave of militancy and violence by an ignored and too often cheated minority group.

Notes

1. U.S. Bureau of the Census. Current population reports: technical studies, 1966, series P-23, no. 18.
2. Ibid.
3. California. Fair Employment Practices Commission. Negroes and Mexican-Americans in south and east Los Angeles, 1966. San Francisco, 1966.
4. California. Fair Employment Practices Commission. Californians of Spanish surname. San Francisco, 1967.
5. The bibliographies are:
    American Council on Race Relations. Mexican-Americans: a selected bibliography. Bibliography series

no. 7. Chicago, The Council, 1949.
California, University, Los Angeles. Graduate School of Business Administration. Division of Research. Mexican-American Study Project. <u>Advance report no. 3 (bibliography)</u>. 1965 and 1967.
California, University, Santa Barbara. Library, Reference Department. <u>Mexican-Americans: a selective guide to materials</u>. 1969.
Oakland Public Library. Latin American Library. <u>Chicano: a selected bibliography</u>...1969. <u>Mexico and Mexican-Americans: a selected list</u>. 1967.
Pan American Union. <u>Mexicans in the United States</u>. Bibliography series no. 27. Washington, D.C., 1942.
Sacramento State College. Library. <u>Mexican-American bibliography</u>. Sacramento, 1969.
U.S. Inter-Agency Committee on Mexican-American Affairs. <u>A guide to materials relating to persons of Mexican heritage in the United States</u>. Washington, D.C., 1969.

6. <u>Los Angeles Times</u>, March 17, 1967, section C, p. 1-4.

American Indians
Search for Fort Hall's Library Service

by Gerald R. Shields & George Sheppard

Reprinted by permission from the October 1970 issue of American Libraries (1:9), p. 856-860. Copyright 1970 by American Library Association.

Among the Indians in and around the Fort Hall Reservation that is draped over the shoulders of Pocatello, Idaho, the suicide rate is nearly six times the rate for the non-Indian in the state. And in the two days we visited in the area, we were to be softly reminded time and time again that it was mostly the 18- to 25-year-old men that took their lives.

George Sheppard, teaching in the library school at Idaho State University in Pocatello and married to a member of the Bannock tribe at Fort Hall, had agreed to take me around to see what kind of library service was available. Our concentration was to be libraries, but you can't be in the area for two days without discovering the facts and the painful truths that have been "exposed" with political regularity. The visit of Bobby Kennedy in 1968 was still spoken of and remembered as another period of hope that had died along with him in Los Angeles. (We won't go into the sociological conditions here, but would recommend the February 1970 issue of Ramparts if you would like to explore on your own.)

"Recent research indicates that mental health problems are increasing among Indian students in proportion to their daily confrontation with non-Indian culture. This value conflict has caused serious problems of identification for Indian youth resulting in alienation and anomie, not only from dominant non-Indian groups but also from his own Indian groups as well."[1] Translating from the text to reality, we saw this demonstrated during a visit with several members of the ethnic and social extracurricular Indian Club at Blackfoot High

340

School.

    We had been talking with Myrle Wallace, librarian for the high school. She was quick to point out the extent of her work load. We were shown the backlog of books waiting for processing going back to 1968. She was the only professional there, she said, and was obviously put out that the audio-visuals had been added to her duties. She pointed to the set of rules for faculty use posted near the circulation desk. No last minute orders or switch in plans could be allowed. They were impressive and depressing rules.

    She introduced us to Peter Lipovac, in charge of Indian education for the nearly 500 Bannock Shoshone students among the twelve hundred enrollment. He had just arrived in the library with about eight members of the Indian Club. Now in his late twenties, Peter Lipovac had started as a VISTA volunteer on the reservation, and by the end of his service had become one of the few whites to be accepted by the tribe and in particular by the youth.

    It was the last hour of the day and we were seated around a study table trying to be informal and at ease. It was monosyllabic and strained until Mrs. Wallace was called away. I am certain she didn't know that when she left the authority symbol went with her.

    The students began to talk. Several of them were able to cope with the put downs that go with being in a minority group and they were quite vocal. They expressed themselves with sincerity and with the slightly "up you" attitude practiced by so many of the now people. (I remember learning to talk that way when I was an enlisted man speaking to an officer.)

    Off to one side, not quite in the group, were two young men. They weren't as fashionably dressed. They kept their eyes down and their faces blank--the classic cool of the alienated. It was obvious they were not part of the articulate group. They answered our questions with mumbles, and when we asked something for which they could not determine the answer desired, they just shrugged.

    We talked of the use of the library and found that it was low. Lipovac showed us the audiovisual equipment in a library closet. It was not impressive. He explained the need for production equipment and materials to help the In-

dian student develop projects related to social studies and
the language arts. Media labs and allied equipment are lacking in all of the surrounding schools. He became excited
and his enthusiasm was infectious as he spoke of answering
needs in this sprawling, sparsely populated area with a mobile unit that would serve both print and nonprint needs of
the students and the tribe. He sadly noted that there was
no dearth of ideas, just a lack of funds. One of his students
footnoted, "It is not so much for me. It is for the younger
kids coming along."

It is not so much for the now but the future that Mrs.
Joyce Hernandez, then chairman of the Education Committee
for the Tribal Council, was critical of what few books they
had been able to collect for a library operated by the Council at their center. She complained that most published material often assumed that all Indian culture was essentially
the same and had the same values. She wanted the children
to know of the heritage of their tribe, the cultural values,
and the meaning of its customs. The only hope she could
see was for the tribe to create their own materials.

As I listened to her talk in the basement of the Tribal Council offices, I could see the mobile unit that Peter
Lipovac dreamed of moving through the reservation, recording the heritage of the tribe.

The need for Indian identity was recognized by every
school we visited. They all had developed a collection of
books and a few nonbook materials about the general subject
of American Indians. Special funds were the major source
for these collections.

Mrs. Hernandez, in voicing her feeling of the need
for local material, told of a tribal member who wants to
write a biography of a former chief whom he admires and
feels was not well represented in histories written by non-Indians. She said that if he were encouraged, he would
write a history of the tribe as well.

Her handsome face clouded and she threw a challenge
at me, "Where can he go for financial assistance or some
assurance that someone would be interested in publishing
such material?"

"How much do you think he would need to get started?"
we asked.

The Social Prerogative

"A few hundred would help him develop the background material," was the answer. There was an edge to her voice that seemed to say, "I'm waiting to hear your glib promise."

We didn't promise anything, but we said that we would ask and see if we could find a source. The words fell lamely off of the tongue.

We fell silent for a moment thinking of the exciting potential. The oral tradition at Fort Hall has not disappeared and would be an excellent source if the people felt that their efforts were to supply their history and record of the life style. Several members could be trained to use recording equipment, high school students could transcribe, and maybe college students, home for the summer, could compile it into a printed form. It is important that it be an all-tribe effort. It should be made possible to record tribal ceremonies and dances that are now part of holidays and festivals such as the "All Indian Day Festival" in August.

We could remember visiting the collection at Fort Hall Elementary School. Lloyd Broadhead, principal, knows his collection of Indian material well because he has involved himself closely in the selection. (There is no librarian.) There are, he says, few books about contemporary Indian life to which the student can relate. Broadhead will speak almost wistfully about having members of the tribe both on and off the reservation record their experiences and have them processed into forms usable for both the reader and the nonreader.

It will not be enough to add materials which will implement the student's understanding of himself. The materials will have to have some meaning within the curriculum. In all of the schools we visited, the books on Indian culture and history were marked and shelved in a distinctive way. They seemed to be waiting for visitors like us to come along so that they could be pointed to quickly and surely. This, in an area that only since recent civil rights legislation took down their signs that denied or segregated the Indian. And, if you listen in the hotel bar or dining room in Pocatello, you can hear complaints from local whites that the Indian is getting all of the attention and the money.

It is likely that the segregation of certain curriculum items will have to continue in order to meet the very special needs of the young Indian in general studies. Research indicates that by the sixth grade the Indian student's achievement level has dropped two or more grades below the national norm. But norms are only indicative. One man's norm could well be another man's abnorm, attributable, in part, to isolation and lack of social and cultural opportunities associated with more affluent and populous areas.[2]

Fort Hall is no different than other Indian reservations. It is located in a sparsely populated school district which has difficulty maintaining service for its own population, let alone for the Indians whose lands provide no tax support. Add to this teachers with a culture and value system foreign to the reservation child, and the problems seem insurmountable.

Daniel Honahni, working with "Project Necessities" (an independent firm engaged in research in school curriculum development for the Bureau of Indian Affairs--BIA) reports that a survey of BIA schools indicates that the main objectives of teachers and Indians differ. Teachers are more concerned with the "socialization" of the Indian than his academic achievement. The students, on the contrary, realize there is a need for intellectually challenging studies and are ready to accept needed additional help in math, language, and science.[3]

But extra help is not readily available. Elementary school principal Broadhead says that the fourth to eighth grade is the crucial time. The need for specialized materials to meet these recognized needs is most important and most usually absent in schools serving minority groups.

The use of media to provide visual and audio experience needed by these special students should be integrated into the instructional program. Yet one elementary school had few audio-visual materials and had to depend on circulating materials that come from the district office. Admittedly, this pattern is repeated all across Idaho and most everywhere in the U.S. But here in Fort Hall is a poignant example of the need for centralized media services within the schools to meet those rare moments when motivation and interest of the student can be met, and the educative process can begin to have meaning and purpose.

In the elementary schools having the most Indian enrollment there was no professional or clerical library personnel. The room housing the library in one school was little more than a storeroom. It had no table or chairs. There were no audio-visual materials, periodicals, or basic reference sources. Many of the books were ancient and in need of repair. There was no catalog. Students could not check out materials from the library. Teachers carry books to class and control circulation from that point. The collection seemed to be primarily recreational with few curriculum materials in evidence.

We don't mean to imply criticism of the personnel of the school districts. They are well aware of the needs but find little money available for education. We were told that the shortages found here were typical of the entire Intermountain area. Yet we could not help but think of the suicide rate. In Fort Hall there is a group fighting for survival, a reason to live. Isn't it possible to provide some alternative to anomie and suicide?

The Blackfoot Public Library is little used by Indians according to its librarian, Mrs. Bowman. During our talk with the Indian students at the High School, they said that they never went there. They wouldn't say why, but it is possibly attributable to the past history of the town in its discriminatory practices.

Public libraries came up for considerable discussion with the Indian students. They explained that demanding bussing schedules prevented after-school use of the high school library, and the junior high did not have a library. However, there was a library in the Tribal Council Center.

The Bureau of Indian Affairs (BIA) has never been very active in supporting library service, and a few years ago when the Center was built (it is primarily a gymnasium-dancehall type of building), a room was set aside for a library. It has never had the services of a librarian according to Mrs. Hernandez. Funds for the collection have been meager. The high school students said that most of the materials were donated and didn't relate to their school needs and personal interests. (When we visited the facility we were startled to find a sizable collection of Marquand novels taking up space in the two stack rows that make up the library.) The students would like current encyclopedias and dictionaries. They said that study carrels with typewriters could provide refuge from family pressures and peer taunts for being studious. One of the girls said that she had worked there the previous summer and about died of boredom because only an occasional person would wander in to seek a book.

We asked about bookmobile service. They had little to say of the service being supplied from off the reservation. They spoke of the bookmobile in terms you would more likely expect to hear in a meeting of library school students. They wanted it to be on constant tour of the reservation, stopping at the homes scattered over the fifty mile radius. They thought it should have tapes, films, magazines, and pictures. They said the older people liked the stories of the early West and they would welcome copies of magazines such as True West and Frontier Times. (It was obvious that Peter Lipovac had been sharing his dreams with them.)

They complained of the often dull jobs provided under the Youth Opportunity Program and wondered if the time could be better invested in providing library service to outlying areas.

As pleasant as it was to an old librarian's ears to be talking to the students about expanding library service, it was the conversation with Mrs. Hernandez about public library service that was the most exciting. She could see the direct relationship between educational needs and library service from her first hand knowledge working with the Education Committee. We discussed the possibility of the tribe establishing their own public library service. She was interested but wary. It would take federal aid, and past experience in other areas had taught her that it would be difficult to find the help necessary to run the project. And it was obvious that past experience made her suspicious of any outside agency or individual coming in to run a project. It happened too often in the past that the outsider inflicted his own standards and took control of the program away from the community.

At this point in our conversation Tribal Council Chairman Arthur Hayball joined the conversation. He was well aware of the bookmobile service and the inadequacies of the Tribal Center library. He asked if we knew of funds that would be available to the tribe to develop more adequate service. His concern was primarily for the young. He said that those few who do attempt to go on to college will not have the advantage of knowing how to use a library. And he added softly, with just a trace of a twinkle in his eye, "After all, going to college is mostly using libraries." He had been doing his homework.4

In two days we had learned a little about the hopes and dreams of a minority group struggling for their right to maintain their identity. How often as we watched and listened did we note that the needs and the inadequacies matched those in the big urban ghettos and barrios. What were the solutions? Our guess could be no better than the next one, most likely.

We were careful not to make any promises or hold out any hopes. We repeatedly told the people to whom we talked that we were just trying to learn for ourselves what the problems were and hoped to assist someone in finding a way to help.

What do we think of the Fort Hall situation? If we would recommend anything it would be that funds be found to help the tribe develop materials on their own culture for the use of the young. That is the most basic need. We would like to see a specially funded project which would let Peter Lipovac have that dream of his to send a mobile unit moving through the reservation, ready to help young and old explore their own lives and their futures through the use of all kinds of media. And closer to our prejudiced hearts would be the providing of funds to the Tribal Council for the establishment of their own library service.

It must be stressed here that any projects with the Tribal Council must be controlled by the Council or another body of local residents that organize to push for development of this service. The Indians must want the service and must set the policies for the type of service desired. We are certain that the State Library would be in a position to offer considerable help, but if it is to approach the tribe it should be with the understanding that, like so many social groups, the Indian has become tired of being told what can be done for him; he wants to know what can be done with him, under his control.

Notes

1. Bryde, John. "A Rationale for Indian Education." Journal of American Indian Education, VIII, January 1969.

2. Thompson, Heldegard. <u>Education for Cross Cultural Enrichment.</u> U.S. Bureau of Indian Affairs. 1964.
3. Note: Mr. Norman Van Houtten, Indian councilor in the Pocatello school district, reported that in the Highland School three new classes have been added which are designed for Fort Hall students. They are in consumer economics, a special art class, and an arts and crafts class using resource people from the reservation. It is a start but an additional effort is needed in language arts, science and mathematics.
4. Bass, Willard. <u>American Indian High School Dropouts and Graduates in the Southwest.</u> Southwestern Cooperative Education Laboratory, 1969.

Plus ça Change

by Jesse H. Shera

Reprinted by permission from the March 15, 1970 issue of Library Journal (95:6), p. 979-986. Copyright 1970 by R. R. Bowker Co., a Xerox company.

"Here was a new generation... grown up to find all gods dead, all wars fought, all faith in man shaken," wrote F. Scott Fitzgerald in This Side of Paradise. Except for the reference to the first World War, which to our sorrow we found was not Armageddon after all, Fitzgerald's words could have been written today. In many ways the sixties were not unlike the twenties. Our own parents blamed everything on "The War," as they looked with consternation and dismay across the generation gap of the "roaring twenties." Indeed, it must have looked that way to an America, exhausted with the dreary story of a brutal war and its sordid settlement at Versailles spread before their resentful eyes by such books as Sir Philip Gibbs' Now It Can be Told, John Dos Passos' Three Soldiers, E. E. Cummings' The Enormous Room, and, for those who had the determination to pursue it, John Maynard Keynes' Economic Consequences of the Peace. Forgotten was the excitement and adventure of Arthur Guy Empey's Over the Top, Coningsby Dawson's Carry On, Frances Huard's My Home on the Field of Honor, not to mention Edward Streeter's Dere Mable.

It is scarcely surprising that a generation which, during the years of the First World War, had discovered the ease with which legislation, propaganda, and even intimidation could be used to compel at least the appearance of conformity and acceptable conduct should have viewed the uninhibited twenties with a feeling akin to horror.

The revolt of youth against the restraints of a Mid-Victorian childhood climaxed by a war "to end all war" was in the making. World War I had brought with it, as all wars have, the proliferation of legislative controls for the regulation of conduct, and restraints were not difficult to maintain even after the signing of the armistice. Protest was almost inevitable. In April 1920, F. Scott Fitzgerald, just out of Princeton and, therefore, one who certainly should "be with it" so far as youth was concerned, published This Side of Paradise: "None of the Victorian mothers--and most of the mothers were Victorian--had any idea how casually their daughters were accustomed to be kissed," wrote the young Princetonian who, five years later was to establish himself as a writer of importance with the appearance of The Great Gatsby: "...Amory saw girls doing things that even in his memory would have been impossible...talking of every side of life with an air half of earnestness, half of mockery, yet with a furtive excitement that Amory considered stood for a real moral let-down. But he never realized how wide spread it was until he saw the cities between New York and Chicago as one vast juvenile intrigue." One well-nurtured Fitzgerald heroine brazenly confided, "I've kissed dozens of men. I suppose I'll kiss dozens more"; while a young lady observed philosophically, "Oh, just one person in fifty has any glimmer of what sex is. I'm hipped on Freud and all that, but it's rotten that every bit of real love in the world is ninety-nine per cent passion and one little soupçon of jealousy."

Such books as Warner Fabian's Flaming Youth and Percy Marks' The Plastic Age may have opened the astonished and disapproving eyes of our parents to the glitter of rebellious youth of the twenties--the gin parties, the petting, the sex, the "indiscretions" of cigarette-smoking "flappers" with their bobbed and shingled heads--but it remained for Main Street and Babbitt, and most of all, perhaps, Mencken's American Mercury to lay bare the real malaise that was infecting society. For, if there was a flask in the hip pocket of every raccoon-coated youth who cheered on "The Four Horsemen" or "Red" Grange, the green cover of the Mercury protruded from beneath every arm.

In his searing photographs of Gopher Prairie and Zenith, Lewis portrayed the superficiality and hypocrisy of the façade of American life, and in George F. Babbitt there was incarnated the arch-enemy of the enlightened and the stereotype of American free enterprise. If anyone doubted the essential validity of Lewis' sharp pen, it was given credence by the revelations of Senator Walsh's investigation into the financial dealings of Secretary Fall and the Teapot Dome scandals of the Harding administration. Nevertheless, de-

The Social Prerogative

spite such machinations within the Republican party, Coolidge was returned to office in 1924, and Oscar W. Underwood probably lost the democratic nomination that same year because he dared openly to oppose the Ku Klux Klan. Nationalism, which had been glorified during the World War, assumed a particularly virulent form during the Harding-Coolidge era, when criticism became un-American. The spirit of "normalcy" manifested itself in a variety of ways: revision of history texts, insistence that teachers subscribe to loyalty oaths, denial of citizenship to pacifists, deportation of aliens, suppression of economic unrest through criminal syndicalism, and criminal anarchy laws climaxed by the Sacco-Vanzetti trial, purging of legislative and other bodies of "Socialists," repudiation of liberalism in all the arts, celebration of fundamentalism in religion which reached its peak with William Jennings Bryan and the "Monkey Trial" in Dayton, Tennessee, and legislative and judicial emasculation of federal and state bills of rights. Those were times that tried the souls of youth, and it is hardly surprising that youth reacted in protest and struck out in its own way.

The stage was indeed set for the advent for the "Bad Boy of Baltimore," whose American Mercury replaced the ill-fated Smart Set. The new journal began where its predecessor left off, and was an immediate success. By 1927 its circulation had soared to 77,000, a relatively small figure in comparison with today's statistics, but remarkable in the twenties for a journal so young. Its editor became, as Walter Lippman wrote, "the most powerful influence of this whole generation of educated people." The pages of the Mercury were filled with ridicule of religion, morality, patriotism, prohibition, prosperity (especially Coolidge prosperity), democracy, socialism, academic pomposity, Bruce Barton's revision of the Christian doctrine for the glorification of the higher salesmanship, and what Mencken himself called "the bilge of idealism." At the same time, its editor championed such writers as Willa Cather, Sherwood Anderson, Theodore Dreiser, Sinclair Lewis, and James Branch Cabell. He seriously questioned, as he said, "that civilized life was possible under a democracy," and again he declared that he was "against patriotism because it demands the acceptance of propositions that are obviously imbecile--e.g., that an American Presbyterian is the equal of Anatole France." He fought anything that threatened personal liberty, and soon became the darling of the young intellectual iconoclasts. The pages of the Mercury were fresh, startling, and delightfully destructive, and its popularity on scores of college campuses was unchallenged by any other publication. Yet much of Mencken's vindictiveness was little more than name calling--mountebank, charlatan, swindler, numbskull, swine, witch-burner, homo boobiens, and imbecile. It was not easy to be coolly analytical in the face of such a prose style as he commanded. Though the intellectuals had been on the offensive against the absurdities of the twenties, Mencken gave them added courage and such magazines as Harper's, The Atlantic, The Forum, began to reflect more boldly than they had in the past, and perhaps even more than they would admit, the views of the intellectually rebellious minority. In a curious kind of way Mencken stood to the youth of the Coolidge era as 40 years later the Kennedys and Eugene McCarthy were to rally the young of their generation. Though their styles were different (Mencken's voice was strident), each in his own way spoke to youth with spectacular success.

The credo of the intellectuals during these years of revolt can be summarized briefly as: belief in a greater degree of sex freedom than had been sanctioned in the past; defiance of the enforcement of morals, exemplified in the Volstead Act, by legislation; rejection of all forms of censorship; skepticism of religion, particularly organized religion; scorn for the great bourgeois majority; distrust of the military; "debunking" of the great and the near-great; fear of mass production and mechanization; opposition to capitalism and its economic and social hypocrisies; and disillusion over the consequences of the Treaty of Versailles. Not all of the young intellectuals who subscribed to these tenets were willing to accept all of these propositions, but any who accepted none were suspect among the enlightened. As Frederick Lewis Allen wrote in Only Yesterday, "The prosperity band-wagon rolled on, but by the wayside stood the highbrows with voices upraised in derision and dismay."

By the wayside crying out with derision and dismay, indeed! The young rebels who vocally opposed standardization and repression, and who were so devoted to the cause of freedom, could not answer the question--freedom for what? Uncomfortable though the house of Babbitt was, there was little to be gained from having one's freedom but not knowing what to do with it. A few of the "lost generation" dashed off to Paris to be free of Buffalo or Iowa City, as Richmond Barrett wrote in Harper's, but after being excessively rude to everybody they met and after tasting a few short and tasteless love affairs and soaking themselves in

The Social Prerogative 353

gin, finally passed out under the tables of the Café du Dôme. It was the age about which F. Scott Fitzgerald wrote in <u>All the Sad Young Men</u>, but it was also an age in which many clung to the old values of the essential common decency of man.

>The mountain's steeple;
>The folk that people
>   The plains and valleys below,
>Are ten times nicer
>Than Lewis, Dreiser,
>   And Sherwood Anderson know.

Thus wrote Arthur Guiterman in a spirit that mirrored that of many during these troubled years. One may call it nostalgia for those far-off happy years before 1914 or one may call it wishful thinking, but there were a surprising number of people who believed in, or thought they believed in this simple faith in basic human goodness.

But it was probably Walter Lippman in <u>A Preface to Morals</u>, who most keenly perceived and penetrated to the central issue: "What most distinguishes the generation who have approached maturity since the <u>debacle</u> of idealism at the end of the war is not their rebellion against the religion and the moral codes of their parents, but their disillusionment with their own rebellion. It is common for young men and women to rebel, but that they should rebel sadly and without faith in their rebellion, and that they should distrust the new freedom no less than the old certainties--that is something of a novelty." Lippman tried to lay the foundation for a new system of ethics and beliefs that would satisfy everyone, and for a brief time, humanism--under the leadership of such academicians as Irving Babbit and Paul Elmer More--enjoyed a degree of popularity among the intelligentsia, but no one quite knew what humanism meant or what brand of humanism was being discussed. There was also an attempt to find in the scientific philosophizing of Alfred North Whitehead, Sir Arthur Eddington, and Sir James Jeans the basis for a new ethic. Nor had the old liberalism been entirely swept away, a politically progressive Catholic was nominated for President in 1928, only to go down to defeat. But there was unmistakable evidence that a search for new values had begun, a search that would explode in new and quite unanticipated directions on Wall Street on "Black Tuesday" of October 1929. Main Street would never again be the same.

To all of these currents and eddies in the life of a
nation the librarians were largely oblivious. If they showed
any concern at all for happenings beyond their own cloistered
walls, it was in the establishment by ALA of its national
headquarters and the "expanded program." Attempts to
"professionalize" the craft were gaining some headway, especially as related to the training of librarians, and attempts
were being made to determine exactly what it is that librarians do when they are working. Such concern as there was
with the world outside was largely reserved to an interest in
the re-establishing of European libraries devastated by war,
and to efforts to spread library practice throughout the earth.
But mostly the librarians devoted themselves to burnishing
and tending the local lamp of learning, and if their libraries
subscribed to the Mercury, the Nation, or the New Republic,
their issues were probably kept in a file cabinet behind the
desk where it was available on request. Many were grateful that the New Yorker was beginning to replace the Mercury in the required reading of the literati.

The crash of the stock market and the economic ca-
tastrophe that it precipitated was, in a sense, both a fulfill-
ment and a refutation of youthful prophecy. Certainly it revealed the myth of eternal prosperity and the instability of
its tinselled façade. The "higher learning" had been right in
condemning the "higher salesmanship." Raucous gin-drinking
youth of the twenties came face to face with economic hardship and met the challenge. The cigarette-smoking "flappers," over whom their mothers had agonized, had become
mothers themselves, and doing, by the way, a creditable job
of rearing their own children in the face of economic depri-
vation, and frequently even the necessity to work themselves
to support unemployed husbands and fathers. Youth had been
right too, about the hypocrisy of prohibition and the futility
of morality through legislation; that fiction was revealed in
all its starkness in a blaze of gunfire in a Chicago garage
on St. Valentine's Day of 1929.

But the youth of the twenties had also been tilting
with a windmill or two: Fundamentalism in religion, and
Babbittry (which would be reborn a generation later in "the
ugly American" and, therefore, may not qualify as a windmill). Youth had been wrong, too, in excessive devotion to
Mencken whose negativism was really anti-intellectualism,
and who was scarcely qualified to lead "the children's cru-
sade." The Great Depression gave youth a new focus, and
it may have been a kind of testing time for the holocaust of

the forties. The era of "debunking" had ended, and Elmer Gantry, Sinclair Lewis' hypocritical minister, was dead. Economic problems were the major concern of youth in the thirties, and if Lewis were read, it was It Can't Happen Here, rather than the earlier, and better, works. The corporation and the economic system that supported it were the bêtes noires of the era. From the ragged sleeve of the raccoon coat, if any such had survived, there protruded, not the green cover of the Mercury, but A.A. Berle's and Gardner Means' Modern Corporation and Private Property, or Thurman Arnold's Folklore of Capitalism.

Youth was steeped in "social significance" and it fought with all the undernourished vitality that it could muster against "big navies," the armament merchants, the rising tide of fascism polarized by the Spanish Civil War, the waste of natural resources, and the degradation of that third of a nation that was "ill-housed, ill-clothed, and ill-fed." Youth looked with hope to the Soviet Union, joined the Abraham Lincoln Brigade in Spain to fight against Hitler and Mussolini, and, at home, attacked the American Liberty League.

Yet for all our Weltschmerz, those of us who lived through this trying time found a certain joy in holding high the banner of the New Deal, like Eagle Scouts. What gorgeous, disorderly, far-off days they now seem. "Hope grew 'round us like the twining vine." Nothing seemed beyond the realm of possibility, and from 16th and Pennsylvania Avenue came that ever strong and reassuring voice, admonishing, challenging, inspiring. Youth followed the voice, as a generation later it was to follow the Kennedys and Eugene McCarthy, like mystics called to worship by the bell of a distant shrine, like Chaucer's Pilgrims on the road to Canterbury--and just as motley. The thoughts of youth are always "long long thoughts," but we were intoxicated with thinking.

The blast furnaces of Gary and Pittsburgh and Youngstown were cold, but there was a bright glow in the night sky over the industrial centers of Russia and youth looked to the east with hope. Looked to the east, but with eyes closed to the purges of Stalin and the suffering that the Soviets had wrought. By the end of the decade the thunderheads of war lay black and meanacing on the eastern horizon. In Africa, a "sawdust Caesar" had laid low The Lion of the Tribe of Judah. In Austria, Seyss-Inquart had proclaimed Anchluss with Germany; and in Germany itself Hitler, with whom one really couldn't do business, had annexed the Ruhr, turning its industrial might to his own nefarious ends. In France, Leon Blum and Edouard Daladier were forcing the government increasingly toward the extreme Right. Across the Pyrenees, the battle-scarred fields of a prostrate Spain were a testing ground over which three mighty military machines had refined their techniques in mass homicide. And at No. 10 Downing Street an aging Neville Chamberlain, who had just returned from Munich, was brandishing an umbrella and crying, "I believe it is peace for our time." But almost as he spoke, the heavy artillery of the Nazis, with the British prime minister's sanction, was rumbling across the Czech border. On this side of the Atlantic, youth had been told that it had nothing to fear but fear itself, but in those dark days fear seemed quite enough to cause anyone concern, and disillusioned youth was ready to admit that it had been lying to itself about Russia. That admission may have been the bitterest pill of all.

Drastic reductions in income which compelled shortened hours of library service, curtailment of book funds, and reductions of salaries and staff, all brought the librarians to the realization that "no man is an island," and that the bell was tolling for them, too. This revelation of the library as a part of the social fabric, of the public sector, undoubtedly helped prepare the way for the arrival of Louis Round Wilson at the University of Chicago and his insistence that the library was a social phenomenon and should be studied as such. The Great Depression having rekindled interest, particularly among the youth, and a certain sympathy for the Soviet experiment, once again the threat of censorship and the witch-hunt flourished. In the face of these threats, the ALA pursued its generally placid way. Of course these events were regrettable, the Establishment admitted, but the profession would have to tailor its garments to conform to the available fabric, and in those days the ALA was short of yard-goods. The association was a tightly closed corporation in the days of the consulship of Carl H. Milam. If there were a sword suspended above the head of this "Damocles," he would not look up and eventually it would probably disappear. A decade later that sword was to come crashing down, but that is another story.

But within ALA, there was a militant band of Young Turks, few in number, geographically dispersed, and pitifully weak in economic resources, who knew what it wanted and set forth with determination to achieve its goal. Fortunately, there were on the side of the young three figures whose

The Social Prerogative   357

names will be etched forever in the minds and hearts of the
youths they encouraged--Charles Harvey Brown, distinguished
director of the Iowa State University Library, and a recognized leader in the academic world; Marian Manley, librarian of the pioneer Business Branch of the Newark, N.J. Public Library and disciple of John Cotton Dana, that iconoclast
of an earlier day; and Stanley J. Kunitz, poet and progressive editor of the Wilson Bulletin, the name of which was
later changed to its present familiar title as an implicit denial that it was for the birds. Kunitz stood to the Young
Turks of the thirties much as Library Journal's Eric Moon
and John Berry have to the young activists of the present
generation. The WB, like the Mercury, had a green cover
in those days, a coincidence into which one can read nothing
of significance, but its pages were always open to protest,
and it gave its youthful contributors a rallying point and a
voice.

    Despite the slamming of bank doors and the general
financial panic that marked the last year of the Hoover administration, enough young librarians were able to scrape
together sufficient funds to attend the New Haven convention
of the ALA in 1931, and there organized the Junior Members
Round Table. What the group wanted was "involvement, "
but the problem of how to become involved was one to which
no one seemed to have a valid answer. Projects, rather
than direct action in the politics of the association, seemed
to offer the greatest prospect for success, and accordingly,
the group undertook two activities: the compilation of a subject index to library literature that would carry forward
Cannons' Bibliography of Library Economy, 1876-1920, and
a survey of opinion concerning the effectiveness of library
training. The first was brought to successful fruition under
the able leadership of Lucile Morsch, and was published by
the ALA under the title Library Literature, 1921-1932.

    The critique of library training was far less satisfac-
tory in execution than was the bibliographic undertaking.
The survey of opinion as reported in LJ for July 1933 (p.
585-589) was based on a very limited seven-point questionnaire sent to a "highly selected" sample of recent library
school graduates. The results indicated that, in general,
the 77 students who replied tended to favor: 1) the selection
of students from those who held the baccalaureate degree and
had some previous experience in library work, and had indicated in an interview that they possessed such desirable
personal traits as adaptability, sense of humor, intelligence,

and calm temper; 2) approval of existing faculties as being well qualified by virtue of diversified experience, though "their teaching could be made more practical, broad, and inspirational"; 3) emphasis upon broad principles rather than a "mass of technical details to be mastered"; 4) existing methods of teaching cataloging, while criticizing the teaching of reference work and library administration for being overburdened with detail; 5) the making of courses in children's work, story-telling, and advanced cataloging "optional"; 6) the continuation of practice work as a requirement, though improvement in the enrichment of the student's experience would be desirable; and 7) the interrogation of library school directors concerning their policies regarding restrictions on enrollment, standards for faculty appointment, objectives of their schools, teaching methods, and alumni contacts. When one rereads, a generation later, the results of this inquiry, it is difficult to avoid the uncomfortable feeling that, except for minor variations, a comparable questionnaire would produce much the same responses if given today. How very familiar it all sounds: the battle between theory and practice; the relevance of the curriculum; admission policies, standards for faculty appointment, evaluation of teaching methods, and relationships with alumni. Is it the schools or is it the students who have not changed, or is it both?

Whether such undertakings as these were appropriate to the desires and needs of the Junior Members was questioned by many. Among such skeptics were Leon Carnovsky and E.W. McDiarmid, both of whom were at that time students in the University of Chicago's Graduate Library School. They urged strongly that the newly-organized group should set itself to the task of formulating a social philosophy of librarianship. In the January 1934 issue of <u>Library Journal</u> (p. 32-33), they wrote, in part:

> If ever there was a time when a philosophy was needed it is the present. Today when librarians are faced with the necessity of proving the library's importance to the community, they are rarely able to relate their activities to the social process. What librarian is not faced with the problem of presenting evidence to validate his claim to continued support in the face of greatly reduced municipal income?... The Junior Members' Round Table amply makes up in range what it lacks in length. Among its members are numbered representatives of all types of libraries, and all branches and depart-

ments of library activity.... Whether a definite philosophy of librarianship would ultimately emerge from the group's deliberations it is impossible to say; but there can be no doubt that from a sincere effort to determine "whither librarianship" the profession would immeasurably benefit.

Because of the criticism that the new group lacked a program, six objectives were adopted at the 1933 Chicago conference of the ALA, and these were set forth in the ALA Bulletin for March 1934 (p. 139-140) by Foster E. Mohrhardt:

To sponsor special meetings to discuss professional problems of concern to the younger librarians.

To increase the participation of young librarians in ALA conferences and other professional activities, including membership on ALA committees and participation on conference programs.

To promote studies that would benefit the profession of librarianship.

To encourage young librarians to join the ALA.

To plan various social activities.

To cooperate with the ALA in promoting its programs, plans, and activities.

Such statements were certainly general enough, and it is to be noted there were no "demands," no threats of secession, and no particular suggestion of social consciousness. Rather the program was largely self-serving; the young outsiders wanted some of what the "in group" had. Expressed or not, economics was in the background, and what the Young Turks really wanted was something that would increase upward mobility and earning power. Thus, Arthur Berthold, writing in "What of the Junior Members?" in the December 15, 1933 Library Journal (p. 1039-40) raised the question of whether the newly-formed round table was not actually an organization paralleling ALA itself, and urged a further clarification of the group's objectives, a cohesive program of action, and representation on important ALA committees so that the goals could be realized. The present writer, in his valedictory to the Juniors (ALA Bulletin, March 1938, p. 181-184), took much the same position as that of Berthold, and attributed much of the failure of the Round Table to form an adequate program and set of professional goals to the great diversity of disparate interests represented in the group.

In 1928 Stanley J. Kunitz, summa cum laude from Harvard and distinguished young poet in his own right, assumed the editorship of the Wilson Bulletin, a position which he held until 1943. In 1943 he invited Arthur Berthold to edit a monthly column entitled "The Young Librarian," and thus established his journal as something of an official voice for the young dissenters. In these columns were discussed such topics as: library training, librarianship as a science; the objectives of the public library; the impact of the National Youth Administration on the young librarian; the librarian's use of leisure (of which it might be said, parenthetically, he, or she, had plenty in those days). There was also the department called "The Roving Eye," which was available to any who wished to unburden themselves concerning the problems of youthful professionalism, and not a few did. Sandwiched in among special contributions dealing with school and small public libraries were features such as: Gretchen Garrison's "Public Libraries and the World View," Ortega y Gasset on "Man Must Tame the Book," and William Fielding Osborn's "The Library and the New Social Order." After reviewing the social role of the public library in the decade of the thirties, Osborn concluded with a statement from H.G. Wells, that colleges and universities should have "professorships of foresight," as well as professorships in history, and Osborn adds, "We might have in our libraries many chairs of foresight as well as in our universities the better to feel our way and be prepared for the problems of the future" (April 1934, p. 447). Thus was the plight of youth in the decade of the depression reviewed again and again by many voices, young and old, under the sympathetic editorial eye of Stanley Kunitz.

Two "battles" stand out in the memory of this writer as arousing particular concern: the segregation of Negroes at ALA conventions, and the famous case of the discharge of Philip O. Keeney, for alleged "communist" activity, from the post of librarian at Montana State University in Missoula The Keeney case became something of a cause célèbre among the young dissidents, for, despite the fact that the defendant had been cleared of any wrong-doing, in published and widely distributed reports of investigations by both the AAUP and the American Federation of Teachers, the ALA refused to

The Social Prerogative 361

intercede, using as the excuse that no funds were available for such defense. We still recall the sting in the observation by both teacher associations that, in view of the failure of the American Library Association to conduct its own inquiry, the two investigating teams were compelled to assume that Mr. Keeney was professionally competent.

So struggle against the indifference of the Establishment to the relation of the library to the problems of the world continued until the Wehrmacht swept all else but global war before it and library professionalization seemed by contrast puny indeed. When the decade of the forties dawned, youth was indeed becoming involved, but not in the politics of ALA.

With the surrender of Germany and Japan came a time of renewed hope and belief, marred only by the terror of the Bomb, that the lights would go on again all over the world and that there really would be bluebirds over the white cliffs of Dover. In the years that followed, young librarians were much too busy advancing their professional educations with the largess of the G. I. Bill to worry much about the Establishment. Nevertheless, the Milam dynasty was overthrown, and many former Juniors were coming into power. In the world outside, there was a brief rekindling of the old spirit with the third-party candidacy of Henry Wallace in 1948, but he was betrayed by some unfortunate associates, and anyway, Harry Truman--"good old Harry"--was doing quite all right, except, perhaps, for Korea. In '52 and again in '56, youth fought vigorously for Adlai Stevenson, but the country was weary of internationalism, even as it had been at the close of Woodrow Wilson's career, and was ready for retreat to "normalcy" with Eisenhower and the "father image."

With the election of John Fitzgerald Kennedy to the Presidency, the dream of youth seemed to be on the point of realization. The mystique of this dynamic young Irishman who had promised to get the country moving again was the very personification of the spirit of reform and innovation. But the dream was ended with three rifle shots in Dallas, and what had begun in hope ended in tragedy and frustration. "For a time," wrote Walter Lippman (or was it "Scotty" Reston?) "the worst in American life seemed to have prevailed over the best," and it was to be a different time, a sadder time, after Dallas.

In large measure Johnson reaped the harvest of which

Kennedy had sown the seed. Never before had the country seen such a massive outpouring of social legislation as that which was placed on the federal statutes between 1964 and 1968. But Johnson's social program also wrote finis to the New Deal, for his administration saw the realization of the social goals of Roosevelt and we found that they were not enough. It was the unnecessary and miserable war in Vietnam that brought Johnson down, yet history has within it a self-correcting force and, if we read the record aright, he, like Truman before him, can await the verdict of posterity with considerable confidence. Perhaps the year 1968 may be seen as the climax, the watershed of the decade--strife in the city streets, the meteoric rise and collapse of the McCarthy campaign, the dream of Martin Luther King and the youthful promise of Robert Kennedy both terminated by the assassin's bullet, and the defeat of Hubert Humphrey--indeed it was a different time, a sadder time, after Dallas. So the sixties came to a close; they were sad, sassy, and sexy, or as Clifton Daniel characterized them, a time of "morals, manners, money, and the moon."

The paradoxical sixties, with all their inconsistency and internal contradictions were poetically eulogized by at least one scientist, John Walsh. He wrote, in part, in "A Not Too Fond Farewell" (Science, December 26, 1969, p. 1605):

> Engendered on the New Frontier,
> Change was in the atmosphere;
> With Berkeley, Watts, and Vietnam
> Turbulence succeeded calm.
> On the campus things grew hotter.
> Up against the wall, O. Alma Mater!
> Teach-ins, sit-ins, power grabs
> Penetrate the ivory labs....
>
> And looking back, as on a graph,
> The Sixties rate this epitaph:
> For science, big and little both,
> An end to exponential growth.

The 20th Century had begun in the naïve belief that science and its burgeoning technology would solve all social problems, and that the realization of social justice would be possible without sacrifice of personal freedom, but it hadn't worked out that way. "We are a society bemused in its purpose yet secretly homesick for a lost world of inward tranquility," wrote Loren Eiseley in The Unexpected Universe.

Against such a backdrop of paradox, instability, and ambiguity it is not difficult to see a generation of youth frustrated, alienated, and in some quarters despised. Because youth today is economically more secure than it had been in the thirties, it has more time now to indulge in its social consciousness and Weltschmerz with more real freedom than ever before (though youth never regards itself as being free), so one may expect an increasingly intensified polarization in our social and political life. It is this latent sense of economic stability, security one might even call it, that has engendered in the youth of today an indifference to money that makes the single great difference between the youth of today and their counterpart in the thirties. With unemployment and misery on every hand, one did not, in those days, lightly cross swords with the Establishment, but recoiled from anything that might jeopardize his job if he were fortunate enough to have one. Thus, there is something reassuring about the emergence of reform from opulence rather than from those "shirtless ones" who had nothing to lose but their poverty. The shift in concern from economic to social values must be regarded as a healthy sign even though the elders may complain about the ingratitude of a generation that would bite the hand which has fed it. Was an earlier generation too much aware of the parental sacrifices that made its education possible? The question is not an easy one to answer. Conformity may not necessarily be the highest expression of gratitude. What parent, at one time or another, has not learned to his chagrin or embarrassment that Papa doesn't always "know best"?

The "happenings" at Bethel, New York, in Texas and California, and on the Isle of Wight, and the Washington Peace March against involvement in Vietnam were expressions of youth glorifying itself, seeking its own identity in the companionship of its contemporaries--its own kind. One may deplore its tactics and its excesses, but its determination to realize a better, more honest, less hypocritical world than that in which it finds itself should not be discounted and dismissed as adolescent naiveté. If we of an earlier generation deplore boys with beards and long hair, we must not forget that our elders looked with stern disapproval upon girls with lipstick and short hair. Such aberrations in tonsorial convention are but the symbols of protest, and though those of us who have come out of an earlier age may not find them appealing, they are basically unimportant. We of the twenties certainly did not regard the "flapper" as being physically repulsive or her smoking of a cigarette as an open invitation to seduction. "Why is a flapper like a bungalow?" our elders were wont to ask, and the approved response, "Because she's painted in front, shingled behind, and has no attic." In those days, too, it was not always easy to "tell the boys from the girls."

Once again the shock-waves of youthful frustration, discontent, and protest have reverberated in the smug little world of the librarians. The profession is in "one of those periods of testing out in which either good or evil will come," William Dix, the newly-elected president of ALA observed in his inaugural address at the 1969 Atlantic City convention. He went on to say, "...many people, most of them young, have realized that there are a number of wrongs in our society, have determined to right them promptly, and are in the process of attacking a number of our concepts and institutions which they believe, correctly or incorrectly, share some of the blame for the present situation. They have done a great service in disturbing our complacency. In the process, some of the revolutionaries have adopted tactics or ideological positions considerably at variance with what we used to believe were basic liberal positions." But "liberalism" for the newly-elected president was little more than an echo of the once vibrant spirit of the New Deal, and his key to the current problems of change was "understanding." The business of librarians, he said, is understanding. "This, I submit, is the real objective of all our techniques, and programs, and projects...for all kinds of people...to bring them understanding of man and the nature of the universe, of the means of livelihood and the uses of leisure, of human dignity and fallibility, of justice and humility."

The address was a sermon rather than a call to action, and despite his appeal for "understanding," and the obvious sincerity in his desire to sympathize with the problems of youth, there was in his peroration little real evidence that he understood the changes taking place either in society or in librarianship. "I submit that the most effective response to the challenge of these difficult and exciting times may be to do better--much better--what we have always tried to do."

As we listened to the demands of the young activists, the new constituency, and the response from the new leader of the Establishment, we were back once again in Chicago in

1933, along with the other "Sons of the Wild Jackass," pounding at the doors of, not 50 East Huron street, but, as it was in those days, 520 North Michigan Avenue, demanding involvement and participation. "To do better what we have always tried to do." Hang yourself, brave Crillon, we fought at Arques, but you were not there! The issues of yesterday and today--one could almost pair them off--Spain and Vietnam, little navies and ABMs and MIRVs, and some of the issues were identical--peace, involvement in the activities of the ALA, Negro (now black) segregation, library unions, condemnation of library education, intellectual freedom, the right to preserve the integrity of acquisition policies. The actors are different, but the script is much the same.

Recently a very close friend of ours, who is young in years but rich in wisdom, wrote to us, "There is a great need for a rebirth of professional dedication and enthusiasm." Professional dedication and enthusiasm--she might well have added "a sense of humor," though, blithe spirit that she is, there is no need to remind her of that. The younger generation does seem to lack a sense of humor, a sense of relationship of values. It is all very well to wear a crown of thorns and, indeed, every sensitive person carries one in secret, but in public it should be worn, if at all, cocked over one ear. In the same communication, our friend also observed that she was a "little weary of having so much of the blame laid at the door of the library schools," but that may be a consequence of having graduated from a school of very special excellence, a possible explanation that we shall not pursue. There is no doubt that library education in general has many shortcomings for which it must accept responsibility.

But there are, it seems to us, three important differences between the position of the young dissidents in the profession today and those of us of an earlier generation. Today there is in the youth a conspicuous lack of a sense of history, a feeling that they are the first to pound their fists against the pillars of the Establishment, whereas in the thirties we were painfully aware of history, especially the socio-economic history in the continuum of which we saw ourselves. "In our streets and on our campuses," wrote Eiseley, "there riots an extremist minority dedicated to the now, to the moment, however absurd, degrading, or irrelevant the moment may be. Such an activism deliberately rejects the past and is determined to start life anew--indeed, to reject the very institutions that feed, clothe, and sustain our swarming millions." Those who would remain ignorant of history are, indeed, bound to repeat its errors, and we can see little evidence that the new constituency has profited from the mistakes we made, indeed we doubt that they even know we made them.

Furthermore, these young librarians are free from the economic restraints that plagued us at every turn and hence they have more freedom than did we to exhibit their courage and appease their social consciences by wearing them, if not their hearts, on their sleeves. This blessing is not entirely unmixed. Certainly no one would ever want the young to have to heal the scars of a depression, scars which we have found never really completely heal; but a little hunger, just a little hunger, can be of real therapeutic value, a kind of catharsis, from which can emerge a deeper understanding of man and his problems.

Finally, the young activists have been able to articulate their needs and desires with such effectiveness as to arouse honest sympathy in the Establishment. Perhaps this success testifies to their persuasiveness, perhaps it is because the Establishment itself has not forgotten its own youthful struggles, for the dissenters of our day are the Establishment of the present. But whatever the reason, certainly youth gained a hearing in Atlantic City that we never did achieve until the passing of time gave us control by default. The meetings of the Council and the membership of the Association are "open," and perhaps that is an accomplishment in which all can take pride.

We of an earlier generation must constantly remind ourselves that just as the young rebels of our day are the Establishment now, so those who today strike at the pillars of society must themselves support the structure tomorrow. This is the way it should be, this is the way the world progresses. Youth must be heard and it must be heeded. "I would be very unhappy," our young friend wrote, "in a profession in which there is no room for growth and improvement." A major responsibility for promoting that growth and improvement must, of necessity, rest upon the shoulders of the young. "Youth is the only wealth," wrote Christopher Morley in Where the Blue Begins, "for youth has Time in its purse."

President Dix was entirely right in emphasizing, in

his inaugural address, the need for "understanding." We do not need, nor should there be, a "silent majority." A silent majority is the stuff of which totalitarianism is made. A bridge of communication must be built across the generation gap; this is one of the great responsibilities of the library schools. Building bridges of communication across generation gaps is what education is all about. The building of such a bridge will not be easy, it never has been; and, one must add, the older generation must, in large measure, bear the burden of its construction. It is the older generation that possesses the greater share of power, and responsibility resides where the power center is.

But the dissidents, too, must assume their share of the burden. They must act with a sense of responsibility and purpose. They cannot forever indulge themselves in the luxury and self-deception of hedonism. They must not give themselves over to self-pity. They must not robe themselves in the pontifical cloak of Rightness. They must not forget that in those great symbols of the intellectual life, the Medieval universities, especially in Bologna and Paris, the bid for student power came to grief when the aggressive traits of its leaders engendered such abuse and chaos, that it became necessary that oppressive authority be taken over by the state, and the university system was set back for generations. As Jacques Barzun has said, we do not want to return "to 1266 and all that," but there are some disquieting indications that the bid for "student power" has affected adversely governmental support for higher education and might eventually lead to state and political control. Irrational conduct breeds irrational response, and from such confrontations no one profits. The generation gap must be bridged rationally.

Three hundred years before the dawn of the Christian Era, Chuang-tsu posed the great question of all communication--"How shall I talk of the sea to the frog," he asked, "if it has never left the pond? How shall I talk of the frost to a bird of the summer land, if it has never left the land of its birth? How shall I talk of life with the sage if he is the prisoner of his own dogma?" Unfortunately, there are prisoners of their own dogma on both sides of the generation gap.

In the early years of his professional career, the present writer, himself one of the dissenting voices, captioned a report for the Wilson Bulletin, on the 1936 ALA convention at Richmond, Virginia, with the words of Figaro in Beaumarchais' Barber of Seville, "Je me presse de rire de tout... de peur d'être obligé d'en pleurer." Today we are still infected with Figaro's cynical pessimism, but we have more hope than we did in the thirties. Even then we saw the menacing shadow of Hitler and the gathering thunderheads of war, and we were attempting to prepare ourselves emotionally for the deluge. Certainly the social problems of today are not insignificant--overpopulation, destruction of the environment, the plight of the cities, racial confrontation, intellectual freedom, war, poverty; we are pressured from every side and we can see no clear solutions. But a quarter of a century of working with students has given us confidence in their capacity to meet these monumental problems head on, and we have not forgotten the "flappers" and the dire predictions about them. Admittedly, the youth of today has a perilous knife-edge to travel, and there are times when they make it very difficult to love them, but we are still very much on the side of youth and we want to stay there. If there is no hope in youth, there is no hope.

So the wheel of fortune turns, ever changing yet ever the same, but never quite the same, either, for it rolls inexorably into a future that we can neither know nor comprehend, a future compounded of menace and promise, of dreams shattered and goals achieved; yet, with all its folly and all its wisdom the heritage of the young.

The Disadvantaged Majority:
Women Employed in Libraries

by Anita R. Schiller

Reprinted by permission from the April 1970 issue of
American Libraries (1:4), p. 345-349. Copyright 1970
by American Library Association.

In most professions women are the disadvantaged minority. In librarianship they are the disadvantaged majority. Although librarianship traditionally has been open to women's employment, and today about four out of every five librarians are women, their salaries tend typically to be lower than those of men librarians. The top positions in the largest institutions are held increasingly by men, and there appears to be a growing trend toward greater inequality between the sexes in the library profession. A national study of academic librarians in 1966-67 showed, for example, that the median salary for men ($8990) was about $1500 higher than that for women ($7455), that men were about twice as likely as women to be chief librarians, and that men who were not chief librarians tended to earn more than women who were.[1] The findings show further that as experience increases, median salary differentials between men and women grow progressively wider, even where educational levels of the two groups are equal. These findings highlight the need to examine the question of equality of opportunity for women in librarianship.

Although many previous studies of librarians reveal similar kinds of inequalities, the status of women in the profession has not been singled out as a matter of special concern, and little serious attention has been devoted to the subject. A check of Library Literature from 1921 to date shows, for example, that in the past fifty years only one published monograph has appeared on women in librarianship, and this was done recently in Great Britain.[2] Three master's theses and occasional articles have attempted to assemble some basic data, but even when taken together the picture they drew is sketchy, at best. The index to the 1969 Bowker Annual..., a basic source of current information about libraries and librarians, contains only one reference to women, and this is for the address of the Women's National Book Association. And despite the fact that library manpower has been considered as a top priority professional issue, there has been little, if any, attempt to examine the special kinds of personnel problems which relate to women librarians, even though they comprise the numerical majority of the profession.

When then, when there are alarming signs of growing inequality of opportunity for women in librarianship, does the profession seem so basically unconcerned about uncovering the facts and examining the issues? Although other professions have begun to consider how women can be attracted to their ranks in larger numbers, and several professional associations recently have passed specific resolutions aimed at improving the status of women in their respective fields, the library profession has remained remarkably aloof from this matter. Many librarians, it seems, would prefer it if the subject never came up at all, or better still, if women had never entered librarianship in the first place. Just think how this would have changed the librarian's image!

It is important to bring this view out into the open, for because the majority of its practitioners are women, librarianship is different from most professions, and reluctance to discuss the status of women librarians may have something to do with this important fact. Librarians esteem the contribution they make toward society, and they seek to win the public recognition they believe the profession deserves. By calling attention to the problems of women in librarianship, public attention would continue to dwell on the fact that many librarians are indeed women, and this is no mark of prestige for any profession. Furthermore, studies of librarians consistently show that men librarians, as a group, are typically younger than the women, and the profession, by attracting more men, would undoubtedly benefit from a lowering of overall age levels as well.

It is not, then, in the best interest of the library profession simply to ignore the question of women as long as it can, hoping that women eventually will cease to enter the field, and join the other professions which claim to want them? This, indeed, may be the implicitly desired goal of the present policy of the American Library Association. A do-nothing policy has an apparent appeal. But can the ALA continue to countenance basic social injustice within the profession which it represents? In its attempts to improve and upgrade librarianship, can the Association continue to ignore the status of the majority of its members? And can it remain impervious to the aspirations of this majority, while a movement for the rights of women is gaining worldwide momentum?

The United Nations Declaration of Women's Rights, adopted by the General Assembly on November 7, 1967, states that "discrimination against women, denying or limiting as it does their equality of rights with men is fundamentally unjust and constitutes an offense against human dignity." (Article I) This document goes on further to state that "all appropriate measures shall be taken to educate public opinion...toward the eradication of prejudice and the abolition of customary and all other practices which are based on the idea of the inferiority of women." (Article III) While there are undoubtedly certain social conditions, in addition to open job discrimination, which contribute to the low status of women, and while these may operate much more subtly, if we genuinely believe in equality of opportunity, why don't we say so? In its reluctance to commit itself on this issue, the library profession has accommodated itself to social prejudice.

An interesting sidelight, which illustrates how out-of-touch with the times we are, is provided by the subject headings librarians have devised to categorize the attainments of women in the various professions: The Library of Congress Subject Headings...for example, uses the term "Women as authors," not "Women authors"; "Women as physicians," not "Women physicians"; "Women as librarians," not "Women librarians," etc.[3] (Yet when we come to "Women as criminals," we are advised to refer to the heading "Delinquent women.") While it is delightful to note the cross reference "Women, see also Charm," and disturbing to find the heading "Women as colonists," it is clear that this terminology, which arose in a bygone age, is not in keeping with present conditions. The view that we should not seek equal opportunity between the sexes is similarly, but much more seriously, out-of-date.

Librarians today are in a unique position to challenge popular prejudice by actively seeking to promote genuine equality within the library profession itself. By seeking to improve conditions of employment, and by raising educational standards at all levels of the profession--the bottom as well as the top--librarianship can strengthen its own position. Librarianship cannot upgrade itself without upgrading opportunities for women who constitute the majority of the profession. Nor should it expect to gain the public esteem that it seeks by tacitly endorsing inequality of opportunity, and furthering, by its own inaction, the all-too-familiar image of librarianship as a passive, unchallenging, and low-paid profession. If librarianship has sufficient self-respect for its own contribution, it will not belittle itself by following other professions backward into the nineteenth century to exclude women from its ranks or to keep them in less privileged positions, while other professions begin now to lower the barriers to women's advancement. On the contrary, since librarianship opened its doors to women well before most other professions, it can lead the way toward full social equality within the professions by seeking to become the first profession to establish equal career opportunities between the sexes.

The library profession should be able to compete on equal ground among all professions for the most talented and capable recruits of both sexes. There is no good reason why librarianship should lose competent women recruits to other professions because it fails to offer women equal opportunities for advancement. Yet this may occur, if librarianship fails to improve the status of women while other professions offer them increasing opportunities for study and advancement. Similarly, there is no good reason why librarianship should lose competent men recruits to other fields because it fails to offer competitive rewards.

The best interest of the library profession cannot be served by continuing to allow unequal opportunities for women. By recognizing and facing this important social issue, and by seeking consciously and deliberately to change, rather than accept, popular prejudice, librarianship has everything to gain.

What then should the ALA do to promote equality of opportunity within the profession? First, the ALA should openly state its willingness to deal with the issue, and express its conviction that equal opportunities for women should be provided. A formal resolution recognizing this commitment should be drawn up and endorsed by the Association.

Second, the ALA should initiate and support a com-

The Social Prerogative 373

prehensive research program, designed to examine the status of women in librarianship and to determine how present conditions operate, overtly or subtly, to prevent women from achieving and maintaining equal status with men. The findings of these research studies should be widely disseminated among the profession, and used as a guide to official policy.

Third, the ALA should open up the channels of communication for discussion of equality of opportunity within the library profession. This subject should receive a prominent position on the agenda at the Association's next annual conference, and an open forum column should appear regularly in American Libraries.

Together, these three proposals: acknowledging an interest in improving opportunities for women, supporting research on the status of women and on the nature of discrimination, and encouraging expression of professional opinion on this important subject, constitute some minimum and immediate steps for action by the ALA.

Fourth, the ALA should establish a special committee on the status of women or some other suitable organizational body to develop procedures to deal with specific instances of reported discrimination. This committee might also be charged with setting up some mechanism for publicizing top-level job opportunities as they become available, so that qualified women candidates can be considered for these positions.

Fifth, the ALA should announce a stated minimum salary for all librarians which is consistent with going minimum salary rates for comparable educational qualifications in other professions where women do not necessarily predominate. Institutions which fail to approach this basic minimum should be censured by the Association.

Sixth, the ALA should support measures designed to promote the rights of women, both in the librarian's professional work and through cooperation with other professions.

Seventh, using the findings provided research studies, and recognizing that far-reaching programs may have to be considered to bring about fully equal opportunity in the library profession, the ALA should seek to develop a comprehensive long-range action program, designed to restructure present arrangements and effect significant change and improvement.

The following specific illustrations are offered as some possible examples of activities which might be undertaken within the overall framework suggested above:

> Statistical indicators which show the salaries and status of men and women librarians, and how the relative position of men and women in librarianship compares to that in other professions should be developed, both to reveal present conditions and to show trends over a period of time.
>
> A study on the status of women in contemporary life should be issued as part of the "Reading for an Age of Change" series.
>
> Subject headings which reflect customary prejudice toward women should be reconsidered and revised.
>
> A special fund to support advanced and continuing education for women of particular promise should be considered.
>
> Child care facilities should be instituted, perhaps in conjunction with other associations and institutions in local areas, to encourage the continuing employment of professionally trained women librarians.
>
> An interdisciplinary conference on improving career opportunities for women could be sponsored jointly by the ALA and other professional associations.

These proposals and suggestions are offered to launch a discussion on an important issue which has been seriously neglected. It is hoped that they will be refined, improved, or replaced by better ones which seek similarly to promote the interests and aspirations of the library profession and its members. [4]

Notes

1. Schiller, Anita R. <u>Characteristics of Professional Personnel in College and University Libraries</u>, Illinois State Library Research Series, No. 16. Springfield: Illinois State Library, 1969.

2. Ward, Patricia Layzell. Women in Librarianship: An Investigation into Certain Problems of Library Staffing, Library Association Pamphlet, No. 25. London: Library Association, 1966.
3. Library Literature used the term "Women as librarians" until 1952, when the wording was changed to read "Women librarians."
4. On January 22, 1970 the American Library Association, LAD/PAS Committee on Economic Status, Welfare, and Fringe Benefits passed a motion instructing the chairman to appoint a subcommittee to gather facts relating to alleged sexual discrimination within the library profession. Such a subcommittee has now been appointed. As part of the fact finding program librarians are requested to report alleged cases of sexual discrimination in the profession to the subcommittee. These reports will be analyzed to assist the committee in assessing the need for remedial programs.

Report of alleged sexual discrimination shoud be forwarded to: Pauline Iacono, chairman, Subcommittee Investigating Sexual Discrimination, c/o Coe College, Cedar Rapids, IA 52402.

Law Library Service to Prisoners--
The Responsibility of Nonprison Libraries

by O. James Werner

Reprinted by permission from the May 1970 issue of
Law Library Journal (63:2), p. 231-240.

I. Prisoners' Need for Library Materials

At the beginning of 1968, there were 196,000 inmates of Federal and State prisons in the United States,[1] about 10 percent of them in Federal penitentiaries. As experience has shown, not all persons convicted of crimes are guilty, nor are all of them given the protection that the law requires from the time of arrest until their conviction. Law reports contain numerous cases in which prisoners have been freed because of improper treatment that violated their constitutional rights. A question that is receiving increased interest is: How are indigent prisoners, who claim they are illegally in prison, to find effective relief in the courts when they cannot afford legal counsel? If they had a right to (free) counsel, they would, of course, exercise it and not bother law librarians about cases and statutes that they think might help them. However, the courts have not yet declared that they have such a right.

The indigent prisoner who believes that he is illegally incarcerated must himself initiate whatever legal action is available to test the legality of his imprisonment.[2] It is from this fact that a need arises for law library service to prisoners. Whether it is desirable to provide such services rather than some alternative method of assistance is a question that will be discussed later. The situation that exists today is that alternative services are so inadequate that prisoners have nowhere else to turn but to the libraries for the minimum information they need to initiate legal actions on their own behalf.

Are the libraries in prisons at all adequate to provide

these basic services? In general, prison libraries have been found wanting, even as to their nonlegal materials. In 1966, the American Correctional Association (ACA) and the Association of Hospital and Institutional Libraries (AHIL) found that libraries in 150 prisons lacked about 1,000,000 books overall.[3] It was said by the chairman of AHIL that prisons are at the bottom of the list insofar as library materials, staff, services, facilities, and financing are concerned. In the same year, the State Library of Indiana surveyed prison libraries in that State and found that 75 percent of the material in their collections was useless.[4] If matters have improved much since 1966, it has not yet been reported in the literature.

Morris L. Cohen, in his article in Prison Journal,[5] states that holdings of law books in prison libraries are particularly poor. He reports that in most States the prison libraries' holdings of law books "are quite small, the sets incomplete and the sources out of date." Consequently, even if inmates could make liberal use of their prison libraries, the legal information they seek would not be available there. They must turn to libraries outside the prisons.

Besides the obvious need for legal information relevant to their imprisonment, inmates also need legal information to help them solve family, personal, and financial problems that exist while they are in prison. Though it may not be prudent for a prisoner to act as his own attorney, the man who cannot afford professional services has no other choice.

Finally, it has been suggested that there is therapeutic value to prisoners in gaining a better understanding of their legal rights.[6] Cohen reports that a majority of State prison officials, responding to an informal inquiry, indicated that access to legal materials did not adversely affect prisoners' morale, discipline, or rehabilitation and that positive effects on the prisoners were most frequently noted.[7]

One writer has noted, in regard to a now famous convict's legal activities while in prison, that

> The prison officials did not mind Gideon's legal activities--indeed they seemed to regard them as therapy. One said, "Usually when they are trying to get out legally, you know they walk on their toes around here."

...An assistant warden said: "Our feeling is: Boys, if you can get out of here legal, we're with you."[8]

II. Legal Aspects of Prisoners' Access to Legal Materials

The question of whether a prisoner has a legal right of access to law books and other legal materials has not been judicially determined, despite the California Supreme Court's statement that a convict has no legally enforceable right to engage in legal research.[9] The present situation was aptly described by the U.S. Court of Appeals, Ninth Circuit, which said: "Courts are currently struggling with the question of the extent of a prisoner's right to have access to legal materials...the Supreme Court has not yet spoken on the subject and the law can hardly be said to be settled."[10]

There are cases involving regulation of the use of prison libraries and law books in the possession of prisoners, but the point at issue in such cases was not whether the prisoner had a right to legal materials but whether the library regulation improperly prevented him from challenging the validity of his conviction,[11] or whether the regulation limiting the amount of library materials a prisoner could possess did in fact deprive him of effective access to a court.[12] Until a case arises that squarely faces this issue, the best that can be done is to see what inferences might be drawn from those cases that involve access to the courts.

The most compelling reason for allowing prisoners access to legal materials is to aid them in presenting possibly valid claims that their rights have been violated in the process of committing them to prison. Although it has been held that an indigent prisoner has a constitutional right to State aid in seeking a post-conviction remedy,[13] based on the 14th amendment requirement of equal protection of the law, the case did not reach the question of whether the indigent prisoner was entitled to free legal counsel.

The remedy most often sought to enable an unlawfully incarcerated person to obtain his freedom is the writ of habeas corpus. It has been frequently held, however, that one has no constitutional right to the assistance of counsel in a habeas corpus proceeding,[14] on the ground that it is not a proceeding that is criminal in nature and therefore does not come within the sixth amendment provision that in all criminal prosecutions the accussed shall have the assistance of counsel. A court, however, may in its discretion appoint counsel for a prisoner who petitions for a writ of habeas corpus.[15]

It would seem, then, that whether it will ultimately be found that a convict has a right to legal materials depends upon whether or not such materials are necessary to him in his endeavor to gain access to the courts. Some writers have argued that courts should find that the doctrine of access to the courts implies access to adequate legal materials.[16] It was argued by the prisoner petitioners in Gilmore v. Lynch[17] that prison regulations relating to the contents of the prison library and prison policy regarding the obtaining and keeping of private law books and court opinions by prisoners violated the due process and equal protection clauses of the 14th amendment. They contended that the regulations infringed upon their right of access to the courts and discriminated between indigent and affluent prisoners, in that the latter could afford counsel who would perform legal research for them. The court held that substantial constitutional questions were presented by these allegations and that a three-judge court could be convened to test the regulations. However, further proceedings following the remand have not yet been reported.

Until recently, Federal courts have been reluctant to interfere with the administration of prisons, even when prison regulations sometimes hindered inmates' access to the courts. A "hands off doctrine"[18] was followed unless the prisoner had actually been denied access to a court.[19]

A Federal district court has held that reasonable access to a book of rules of procedure for a State court was part of reasonable access to the courts where the prisoner, not represented by counsel, had a suit pending before the State supreme court.[20] After stating that reasonable access to the courts is a right given by the due process clause of the 14th amendment, the court said: "In the context of this case, reasonable access to the courts means a right of a prisoner to prepare, serve, and file legal papers and prosecute legal actions affecting his personal liberty."

The court in Hatfield v. Bailleaux[21] recognized that access to the courts means the opportunity to prepare documents necessary or appropriate to commence and prosecute court proceedings, but it denied the prisoners' suit to enjoin prison officials from enforcing regulations limiting the time and place for doing legal research and restricting the acquisition and retention of law books by prisoners. The court found that the regulations did not in fact deprive the inmates of reasonable access to the courts, and it said: "The fact, if it be a fact, that access could have been further facilitated without impairing effective prison administration is... immaterial."

A 1969 case that offers some guidance on the direction the law was taking before the recent changes in the composition of the U.S. Supreme Court is Johnson v. Avery.[22] In that case, a life prisoner in the Tennessee State Penitentiary filed a "motion for law books and a typewriter" and sought relief from his confinement in the maximum security building where he had been placed for violating a prison regulation. His motion was treated as a petition for a writ of habeas corpus by the district court, which ordered his release from disciplinary confinement and held the regulation void. The regulation forbade inmates from assisting other inmates in preparing writs or other legal papers. The Supreme Court held, 7 to 2, that the State may not enforce such a regulation unless and until it provides some reasonable alternative to assist inmates in the preparation of petitions for postconviction relief. The court pointed out that "...the initial burden of presenting a claim to post-conviction relief usually rests upon the indigent prisoner himself with such help as he can obtain within the prison walls...." It approved the conclusion of the district court that "...[f]or all practical purposes, if such prisoners cannot have the assistance of a 'jailhouse lawyer,' their possibly valid constitutional claims will never be heard in any court."[23]

If the courts extend much further the principle that "access of prisoners to the courts for the purpose of presenting their complaints may not be denied or obstructed"[24] (emphasis added), then it seems reasonable that eventually it may be found that hindering a prisoner's access to legal materials in effect obstructs his access to the courts. This might be so despite the oft-repeated statement "that a petition for a writ of habeas corpus properly contains allegations of fact alone, and that legal arguments are not a proper part thereof."[25] A prisoner's petition will not receive sympathetic consideration by a court if it is a rambling description of every fact concerning his arrest and trial. He needs to know enough law to recognize possible defects in his judgment or sentence and to state only those facts that are legal-

The Social Prerogative 381

ly relevant. Therefore, in the future, a court might say that, for all practical purposes, if prisoners cannot have access to legal materials, their possibly valid constitutional claims might never be seriously considered in any court.

A recent case that relied upon Johnson v. Avery offers some indication of how prisons may begin to provide assistance to inmates working on their own legal matters. In Ayers v. Ciccone,[26] a prison was enjoined from enforcing a regulation that prohibited prisoners from assisting other prisoners in legal matters. The injunction was terminated, however, after the prison instituted a program of preliminary legal assistance under which a consultant was hired to help inmates with their legal matters for 12 hours per week, or for a longer time if needed.

While it appears that prisoners have no presently recognized right of access to legal materials, there are some State prison systems[27] that have assumed responsibility to provide some basic legal information for inmates. But the implementation of such policies, as well as the number of States that have them, cannot be considered adequate, in view of the continuing requests libraries receive for legal materials. Some hope for future improvement is indicated by the 1966 statement of the director of the Florida Division of Corrections: "I think it is apparent that the day is coming when legal services will be an integral part of the institutional program."[29]

III. Present Law Library Service to Prisoners

In an effort to find out what kind of law library service prisoners now receive from nonprison libraries, the writer sent a questionnaire to the libraries of the largest law schools, the largest county libraries, and the State law libraries in each of the 50 States, the District of Columbia, and Puerto Rico. In the case of States not having State law libraries, the questionnaire was sent to their supreme court library. A total of 155 questionnaires was sent, 93 of which were returned. The percentage of replies from each type of library was as follows:

Libraries That Returned Questionnaire

Private Law School Libraries   64.0%
State Law School Libraries   56.8
State Law Libraries   62.5
State Supreme Court Libraries   56.2
County Law Libraries   48.5

The first half of the questionnaire dealt with library policies on service to prisons and inmates, while the second half dealt with library experience in servicing them. Looking first at the replies concerning policies, the survey indicated that State law school libraries are the most willing to provide service to the various penal institutions. The percentage of libraries in each group willing to lend law books or photocopies of legal materials was as shown in Table 1.[30]

The survey indicated clearly that the thing law libraries are most willing to do is to furnish photocopies of material in law books and periodicals, for which they usually charge from 5 cents to 15 cents per page and often require payment in advance. Table 2 shows the percentage of libraries in each group that are willing to provide various types of library materials to inmates or to their prison libraries.

The percentage of libraries willing to lend books is probably smaller than the above figures indicate because some of the libraries did not clearly distinguish between loans and photocopies of the same type of material.

In general, the reporting libraries preferred to lend materials to prison libraries rather than directly to inmates. The percentage of libraries in each group willing to lend to either was as shown in Table 3.

Loan periods varied from 3 days to 3 months, although the most popular periods were between 2 and 4 weeks. One State law library loans materials to prisoners for 3 weeks but will let prison libraries borrow for a 3 month period.

The libraries' willingness to provide reference service to inmates varied considerably, depending upon which penal institution the prisoners were in. The most widely available service is the reference service that supreme court and State

Table 1. Libraries Willing to Make Loans[31]

Will loan to	Priv. L. Sch.	St. L. Sch.	St. L. Lib.	Sup. Ct. Lib.	Co. L. Lib.
Own State prison	6.2%	48.0%	40.9%	22.2%	17.6%
Own county jail	6.2	40.0	13.6	22.2	35.3
Own city jail	6.2	40.0	13.6	22.2	5.9
Federal prison in State	6.2	44.0	8.1	0	5.9
Out-of-State prisons	0	36.0	4.5	11.1	0
Other county jails	0	32.0	4.5	0	0

Table 2. Libraries Willing to Lend Various Materials

Type of material	Priv. L. Sch.	St. L. Sch.	St. L. Lib.	Sup. Ct. Lib.	Co. L. Lib.
Reporters	18.7%	32.0%	36.6%	11.1%	29.4%
Statutes	18.7	28.2	31.8	11.1	29.4
Textbooks	12.4	44.0	31.8	0	23.5
Legal fiction	12.4	40.0	13.6	0	11.8
Periodicals	12.4	28.2	22.7	0	29.4
Court rules	12.4	28.2	4.5	0	17.7
Legal dictionaries	12.4	12.0	13.6	0	17.7
Legal biographies	6.2	32.0	22.7	0	5.9
Practice books	12.4	20.0	4.5	0	5.9
Photocopies	62.5	80.0	59.0	66.6	29.4
Records/tapes	6.2	4.0	4.5	0	0

Table 3. Libraries Willing to Lend to Inmates and Prison Libraries

Will lend to	Priv. L. Sch.	St. L. Sch.	St. L. Lib.	Sup. Ct. Lib.	Co. L. Lib.
Prisons	12.4%	44.0%	36.6%	0	23.5%
Inmates	6.2	32.0	27.3	0	17.7

law libraries offer to inmates of their own State prisons. Table 4 shows the percentage of libraries in each group willing to provide reference services.

A few libraries indicated they were willing to provide services but that they had little or no prisoner requests. Only eight of the reporting libraries said they received over 100 requests for legal materials from prisoners during the past year. Most of them received from 1 to 10 requests. The percentage of libraries in each group receiving requests was as shown in Table 5.

The Law Library of the California State Library indicated that it received between 6,000 and 7,000 requests for materials during the past year. Because of the number of requests, the library found it necessary to set a limit of five requests per inmate during any 2 week period. Even then the number of loans it made during the year amounted to about 5,000. The Law Bureau of the Pennsylvania State Library estimated that it received over 1,000 requests during the last year. The percentage of libraries in each group that made loans to inmates was as shown in Table 6.

Again, some of the above figures include libraries that furnished photocopies rather than actual book loans. It should be kept in mind also that many of the libraries that did not report loans did provide photocopies of materials requested. The only library that reported any losses resulting from loans to prisoners reported substantial losses from the special collection it maintains for loans to prisoners.

Not many of the reporting libraries answered the question about the attitudes of prison officials regarding law library service to inmates. Some libraries stated they had no contact with the officials; through correspondence they dealt only with the prisoners or prison librarians. The percentage of libraries in each group reporting on official attitudes was as shown in Table 7.

The materials most often requested by prisoners were reporters (or cases) and statutes. The percentage of libraries in each group that received requests for the various types of material was as shown in Table 8.

Reference service to prisoners, judging from the survey, has been rather limited, although the Law Bureau of the Pennsylvania State Library reported answering about 300

Table 4. Libraries Willing to Provide Reference Services to Various Institutions

Service to	Priv. L. Sch.	St. L. Sch.	St. L. Lib.	Sup. Ct. Lib.	Co. L. Lib.
Own State prison	31.2%	44.0%	54.5%	55.5%	0
Own county jail	31.2	44.0	40.9	33.3	23.5
Own city jail	18.7	44.0	31.8	44.4	11.8
Federal prison in State	25.0	44.0	36.6	22.2	0
Out-of-State prisons	12.4	40.0	36.6	33.3	0
Other county jails	12.4	40.0	31.8	22.2	0

Table 5. Libraries That Received Requests for Legal Materials

No. of requests	Priv. L. Sch.	St. L. Sch.	St. L. Lib.	Sup. Ct. Lib.	Co. L. Lib.
1-10	56.2%	32.0%	27.3%	33.3%	29.4%
11-50	0	28.2	9.1	11.1	11.8
51-100	0	8.0	4.5	0	0
Over 100	0	4.0	18.1	0	0

Table 6. Libraries That Made Loans to Prisoners

No. of loans	Priv. L. Sch.	St. L. Sch.	St. L. Lib.	Sup. Ct. Lib.	Co. L. Lib.
1-10	6.2%	12.0%	9.1%	0	23.5%
11-50	0	12.0	18.1	0	5.9
51-100	0	0	0	11.0	0
Over 100	12.4	0	22.7	0	0

Table 7. Libraries Reporting on Prison Officials' Attitudes

Attitude of officials	Priv. L. Sch.	St. L. Sch.	St. L. Lib.	Sup. Ct. Lib.	Co. L. Lib.
Cooperative	12.4%	0 %	27.3%	0 %	0 %
Hostile	0	12.0	4.5	0	5.9
Indifferent	6.2	12.0	4.5	11.0	5.9
Mixed	12.4	4.0	0	0	5.9

Table 8. Libraries Receiving Requests for Various Materials

Material requested	Priv. L. Sch.	St. L. Sch.	St. L. Lib.	Sup. Ct. Lib.	Co. L. Lib.
Reporters	43.7%	40.0%	36.6%	22.2%	29.4%
Statutes	31.2	36.0	45.4	22.2	29.4
Textbooks	12.4	4.0	13.6	0	5.9
Legal dictionaries	0	0	4.5	0	0
Legal biographies	0	0	0	0	0
Legal fiction	0	0	0	0	0
Periodicals	18.7	0	4.5	0	5.9
Court rules	0	4.0	4.5	0	0
Practice books	0	0	13.6	0	5.9
Photocopies	12.4	32.0	22.7	11.1	0
Records/tapes	0	0	0	0	0

Table 9. Libraries That Answered Reference Questions

No. of questions answered	Priv. L. Sch.	St. L. Sch.	St. L. Lib.	Sup. Ct. Lib.	Co. L. Lib.
1-10	25.0%	32.0%	18.1%	22.2%	5.9%
11-50	6.2	12.0	9.1	11.1	0
51-100	0	0	4.5	0	0
Over 100	0	4.0	4.5	0	0

The Social Prerogative 389

questions during the last year. A number of the libraries seemed to think that reference service amounted to the practice of law and shied away from it on those grounds. Eight of the private law school libraries and seven of the State law school libraries said that they refer most reference questions to their student legal aid services. The public defender was mentioned by three State law school libraries, a State law library, and a county law library as the office to which they normally refer reference questions. The percentage of libraries in each group that did not answer reference questions was as shown in Table 9.

One State law school library sends a form letter to inquiring prisoners, stating that the only service it can render is to give the number of pages and the cost of copying an item if it is requested by citation. It will send the copy if the prisoner will pay 10 cents per page in advance. It also refers prisoners to the American Civil Liberties Union for civil rights questions and encloses a copy of the State post-conviction remedy statute.

Comments made by the reporting librarians provide an impressionistic view of the pros and cons of law library service to prisoners. A representative selection of comments follows, grouped by the type of library:

Private Law School Libraries

I wish county and State law libraries would provide a fuller service to local prisons here.

Our library attitude is strongly in favor of more service [to prisoners], a national program is needed, and dollars must be made available to support such a service.

Since the attitude of prison officials and the State libraries that should serve prisons is less than one would expect, a library that is willing to serve prisons will be innundated with requests.

Letters from inmates themselves come occasionally ...these requests are never granted.

I doubt if I would loan any material; but the decision would probably be with our dean.

State Law School Libraries

Our law library does not hold itself out to practice law.

We do not provide such service.

We're willing to answer all questions regardless of source, and we'll try to lend or copy any type of material requested.

All contact with prisoners in past years has been excellent; they were most cooperative.

I feel prisoners have need for law library services and that we ought to bend over backward to see that they get them...they have little enough in the way of constructive pursuits to occupy their time...."

The number and accuracy of [prisoner inquiries] manifests a surprisingly sophisticated and widespread awareness of legal matters among inmates.

Wish that we could do more.

State Law Libraries

We wish the Department of Corrections would provide better basic libraries.

As we have always (in this century) been willing to lend law books anywhere within the State, service to [prisons] represents no particular problem.

We have tried to interest State authorities to establish unit law libraries in State prisons without success.

For the most part, we have found the prisoners moderate in their demands. Except for a few who claimed to be indigents, they pay promptly for the cost of Xeroxed work.

Our experience thus far has been that prisoners are only interested in actual decisions that may have some direct helpful effect on their own personal status.

We did at one time Xerox copies for [prisoners] and they would pay 10 cents a sheet, but the requests became so numerous that the Executive Council ruled that people who want Xeroxing done have to come in person...[one prisoner] would tell the other and it became such a nuisance--about all we were doing was 'working' for the prisoners.

...our staff and book budget are barely enough to take care of our own supreme court and other legitimate patrons.

Our State law library does not have a policy of loaning materials to anyone but attorneys.

State Supreme Court Libraries

I would like to know to whom I could refer the prisoners for the help they request.

Our library is quite willing to lend any materials which circulate at all to prisons and prisoners... we will also make photocopies of noncirculating materials....

With a staff of two and meager copying facilities, we try to discourage requests or refer them to another department.

If you do research for one you will have to do it for all, and pretty soon you will be using all your time for the prisoners. We cut out research altogether.

County Law Libraries

It is our policy to Xerox the material specifically requested and send it, gratis, to the prisoner.

Our library maintains a criminal law library...located in the central county jail...available to prisoners on court order.

...we consider the State library as the proper source for prison inmates.

...it is the policy of this library not to lend books except for use in the courthouse complex....

We don't loan to any laymen.

IV. Some Proposals for Legal and Library Services to Prisoners

Various solutions, which are to some extent alternatives to law library service, have been offered for the problem of post-conviction relief for indigent prisoners. The following list of proposals illustrates the current trend:

1. Extend constitutional due process to include a right to counsel for inmates seeking post-conviction relief.[32]

2. Establish a legal ombudsman to investigate prisoners' cases, unfair policies, procedures, and rules that apply to inmates seeking remedies.[33]

3. Establish a public defender to investigate and file collateral attacks, and to advise prisoners whether their complaints entitle them to relief.[34]

4. Permit laymen--in or out of prison--to act as "next friends" to help prisoners preparing papers or claims, so long as such laymen do not hold themselves out as practicing law.[35]

5. Establish a system under which regulated prison trusties would advise other prisoners of their rights, such "jailhouse lawyers" being selected by prison officials for their scholarship and character.[36]

6. Distribute to prisoners legal pamphlets, such as the series prepared by the Minnesota Correction Service in cooperation with the Minnesota Bar Association, containing vital information about post-conviction relief and procedures.[37]

The writer favors a proposal close to that of Mr. Justice Douglas, based on the same reasons he adduces; namely, that

> ...more and more of the effort in ferreting out the basis of claims and the agencies responsible for them and in preparing the almost endless paper work for their prosecution is work for laymen. There are not enough lawyers to manage and supervise all

The Social Prerogative 393

of these affairs; and much of the basic work done requires no special legal talent.[38]

The writer feels, however, that not just any laymen should be relied upon to assist prisoners in preparing the initial letters or petitions to get their cases before the courts. What is needed are laymen who have been specially trained to interview prisoners and to advise them what they may do in regard to their petitions, at least to the same extent that prison officials advise them what they may not do (without being accused of practicing law). These trained laymen could serve the same function that administrator-interviewers do in Social Security offices across the country, providing basic information and helping fill out forms or write petitions. The instruction these laymen would receive should be given by lawyers, or possibly by persons who have been instructed by lawyers. It would probably be best if they were not employees of the prison, otherwise the prisoners might be reluctant to place their trust in them.

Where should nonprison law libraries fit into this picture? Until the "millennium" arrives when any prisoner seeking post-conviction relief can obtain legal counsel to initiate and to carry out court action on his behalf, or until adoption of the more realistic proposal to permit trained laymen to assist prisoners, nonprison law libraries should at least provide, within reason, photocopies of legal materials upon the request of prisoners or prison librarians. If a national policy were adopted whereby the law libraries in each State--including State, law school, and county libraries--assumed the responsibility of servicing prisoners within that State, the burden would not fall too heavily upon any one library.

The cost of labor and materials is most often given as the reason for not providing such services. However, some prisoners can pay for the service, and the writer's survey indicated that law libraries generally provide copies only for payment. By charging realistically for the copies, no library need refuse such service because of the costs involved. The cost of service to indigent prisoners presents a more difficult problem. One possible source of funds, if the inmate's institution will not pay, is grant money specifically requested by libraries for such purposes. Law libraries supported by public funds might reasonably be expected to absorb the cost of services to indigent prisoners within their own State, up to some small percentage of their budgets, such as 1/2 of 1 percent.

A service that law libraries can provide at very little cost is to send prison libraries their superseded advance sheets for reporters, the General Digest, U.S. Code Congressional and Administrative News, and their superseded State session law service paperbound volumes. Of less value, but still of some use to prisoners, would be superseded volumes of American Jurisprudence 2d and Corpus Juris Secundum in the areas of criminal law and procedure, evidence and domestic relations, as well as the superseded volumes of Martindale-Hubbell, containing the law digest and court information.

It should not be a hardship for law libraries to make interlibrary loans to prison libraries, with the understanding that the materials would be used in the library with adequate supervision. Even that restriction might be unnecessary in many cases. The University of Washington Law Library, for example, has been making interlibrary loans to prisoners at the Washington State Penitentiary for a number of years without such restrictions.[39]

The services described thus far are feasible shortrun measures that can be taken at the present time, but it is the writer's opinion that ultimately law library service to prisoners can best be provided by basic legal collections in prison libraries, such collections as those described by Charpentier[40] and Cohen.[41] Law librarians individually can help strengthen prison collections through donations of worthwhile duplicates and superseded materials, and by advising prison librarians on book selection, but long range results might best be attained if the American Association of Law Libraries would join forces with the American Correctional Association (ACA) and the Association of Hospital and Institutional Libraries (AHIL) to persuade legislators to provide adequate and regular appropriations for prison libraries, including basic legal collections.

The long, slow road of educating the public and its legislators is not an inviting one, but nothing less than State and Federal money will be sufficient to establish and carry on the kind of prison library program that would suffice until better legal or sublegal services are available to prisoners. If law librarians are reluctant to start down that road, they will continue to be vexed by prisoners' requests and will have to live with their consciences, knowing that they are not adequately providing a needed service and that they are not doing anything about it.

Notes

1. Britannica Book of the Year, 1969. Chicago: Encyclopaedia Britannica, 1969, at 629.
2. See Johnson v. Avery, 393 U.S. 483, 488, 21 L. Ed. 2d 718, 89 Sup. Ct. 747 (1969).
3. "Prison Libraries Below Standard According to AHIL-ACA Inventory." 91 Library Journal 1189 (Mar. 1, 1966).
4. "Indiana Prison Library Survey by State Library," 91 Library Journal 5352 (Nov. 1, 1966).
5. Cohen, Morris L. "Reading Law in Prison," 48 Prison Journal 21, 23 (Spring-Summer 1968).
6. Wainwright, Louis L. "Legal Information and Resources for Inmates," American Correctional Association Proceedings, 1966, at 236.
7. Ibid. at 25.
8. Lewis, Anthony. Gideon's Trumpet. New York: Random House, 1964, at 98.
9. See People v. Chessman, 44 Cal. 2d 1, 279 P. 2d 24 (1955).
10. Gilmore v. Lynch, 400 F. 2d 228, 230 (9th Cir. 1968).
11. Haughey v. Rhay, 300 F. Supp. 490 (E. D. Wash. 1969).
12. Konigsberg v. Ciccone, 285 F. Supp. 585 (W. D. Mo. 1968).
13. Griffin v. Illinois, 351 U.S. 12, 100 L. Ed. 891, 76 Sup. Ct. 585 (1956).
14. E.g., Brown v. Johnston, 91 F. 2d 370 (9th Cir. 1937), cert. denied 303 U.S. 728 (1937); People v. Reagan, 391 Ill. 419, 63 N.E. 2d 874 (1945); Manning v. Brierley, 392 F. 2d 197 (3d Cir. 1968), cert. denied 393 U.S. 882 (1968).
15. Millslagel v. Olson, 128 F. 2d 1015 (8th Cir. 1942); Dorsey v. Gill, 148 F. 2d 857, 864 (D.C. Cir. 1945), cert. denied 325 U.S. 890 (1945).
16. Note, 110 University of Pennsylvania Law Review 985, 994 (1962); Squillante, Alphonse M. "Does the Self-Defending Defendant Have the Right of Access to a Law Library; Gideon's Corollary?" Missouri Library Quarterly 201, 211 (Sept. 1968).
17. Gilmore v. Lynch, 400 F. 2d 228 (9th Cir. 1968), cert. denied 393 U.S. 1092 (1969).
18. See Banning v. Looney, 213 F. 2d 771 (10th Cir. 1954),

cert denied 348 U.S. 859 (1954). Doctrine discussed in Note, 72 Yale Law Journal 506, 507 (1963).
19. Ex Parte Hull, 312 U.S. 546, 85 L. Ed. 1034, 61 Sup. Ct. 640 (1941).
20. Mayberry v. Prasse, 225 F. Supp. 752 (E.D. Pa. 1963).
21. 290 F.2d 632 (9th Cir. 1961).
22. 393 U.S. 483, 21 L. Ed. 2d 718, 89 Sup. Ct. 747 (1969).
23. Ibid. at 488.
24. Ibid. at 485.
25. See State v. Gladden, 240 F.2d 910, 912 (9th Cir. 1957).
26. 303 F. Supp. 637 (W.D. Mo. 1969).
27. Wainwright, op. cit. at 236.
28. U.S. Bureau of Prisons, Policy Statement no. 2001.1, Jan. 21, 1966.
29. Wainwright, op. cit. at 238.
30. The abbreviations used are as follows: Priv. L. Sch. for private law school libraries; St. L. Sch. for State law school libraries; St. L. Lib. for State law libraries; Sup. Ct. Lib. for State supreme court libraries; Co. L. Lib. for county law libraries.
31. These percentages, and the percentages shown later, represent the fraction of reporting libraries that are willing to provide the service indicated or have had the experience indicated. For example, of the State law school libraries that answered the questionnaire, 48 percent of them indicated a willingness to lend legal materials to their own State prisons.
32. Larsen, "A Prisoner Looks at Writ-Writing," 56 California Law Review 343 (1968).
33. Spector, "A Prison Librarian Looks at Writ-Writing," 56 California Law Review 365 (1968).
34. Krause, "A Lawyer Looks at Writ-Writing," 56 California Law Review 371 (1968), and Wainwright, op. cit. at 237.
35. Mr. Justice Douglas concurring, Avery v. Johnson, 393 U.S. 483, 498 (1969).
36. Mr. Justice White dissenting, Avery v. Johnson, ibid. at 502.
37. Wainwright, op. cit. at 238. Reports indicated their use reduced frivolous writs and prisoner frustration.
38. Op. cit. at 491.
39. Parkany, Betty. "A Prisoner and a Law Book; How Should They Be Brought Together?" Paper prepared for School of Librarianship, U. of Wash., Aug. 20,

1965, at 11.
40. "Law Collection for Penal Institutions," American Correctional Association Proceedings, 1966. Pp. 230-35.
41. "Reading Law in Prison," 48 Prison Journal 21-27 (Spring-Summer 1968).

When Readers Become Suspect

by Reese Cleghorn

Reprinted by permission from the July 9, 1970 issue of South Today (2: Special Edition), p. 1-2.

The federal government, through the Treasury Department, has begun a systematic effort to obtain the names of people who check library materials about explosives and, in some cases, books loosely described as "subversive" or "militant."

Investigators of the Treasury's Internal Revenue Service have been quietly visiting libraries for at least two months seeking the information. The result is believed to be the nation's first coordinated effort to gather intelligence information that makes Americans suspect because of what they read.

Numerous librarians and officials of the American Library Association, questioned during the past few days about the Treasury agents' visits, confirm that the investigators have sought the titles and the names of borrowers of books listed under the heading "Explosives" in library catalogues and, in some cases, titles suggesting contents related to guerrilla warfare. Beyond that, in at least one library system an agent simply requested that the librarian provide the names of people who have checked out "militant or subversive" books. When she refused, the investigator angrily lectured her on refusing to cooperate with the government.

In another library, agents succeeded in obtaining the names of people who had checked out books on guerrilla warfare by Che Guevarra, the Cuban revolutionist, and François Sully. The librarian willingly provided the names, which included those of two teen-agers who apparently were working on term papers.

The federal agents in some cases, upon meeting re-

The Social Prerogative

sistance by librarians, have suggested that they might obtain subpoenas for the information, which presumably would place the burden upon the librarians themselves to laboriously extract the desired information from microfilmed records. And in another case the agents, after a refusal from a librarian, contacted the city attorney's office, which opened the library files by advising the librarian in writing that, contrary to library tradition, all library records were public information.

Inquiries for this report have revealed that the agents' activities are not simply localized, pertaining to specific investigations, but part of a nationwide campaign to gather the names of readers of certain kinds of books. Before the inquiries, the American Library Association, through its Office for Intellectual Freedom in Chicago, knew of one library's experience with the investigators but was unaware that the Internal Revenue Service was gathering the information elsewhere.

It has now been confirmed that the IRS is gathering the information nationally, through its Alcohol, Tobacco and Firearms Division, under a very broad construal of IRS enforcement powers authorized by the Gun Control Act of 1968. That act defines destructive devices (including explosives, mines, missiles and poison gas) and provides that anyone manufacturing them must file an application with the Secretary of the Treasury and purchase a tax stamp.

Librarians are uncertain about what is done with the names of readers once the IRS has obtained them. In recent weeks, Sen. Sam J. Ervin Jr. of North Carolina, chairman of the Senate Subcommittee on Constitutional Rights, has charged that the use of government computers to amass files on suspect citizens is in itself a threat to Americans' freedoms.

When asked whether agents have been gathering names of book borrowers, Harold Serr, director of the IRS Alcohol, Tobacco and Firearms Division, said: "I wouldn't swear that they haven't, because when you are looking for information you go wherever you can find it. But unless they are working on a particular person, I don't think it would be worthwhile to find information that way." Although his office has not specifically directed investigators to gather names of book borrowers, he said, "it's possible that some investigator is looking for this." ...

He said his division has been asked by the McClellan Committee "to collect certain information on explosives, the number of bombs, and so on. We have asked our people to give us certain information about what the local requirements and rules are with regard to explosives. I am sure they have been doing a certain amount of research to find out how things are run."

Following are the particulars of a number of Treasury efforts to obtain library information:

On July 1 and on other days... investigators called at libraries throughout metropolitan Atlanta. In a few cases they found immediate cooperation, but in most they were turned back--temporarily, at least--by the objections of librarians and the difficulties of obtaining information from highly-systematized microfilm records. How persistent they will be in pursuing the names they are seeking remains to be seen.

Carlton Rochell, director of the Atlanta Public Library, was attending the American Library Association convention in Detroit when an investigator identified as Charles D. Lowe visited the city's main library. The investigator was told that it would be impossible to immediately obtain the names of borrowers of particular books but that, if he desired, he could have access to the large numbers of microfilm reels which record some 150,000 book transactions each month.

When Mr. Rochell returned to his office that week, he told supervisory staff members that the library's records were private. "I said that I feel when a situation involves a member of the public and his reading matter, this is a trust between the librarian and that person," Mr. Rochell said. "We won't provide such information unless required to by subpoena."

On July 6 Mr. Rochell called Robert P. Lane, who is Georgia chief special investigator for the Alcohol, Tobacco and Firearms Division of the IRS, to inquire about the agents. "He said they were doing this in connection with the Gun Control Act of 1968, destructive devices section," Mr. Rochell subsequently related. "He said the idea of visiting the libraries was provided as an 'investigative lead' by his regional office. They were trying to find out, first, what is available in the libraries and, second, who might be reading it."

The Social Prerogative

Mr. Rochell asked whether the IRS had specific books in mind. "He said they really didn't, that they were looking to see what might be available." Mr. Rochell said he expressed his concern about the whole process and that Mr. Lane said he would relay this concern to the regional office.

In addition to the main office, the agents visited only one Atlanta system branch, insofar as Mr. Rochell could immediately determine. It was the Inman Park branch, which serves a lower-income area that is racially transitional and where a substantial number of "longhairs" and Cubans live.

Agents made a much more extensive visitation the same week to branches of the library system of DeKalb county, a largely middle-class "bedroom community" that includes some of Atlanta and a large part of its suburban population. At first there was some incredulity, and suspicion that the agents might be rightwing extremists with phony credentials....

Mrs. Tomlin E. Brown, in charge of DeKalf's Avis G. Williams branch, said the agent mentioned no specific books or authors. "He was concerned with the phrase 'militant and subversive material,' " she said. She also recalled that he asked her whether the library would "flag" certain "subversive" books so that agents could easily determine who had checked them out. "I said I would resist such a move as severely as I could," she says. "I said I would do so only if commanded to do so by the director of the system. ... I explained that I happen to be an old-fashioned librarian and that anyone coming in the door of a library I am in charge of can read what he wants and in privacy."

It was at that point, Mrs. Brown recalls, that the encounter became a personal conflict. "He said, 'I detect a feeling of hostility on your part. I don't believe we should pursue the conversation.' I said I didn't feel hostile toward him but toward what he was doing. He hit the roof. He shouted: 'Do you mean to tell me that you would allow patrons to use militant and subversive material at this library toward the purpose of overthrowing the government?' I refused to answer. I told him that was as if I asked him whether he had stopped beating his wife. He was livid when he left, and I was, too."

An agent who called at another branch in the DeKalb County system, Brookhaven, found it easier to obtain what he wanted. The borrower records at the Brookhaven branch are less complex than at some other libraries. It is a relatively simple matter to correlate the numbers of patrons with the numbers on the check-out records for particular books.

Mrs. Matty Dodson, head librarian at the Brookhaven branch, said the agent checked the catalogue and asked about borrowers of two books: "Guerrilla Warfare," by Che Guevarra, and "The Age of the Guerrilla," by François Sully. "One of these books had gone out only twice," Mrs. Dodson said. "The one by the man with the C-h-e name had gone out nine times since 1962. He got the names of the ones who had checked it out in 1968 and 1969." There were only two names, Mrs. Dodson said: both of teen-agers who, she thought, were working on term papers.

After the agents' visits to the DeKalb branches, Mrs. Brown contacted Dr. Venable Lawson, of the Emory University library school in suburban Atlanta, who is chairman of the Intellectual Freedom Committee of the Metropolitan Atlanta Library Association. Still believing that the whole matter was so bizarre that the libraries' visitors might have been imposters rather than federal agents, Dr. Lawson checked one agent's name he had been given, "Charles D. Lowe," and learned that the local Alcohol, Tobacco and Firearms Division does have an agent with that name.

Dr. Lawson was prepared to ask his local committee to denounce what he considered grave intrusions upon First Amendment rights. He responded to a request to withhold action until it could be established whether the agents' visits were a local phenomenon or part of a national pattern.

Mrs. Judith Krug, director of the American Library Association's Office for Intellectual Freedom in Chicago, knew of only one instance of Treasury inquiries when she went to the library association's annual conference in Detroit during the first week of July. It involved the Milwaukee Public Library, and at the convention one session heard a brief report on that episode.

"Then I started hearing comments about other places," Mrs. Krug said. "I know there was one reference to such an occurrence in Colorado and one in Wyoming, but this was second hand. It was very frightening to me. The Intellectual Freedom Committee discussed it only in very general terms." Just after the convention she was told about the Atlanta incidents "and I saw it fit exactly the same pattern," she said.

Miss Vivian Maddox, assistant city librarian in Milwaukee, relates this sequence of events which began the first week of May:

"A Treasury Department agent appeared here, asking a supervisor about books on explosives. He was sent to my office, and we had a lengthy talk. He said if we were served with a subpoena for the records, we would have to do all the work, but if we would just let them do it they would do the work. I still refused. An assistant city attorney called the next day and said the library's records are all public. I asked him: 'Are you bringing this up because of the Treasury Department request?' He said, 'Yes.' "

Miss Maddox said Milwaukee's head librarian, Richard E. Krug, then talked to the city attorney's office and asked for the legal ruling in writing. It arrived a day or two later, she recalled. Mr. Krug then ordered release of the information. The library has information indicating that the agent who first called was M. Michael Geraty.

It was later ascertained that the Treasury Department's interest in Milwaukee has been narrowed to 15 books, principally volumes on explosives, and 10 borrowers of them. Circulating records for the period January, 1969, through April, 1970, were checked. In Milwaukee, Miss Maddox said, no general interest in "subversive" or "militant" books was expressed. She said the agent, however, not only threatened a subpoena but also suggested the librarians should cooperate because of national unrest and disturbances.

Miss Maddox believes that some of the books in which the Treasury Department was interested would, in fact, inform a reader how to make explosive devices.

The Board of Trustees of the Milwaukee Public Library met during the first week of July and considered a resolution that might prohibit release of information about borrowers in the absence of a court order or strong evidence of a serious need for the information.

But the resolution was delayed, pending consultation with the city attorney's office. Thus, in Milwaukee, the matter remains unresolved and the Treasury Department already has obtained the names of borrowers.

In another Georgia incident, Dr. Lawson ascertained that two Treasury agents visited the Cobb County-Marietta Public Library, 20 miles from Atlanta. He said the acting director there, Mrs. Josephine Stratton, was asked about the book retrieval system, check-outs, and books on bombs and explosives. "They also found a book written by an ex-Communist, eight or nine years old, listed in the catalogue," Dr. Lawson said. "But it had been lost. They had preceded this visit with one to the county police department."

These various inquiries into the federal agents' efforts suggest a widely varying response on the part of the librarians. In some cases the agents found ready cooperation; in some, direct rejection; and in some, permissive responses grounded, however, in the knowledge that microfilm recordkeeping systems themselves impose a formidable obstacle to obtaining the information desired.

The posture of the American Library Association is clear, however. In its "Library Bill of Rights," the association holds that information about what people read is held in trust and should not be divulged.

"How would it be," said one librarian, "if we readily released, for instance, names of people who have checked out books on sexual deviations? That would create suspicion about people that would have no basis at all."

Up Against the Stacks:
The Liberated Librarian's Guide to Activism

by Carolyn Forsman

Reprinted by permission from the July-August 1970 issue of Synergy (28), p. 6-12.

The MLS "Movement" first became visible in San Francisco in June 1967, when librarians organized a picket line protesting the pro-Vietnam speech of General Maxwell Taylor at ALA. The next year, at Kansas City, a petition of several hundred signatures was presented to ALA asking for the formation of a Round Table on the Social Responsibilities of Libraries within the ALA structure. This was approved, in what was considered the astonishingly short time of six months, and the wheels were in motion. The Social Responsibilities Round Table (SRRT, pronounced "Sirt") has since served as an umbrella for national Task Forces on specific issues as well as for local "affiliates." Since its formation, other more or less defined groups have formed and disbanded independent of SRRT: 321.8, the National Freedom Fund for Librarians (NFFFL), the Congress For Change (CFC), the Black Caucus. Memberships have often overlapped. There is more freedom and less structure outside SRRT. Nevertheless the groups have cooperated in areas of mutual benefit and concern.

To organize, it became evident that a mailing list of potential activists was necessary, whether or not they were members of any library association. The SRRT was a beginning, but it was topheavy with organizational members and also excluded non-ALA members. The National Call for Library Reform set up a p.o. box to solicit names for this purpose. It has just been absorbed by the SRRT Clearinghouse, not to be confused with the SRRT official mailing list, which is responsible for keeping an up-to-date list to be used by other groups as well as by SRRT Task Forces and affiliates, when there is a need for action, monetary support or organization at the grass roots level. In the minds of many librarians who consider this a top priority is also the possibility of using this list in the future as the nucleus for the formation of an alternative association to ALA when and if...

Closely related to the mailing list was the need for a communications medium. The national library press, though sympathetic, was and is unable to overcome its four to six week deadlines, which made most calls for action history. The SRRT Newsletter was the first attempt, and was generally unsatisfactory for that purpose, since it was quarterly. Fourth John (4J) inspired by the CFC concept of a "letters journal," was the latest attempt and has been more successful. In addition, some groups notified their own members of issues, sometimes within 24 hours, as 321.8 did.

The various groups have all needed money. SRRT is funded through ALA membership dues. Other groups have solicited funds for printing, postage, buttons, and telephone calls at meetings or through mailings. The sale of buttons has also been a profitable enterprise. Libraries to the People was the first such button, appearing at Atlantic City, June 1969. 321.8 appeared in September 1969, and Detroit, June 1970 saw 2 others competing for donations, F*ck Censorship and American Ladies Association, and two that were free and not associated with any group, P.O.W. (Power of Women) and S.I.R.T. (Social Irresponsibilities Round Table). A Librarians for Peace button is being considered, as well as Intellectual Freedom stamps.

The groups differ in membership, purpose and accomplishment, but one element common to most of them is an almost too conscious fear of institutionalization, leaders, and personal power. What results from this is most evident in the structure of the national SRRT, which is compelled by ALA bylaws to have a written formal organization. Its constitution is called Organization and Action and is unlike any other. Instead of a president or chairman, there is a Coordinator, elected from among the ten members of the Action Council, who are themselves elected by the membership from volunteers, who place themselves in nomination, accompanied by a platform statement. When it is necessary to have SRRT represented in ALA, it is not the Coordinator who is automatically chosen, to prevent him from being co-opted. Members of Action Council are limited to the number of other positions they can hold in ALA. Instead of standing committees, Task Forces are formed at the will of any group of members. These Task Forces are problem oriented and go

The Social Prerogative 407

out of existence at the end of the year unless purposely continued by interested members. All members of Task Forces are volunteers, not appointees.

Just what has been the substance of the activists, insurgents, radicals, reformers, and DWHY's (Dissident-What-Have-Yous, a phrase coined by Fay Blake)? How has Social Responsibility been interpreted? The best operational definition is via a survey of the groups, caucuses and movement that have emerged: their history, the issues as they saw them and the action they took.

A. L. A.   S. R. R. T.   (Social Responsibilities Round Table)

Action Council Coordinator: Patricia Schuman, 10 W. 16 St., NY, NY 10011.

History: The largest, oldest and most well-known activist group. Begun in Kansas City, June 1968, and officially approved by ALA at Midwinter, 1969. First Coordinator was Bill DeJohn. Official membership was 1100, as of May 1970.

Organization: A 10-member Action Council, who serve 2-year terms. A 6-member Clearinghouse, responsible for communications. Task Forces. Local affiliate groups.

Issues and Actions: Best described through the Task Forces (see p. 8).

Communications: See description of the Clearinghouse (see p. 10).

Bibliography: LJ, March 15, 1969, p. 1110-11.

Eubanks, Jackie. "Confessions of a Middle-of-the-Road Militant," American Libraries, May 1970, p. 437-39.

Schuman, Patricia. "Social Responsibilities--A Progress Report," LJ, May 15, 1969, p. 1951-52.

SRRT TASK FORCES

Action Councilor responsible for SRRT Task Forces: Gay Detlefsen, 527 W. 110 St., NY, NY 10025.

Task Force on Gay Liberation

c/o George Hathaway, Clearinghouse Secy., Brooklyn College Library, Brooklyn, NY 11210

History: Formed during the Detroit ALA annual meeting. It was first organized as the Gay Liberation Caucus, in the two fliers it put out at the convention. Three meetings were held, attended by over 100 librarians. Next meeting NYC, September 13.

Issues: "The revision of library classification schemes to remove homosexuality from the realm of sexual aberrations, to encourage all libraries to build objective collections on homosexuality, and to make these collections easily available to all."

Task Force on Minority Recruitment

Coordinator: James Wright, Rochester Public Library, NY 14603. Organizing a preconference for Dallas, June 1971.

Task Force on the Reprinting of Black Literature

Coordinator: Ray Brazey, 3M Library, NY. Surveying the review media as to their coverage of the many reprints.

Task Force on Intellectual Freedom

Coordinator: Jean Anne South, 6040 Kennedy Blvd. East, Apt. 2L, West New York, N.J. 07093.

History: One of the original Task Forces, it was renewed at Detroit.

Issues: Will concentrate on the Internal Revenue Service's intrusion into the Library circulation records. Will work to get state associations to take action on the issue. See also the National Freedom Fund for another expression of action in the area of intellectual freedom.

Task Force on the Status of Women in Libraries

Coordinator: Kay Cassell, 1 Highgate Dr., #406, Trenton, N.J. 08618.

History: In November 1969, during the Washington, D.C.

Moratorium, signs proclaiming "NWLFFL" (pronounced Waffle) standing for the National Women's Liberation Front for Librarians, appeared. Also referred to as Women's Lib, this loosely organized group produced the American Ladies Association button, which first appeared in May 1970, at the Philadelphia meeting of the national SRRT affiliates. Simultaneously a Women's Caucus was being formed by Ruth Beasley in Bloomington, Indiana. At ALA, Detroit, this June the two groups merged and formed the above task force within SRRT.

Issues: Discrimination in promotion and salaries; under-representation of women in library education, on ALA staff, and in library administration; working conditions to enable women to reach their potential, such as day care centers for working librarians and maternity leave. They will pressure other library periodicals to follow the example of American Libraries in its policy against sex discrimination in advertising. As librarians they are concerned with the lack of bibliographic control of women's liberation literature, and the image of women in career guides and children's books.

Actions: A resolution, "Equal Opportunities for Women in Librarianship," was passed unanimously by the Task Force and will be presented to ALA at its next membership meeting. Another resolution asking, among other things, that ALA not hold meetings where sexism was practiced, was introduced at the Detroit membership meeting by individual members of the Task Force. This was greeted with laughter and defeated by the largely female audience!

Communications: A newsletter is being planned to be sent to the mailing list of already over 200 librarians. The SRRT Newsletter will be used until then. Local affiliates are encouraged and already exist in Mass., Ind., Ill., Calif., N.Y. Men are allowed but not unanimously welcome.

Buttons: American Ladies Association buttons are still available from Gay Detlefsen. At Detroit, another women's liberation button appeared: P.O.W. in the "conventional pink," but set against black. It stands for the Power of Women, according to Shirley Olofson, who got the national Junior Members Round Table of ALA to underwrite it and distribute it free at their booth.

Bibliography: Barber, Peggy. "Ladies in Waiting," Synergy, Dec. 1969. p. 22-25.

Freedman, Janet. "The Liberated Librarian," LJ, May 1, 1970. p. 1709-11.

Schiller, Anita R. "The Widening Sex Gap," LJ, March 15, 1969. p. 1098-1100.

----"The Disadvantaged Majority," American Libraries, April 1970. p. 345-49.

Schuman, Patricia and Ellen Gay Detlefsen. "The Women's Liberation Movement I," Wilson Library Bulletin, May 1970. p. 962+.

SRRT AFFILIATES

Action Councilor responsible for affiliate groups: Jackie Eubanks, Brooklyn College Library, Brooklyn, N.Y. 11210.

Non-ALA members can affiliate with the national SRRT by forming a local group, which will receive a subscription to the national newsletter for $1. Most local SRRT's have used the structure of the national as a model. There are Coordinators and Task Forces and very simple constitutions. Some are within state library associations. Not all are called SRRT. Some encompass an entire state, others only a city. Activities are reported in the national SRRT newsletter. There is the possibility of a newsletter just for affiliate groups. At least three local groups have their own newsletter:

COLT (Colorado Librarians in Transition) publishes the Silver Bullet. Barbara Wagner, 129 Dartmouth Trail, #4, Fort Collins, Colo. 80521.

New Jersey Social Responsibilities Group publishes a Newsletter. c/o Martha Williams, Princeton Public Library, Princeton, N.J. 08540.

New York Librarians Social Responsibilities Round Table publishes Response. Box 2688, N.Y., N.Y. 10001.

SRRT CLEARINGHOUSE

Secretary: George Hathaway, Brooklyn College Library, Brooklyn, N.Y. 11210. Responsible for the publication of the official national SRRT Newsletter, quarterly; first issue May 1969. Reports on the activities of the national Task Forces, the local affiliates, and other activist groups. It goes to all official members, i.e. ALA members who paid $5. It is also available to non-ALA members for $2.

In addition, the Clearinghouse has compiled and updates an extensive file of librarians interested in social action. It includes the memberships of the National Call, of 321.8 and other groups as well as SRRT. Recently updated entire mailing list. It hopes to put the list in machine readable format so that there will be access to it geographically.

BLACK CAUCUS OF A.L.A. Chairman: E.J. Josey, Chief, Bureau of Academic and Research Libraries, Division of Academic Development, N.Y. State Education Dept., Albany, N.Y. 12224.

History: First organized at ALA, Kansas City, June 1968, it was reactivated at ALA Midwinter, 1970. Over 200 black librarians met again at Detroit, June 1970.

Organization: The caucus is purposely independent of SRRT or any other ALA structure because of a belief in the need for self-determination. But it will continue to join with SRRT or any other group in specific issues of mutual benefit.

Issues: The second class citizenship of blacks in ALA, the profession, and society. It is a united front to make blacks full and equal partners and will work for the full utilization of black librarians in ALA and in libraries. It points to the small number of blacks serving on the ALA Council and to the fact that there has never been a black ALA president. Other areas of concern are discrimination in the promotion and hiring of blacks, lack of recruitment of blacks into the professions, and institutional racism as practiced by libraries.

Action: Successfully brought to ALA Council at Midwinter a resolution in support of Carrie Robinson, a black librarian who had brought suit against the state of Alabama, charging discrimination in promotion. Rumors are it will nominate a candidate for ALA President. A Planning and Action Committee reported to the Caucus at Detroit. Its position paper will be strengthened and improved and brought again to the Caucus at Midwinter, 1971. If accepted at that time, it will be released. The Caucus has supported a stronger version of the new LSCA bill than that supported by ALA, in its provisions for library service to the disadvantaged.

Communications: There is no formal newsletter. Members are kept informed by memorandum as the need arises.

CLOUT

Concerned Librarians of University Training, was formed in Sept. 1968 at the Syracuse Library School. It was active in the CFC and in forming a national students group. It is currently an affiliate of SRRT. An SRRT Task Force has been set up since Detroit on Library School Student Affiliates. Nancy Hansen is Coordinator. 275 Clinton Ave., Brooklyn, N.Y. 11205.

CONGRESS FOR CHANGE

In March 1969 representatives from library schools met at the U. of Maryland to plan for a national conference of library school students and other activist-oriented young librarians on June 19-22. It was more an experience than an organization. At ALA in Atlantic City, it became a symbol of young activists, as the resolutions that had been passed were presented to the ALA membership. They covered the range of issues from ALA election reform, to library education and recruitment, and the social issues of Vietnam and ABM. It was the spark for the Fourth John, and the National Call for Library Reform. It was also hoped to organize a national student organization. At Detroit, 22 library schools were represented at another meeting to discuss this possibility. Bob Wedgeworth at the Rutgers Library School volunteered to pursue it.

FOURTH JOHN. Tom Bonn, Editor. Box 457, Etna, N.Y. 13062.

History: The idea of a "letters journal" grew out of Congress for Change. The first issue of the 4J followed Midwinter 1970. A five-page compilation of letters from individuals to the "group," each letter correctly identified by volume, issue and number for later identification, it was mailed to 75 persons, who in turn copied it for further distribution in their area. There were 8 issues by the time of the ALA convention in Detroit, where the future of 4J was discussed. It now plans to continue on a subscription basis of $5 with the hope of being able to hire a part time editor. Its purposes as stated in issue nine are (1) to improve communication, (2) to broaden the base of the movement, (3) to be a cathartic repository. The origin of the title is derived from an answer to a reference question Tom Bonn heard. Q: I notice that you have a rest room in your library marked "Third Sex." Why? A: Yes, and you should see the fourth john...

LIBRARIANS FOR PEACE

This author has not been able to identify any one national organized group. But there are activities under this movement. Librarians participated in the Nov. 1969 Moratorium in Washington D.C. and San Francisco, marching under that banner. N.J., N.Y., and California have Librarians for Peace groups. The N.J. group published a bibliography on Draft Counseling. Columbia Library School students published a compilation of documents on Cambodia. UC Berkeley also provided antiwar resource material.

LIBRARIANS FOR 321.8. Chairman: John Forsman, 6910 Carleton Terrace, College Park, Md. 20740.

In August, 1969, a group of librarians from the Washington, D.C. area met to continue the push towards democratization of the ALA that had begun at Atlantic City in June 1969. A statement was printed and distributed at over 30 state library associations during the year. It called for platform statements by all candidates for Council and the Presidency, roll call votes, sanctions against librarians who violated the library Bill of Rights, and increased staff for the Office of Intellectual Freedom. It polled all nominees in regard to the statement, and, with the help of SRRT, ran 10 candidates for Council. It issued a second statement in the Spring of 1970 which was also distributed at state conventions, which proposed other election reforms: the abolishment of the office of second vice president, elimination of divisional at-large councilors, a provision to remove councilors who do not attend meetings. These reforms have yet to be implemented. In June it took on a swift and successful campaign to kill the 5% amendment to the ALA bylaws, that would have prevented nomination by petition.

Communications: Memoranda were sent out as needed to its several hundred members. It is currently looking for another group that would like to continue this effort.

Buttons: 321.8, Dewey for Democracy, available at 10¢ apiece in bulk rate for local groups.

NATIONAL CALL FOR LIBRARY REFORM. Box 10150, Pittsburgh, Pa. 15232.

History: Organized after the impetus of the CFC and ALA Atlantic City, it urged librarians to organize around the issues of restructuring of ALA, library education reform, community participation, library unions, the social and political issues of war, racism and poverty, intellectual freedom, a national union of library workers. The entire statement was printed in the SRRT newsletter of Sept. 1, 1969, as well as LJ. Its mailing list was absorbed by the SRRT Clearinghouse.

NATIONAL FREEDOM FUND FOR LIBRARIANS. Box 10174, Pittsburgh, Pa. 15232.

A defense fund, organized in the fall of 1969 in response to the firing of Ellis Hodgin from the Martinsville, Va. Public Library. It was formed as a temporary fund with the hope that ALA would create a similar fund, at which time it would turn over its remaining donations to it. There is now the possibility that the LeRoy Merritt Humanitarian Fund, in the process of being set up within the Freedom to Read Foundation, will fit this. A press release is expected shortly from the Board of Directors of the NFFFL.

In the three years since San Francisco, the activists have become more sophisticated and varied in their responses to the social issues they have interpreted as library concerns: moving from hastily formed picketing to petitions and finally to resolutions at Kansas City and Atlantic City; then to planned political pressure, investigation, reports, and fund raising at Detroit this year. Librarians may be affiliating with other professionals around specific issues. The beginnings of this can be found in the anti-Vietnam ads in the New York Times and San Francisco Chronicle and the Publishers for Peace booth at ALA, where librarians bought their buttons.

EPILOGUE:

LIBRARY GERMULE

(Reproduced by permission from the April 1970 issue of Wilson Library Bulletin (44:8), p. 839-847. Copyright 1970 by the H.W. Wilson Company.)

LIBRARY GERMULE

THE INCIPIENT GERM OF LIBREMIA LITERATIASIS, FOUNDED APRIL 1970;
FORMERLY THE LIE-BERRY JERKEL, ALA BULLSHOOTER, AND WILSOME LIBRARY BULLOCK

BURN EVERYTHING AND DROP DEAD: A MESSAGE OF FAITH IN THE PROFESSION

Libraries stink! Librarians are idiots, creeps, lice, and scum. Books ought to be burned, and the readers with them—those phony, irrelevant culture vultures! Those prurient patrons of porno and pap!

Sometimes a journalist has to stop cold in his tracks and impale his guts on the typewriter. That is, if you're a journalist. If you've got any guts. We wouldn't know.

But we know about libraries. And we OBSCENITY them!

Librarians are no better. They were never any better. In the beginning, they were tools of the Pharaohs; then, tools of the dogmatists; tools of the capitalists; tools of the military-industrial complex; tools of the establishment; and, finally, tools of the revolutionaries. And in all this time, why hasn't one solitary librarian seen the true and soulful, the crying NEED of the profession?

A bigger toolbox.

Think about it.

Oh, you librarians—you've got everyone snowed. But not *LG*. We're objective; we haven't been in a library in *years*.

You dare to call yourselves *hip,* you fools and featherbrains? You dare to call yourselves *involved,* you copouts and dropouts? You dare to call yourselves *activists,* you schmatas and schlumpadinks? GET WITH IT! Better yet, get OUT OF IT—because you've already been there for ages, baby!

But if you're going to stay in, if you're going to be NEW YORK swingers and dapper dingalings in the din of battle, in the heat of the fray, then THROW AWAY THOSE BOOKS, Mac. Can the computers. Give "Information" back to the operators. Give the budget to *LG*. As for you? Baby, we want you in the soup kitchens—if you can stand

EDITORIAL

the heat! We want you with the Weathermen! We want you with the Minutemen! We want you in the prisons—in solitary and death row, baby! We want you in the flop houses, the bawdy houses, the bug houses, and the funny farms! We want you in the streets, on the rooftops, and in the sewers! We want you out of the library and into the *funk,* baby!

Because that's where it's happening!

Because that's where the action is!

But mainly, because that kind of stuff makes a lot better copy for us than "How We Licked Our Labels in the Little Pee Dee Public."

Epilogue

Letters

"We get letters—and the last laugh."
—*Ed.*

False Firing
P. O. Job
Jilted, Calif.

May I respectfully point out some small corrections regarding your cover story for the last four months? I did not fire Gideon Quickfingers because he put the *Evergreen Review* on the shelves. I fired him because he *removed* it from the shelves, six bound volumes for his home library, in addition to a twelve-year run of *Playboy*, a set of encyclopedias, and, in the course of his tenure, 228 assorted reference works, record albums, and expensive folio volumes. Furthermore, he has been convicted of selling drugs in the Young Adults Section, setting fire to his supervisor's house, molesting the Acquisitions Librarian, and embezzling the overdue fines. When I sent him to the ALA conference in Atlantic City, he turned up in Monte Carlo, with a $12,50 gambling debt charged to the library. Even after these questionable practices, however, I tried to keep him on, hoping to channel his remarkable energies into constructive library work. The axe did not fall, I assure you, until Mr. Quickfingers cashed in my insurance policy of thirty years over a forged signature and ran off with my wife to Tierra del Fuego.

ED. NOTE—Come off it, P.O.! Your wife is a *dog*. But if there's any truth to your fantasy, rush me a picture of the two of them down there, maybe sitting on top of all the stolen loot and thumbing their noses to the north. We'll call it "Safe from the Fat Cats" and run it as a cover between a cover I just did—a beautiful photo of a piece of slush—and our usual cover of Jerry Rubin shooting one of the New York Public Library lions in the mouth with a toy machine gun.

Loyalty Oats
Lovitore Leavitt
Lagoochie, La.

I am sick of hearing the unwashed slobs of our profession mouthing off against loyalty oaths, one of the bulwarks of a free society. Yes, there are some librarians who simply cannot find it in their conscience to swear allegiance, as a condition of their employment, to the United States of America, right or wrong. They call these people Communists.
Is it so much to promise to cherish, honor, and protect that which we, as decent citizens, already hold so dear? My husband, who is a librarian, has always been devoted to me in a manner second only to love of country, and yet he gladly took the marriage oath some fifteen years ago. He would gladly take it again today.

ED. NOTE—Your husband may have taken the oath, but it's his *oats* that he's been feeling for the last ten years or so, according to what we see at the professional conventions. And it's not only gals—it's the booze, too. Perhaps he ought to take the AA Pledge, but he seems to be having enough fun under the one oath.

Classified Information
Manny Powers
Recession, Ky.

The "Positions Wanted" section of LG's classified ads has been running about three times longer than "Positions Open." Could it be that the library manpower shortage is one more myth perpetuated in your editorial pages? What I see everywhere is a manpower surplus.

ED. NOTE—Will you please shut your mouth about the manpower surplus until we've used up all the "shortage" articles? Why is everyone always counting and *measuring* things in LG?

Counting Letters
Penvelope Steamer
Stamplicker, Mass.

I have counted the number of *different* people writing letters to *LG* in the last fifteen years. Although the letters in that period totaled 4,176, the number of individuals writing them was only twelve.

ED. NOTE—That makes you number thirteen, Miss Steamer, and we wish you all the luck that goes with it for sticking your nose into our mail.

Next month in LG--

An

entire

issue of

ADS!

NEWS

93 MILLION MICROBOOKS SWALLOWED BY HIPPIE

An exciting breakthrough in microstorage of information has ended in disaster for the developers and a bum trip for a misguided user. Library Science Dynamics, Inc. (LSD) of London and New York has developed a process by which information in books could be coded chemically and stored in one two-millionth of the space required for genetic information in DNA. Although the method was known as early as 1909, it was not until sixty years later that private researchers—two generations of them—completed the transfer of 93 million library books into a single drop of "information acid," as it was called. Ready for analysis and retrieval by a special computer, the drop was stored in a sugar cube, and an announcement of the breakthrough on worldwide television was scheduled to coincide with National Library Week.

It was on the eve of NLW that Mansard Moody, profligate son of Lord Moody of Chadwick, discovered the cube in his father's private refrigerator. Lord Moody, President of LSD, Inc., was away on business and had not expected his son to come to the country estate that evening with his coterie of hippies and drug freaks. "Daddy's a head!" young Moody exulted to his friends, and promptly popped the cube in his mouth.

Within twelve minutes, the entire contents of 93 million library books were in his brain. His amazed cohorts reported that, in addition to his hair turning white, his eyes bugging out, and his feet leaving the ground, a cloud of yellow smoke blew from his ears and his fillings shot sparks for an hour and a half.

When Lord Moody returned home and Mansard had recovered from the initial shock, father confronted son for the first time.

"Bad show," he told him. "Hard cheese on libraries, losing that sugar cube. But see here, Old Boy—now that the wisdom of 93 million books is in your brain—what *is* the secret of life?"

Mansard threw his head back. His eyes became pinwheels. His nose snorted fire. Lightning flashed from his fingers and toes. Finally, when the fireworks subsided, his lips began to move slowly, and he beckoned his father closer so that the priceless words might not be lost upon the cosmic ether surrounding the puny world of man.

"*Not on shelf*," he whispered, and was never heard to speak again.

LIBRARY OF CONGRESS BUILDING TAKEN OVER BY DEFENSE DEPARTMENT

The Library of Congress' proposed Dolly Madison Memorial Building, an enormous structure designed to relieve the Library's critically overcrowded facilities, will be financed and occupied by the Defense Department now that Congressional building appropriations to the Library have been deferred for the twenty-third time "without pride or prejudice." Whereas the Library—which spends millions of dollars a year renting temporary space—would have faced even more devastating expenses if building funds had not been approved before construction costs soared out of reach, the Pentagon has no such fiscal apprehensions. "We've got money and villages to burn," cracked one official.

It is expected that the Defense Department, no stranger to LC facilities, will use the monolithic structure as a fortress against Black Panther attacks on the neighboring Rayburn House Office Building, its swimming pool,

Mansard Moody, right, and fellow hippie warm up to cube of "information acid"—packing the punch of 93 million library books.

Epilogue

and the Capitol Building. Moreover, it is anticipated that a rank of howitzers trained on the chambers of both Houses will have an accelerating effect on appropriations for Defense in the future.

MIDWESTERN LIBRARY SYSTEM DIRECTOR ON MAGNETIC TAPE

A group of Midwestern city libraries linked in an experimental HURT (Heartland Urban Relay Terminals) system found its system director transferred to magnetic tape when a new computer terminal he was operating went haywire. The director, Marc Frotranski, was experimenting with the output of a program he had designed in order to display, on a cathode ray tube, the anatomy of a shapely research assistant at a Chicago terminal. Unknown to Dr. Frot-

---

POSITION AVAILABLE: Library seeks reference assistant. Responsible for knowledge of and experience in Etruscan pots, tatting, lute tuning, Hepplewhite furniture, igneous rocks, Nepalese temple art, and libraries to the people. Send recent photo. No weirdos please.

---

ranski, the Chicago terminal had been smashed by a band of Weathermen just minutes before. When Dr. Frotranski switched on input to query the computer, there was a bright flash, a crackling of electricity, and when the smoke cleared away, zero Frotranski. A week later, during the investigation, the following message appeared on a CRT screen in Peoria: HELP—I'M TRAPPED ON MAG TAPE—M.F.

ALA BOUGHT BY PLOYBOY MAGAZINE

Angered by the failure of libraries to acquire and disseminate the nation's most literary mass-circulation magazine, Ployboy Magazine, Inc., has purchased American Libraries Associated of Chicago, lock, stock, and ACRL. *Ployboy* owner Huge Hefty has announced the following plans of the new conglomerate: the Children's Services Department will become the Bachelor Services Division, and its staff members will move into the *Ployboy* mansion at once; the Kingdom of Monaco will be purchased for the 1975 ALA Convention; a Committee on the Shape of ALA will be headed by an ex-Ploymate; and a new magazine, *ALAboy*, will be published to replace, hopefully, all existing periodicals in the field.

EGGBERT HEEVER TO HEAD AGENCY INVESTIGATING LIBRARY BORROWERS

The Administration has named Federal watchdog Eggbert Heever to head a new agency that will weed out undesirable library borrowers and, in the process, phase out all library service—highly suspect to the White House for some time. Effective immediately, all library circulation procedures will require fingerprinting, and a computerized record will be kept of patrons borrowing any but USIA-approved titles. Mr. Heever has pledged to tap into telex and other library network wires in order to nab criminal types at the point of circulation. In addition, borrowers taking out more than five books a month will be photographed; those taking out more than ten will be subpoenaed to show cause why they should be reading to that extent.

POSITION WANTED: Male, age 33, would like to be slave to female or females. Your wish is my command. POSITION AVAILABLE: Hard-working young man sought by busy urban public library. Must be original thinker. Contact Maj. Alice, librarian.

RESEARCH ON RESEARCH

The study described below was done under the aegis of the Office of Edification, which granted $387,000 to design the questionnaire and $463,-000 (supplementary) for the keypunching of the responses.—Ed.

Our study was an 'umble attempt to evaluate the effectiveness of questionnaires in the gathering of data. As one respondent put it, "It was the best questionnaire I received today." The questionnaire on questionnaires, a multiple-choice instrument, allowed respondents to specify any one of six cogently-worded responses to a series of 3,158 questions. As we said in the covering letter, "It will only take six weeks of your time to fill up (er, out) this questionnaire."

A few respondents claimed it was an "opinionaire," but, as professionals know, it was truly a "questionnaire," since each statement ended with a question mark (?). We do not intend to confront these dissidents; rather, as true professionals, we will simply disregard their responses and thus reduce our sample to a manageable number of seventeen.

Except for a few hundred IBM cards, which were lost while playing blackjack last Tuesday, all responses have now been keypunched. Within eighteen months, the programs for analyzing the responses will have been written, and full details of this important study will be available.

Of course, it will take some time to apply the chi-square formula to the summarized data, so levels of significance will only be approximate in the preliminary report. It is our understanding, however, that no grants will be made by the Office of Edification for studies utilizing the questionnaire method until our results are in.

Watch for the full report of the ?/? study, which will be available from EARACHE at the appropriate time.

NEWS IN BRIEFS

An extensive collection of books, pamphlets, and ephemera, including many caries, classified by kind, has been given to the dental school library of Molarsburg State University, Incisor, Pa. The works deal mainly with the development of therapeutic chewing gum, but there are also thousands of x-rays which have been photographically reduced to save space. Material on aid to impacted areas is also included.

Word has just arryvd that a 1st-edition Dui (1876) wuz found at the Lake Plastic Club, where it had apparently been hiddn in the cornerstone. Speculation is that it wuz found during the recent NYLA meetings, when Reginald Pangloss wuz looking for the lost gavl. A blu-ribbn committee wil select the most appropriate larj research libraries, jeografically, to receive one leaf each of the long-lost volume, thus sharing with the yung the knowlej to be found only in the work of a genius.

WORLD OF PRINT

A new edition of *The Universal Directory* has been published by the R. R. Bupkiss Co. This famous work has been completely revised and appears in 177 volumes, listing every person known to have learned to write left-handed since the beginning of time. Now arranged chronologically instead of alphabetically, it will serve researchers even better than in the past. Price, $1,679 U.S., $1,996 elsewhere.

POSITION WANTED: Cataloger in Hindi-Sanskrit seeks position in rural library. Sincere.

BRICKS AND MORBID

Architect Andrew Weirdhol's unusual library tower—shaped exactly like a copy of the bestseller "Nakeder Came the Stranger"—has been awarded top honors by BLIGHT (Build Libraries in God-High Towers), Inc., a subsidiary of Amontillado Bricks and Mortar, Ltd.

One enters at the base of the book-spine through an orifice disguised as a Dewey Decimal point, rides a heart-shaped elevator to the "blood pressure" (floor) desired, and follows Cupid's arrows to the book of his dreams. The library's professional staff consists of three psychiatrists, an astrologer, a talking chicken, and two strangers.

"Libraries are built on and sustained by bestsellers," commented the architect. "It's high time that form followed function."

MUSIC

Librarian's Tears Flow on the Chart
(Sung to the tune of a *Hair* song.)
Digital
Facsimile
Cathode Ray Tube
Heuristic
Father,
why do these words
sound so mystic?
Information
can be fun
Join the
On Line
GIGO
Keypunch
Software
Every
one....

WASHINGTON REPORTS
(Reprinted from the ALA Bullshooter and Wilsome Library Bullock)

Reorg of DLSEF OKD by HEW under HEA, SHEA, and ESEA Rider.

Now HEA de wo'd o' de Lawd: O', de DLP bone connected to de BAVTE bone; de BAVTE bone connected to de DCSS bone; de DCSS bone connected to de DASDC bone; de DASDC bone connected to de ASECE bone; de ASECE bone connected to de OE bone; de OE bone connected to de HEW bone—now HEA de wo'd o' de Lawd! Dem bones, dem bones, dem dry bones....

Copyright Bill Finally Due for Passage

Thanks to the Head Acid Officer at the Lyeberry of Congress, the Shrewsworth Institute has developed a paper which will self-destruct within twenty-four hours. This advance has so allayed the fears of authors and publishers about unauthorized copying of their works, that former stringent penalties for such copying in libraries are no longer needed. As a result, legislators have now put the finishing touches on the new copyright bill. The bill still retains the injunction to erase all magnetic tapes automatically, and severe penalties are included for hardcore use of software.

The Institute staff had first worked on inks which would fade within twenty-four hours, thus answering the authors' and publishers' demands for protection. It was pointed out, however, that getting rid of the paper itself was far better, since some unfair user might treat the ink to make it permanent again.

As a first experiment, the copyright bill itself will be printed on the special paper. If it works, all parties will be gratified.

Epilogue

MAN, THEM ANGLO RULES were right on the case for a year or two, baby, but the times, they are a changin', and I wanna tell it to you like it is, big daddy—I wouldn't catalog a *matchbook* today with that jive Wasp code they call THE RULES. Yippie! Like they had some 125 cats laying down those Anglo changes in old D.C., Pig City, and the heartlands—man, they could have cataloged the Milky Way in all that time with the *Angry*-American Rules—the heavy rules, the truth and soul rules that catalog it like it is and where it's at!

And now I'm gonna lay the underlying principle on you: Anarchy!

Anarchy is what's happening in books and media, baby. Do your own thing. Publishers do it, and that's how you gotta pick it up, or else blow your scene, bum trip, bad vibes, and never get your head together. So, brothers, when that book truck comes by—burn it! That's liberation. That's the right start. Then you're ready for some groovy cataloging. Freak out!

PART I. Entry and Heading

Main and added entries. For the main entry, try some finger-lickin' spareribs and greens, coexistence water bagels, *enchiladas de arroz*, and *cervelles au beurre noir*, with a side of macro rice and crunchy granola. If there's any room left for an added entry, *pesche imbottite alla mandorla* is recommended, but keep the flame low and don't get any *tagliarini* on your title page.

Works with authorship of mixed character. These are the grooviest kind, but don't try to cross State lines with them or flaunt them in Chicago.

Works by chiefs of state, heads of governments, etc. Treat as fiction.

CATALOGING IT LIKE IT IS

by
WRIGHT ONN

PART II. Description

Principles of descriptive cataloging like it is. Man, forget those jive objectives of the Anglo rules: "to state the significant features of an item with the purpose of distinguishing it from all other items. . . . " If a work can't distinguish itself, ain't no cataloging in the world gonna make up for it, right? Right! So the *real* objectives of descriptive cataloging are 1) for the cataloger to find where his head is at and express himself, and 2) for him to get a message to the people—about anything! The only limitations are the cataloger's supply of mind-expanding drugs and that

Wright Onn overthrows traditional cataloging.

little hole at the bottom of the card, which can contain only one message: existential nothingness. Organization of the description should be strictly according to the *I Ching*, documentation is based on astrological factors, and style is derived from Mailer, Roth, Hesse, Ginzburg, Marcuse, Vonnegut, Cleaver, et al. Now of course if your thing happens to be straight elements like title, author, edition, imprint, collation, and so on, that's cool, too, but if you're up against the wall, better save that stuff for Habilitationsschriften and Rektoratsreden. For *truth* in cataloging, let this LG card be your guru-vee guide.

Onn, Wright (cataloger)
    I love you, library user. Vanity-Press-Me 2001
    Mutilated p.—dirty pix—maps—x-ray—teardrops

        A steamfitter's manual (but on acid, a charmingly illustrated child's coloring book). The cataloger next to me is hostile. I want to grok her. I feel . . . disembodied. Libraries to the people! Once I drank red wine with fish. This card will self-destruct in twelve seconds. Life is an analytical entry.

    1. Man—Description and travail   2. Smoked salmon—Bagels and cream cheese   I. Touch me

321.8 Libra, Scorpio rising
LG Cards Inc.   Under   588-8400 (nights)
                          30

LIBRARY WAYOUTREACH
by POLLYANNA PLASTICENE

SERVING THE UNSERVED, reaching the unreached, dressing the undressed—this is my life as a free-floating professional, all 278 pounds of me. When my library began to come between the people and their books, I set out as an independent agent to answer the long felt needs and brief cotton wants of proles and patricians alike. Now, as I wander the world, there are books in my baggage, and Heaven help the poor baby I suspect to be a nonreader.

The Unseated

Huddled masses are my meat. My first bite was in a rush-hour subway car at Grand Central Station. Yes, here were my clients—their book-hungry eyes bugging out from the crush of humanity, with little to feed upon but the tawdry face of Miss Subways gleaming down from her cheap cardboard placard. It was then that I first reached out and cried, "Your free-floating librarian presents a one-minute review of a book written just for you!" Immediately, two New Yorkers began to show interest in the only way they could have known, one grabbing my purse, the other stabbing me gently in the hip with a stiletto. *"Subways Are for Sleeping* is a charming collection of short stories," I screamed, "with a cast of delightful characters familiar in some sense or another to each and every one of us. Available in an inexpensive paperback edition, it—" Not another word could I say to these happy book perverts—er, converts —who all at once rushed through the open door to 59th Street to buy as many books as their few pennies would allow and who positively *trampled* me in their new-found delight. "CREEP!" one called to me, and, indeed, taking his relevant user's advice, I crept away to escape the newly-literate zealots.

The Unsober

How do you reach a drunken Bowery bum swilling his white lightnin' in a heap of refuse in a dank and darkened doorway? How do you turn him on to books?

First you call yourself a *project* and give it a name. "Books for Bowery Bums" might get you $50,000 in grants under the right administration, and 50 years under the wrong one. You begin to relate to the bum as a person. (Perhaps you are already related to him. Remember Candy, finding her poor father under the most unlikely circumstances?) In educational terminology, of course, this is called *reaching the whole drunk*. You find out his reading tastes. He likes to read Gallo labels? You get him Gallo labels—pasted in a book, not on a bottle. "Hey, theshe booksh are shwell," he might reward you. You find out his informational needs. Where can he get a free drink? Why, at that half-

It matters not how looketh the librarian, but how he reacheth out...

"You begin to relate to the bum as a person... He might reward you."

Epilogue

way house, the public library. You don't tell him the drink is knowledge, the bar is the circulation desk, and that the "barmaids" are professional, but not for sale. If he refuses to move, propagandize him into action. Plaster his doorway with posters: "Book Benders are Best"; "Booze up with Books"; "Literature Lubricates"; "Lush up at your Library"; "Get Rigid—Read!"

My own experience was with a drunken bum in the doorway of the Filmore East Rock Theater, who told me he was "Jest havin' a taste until Mr. Jolson goes on." "There are many fine *books* about Mr. Jolson," I explained. "Get lost," he suggested. "Get *The Lost Weekend*," I countered, "Jackson, Charles, available in paperback." His further rudeness only prompted me to sit beside him for the next few hours, he with his Thunderbird, I with a Gatorade, until, at last, I found his hook for books: the man was having an *identity crisis*. When I explained to him that through reading he could finally discover, as Kierkegaard phrased it, "that self which one truly is," he was off like a champagne cork to the public library.

When I saw him next, he was sprawled out in the doorway of—yes —the Main Branch.

"Didn't you find a book?" I asked.

"Yesh," he said. "I found a the-shawrush."

"But did you find your *identity?*"

"You bet your shweet shwazzle!" he wept. "I'm a cock-eyed, half-corned, juiced-up, laid-out, looped-legged, rum-dum, salted-down, slopped-over, stone-blind, tangle-footed, well-oiled, wing-heavy, zig-zag dipsomaniac."

"But a *reading* one," I reassured him. "A *reading* one," and off I floated, freely, way out, searching for the unserved, the unreached, the undressed . . .

BUYERS' GUIDE

Automatic Cataloging Machine

You put any book or periodical in the top, turn the handle, and—presto! A full set of catalog cards pops out of the bottom drawer. How does it work? A tiny cataloger inside gets bumped when you grind. As the bits of book come through, she goes to work. Write to Peppercorn Surplus, Inc., Gnome, Alaska. Price is only $8.95 (tiny cataloger not included).

Print-Out Terminal

Hook this baby to the juice, and watch those words come flying. Developed over a period of forty years by Dr. Kenneth Plucker, librarian of the Poultry Science Institute, the terminal can be adapted to any language or format. Rent from Dr. Plucker at $600 a month, or go pluck your own.

Labor-Relations Aid— Management

Turn troublemakers into team workers! No two staff members are so independent that they can't get together with the help of this simple device. Specify neck size; one dollar per dissident to: Legree Enterprises, Lynchburg, La.

Circulation System

They say it's good for the circulation—so why not in libraries? It's already marked with call letters; place it on the shelves accordingly, with a cross-reference to T-totalers. Won't make the shelves more compact, but watch how tight the patrons get! Also comes filled with white paste as a novelty dispenser for dry libraries. Specify teak or cherrywood body, gold, platinum, or uranium tap. $785 from Rum at the Top, Eerie, Pa.

PROFESSIONAL READING & THE BOOK REVIEW

LIBRARY BOUND

RAM, BUCK. *A Casebook on Library Binding*. 84p. index. bibliog. appendixes. samples, artifacts, facetiae. Shoecrow. 1971. $42.98. SBN 923784-109-X. LC rejected.

Setting aside the fact that this book was itself not bound, but cased in, one must face the rigor of terminology from the outset. The author, Buck Ram, has admirably distinguished between case-in, case book, and casein, the last-named binding all together neatly into a tautology.

The samples included in a pocket at the back are invaluable; I will only mention the *Encyclopedia of Library and Information Science*, thoughtfully provided on microfiche to allow for subsequent volumes. Among the artifacts included is a saddle-stitched, year's volume of *Ployboy*, untrimmed to allow viewing of the full-edge full-color photo of the Ploymate of the Year. (I wonder how many libraries have unthinkingly allowed their binders to trim all three sides? This error is second only to stripping the ads, which, heaven knows, are immodest enough as it is.)

Ram lends his authority in giving the following advice to librarians on collation: don't do it! It is the binder's job only to see that the index is bound in front and the contents in the rear. Librarians who insist on giving detailed instructions are striking at the very spine of the binder's professionalism. Confine yourselves to aesthetic considerations, such as full calf, midcalf, kneelength, etc.

As to minor quibbles, I think it a mistake to have included in the index the entries for the *Encyclopedia* and *Ployboy*; this forced a reduction in type size from Bourgeois to Diamond, which will probably make the book unacceptable to Third World students. They have been striving to eliminate elite type, as we all know, and this will merely bring out the felt pens to proclaim, *"Épater la bourgeoisie!"*

In summary, this book should be purchased in quantity for library school use, especially because it is destined for paperback publication soon. Then it will be suitable only for those schools which have laboratories, for the first assignment will be to rebind one's textbook. The idea, I admit, does have a certain charm, though.—*Malfolio Octavo, Distinguished Professor of Pagination, Boshkosh State College, Wis.*

THE CONTEMPORARY SCENE

PUGH, Montbretia, ed. *To Nicodemus O'Shaughnessy Grubb, With Love*. A most timely festschrift of reminiscences of this little-known drunk, illiterate lyric poet to mark the tenth anniversary of his death in an Irish bog at the age of 93. One's heart aches ineffably as one turns the pages of his crucial *Gutstring Gropings* (1927), pondering what might have been had the wan snowdrop that was Grubb's talent e'er flowered into shy maturity. *O tempora, O mores, timeo Danaos et dona ferentes, adeste fideles laeti triumphantes, gluteus minimus* are phrases that leap to mind. One does, oneself, sensitively, tentatively, putatively feel, or, rather, as it were, sense, that his major poems can only be the sonorous *Soultwitch*, and the heart-rending *A La Récherche du Grubb Perdu*. One quotes:

> Soultwitch
> My heart
> Goes out to
> Roaches.
> O, World,
> O Weary Brutal World
> When, O, When
> O, When
> O
> When
> Will You Learn
> That Roaches, Too,
> Are Human?

> *A La Récherche*...
> Tuesday
> Tuesday
> Tuesday
> Tues-
>   day
> is the
> Day
>   After
> MONDAY.

Also included is the full text of Grubb's diary expressing his philosophy of life (basically: "The past is gone, the future is not yet come, and the present is today— maybe.") Recommended for all libraries. 8v., 632 p. each; $1.50 the set.

> *"If we shadows have offended,*
> *Think but this, and all is mended,*
> *That you have but slumber'd here,*
> *While these visions did appear.*
> *And this weak and idle theme,*
> *No more yielding but a dream,*
> *Gentles, do not reprehend:*
> *If you pardon, we will mend."*—Ed.

Contributors

LLOYD ALEXANDER has taught children's literature at Temple University and is a winner of the 1969 Newbery Award for his The High King.

CURTIS G. BENJAMIN is a consultant to, and former president and chairman of, the McGraw-Hill Book Company.

ROBERT H. BLACKBURN is chief librarian at the University of Toronto.

HENRY M. BRICKELL is a staff member of the Institute for Educational Development, New York City.

VERNER W. CLAPP is a consultant to the Council on Library Resources.

REESE CLEGHORN is the editor of South Today, published monthly by the Southern Regional Council.

SANFORD DORBIN is both editor and bibliographer of Bukowski and a published poet himself.

CAROLYN FORSMAN is a doctoral student at the School of Library and Information Services, University of Maryland.

ERVIN J. GAINES is director of the Minneapolis Public Library.

ROBERT P. HARO is a member of the faculty of the School of Library and Information Services, University of Maryland.

PAUL HEINS served as a judge for the 1970 Children's Spring Book Festival.

FREDERICK G. KILGOUR is director of the Ohio College Library Center, Columbus.

HERMAN LIEBAERS is director of the Bibliothèque Royale Albert 1er, Brussels, and president of the International Federation of Library Associations.

M. B. LINE is librarian at the Bath University of Technology.

DARRYL MLEYNEK is employed in the Los Angeles Public Library.

ERIC MOON is president of the Scarecrow Press.

DAVID PEELE is an associate professor in the Department of Libraries, Staten Island Community College

P.D. POCKLINGTON is city librarian at the Chester Public Library

ROSCOE ROUSE is university librarian at Oklahoma State University, Stillwater.

ANITA R. SCHILLER has recently accepted a position in the University Library, University of California at San Diego.

RALPH R. SHAW is dean emeritus of Library Activities at the University of Hawaii.

GEORGE SHEPPARD is a lecturer at the Library School, University of Idaho.

JESSE H. SHERA is a professor at the Graduate School of Library Science, University of Texas.

GERALD R. SHIELDS is editor of American Libraries.

PAUL SPEHR is a motion picture specialist at the Library of Congress.

NORMAN D. STEVENS is associate university librarian at the University of Connecticut, Storrs.

PAULA M. STRAIN is a member of SLA's Placement Policy Committee (1969/70).

G. THOMAS TANSELLE is a professor of English at the University of Wisconsin.

O. JAMES WERNER is assistant law librarian and instructor in law, University of Texas.

JOSEPH L. WHEELER, recently deceased, was the distinguished former director of the Enoch Pratt Free Library, Baltimore.

Z
671
L7024
#1
1970

SEP 2 1971